Vietnam's Year of the Rat

Vietnam's Year of the Rat

Elbridge Durbrow, Ngô Đình Diệm and the Turn in U.S. Relations, 1959–1961

Ronald Bruce Frankum, Jr.

McFarland & Company, Inc., Publishers
Jefferson, North Carolina

LIBRARY OF CONGRESS CATALOGUING-IN-PUBLICATION DATA

Frankum, Ronald Bruce, 1967–
Vietnam's year of the rat : Elbridge Durbrow, Ngô Đình Diệm and the turn in U.S. relations, 1959–1961 / Ronald Bruce Frankum, Jr.
        p.   cm.
Includes bibliographical references and index.

ISBN 978-0-7864-7815-6 (softcover : acid free paper) ∞
ISBN 978-1-4766-1472-4 (ebook)

1. United States—Foreign relations—Vietnam (Republic)
2. Vietnam (Republic)—Foreign relations—United States.
3. Durbrow, Elbridge, 1903–1997. 4. Ngô Đình Diệm, 1901–1963. I. Title.
E183.8.V5F73 2014   327.73059709'046—dc23   2014006070

BRITISH LIBRARY CATALOGUING DATA ARE AVAILABLE

© 2014 Ronald Bruce Frankum, Jr. All rights reserved

No part of this book may be reproduced or transmitted in any form or by any means, electronic or mechanical, including photocopying or recording, or by any information storage and retrieval system, without permission in writing from the publisher.

On the cover: Ngô Đình Diệm at a diplomatic function, 1956 (United States Embassy, Manila, United States Information Agency Photograph 56-2742, National Archives and Records Administration, College Park, MD)

Manufactured in the United States of America

McFarland & Company, Inc., Publishers
Box 611, Jefferson, North Carolina 28640
www.mcfarlandpub.com

For Jack Joseph Frankum

Acknowledgments

I am indebted to Herb Pankratz, Michelle Kopfer, and Chalsea Millner at the Dwight D. Eisenhower Presidential Library and the wonderful staff at the John F. Kennedy Presidential Library for their assistance during my many visits. I was fortunate enough to receive a Dwight D. Eisenhower Presidential Library Research Grant and John F. Kennedy Presidential Library Research Grant to help defray expenses while researching at these two valuable libraries. Additional assistance was provided by the Millersville University of Pennsylvania Faculty Grants Committee and humanities and social science deans John Short and Diane Umble at Millersville University. Ms. Terri Monserrat read early draft chapters and offered critiques, which only made the manuscript stronger. She and others with whom I have consulted, however, are free from fault for any errors or omissions in this work.

Table of Contents

Acknowledgments   vii
A Note on Source and Names   1
Preface   3

1. Exit the Year of the Pig   7
2. Enter the Year of the Rat   21
3. Conflicting Personalities and Egos   32
4. The Caravelle Carnival   50
5. The French Connection   69
6. The Turning of the Screw   82
7. Turning Points: The November 1960 Coup d'État Attempt   93
8. After the Coup d'État: Saigon Responds   109
9. Returning to Normality   128
10. A New Year with an Old Problem   144
11. A New Plan for an Old Problem   159
12. Vietnamese Democracy in Action   170
13. April 1961 Election and the Departure of Durbrow   184

Conclusion   203
Appendix: The Republic of Vietnam's Economy   205
Chapter Notes   207
Bibliography   243
Index   249

A Note on Sources and Names

The Department of State Central Decimal Files (Record Group 59) is extensively used in *Vietnam's Year of the Rat*. The Central Decimal Files system seems at first to be complex but is in fact simple to use. Each document in the series is stamped with a multi-alpha-numeric code. The first number in the code refers to the primary classification of the document. For this manuscript, classification code 7 (Internal Politics and National Defense Affairs) is used. The next set of alpha-numeric numbers refers to the country code. The Republic of Vietnam's code is 51K while the Indochina code is 51G. Following this data is a subject code. The following codes are used in this manuscript:

.00 (Political Affairs—General)
.00(W) (Political Affairs: Weeka Reports [Weekly reports on South Vietnamese political, military, and economic affairs.])
.001 (Political Affairs: Communism)
.022 (Political Affairs: Government—Territory)
.11 (Political Affairs: Executive Branch of Government—Chief Executive)
.13 (Political Affairs: Executive Branch of Government—Cabinet; Ministry)
.3 (Political Affairs: Judicial Branch of Government)
.34 (Political Affairs: Judicial Branch of Government—Laws; Statutes)
.5 (National Defense Affairs—General)
.5MSP (National Defense Affairs: Mutual Security Program)
.521 (National Defense Affairs: Intelligence Activities—Biographical Data)
.54 (National Defense Affairs: Maneuvers; Troop Movements)
.5511 (National Defense Affairs: Organization—Personnel: Conscription)
.58 (National Defense Affairs: Missions)
.5811 (National Defense Affairs: Missions—U.S.)

The date, which is preceded by a "/," is the final number. Thus, a document stamped 751K.00/4–2860 was one that was filed in the Internal Politics and National Defense Affairs classification for Vietnam under the general subject category of Political Affairs and is dated April 28, 1960. All of the Central Decimal Files listed for the period 1960–1961 in the footnotes come from the microfilm series, *Confidential U.S. State Department Central Files: Vietnam, 1960–January 1963: Internal and Foreign Affairs*. Material from Record Group 59 that is dated before December 31, 1959, is also located in the National Archives and Records Administration at College Park, Maryland, but is available in textual form. This book also uses material from Record Group 84: Records of the Foreign Service Posts of the Department of State and the Foreign Broadcast Information Service (FBIS) files located in Record Group

262. These documents consist of translated abstracts and full stories from Vietnamese language sources. When used, the documents are cited by indicating the date of the actual publication and then the date listed in the FBIS. The page number citations with the FBIS, which use a triple-letter format, have also been modified to a single letter. The *Vietnam Press* is also used in this study. While the reliability of this news source might be called into question because of its close association with Ngô Đình Diệm, this collection contains abstracts and, in some cases, full transcriptions of articles and editorials from Vietnamese newspapers. The following newspapers from this collection are used in this study: *Ah Chau Jih Pao, Buổi sang* (Morning Post), *Cách mạng Quốc gia* (National Revolution), *Chung Juo Jih Pao, Chuông Mai* (Morning Bell), *Dân chúng* (The People), *Lẽ Sống* (Reason to Live), *May Jih Luan Zan, Ngôn Luận* (Opinion), *Sài Gòn Mãi* (Saigon Tomorrow), *Sài Gòn Mới* (New Saigon), *Sài Gòn Thời Báo* (Saigon Times), *Sun Wun Jih Pao, Times of Vietnam, Thời luân* (Commentary), *Tiếng Chuông* (Bell Toll), *Tin Mới* (New Reports), *Tự do* (Freedom), and *Tuan Tung Jih Pao*.

In 1957, Ngô Đình Nhu traveled to the United States in advance of his brother Ngô Đình Diệm who was nearing his second full year as the president of the Republic of Vietnam. While the series of conversations that Ngô Đình Nhu had with American officials covered a variety of significant areas, one conversation stood out. Ngô Đình Nhu had an extensive conversation about how his brother should be addressed. He explained that the American tendency to address the president of the Republic of Vietnam by his first name was inappropriate. Unfortunately for Ngô Đình Nhu, his arguments failed to shift what was already entrenched in Washington circles. Scholars of the Vietnam war have, for the most part, followed suit. The present work honors Ngô Đình Nhu's request by identifying Vietnamese names and places using the Vietnamese spelling and diacritics. The only exceptions are when the Vietnamese name has been altered, or Americanized, or there is not enough information available to determine the full name. This occurs only rarely. In a few more commonly known Vietnamese placenames, such as Saigon and Hanoi, I have retained the English spelling of the word in order to avoid confusion.

It was not uncommon to leave out words in diplomatic transmissions in order to limit transmission time. I have left the quotation in the original rather than fit it grammatically. I did this because the insertion of additional words may change the meaning of the original. While my interpretation of the transmissions may be open for debate, it is important that that debate focus on interpretation rather than insertion.

Preface

Throughout the twenty-five years that the United States was involved in Southeast Asia, between its official recognition of the states of Vietnam, Laos, and Cambodia on February 7, 1950, through the fall of the Republic of Vietnam (RVN) and Cambodia in April 1975, controversy dominated the political arena. In the early years of this turbulent relationship, no figure served more as a catalyst for American frustration than Ngô Đình Diệm. As the founder of the RVN and its first president, Ngô Đình Diệm seemed to offer the only real option to bring Vietnam through the trials and tribulations associated with a country emerging from a colonial past while engaged in a struggle against internal and external threats. However, Ngô Đình Diệm never had the complete trust of his people and peers, either as a result of apathy, jealousy, or the constant struggle for control. Neither did he maintain the confidence of his American allies during their wavering commitment to his continued rule. The American experiment in the RVN started well, while several indicators pointed to a promising future.

However, this experiment was hampered by a clash of culture that was never fully reconciled by either Ngô Đình Diệm and his followers or the Americans in charge of U.S. policy in Southeast Asia. By the fall of 1963, most Americans involved in the day-to-day decisions regarding the RVN believed Ngô Đình Diệm to be a failure who had run his course. Any attempt to continue to prop up the government would only exacerbate a bankrupt American foreign policy in the RVN. When internal discord reached a fevered pitch in the summer and fall of 1963, Ngô Đình Diệm failed to contain the dissent and acted not as a leader of a country ready to be admitted into the community of free nations but, rather, as a despot who relied on others, specifically his brother Ngô Đình Nhu and other close family members and friends, to reverse the tide of discontent. At every move, he was countered by Americans who had grown tired of supporting a man that no longer appeared to serve the best interests of the United States in its international struggle against Southeast Asian communism, nor did he provide any evidence that he planned to act upon, let alone listen to, American advice on how to best accomplish their goals.

Until recent years, most historians who studied the Vietnam War followed the accepted paradigm that Ngô Đình Diệm was a corrupt, inefficient leader who had been placed into a position of power by the United States. He maintained power, so the argument goes, as long as the United States supported him. This work does not challenge the overall assumption offered in this paradigm that Ngô Đình Diệm had failed as a leader by the middle of 1963. However, it does call into question the process by which Ngô Đình Diệm transformed from being the only figure capable of leading his country to an individual whose value had diminished to such an extent that he was expendable. Lost in the effort to prove how utterly corrupt Ngô Đình Diệm was during his tenure as president are the external factors that, in some cases, forced his actions and poor decisions. At no time in his presidency was this truer than during the lunar year 1960: the Year of the Rat.

By studying the year 1960, it becomes possible to delve deeper into the events that helped to shape changing American attitudes toward Ngô Đình Diệm that eventually led to his assassination in November 1963. While the events that occurred in 1960 in and of themselves do not represent major turning points in the relationship between the Vietnamese leader and the Americans, the cumulative effect of the year marked a transition that only became clear in the months leading to his death and America's acquiescence to the coup d'état. Additionally, a more in-depth analysis of the year provides a corrective on some of the myths that have been generated by historians and observers of this period in time. For instance, two major events during the year, the April 26 Caravelle Manifesto and the November 11 abortive coup d'état, have received some attention by scholars, though often only in passing in order to move into the more controversial years 1962 and 1963. As a result, misinformation regarding these events has become entrenched in the Vietnam War historiography. With regard to the Caravelle Manifesto, a document authored by eighteen Vietnamese, in protest of Ngô Đình Diệm's rule, the general consensus was that these Vietnamese protestors were prominent members of the Saigon community who commanded the respect of the Vietnamese people. Several historians have also maintained that the Caravelle Eighteen were arrested by Ngô Đình Diệm for their protest writings.[1]

These two assumptions are misleading or incorrect. For example, historians have suggested that the Caravelle Group did not call on Ngô Đình Diệm to resign and, instead, offered a respectful, apologetic presentation that warned of dangerous change should Ngô Đình Diệm not react to the deteriorating conditions in the RVN.[2] While on the surface this is accurate as the public utterances of the group did not suggest anything more radical than calling upon Ngô Đình Diệm to change his ways, privately members of the group became frustrated enough to begin discussions on the possibility of a coup d'état. The myth that the eighteen members of the Caravelle Group were arrested after the release of their manifesto has also been perpetuated even though this did not occur.[3] While it is true that four members of the Caravelle Group were arrested after the November 11 abortive coup d'état for publicly speaking out for the rebels and calling for the end of Ngô Đình Diệm's rule, this occurred for acts that were considered treasonous rather than for expressing their views in the manifesto some six months earlier.

Likewise, the November 11 abortive coup d'état has received some attention by scholars, usually less than a page or two and sometimes only a paragraph or passing sentence. These scholars conclude that the event, by loyal troops, justified the real concerns of the United States that Ngô Đình Diệm had reached the end of his useful life as the leader of the RVN. In reality, most of the troops that supported the abortive coup d'état did so because they had been tricked into believing that they were going to Ngô Đình Diệm's rescue from an attempted coup d'état. Once these troops realized that they had been lied to by the rebel leaders, they ceased fighting. This was the reason the coup d'état failed rather than the notion that the rebel leaders were unorganized.[4] Likewise, public support for the attempted coup d'état did not bring people dancing in the streets, as Malcolm Browne observed, in expectation that Ngô Đình Diệm's rule was finally at an end. Rather, the result was a subdued demonstration against Ngô Đình Diệm followed by a much stronger pro-government rally after the abortive coup d'état that was organized by the Saigon government.[5] These two events are prominent in the historical writings that cover the period 1960, but much has been neglected save for a few works such as David Anderson, *Trapped by Success*, and Ronald Spector, *Advice and Support*.[6]

While Anderson captures the tension that existed between the American diplomats and military figures involved in the RVN and the conflict between Ngô Đình Diệm and his American military supporters on one side and U.S. ambassador to the RVN, Elbridge Durbrow, and his cohorts on the other, his analysis falls short of really explaining the significance of the year, though Anderson is more concerned with the entire Eisenhower experience in Vietnam from the 1954 Geneva Conference to the end of his presidency. Spector, whose work was a part of the United States Army in Vietnam series, focuses on the American military perspective, and while he alludes to the tension that existed among the Americans and between the U.S. representatives and Ngô Đình Diệm, his objectives take him in another direction. John Ernst, whose excellent work on the role of the Michigan State University Group, covers this period, but he also has different, albeit equally important, objectives to satisfy, while Arthur Dommen provided a complete but clinical analysis of this period.[7]

Despite the abundance of writings on Ngô Đình Diệm and American involvement in Southeast Asia during his rule, he remains an elusive figure. Ngô Đình Diệm had a significant minority of Saigon intellectuals who opposed his government and had access to the American embassy staff. In 1960, this resulted in a negative atmosphere within the American embassy which moved to actively oppose the RVN president during the Year of the Rat. This group, ironically, also helped to shape the historical debate for the next fifty years. Lost in their translation was the fact that Ngô Đình Diệm did have some support from his people save for the Saigon intellectuals and those negatively affected by the failed programs and policies designed to thwart the communist insurgency in the countryside. This assessment does not discount the very real fact that Ngô Đình Diệm had created enemies within the RVN by his actions, or his failure to act. Rather, it is designed to counter the reports and memoranda originating from the U.S. embassy in Saigon that offered a solely negative opinion. While this latter group did not represent the majority, its numbers were significant enough to keep the insurgency alive and keep doubt and suspicion active among the Americans. Additionally, the majority of Vietnamese people living in the countryside were not actively supporting the Saigon government even as they did not oppose it. It was the inability of Ngô Đình Diệm and his brother Ngô Đình Nhu to formulate a program to mobilize the population toward supporting the Republic and the Saigon government that became their greatest failure. This failure had its roots in the Year of the Rat but would become the main cause of the strife of 1963 that led to their deaths.

This book acknowledges the failures of Ngô Đình Diệm during the Year of the Rat, but it also highlights the failed policies of Durbrow and his staff as they selectively reported the events from the RVN and made the conscious decision to work against Ngô Đình Diệm. Both perspectives are necessary for a more complete understanding of the year. Similarly, it explores the role of those Americans who supported the continued rule of Ngô Đình Diệm and their attempts to influence American foreign policy in Southeast Asia. There is little doubt that Ngô Đình Diệm contributed to his own self-destruction in 1963 by his actions, but what must be considered is that the United States and its principle representatives in Saigon also share responsibility for the Vietnamese tragedy.

As such, *Vietnam's Year of the Rat* is a study of the interactions between the principal American agents in the RVN and Washington and their interactions with the prominent

Vietnamese who helped to influenced U.S. foreign policy in 1960 Saigon. It is a story of frustration. Within the American community, two camps emerged that consistently clashed with one another in their attempt to assume a position of leadership in directing America's Ngô Đình Diệm policy. The same is true for the Vietnamese as tension and strife within the Saigon government coupled with the intrigue of Saigon politics produced uncertainty and distrust at a critical point in the RVN's young history. When the interaction between the Americans and Vietnamese is added to this mix, there is no doubt that the year 1960 produced a significant legacy that would help to shape American foreign policy for the final three years of Ngô Đình Diệm's rule.

On both sides of the debate, personality, perspective, and a clash of culture helped to shape the discussion and influence the decisions made during the Year of the Rat. Ironically, each individual involved shared similar objectives: a free and independent RVN that could operate as a productive member within the international community of the Free World and serve as a model for other nations emerging from a colonial past. However, while they shared similar objectives, the means employed to achieve these goals differed. Rather than providing a resolution to the problem of the RVN, these conflicting means to a common end set up the conditions for a failed American policy in Southeast Asia that would not see its conclusion until fifteen years later. The Year of the Rat set in motion the process of failure and the American lament for what was happening with Ngô Đình Diệm in power. While no one in 1960 could have predicted the course of America's involvement in Southeast Asia in the 1960s or the effects it would have on American society in the 1960s and 1970s, this book does offer an explanation to how American policy failed in the decade to come. *Vietnam's Year of the Rat* is not a story of hindsight; rather, it is an attempt to offer a perspective on one of the many significant turning points in the war when the United States was presented with a choice on how to proceed and failed to live up to the challenge of making a different decision.

1

Exit the Year of the Pig

In many ways, the RVN that left the Year of the Pig, the lunar year 1959, had achieved unprecedented growth in its economy, internal security and stability, political infrastructure, and diplomatic position within the community of nations that made up Southeast Asia and the Pacific. Its leader, Ngô Đình Diệm, rose to power during the turbulent period between the fall of the French fortress at Điện Biên Phủ on May 8, 1954, and the July 21, 1954, Geneva Agreements. These two events set in place the conditions that would dominate his country for the next two years and continue to influence his public persona and reputation until his assassination on November 1, 1963. From the time Emperor Bảo Đại called for Ngô Đình Diệm to serve as the president of the Council of Ministers of the State of Vietnam on June 16, 1954, Ngô Đình Diệm directed the accomplishments of several objectives that some in the United States considered to be miraculous. He oversaw the influx of 810,000 refugees from the North who had been given the choice of living under a communist form of government or starting a new life in the South. He also worked with Americans from the United States Navy, United States Overseas Mission, and the Special Technical and Economic Mission to see to the refugees' resettlement and rehabilitation.[1] While the exodus from the north was in its final days, Ngô Đình Diệm had to contend with the Hòa Hảo, Cao Đài, and Bình Xuyên, each of which resisted the return of strong centralized leadership in Saigon that might threaten their political or economic position. In the case of the Bình Xuyên, who had the tacit support of the French, Ngô Đình Diệm faced a determined and well-armed group of men who were motivated to overthrow the president before he could move to eliminate them. Ngô Đình Diệm successfully resisted the three politico-religious groups, diffused their effectiveness and, in a few cases, even managed to convince individual leaders to support his vision for Vietnam through an effective articulation of his political philosophy or with a financial incentive.[2] After dealing with the internal challenge, Ngô Đình Diệm moved to replace Bảo Đại, who he considered an ineffectual ruler because he had sacrificed the struggle of his people for the comforts of France. Ngô Đình Diệm removed Bảo Đại from power peacefully after a national referendum in October 1955 and then proclaimed the RVN on October 26, 1955. He worked with American advisers, including members of the Michigan State University Group, and his trusted colleagues to create a constitution in 1956 and, by the Year of the Rat, had established the beginnings of an effective armed force, an economy that had begun the process of exporting commodities, in addition to a growing list of countries that recognized the Republic with diplomatic relations, and established a land reclamation and redistribution plan that sought to maximize Vietnamese agriculture and animal husbandry while offering the people a chance to work their own land and become motivated to unite against the communist insurgency.[3] While each of Ngô Đình Diệm's actions came with costs, both diplomatic and political, he sought to move his country forward as he consolidated his power base and prepared for the possibility of resistance to his rule. Ngô Đình Diệm had accomplished much in the nearly six years since his self-imposed exile to the United States and Belgium, but he had achieved these goals at an expense that would continue to plague him in the lunar year of 1960.

Ironically, the success of Ngô Đình Diệm and the RVN from 1955 to 1959 was the principle source of the discontent that many within the country expressed. Before 1959, Ngô Đình Diệm's policies greatly diminished the threat of the communist insurgency and resulted in relative stability, but with the calm came a more focused discussion of the principles of democracy and the freedoms expected from such a condition. Ngô Đình Diệm was able to direct some of that focus positively while, at the same time, reinforcing the level of internal security that existed. The election of the National Assembly on August 30, 1959, highlighted the Republic's move toward a more democratic government, while the lack of communist violence during the elections suggested that the overt threat of organized communist resistance had been negated.[4] The Country Team established with the U.S. embassy in Saigon, however, did have some serious concerns about the real progress Ngô Đình Diệm had made toward a democratic form of government.[5] While it conceded that the RVN had as its long-term goal an ideal of democracy and had been successful in building a foundation for such a form of government, it argued that Ngô Đình Diệm had really only made minimal progress toward that ideal: "Vietnam can show only small steps of progress. Furthermore, in great part these steps amount only to the erection of a façade and the reality of the situation remains one of authoritarian control by the regime."[6] This line of thinking, advocated by Counselor of embassy in Vietnam for Political Affairs, Joseph Mendenhall, for the Country Team and Durbrow for the embassy, would influence American relations in the lunar year 1960.

Another concern that explained much of the criticism within Saigon of Ngô Đình Diệm's rule was the Country Team analysis of the "revolution of rising expectations."[7] During the Year of the Rat, the Saigon intelligentsia vocalized its criticism of Ngô Đình Diệm and the Ngô family rule within the RVN. Durbrow, Mendenhall, and Counselor General of the embassy in Vietnam Francis Cunningham all reported conversations they had with this group of intellectuals and reputable Saigon

Ngô Đình Diệm at the Presidential Palace (L. Lawson, United States Information Agency, Photograph 55–20930, National Archives and Records Administration, College Park, Maryland).

businessmen and community leaders, but not once, as a way of explaining their criticism, did the three principle representatives in the U.S. embassy mention the revolution of rising expectations that pervaded Saigon culture. This revolution resulted from the success of the Saigon government in achieving lasting stability in the face of constant pressure and obstacles. With the immediate areas of concern in the capital city eliminated, the Saigon elite had the time and attention to focus on the failure of Ngô Đình Diệm to institute more far-reaching political reforms that would allow for a greater democratic experiment. This criticism, however, did not take into account the nature of that success, nor did it acknowledge the necessity of Ngô Đình Diệm to limit the democratic experiment in order to ensure that Saigon remained a safe haven. While it was not unreasonable to expect from Ngô Đình Diệm greater freedoms and Republican principles as those Vietnamese in Saigon and the American diplomats did in 1960 to 1961, the peasants in the countryside did not enjoy the same luxury to muse over such idealistic concerns.

The level and intensity of the clashes between the communist insurgents and the RVN forces protecting the people in the countryside also showed signs of increasing as the Year of the Pig ended, as seen in a series of December skirmishes and battles.[8] The North Vietnamese and the southern communist insurgents' change in strategy and intensification of their effort to topple Ngô Đình Diệm from power would serve as an additional catalyst to the growing concerns of the American personnel in Vietnam and those Vietnamese critics who believed they could do better. The troubling fact for Ngô Đình Diệm was that this change in communist strategy did not alter the complaints from the privileged in Saigon, nor did it cause Durbrow and his entourage to adjust the intensity of their calls for political reform. Ngô Đình Diệm appeared to be stubborn and even obstinate in his dealing with Durbrow, but his was a greater concern than appeasing the American ambassador or the embassy staff. In the Year of the Rat, the RVN and its president would be contested internally and pressured externally; Ngô Đình Diệm would do nothing less than work to maintain his position and challenge those who opposed his rule. His ultimate objective was an independent and anti-communist government, free from foreign interference and influence, including the United States, and one that stood as a model for other countries emerging from a colonial past on their path to a place within the international community of nations.

The months preceding the Year of the Rat shaped the debate and discussions Ngô Đình Diệm and Durbrow would have in 1960 and 1961. The two men, each strong in personality and vested in their position, would continue to clash as competing means vied for control over a common objective: the independence of the RVN and a stable internal security situation. The intensity of their confrontation was enhanced by individuals in Washington who transferred the divisions in the RVN to the buildings within the U.S. capital. Brigadier General Edward Lansdale, a longtime supporter of Ngô Đình Diệm, would clash with Durbrow and J. Graham Parsons, who served as the assistant secretary of state for Far Eastern affairs.[9] Ngô Đình Diệm and Lansdale would find a willing ally in Lieutenant General Samuel T. Williams and Lieutenant General Lionel C. McGarr, both of whom would serve as the chief of the Military Advisory Assistance Group (MAAG), Vietnam, in 1960. While many issues that had lingered since Durbrow's arrival in March 1957 continued to plague the relationship, the events that followed represented the clash of culture, ideology, and strategy that would eventually culminate in the split between the president of the RVN and America's principle representative in that country.

On December 7, 1959, Durbrow transmitted to the Department of State a copy of a study originating from the U.S. embassy in Saigon titled "Role of the Military in Less-Developed Countries: Vietnam, a Country Team Assessment."[10] The report was drafted by Joseph A. Mendenhall, the recently promoted officer in charge of Vietnamese affairs in the Department of State to the position of counselor of the embassy in Vietnam for political affairs, and William E. Colby, whose official title was political officer and first secretary for the embassy in Vietnam.[11] The study, approved by Durbrow, reflected the state of U.S. thinking on its South Vietnamese ally as well as the conflicting opinion held by members of the American contingent in Saigon. Both Mendenhall and Durbrow took a poor view of Ngô Đình Diệm in the waning months of 1959 while Colby, who was joined by Williams, and then McGarr, were more sympathetic to the plight of Ngô Đình Diệm and tended to advocate a more conciliatory approach in dealing with the president of the RVN.

The study, which really was a Country Team assessment, was significant for a number of reasons, as were Ngô Đình Diệm's remarks to American journalists the next day in an unrelated event. The December 7 assessment highlighted the major concerns for the United States that had been evident in Vietnam since Durbrow's arrival in Saigon in 1957 as well as foreshadowed the major crises, both real and theoretical, that would push Durbrow and Mendenhall further away from reconciliation with Ngô Đình Diệm and, at times, toward active resistance to Ngô Đình Diệm's continued presence in the Presidential Palace in Saigon.

The tenor of the assessment followed the Durbrow-Mendenhall line of thinking as it analyzed the Ngô Đình Diệm government and the progress it had made in the first five years of its existence. It stressed that, while there was no indication of a military-inspired coup d'état in the making, Ngô Đình Diệm had become more authoritarian in his efforts to secure the countryside and move the Republic forward. This movement away from the preferred American model for democracy came at a time, so it was argued, when Saigon was not subject to organized, overt communist competition with its democratic forces. The assessment accounted for this trend, and it was here that Colby's influence surfaced, when it maintained that it was the nature of Ngô Đình Diệm's political philosophy. Ngô Đình Diệm preferred to construct the Vietnamese political system based on Vietnamese traditions rather than an American model. To many Americans and Vietnamese intellectuals in Saigon, this was anathema to their vision of a free and independent RVN. Ngô Đình Diệm adhered to the Mandarin tradition and saw himself as the Gia Long of the twentieth century who, like the former Nguyễn dynasty emperor, united the Vietnamese people at the beginning of the nineteenth century and codified into law the foundation of Vietnamese self-rule until French colonialism asserted itself toward the end of the century.[12] Ngô Đình Diệm was willing to accept American aid; he even encouraged any increase in that aid that he could manage, but he always reserved the right to act independently of American advice. He believed that his way was the best for the Vietnamese people and could not understand why those Americans in Saigon who had little real understanding of Vietnamese history, culture, or tradition tried to interfere in his effort to achieve a strong, independent, and anti-communist Republic. He also constantly struggled against communist propaganda that characterized him as a puppet to the Americans and a lackey to American foreign policy in Southeast Asia. While Ngô Đình Diệm agreed with much of American diplomacy in Asia and was willing to have his country serve as the model nation of the Free World in the region, he did not wish to see any appearance of subjugation or subservience to the United States.

Ngô Đình Diệm also advocated strict discipline of his people if they were to emerge from their current state in 1959 and progress toward the final goal. He equated the effort to a "forced march" by the people toward their final goal. The Country Team assessment highlighted this point as a condition of Vietnam's underdeveloped-country status and as an explanation for Ngô Đình Diệm's high-handed tactics. The study would conclude that such actions, as Ngô Đình Diệm continued to create a "democratic façade" that offered "little life" but provided a "skeletal framework for eventual political evolution in Vietnam," had resulted in two significant problems that, if left unchecked, might result in an organized effort to overthrow the Ngô Đình Diệm government and create a constitutional crisis from which the South Vietnamese might never recover.[13]

The two major problems addressed by the Country Team were Ngô Đình Diệm's strong-handed government from which the president ruled over the people, which had drawn considerable opposition from the intelligentsia in Saigon, and the emphasis of security over economic development, from which Durbrow, Mendenhall, and others in the embassy had experienced a consistent source of frustration as Ngô Đình Diệm ignored or dismissed their advice. The study concluded that Ngô Đình Diệm had made little attempt to hide the fact that he was the one who made all the decisions for his country even if propaganda from the Saigon government asserted differently.

Many of Ngô Đình Diệm's critics made the accusation that he allowed the National Assembly no real power and that the organization was dominated by individuals who followed his lead without question except for a minority number of deputies whose voice was not heard and rarely reported.[14] While this theme would be prevalent throughout 1960, it would intensify as the April 1961 national elections approached. A closer examination of the Vietnamese press, a group that was also seen by Americans who had visited Saigon to be subject to the whims of Ngô Đình Diệm, offers a different perspective and one that provides evidence for the conclusion that the National Assembly did hold power, even for a newly formed organization in a Republic that was less than five years old. In December 1959, the focus of the National Assembly, and the reporting of that organization's activities, revolved around the discussion of the 1960 national budget. Reports from the press suggested that the debate in the National Assembly was lively and controversial, with many departments receiving less than they had requested or even received in the previous year. Some departments, which had been considered close to the Ngô Đình Diệm administration and therefore protected like the Department of Information, had their budgets significantly cut.[15]

The nature and intensity of the debate was even noticed by Durbrow who, in a response to a December 24, 1959, letter from Senator Al Gore (D–Tennessee), noted that more than just the six independent deputies in the National Assembly, including members of the National Revolutionary Movement, were involved in the debate. Durbrow conceded that the deputies had "spiritedly criticized various government operations, raised questions concerning government policies and evidenced an increasing consciousness of the independent role of the Assembly vis-à-vis the executive branch."[16] While Durbrow's main purpose in the letter was to answer Gore's query regarding the disqualification of the August 30, 1959, National Assembly election results for Phan Quang Đán and Phan Khắc Sửu, both of whom represented the opposition and both of whom would receive support from the embassy for their seating in the assembly, Durbrow's observation of the democratic nature of the National Assembly was noteworthy. In a follow-up to the Gore letter, Durbrow reported that the Saigon by-elections for two of the invalidated seats resulted in the election of the former minority leaders in the previous assembly who defeated an official government party candidate and the strong independent Phạm Văn Thùng, who won out over a candidate favored by the National Revolutionary Movement.[17] The debate within the National Assembly over the budget issues received praise from many of the Saigon newspapers. *Buổi sang* applauded the debate in an editorial which suggested that the National Assembly's action showed that the deputies understood their role in the Republic, implying in the process that that role was not one for which rubberstamping was the primary task.[18] During the course of the debate over the budget, deputies of the National Assembly also voiced their protest over what they considered recurring problems in the RVN.

On December 19, during the debate over the section of the Department of Interior's budget connected to political training centers and reeducation centers for political detainees, three deputies, headed by Bùi Quang Nga, raised the question of how these individuals were being treated. He requested that, in connection with the budget, Ngô Đình Diệm grant amnesty to some of the political detainees, or at least reduce their jail time, in celebration of the visit of the Thai king and queen, as well as provide a thorough review of all detainee files with the purpose of either bringing them to trial or freeing them. The main criticism was the number of individuals who were suspected of subversive action but not charged with any crimes who were allowed to remain in the reeducation centers without the benefit of trial. Assemblyman Bùi Quang Nga also called for the release of individuals who had spent a considerable amount of time in the centers and had repented or had been falsely accused.[19] Joining the debate was the independent Cao Đài member Phan Khắc Sửu who represented the intellectual opposition to Ngô Đình Diệm and had gained his seat in the August 30, 1959, election despite active opposition. He argued that the government needed to adopt a policy of clemency rather than hold individuals based on suspicion. Another deputy, Huỳnh Thành Vị, asserted that the provincial security officials who were also funded in the budget under discussion were acting authoritarian and violating the RVN's motto of "Police are the people's friends."[20] Huỳnh Thành Vị, supported by Nguyễn Văn Liên, accused the police of using torture to acquire oral or written confessions.

These deputies were very vocal in their opposition to the current policy, and their positions were reported in the Saigon papers; the argument that the actions by the police sabotaged the efforts of the government of Vietnam were not passed over by Ngô Đình Diệm who would frequently complain to Durbrow and other Americans about his inability to get competent people in place in positions of power and influence in the countryside. It was also worth mentioning that Ngô Đình Diệm responded to this criticism by creating a Directorate General for Political Reeducation Centers on January 13, 1960, headed by the former commander of the Fifth Military Region, Colonel Nguyễn Văn Y.[21]

While the Country Team failed to acknowledge the role of the National Assembly, it did attempt to explain its perceptions of Ngô Đình Diệm's authoritarian approach to governance. The Country Team dismissed this style of rule, concluding that Ngô Đình Diệm had no real desire "to launch into any widespread experiments in democracy when he sees more important work ahead."[22] Ngô Đình Diệm's reasons: the inexperience of his government in politics and decision making for the nation, the effects of French colonialism on dynamic leadership, the need for security and discipline in the face of the communist insurgency, and the lack of trained cadres who were responsible enough to do the work of the Republic without Ngô Đình Diệm's supervision were considered secondary to the Ngô family's adherence to the tradition of the Mandarin who rule from wisdom and experience and led rather than included the uneducated and guideless masses. While the Mandarin tradition was strong in the Ngô family, its necessity, despite what the Americans believed, was strong because of the public reasons that Ngô Đình Diệm had communicated to the U.S. embassy staff in Saigon. There was a sense, however, that individuals like Durbrow and Mendenhall were more willing to listen to the Saigon intellectuals who constantly complained of Ngô Đình Diệm's failure to include them in his decisions. It would be this group that formed the nucleus of dissent in Saigon during the Year of the Rat and would help to encourage, even if it was not actively involved in the planning of, the failed rebellion in November 1960. This group, despite its motives, would continue to have the ear of the American embassy and play a more decisive role in Saigon politics than perhaps it should have during a time of growing communist insurrection and domestic crisis.

Another source of controversy between the U.S. embassy and the Presidential Palace was the existence of the Cần Lao Nhân Vị Cách Mạng Đảng (Personalist Labor Revolutionary Party or Cần Lao Party), which was an organization modeled in secrecy and headed by Ngô Đình Nhu. It became the political party most closely tied to Ngô Đình Diệm's vision of the Republic, serving as both advocate and informant for the president. The 20,000-member-strong party was a serious concern for Durbrow as it represented a movement away from the democratic model that the United States had been trying to construct in the RVN since 1955. American officials in Saigon maintained that the Cần Lao Party represented one of the main obstacles to the democratic process in that it encouraged Ngô Đình Diệm's refusal to concede to political reforms that had been advocated by the American embassy as well as some in Washington.

According to the Country Team assessment, the main function of the individual Cần Lao Party member was to "exert positive influence by applying and expressing the principles of Personalism, and also to keep his party superiors informed of the 'true' situation surrounding him."[23] The implication was that the Cần Lao Party served as the government's eyes and ears, spying on subversives and malcontents to keep the people in order and focused on the Republic in support of Ngô Đình Diệm's rule. The assessment also maintained that the Cần Lao Party organization was used to "provide an extra-legal method of accomplishing results which for one reason or another are not desired to be accomplished through normal government channels."[24] While the assessment focused on this justifiably negative aspect of the political party, the Country Team's analysis suggested that these activities served as the main function of the organization though it begrudgingly added that the party might also serve a useful purpose: "The Can Lao Party, in theory, would provide the cement to maintain control while the government establishes the facades of democratic organization and institutions. It might thus be considered a technique to assist other less-developed countries through their immediate problems toward political democracy."[25] The Year of the Rat revealed that the Cần Lao Party members provided for a more diverse and positive contribution to the RVN that involved action that was not connected to, or identified with, Ngô Đình Diệm.

That Durbrow and the Country Team failed to provide the other side of the Cần Lao Party was not surprising given the atmosphere of frustration and tension exhibited by these select members of the American diplomatic mission in Saigon nor was it surprising that, as the lunar new year came and went, Durbrow and Mendenhall reported to Washington only conversations with Vietnamese opposed to the functions of the Cần Lao Party and never reported on the humanitarian and social programs sponsored or organized by the party.

Another related area of concern was the role of the military in the political life of the RVN. While the military bore the major brunt of the responsibility of protecting the country against the Democratic Republic of Vietnam (DRV) and the southern communist insurgency, it shared very little influence in the day-to-day political affairs of state. The Country Team connected the Cần Lao Party's infiltration of the Vietnamese military with this reality and concluded that there was no military leadership available to serve as an alternative to Ngô Đình Diệm's rule. The theme of replacing Ngô Đình Diệm would run through the lunar year, culminating in the abortive November 11 coup d'état and the realization that the United States had to prepare for a future RVN with Ngô Đình Diệm.

The assessment examined scenarios that might follow Ngô Đình Diệm's death, from a constitutional approach in which Vice President Nguyễn Ngọc Thơ would assume power to a push by the Ngô family to retain power, or a military coup d'état. Even without Ngô Đình Diệm's death, the Country Team predicted a crisis with the April 1961 national elections, scheduled to select the next president and vice president under the terms of the constitution. The assessment concluded that Ngô Đình Diệm would not allow his opposition to express themselves during the campaign season before Election Day. As the events proceeded and the April 1961 presidential election unfolded, it was clear that the dire predictions proved to be unwarranted as the election, still a resounding victory for Ngô Đình Diệm, demonstrated some progression for the RVN toward the democratic model so desired by the United States, as well as how accommodating Ngô Đình Diệm had become in allowing the people and the election process to determine the next president.

The Country Team assessment ended on a positive note even if its conclusions were based on seemingly incompatible factors. It recommended continued support for the Ngô Đình Diệm government even if it was authoritarian, as it was at least working to eliminate those aspects in the countryside that had given rise to the communist insurgency. It also acknowledged that the Saigon government under Ngô Đình Diệm might never attain a Western style of democracy and suggested encouraging the Vietnamese to continue with the form of government that blended democracy with the traditional needs and customs of the people. It would take a little more than a year for Durbrow to put aside this compromise as he pushed for political reforms as a requirement for continued U.S. support. Durbrow's future position was foreshadowed in the assessment as it called for continued pressure on Ngô Đình Diệm to preserve basic human rights and move toward a more representative form of government in order to improve his prestige and counter the communist propaganda emanating from the North. Durbrow used the August 30, 1959, election of the National Assembly as an example of his concern for the distaste of Ngô Đình Diệm's form of representative government. Ngô Đình Diệm had denied seats won in the election to Phan Quang Đán and Nguyễn Tấn, both of whom would play a role in the Year of the Rat and have the ear of the embassy as they discussed Ngô Đình Diệm's rule.

Both men represented the Saigon intelligentsia that Durbrow and Mendenhall believed should have an opportunity to play a more substantial role in the Saigon government. The Country Team assessment recommended that the United States encourage Ngô Đình Diệm to seek their counsel because they represented a wealth of knowledge but also because they were likely to be the leaders in the "second-stage" revolt against Ngô Đình Diệm. What was lost in the recommendation and neglected in the year to come was that individuals like these two men represented a Vietnam that Ngô Đình Diệm did not want. To include them in the discussion was to dilute Ngô Đình Diệm's vision for the future of the RVN.

Another common complaint issued by Durbrow and the Americans concerned the rampant corruption within the Ngô Đình Diệm regime and throughout the countryside. While the acts themselves were criticized, the Americans often pointed to the inability of the Ngô Đình Diệm administration to deal with the perpetrators of the corruption. Corruption did exist in the RVN during this time frame and its proliferation was harmful to the progression toward democracy, but the record does indicate that the Saigon government was not oblivious to the problem nor was it passive in its efforts to alleviate the condition. There were several reports of criminal cases conducted against those guilty of corruption.[26]

The Country Team assessment represented the view of the U.S. embassy at a critical time for the U.S.-RVN relationship. Ngô Đình Diệm had undergone tremendous challenges and had survived attempts upon his life. He had made mistakes along the way, as any new leader would do in an infant country, but he represented the RVN's best hope, at that moment, for a positive future. As the assessment implied, and Durbrow would confirm, Ngô Đình Diệm had not progressed fast or far enough. Time for the Vietnamese was often marked in years or decades rather than hours or days. Changes did occur in the Saigon government and, by the presidential election in April 1961, there appeared to be every indication that Ngô Đình Diệm had moved forward in his goals for the Republic as well as American aspirations for Vietnam's democratic experiment. However, for Durbrow, the Department of State officials associated with Southeast Asia, and the embassy staff, the benefits for the United States' continued association with Ngô Đình Diệm no longer outweighed the costs.

As the Country Team prepared and transmitted its assessment of the RVN, Ngô Đình Diệm was also undergoing his own review as 1959 came to an end. On December 8, he held a press conference, the second of two that day, for a group of touring newspaper men and journalists who were traveling throughout the Far East.[27] The media party made several stops before meeting with Ngô Đình Diệm, which allowed them an opportunity to formulate an opinion on the state of the country under the close supervision of MAAG and General Williams. Several

Ngô Đình Diệm's press conference, circa 1950s (United States Information Agency-United States Overseas Mission-Saigon, Photograph 55–4698, National Archives and Records Administration, College Park, Maryland).

issues emerged from the question-and-answer period of the press interview that begin to explain the nature of Ngô Đình Diệm's rule in the RVN and the constraints the country was under preceding the start of the Year of the Rat.

One of the lingering issues of the Saigon government was land redistribution and security for villages oftentimes isolated from military bases or controlled lines of communication. In response to journalists' observations and questions related to the subject, Ngô Đình Diệm expounded upon the strategy of his government in dealing with this most significant problem. Land redistribution had been a concern since Durbrow's earliest days in Saigon, while Ngô Đình Diệm had used the issue to further the more pressing problem of internal security.

For Ngô Đình Diệm, the creation of economic infrastructure was tied to democracy in the RVN. He argued, as others had before him, that the Vietnamese farmer needed to be able to till his own land not only to feed and care for his family and provide for future generations but also as a means of securing the loyalty of that farmer to the Republic. An individual who owned land also had a vested interest in the survival of the government that ensured that land would remain his own. The nature of the land redistribution and resettlement program continued throughout 1960 and 1961 and would prompt observations on the part of the Americans in Saigon who believed that Ngô Đình Diệm did not have the Republic's best interests in mind.

Another issue that had served as an obstacle for advancing the RVN's prosperity and internal security was the creation of lines of communication throughout the country. As Ngô Đình Diệm remarked in the press conference, only one highway existed from Saigon to the Demilitarized Zone along the 17th parallel, and that road, Route 1, was often blocked during the rainy season by flooding of the many rivers that traversed it. Ngô Đình Diệm had plans for an alternative highway system, but his vision and that of the Americans had caused tension and discord.

Ngô Đình Diệm's position on the road system was simple: the greater the communications infrastructure in the RVN, the more likely that manufactured goods and foodstuffs could flow throughout the country. Improved roads would also allow for the elimination of the isolation of many villages, which were more prone to the communist insurgents, known as the Việt Cộng, and less able to enjoy the benefits of other goods and services offered by the Saigon government.

Ngô Đình Diệm was also given the opportunity to explore his views on reunification with the North, something that other critics of the American involvement in Vietnam would point to as one of the primary reasons why the United States was not justified in its decision to fight in Vietnam. In 1959, Ngô Đình Diệm's position on the issue of reunification was a sophisticated blend of political and philosophical factors that made the event highly unlikely. He argued that reunification was much more than just the physical act of joining geography and terrain. His concern was for his people whom he refused to turn over to a government that he considered inhuman. To negotiate with the DRV and Hồ Chí Minh on the possibility of elections and reunification while the people of the North were not free and the government practiced on the people in order to suppress their basic human rights was to acknowledge that the communist form of government was legitimate, if not desired. Ngô Đình Diệm would never concede this point. Elections, as a result, would not solve the issue of either, even if the politicians in the RVN were victorious. In 1959, the armed forces in the North, which were estimated in numbers of at least twice the size of the South, would have to be completely disbanded and not pose a threat of any future settlement. As the events of the next year would reveal, Ngô Đình Diệm was correct in asserting that the North was less willing than the South in reunification through peaceful elections and in the absence of armed confrontation.[28]

Despite the political unrest with the North, Ngô Đình Diệm still maintained a certain degree of confidence in the internal security and stability of the RVN, despite increased communist insurgent activity. While he was quick to concede that much work needed to be accomplished before true peace would return to the Vietnamese people, he also highlighted the challenges of the five-year struggle he had experienced during his tenure in office. Ngô Đình Diệm had not inherited a country with a homogeneous people, nor was it free from communist insurgents who had the popular support of most of the people due to the struggle against the French over the previous nine years. The people had a near decade-long exposure to the communist insurgency and naturally equated the resisters as the heroes in the struggle against the latest foreign invader. The fact that the people in question lived in the isolated villages that his government had been trying to link together made it even more difficult for Ngô Đình Diệm to reassert some form of presence and control in the countryside.

Given these difficulties, it should not be surprising that Ngô Đình Diệm's plan to regain control of the villages in Vietnam combined with efforts to increase the armed forces, Civil Guard, and Self-Defense Force while encouraging the Thanh niên Cộng hòa (Cộng hòa or Republican Youth) to take a more active role in the village councils even if it meant tampering with the existing system.[29] While there would be short-term problems, many of which would be significant, the long-term results would mean a more unified RVN that could withstand, and perhaps conquer, its communist brethren to the North. Ngô Đình Diệm was careful during the press conference to argue that it was not policy to overthrow the communist government in the DRV. Instead, he argued that the regime had to be weakened from within. Ngô Đình Diệm maintained that the Hanoi government needed to be isolated from the rest of the communist world, but it also had to be blocked from trade with the Free World. Ngô Đình Diệm praised the United States for its support of his country but also warned the journalists that the United States needed to take a leadership role in applying diplomatic pressure on its allies to cease their support, directly and indirectly, to the North Vietnamese. Only then could the scenario occur that would result in the internal deterioration of the communist government in Hanoi.

While this political philosophy had every appearance of being noble, there was a practical aspect to Ngô Đình Diệm's strategy for undermining the North. The RVN had in its military approximately 150,000 men divided into a general staff headquarters, three corps, seven combat divisions, one airborne brigade, one regiment of marines, and supporting troops. The United States was contributing between 60 and 80 percent of the RVN defense budget of VN$6,000,000, which stood at just over 14 percent of the total national budget of VN$43,000,000.[30] American aid was essential to the survival of the Army of the Republic of Vietnam (ARVN) just as American hardware and advisers proved indispensable to the South Vietnamese navy and air force.

While the RVN wanted to eventually do away with American aid, in December 1959 it still required a steady flow of U.S. dollars to fund the development of its armed forces to fight the communist insurgency and prepare for the expected invasion from the North. As Ngô Đình Diệm would comment to the journalists, after 1955 his troops had to operate as both military units and labor brigades to construct and maintain the roads, railways, and bridges as well as build and rebuild the infrastructure of the individual villages that had suffered nine years of war with the French, five years of Japanese occupation, and destruction at the hands of the communist insurgents as they vacated some areas after the 1954 Geneva Agreements. The ARVN had to help the people regain a sense of control over their lives and reestablish a pattern of normality. It also had to help care for the refugees from the North that had fled the communist-controlled government as a result of the 1954 Geneva Agreements. Over 810,000 Vietnamese moved during the 300-day period allowed for by that agreement, but the total continued to increase in the months and years that followed as individuals, families, and small groups risked everything to flee communism in the North. The reality of the RVN situation, in which Ngô Đình Diệm inherited a country that had to build itself from the very foundation, meant that the armed forces played a dual role that took away from their combat readiness and effectiveness by the end of the decade.

As a result of this added responsibility for the ARVN, the issue of the 20,000-man troop increase had been one that also lingered throughout the Durbrow–Ngô Đình Diệm relationship. Ngô Đình Diệm wanted 20,000 extra men to make the ARVN more effective, but he faced constant objections from Durbrow and his staff at the U.S. embassy in Saigon who preferred to use the 20,000-man question as a bargaining chip for American ideas of reform with the Saigon government and specifically directed toward Ngô Đình Diệm. Throughout the Year of the Rat, the 20,000-man debate continued as Ngô Đình Diệm pushed for what he considered a necessary increase to stave off defeat while Durbrow used the debate as leverage against the RVN president.

The question of prestige was not a one-way street though the American's often viewed it as such. While the U.S. personnel did not see the need to go through a self-evaluation of their role vis-à-vis the RVN, they were often on the minds of the Vietnamese leadership. One such case occurred during a December 11 conversation between Durbrow and Nguyễn Ngọc Thơ. Nguyễn Ngọc Thơ complained of the duplicity he believed American visitors to South Vietnam were involved in as they said one thing to the Vietnamese and another to the press. Nguyễn Ngọc Thơ specifically mentioned the case of Senator Al Gore who had recently visited the country and had had high praise for South Vietnam's progress and programs when he met with Nguyễn Ngọc Thơ and Secretary of State for the Presidency Nguyễn Đình Thuận amid an internal controversy over the nature of American aid to the RVN.

The issue that surfaced in December 1959 was the Vietnamese reaction to the United States "Buy American" Plan. The weekly magazine, the *Times of Vietnam*, editorial for December 5 addressed the plan and criticized the United States for its backward thinking and fiscal policy that would negatively affect the RVN toward its road to independence and self-sufficiency.[31] The editorial sympathized with the "Buy American" policy after the Second World War that helped to stabilize and then reenergize Europe but argued that Asian countries, and especially South Vietnam, had not been given sufficient time to rebuild after the Japanese occupation during the war, nor had it the opportunity to develop its infrastructure in peacetime as a result of the First Indochina War and the subsequent communist insurgency that had lingered in the countryside through the 1950s. The editorial cited a meeting of economists at Princeton University that had earlier convened and had concluded that the "Buy America" provision to U.S. foreign aid would only recover about US$200 million which was a fraction of the US$3 billion spent abroad.

The *Times of Vietnam* concluded that the United States would lose much more favor from the Asian nations by this policy than dollars saved: "Surely it is not by hitting at the

Vice President Nguyễn Ngọc Thơ (center) and Secretary of State Nguyễn Đình Thuận (center-right) at the funeral of Colonel Hoàng Thùy Nam, 1961 (United States Information Agency–United States Overseas Mission–Saigon, Photograph 61–13568, National Archives and Records Administration, College Park, Maryland).

poor and sparing the rich that the deficit in the balance of payments of the United States can be stopped. The solution lies elsewhere."[32] This type of financial issue would continue to plague the U.S.-RVN relationship. From the Vietnamese perspective, it made little sense to add requirements for, or restrictions on, spending when that country was at war and fighting for its very survival. Ngô Đình Diệm would repeatedly express this point of view to his American allies, oftentimes with frustrating results as the American perspective held that the United States, as a result of being the source of the funding, had a legitimate right to determine how, when, and where American aid would be directed. In many respects, both perspectives and arguments deriving from them are correct, but, as a result, neither side would be able to fully reconcile the difference over dollars.

Senators Gore and Gale McGee arrived in Vietnam on December 6 for a five-day visit to study American aid to Vietnam. Ngô Đình Diệm received the senators on December 7 at the Presidential Palace, with Nguyễn Ngọc Thơ and Nguyễn Đình Thuận presumably meeting with the senators afterward.[33] Gore then spoke to the news media, criticizing Ngô Đình Diệm and his policies. While the duplicity was a serious concern, the criticism of the programs also offended the Vietnamese who had accomplished much in the three years of active nation building with the help of American aid and technical advice. The Saigon government had a certain pride in its accomplishments even if it recognized that many more tasks lay ahead. Nguyễn Ngọc Thơ maintained, in his conversation with Durbrow, that the United States needed to limit its domestic bickering to its own borders; it also needed to contain its opposition so that domestic conflict did not extend into the international arena. If the United States continued to allow this to happen, it would damage America's role as a leader of the Free World; in short, U.S. prestige would be irrevocably damaged each time critics of the Dwight D. Eisenhower administration in Congress used the RVN as a means of striking out against the Republicans. Nguyễn Ngọc Thơ also warned that Gore's duplicity also aided the communists and negatively influenced the neutrals: "One unfavorable story gave comfort to neutrals in Cambodia and elsewhere, and were seized upon by communists in Hanoi to [the] embarrassment of [the] Diem Regime."[34] Nguyễn Ngọc Thơ maintained that the Americans had the responsibility, as they assumed the position of leadership in the Free World, of acting with "dignity and trust." Gore's actions, and the failure of the U.S. government to respond in defense of the RVN failed to live up to the high standards expected of it by its allies.

Ngô Đình Diệm ended 1959 with a Christmas message, focusing on the "remote village in the middle of the jungle" that was the shared space of the soldier and peasant. He remarked on the service and sacrifice of the individual but also on those who were north of the 17th parallel: "In the midst of the family and popular festivities with which we like to celebrate Christmas, let us keep a special thought for our compatriots in the north, who are enduring a tyranny that is becoming ever more oppressive and who place all their hopes in us. It is by observing the evangelical message in our private and public lives that we will be able to some extent, to justify this confidence."[35] In some ways the speech was symbolic of Ngô Đình Diệm's problems. His tone and message were appropriate, though a Christmas message to a predominantly Buddhist population exposed the possible inconsistencies of his policies. In the final month of the Year of the Pig, Ngô Đình Diệm remained hopeful for Vietnam's future while at the same time encouraged by the state of affairs that existed within his country and among his closest allies. The Year of the Rat would offer challenges to this conviction and test the limits of Vietnamese-American friendship.

2

Enter the Year of the Rat

In his 1960 New Year message, Ngô Đình Diệm praised the Vietnamese people for their effort in building up the infrastructure of a free country in the midst of a communist insurgency and with the handicap of living for so long under French colonial rule.[1] As an underdeveloped country, the RVN had faced a series of disadvantages that had created a disparity between it and the Western nations that made up the international community of the Free World. Ngô Đình Diệm noted that Vietnam still needed to exploit its natural resources, modernize its agricultural practices, develop an industry and individuals to lead it, and garner a collective spirit to move the nation forward. These challenges were all the more difficult because of the institutional obstacles created by French colonialism in the political, social, and cultural structures as well as the potential threat of international communism.

Ngô Đình Diệm continued in his message to explain that the Vietnamese success was a result of their path that respected the individual, the community, and progress. It required the Vietnamese citizen to put aside petty interests for the welfare of the State but also required the individual to sacrifice certain benefits until the Republic was safe: "Having discovered the right path we must now enrich our spiritual and moral life, preach discipline, practice rigorous saving, redouble our efforts so as to render our regime each day more solid, more powerful, more prosperous, and thus prepare favorable conditions for reunifying our country in freedom and prosperity."[2] Ngô Đình Diệm maintained that the RVN, while its condition had been under significant stress, was still in a better situation than many of the former colonies in Asia and Africa. While he did not mention it specifically, this was due in part to the tremendous amount of economic and military assistance provided by the United States.

In the lunar New Year, this aid would come under scrutiny and become tied to American-sponsored reforms that would, at times, recall the old colonial system and create an atmosphere of distrust. What Ngô Đình Diệm did not anticipate was the opposition by personnel in the U.S. embassy in Saigon. These individuals sometimes cajoled the RVN president toward questionable reforms and worked to isolate him from Americans who shared the Vietnamese philosophy and process for change. The Year of the Rat held great promise for the RVN, but it also had, at its core, the potential for great harm. The RVN was irrevocably tied to the United States for its progress and security and needed stable, anti-communist allies in Cambodia and Laos to ensure its survival. The many and varied events during the Year of the Rat would determine the extent to which these factors would succeed or fail.

As 1960 began, the RVN economy gave every indication of improving. In many of the key indicators, including rice, rubber, agricultural staples, fruit, milk, poultry, and tea, the Vietnamese had some remarkable improvement. Ironically, these economic advances were rarely reported by the United States.[3] Yet, if Ngô Đình Diệm felt comfortable with the economic progress of the RVN, he was less optimistic with the diplomatic and military situation and the state of the ARVN as the lunar New Year began. For example, the program to eradicate malaria that paralleled American efforts in Italy after the Second World War had collapsed because members of the teams charged with going out into the countryside refused to leave the cities for fear of their lives. The communists had targeted these teams for assassination because this program, which held too many positives, was directly connected to the Saigon government.[4] It was these factors that the American officials in Saigon focused on and reported back to Washington, rather than the improving economic situation.

The strain in diplomacy between the United States and RVN showed itself early when Secretary of the Army Wilbur M. Brucker visited Saigon.[5] On January 7, Brucker along with Durbrow and Williams met with Ngô Đình Diệm and Nguyễn Đình Thuận. Brucker, who had been in the RVN in 1955, was acquainted with Ngô Đình Diệm and familiar with his struggles. The two discussed the security situation in the country, while Ngô Đình Diệm, in his typical fashion, spent some time outlining the security threat and explaining the increased Việt Cộng activity over the previous eighteen months.[6] The conversation continued for about an hour when Brucker commented to Ngô Đình Diệm that the RVN needed better airports. According to Durbrow, Brucker argued that the RVN required jet-capable airstrips in order to accommodate the U.S. military should the Vietnamese require American assistance against the DRV. At this point, according to Williams, Durbrow turned to Brucker and told him that he could not make such a statement. Williams described Durbrow's language in the exchange as inappropriate and unprofessional given the nature of the conference. Infuriated, Brucker walked out of the conference after bidding Ngô Đình Diệm a good night.[7] The confrontation between Brucker and Durbrow was a prime example of the growing tension that existed between the Department of State and Department of Defense. It also demonstrated the type of manipulation exerted by Durbrow on the Vietnamese.

Durbrow wanted complete control in the handling of Ngô Đình Diệm and did not tolerate interference. His relationship with Williams had strained as a result, while his treatment of Brucker, in front of Ngô Đình Diệm and Nguyễn Đình Thuận, showed the degree to which he tried to manage situations with the RVN president. When Brucker offered an insight that went against Durbrow and the Department of State's vision for the RVN, the ambassador responded forcibly. For Ngô Đình Diệm, who spoke English though he preferred to communicate with the Americans in either French or through an interpreter, the exchange between the secretary and the ambassador was disturbing. Ngô Đình Diệm saw in Brucker an ally who essentially wanted the same things as himself. While the Department of State would argue later that Ngô Đình Diệm used the incident to work one group of Americans against another, it is more likely that Ngô Đình Diệm was embarrassed by the actions of the ambassador whom he saw as a subordinate to the Secretary of the Army.[8]

Because the meeting had broken up in such an awkward way, Nguyễn Đình Thuận telephoned Williams a few hours later and requested that he and Brucker return to the Presidential Palace without Durbrow to continue the discussion. Brucker agreed to go back, but Williams declined in order not to be drawn into the argument between Brucker and Durbrow. Williams, who had been at odds with Durbrow for some time and who would experience even greater consternation as the year progressed, recognized that his involvement in the potential discussions would serve no positive role. Brucker, however, returned to the palace at 9:45 p.m. accompanied by an interpreter, to continue their conversation.

Right before the earlier incident that precipitated the break-up of the meeting, Brucker had been discussing the personnel ceiling imposed by the 1954 Geneva Agreements. The United States had been restricted to 342 personnel though an additional 350 had been added through the Temporary Equipment Recovery Mission (TERM).[9] Brucker had been pressing Ngô Đình Diệm to publicize DRV violations of the Geneva Agreements in order to justify continuing American personnel in the RVN above the 342 level. During the course of the hour meeting, Brucker continued his exchange with Ngô Đình Diệm and Nguyễn Đình Thuận on the MAAG ceiling. Brucker asked a series of questions to the two Vietnamese leaders about the status of the MAAG personnel and the Geneva Agreements.[10] The question of MAAG violating the Geneva Agreements had been brought up by the Polish delegation to the International Control Commission (ICC) who had forwarded their concern to Durbrow. As a result of these concerns, which had reached Washington, a deadline was set to remove the TERM personnel by the end of 1960. When Brucker asked Nguyễn Đình Thuận who had set the deadline, he responded that Durbrow had done so in coordination with Williams.

Williams later refuted this claim, arguing that he had never agreed to coordinate a deadline with Durbrow nor had he been asked. Brucker, who was concerned that this decision had been made because it fixed a timeline to the withdrawal of American personnel from the RVN, then asked Nguyễn Đình Thuận who had reviewed the Vietnamese reply. Again, he stated that both Durbrow and Williams had agreed to the deadline. Williams argued that he had no knowledge of the reply nor would he have committed to a reduction of TERM personnel without Department of Defense approval. As would often be the case in the tenure of Durbrow, the ambassador involved Williams' approval for a plan of his own design, even when Williams had not approved it, when he knew that it might be opposed by the Vietnamese. Durbrow understood that Williams had a better working relationship with the Vietnamese than he did and used that knowledge to push through potentially controversial policy.

The conversation concluded with Brucker reinforcing the need to publicize the Việt Cộng violations of the Geneva Agreements and a brief exchange between Ngô Đình Diệm and Brucker in which the RVN president tried to justify a greater increase of MAAG personnel while still staying within the limits of the Geneva Agreement. Ngô Đình Diệm maintained that French personnel who had vacated the country should be added to the U.S. total. Essentially, as Ngô Đình Diệm saw it, it did not matter where the personnel came from when one calculated the personnel limit under the Geneva Agreements. They could be French or Americans. In his line of thinking, this allowed TERM personnel to remain without fear of condemnation by the ICC.[11] Brucker left the meeting with a reflection of Durbrow's role in Vietnam. He argued that the RVN deserved any help that the United States could supply and that Durbrow, as head of the Country Team, had the authority to determine that aid. However, he maintained that Durbrow "also had the responsibility to be alert, energetic, and active in assisting the government of Vietnam to benefit to the greatest possible degree from any juridical interpretations that could be given to the Geneva Agreements or any other international instruments."[12] Brucker promised Ngô Đình Diệm that he would do all in his power to help maintain the number of MAAG personnel and informed him that he would tell Durbrow of the contents of their meeting.

In reflecting upon the events some ten years later, Williams believed that Durbrow had used his name in his conversations with Ngô Đình Diệm and Nguyễn Đình Thuận in order to calm Vietnamese fears that the United States might disengage from Southeast Asia. Because the Vietnamese trusted Williams but were on less stable ground with Durbrow, the ambassador employed the general's name to reassure the Vietnamese that what he was doing was part of a united American front and, as a result, would most likely not be detrimental to the Vietnamese struggle against the Việt Cộng. The exchange between Brucker, Ngô Đình Diệm, and Nguyễn Đình Thuận reaffirmed the tension between Durbrow and Williams. It was also at this time that Williams exposed Durbrow's duplicity in his reporting of the incident to J. Graham Parsons. On January 8, Durbrow sent Parsons a letter outlining the course of events.[13] Williams would argue later that Durbrow's letter was misleading and was designed to protect himself from any response Brucker might have as a result of their exchange.

As it related to the jet-capable airfield, Williams noted that Durbrow tried to connect his argument to the Geneva Agreements by including airfields at other cities that had never been mentioned in the course of the conversation. Williams maintained that MAAG had always wanted the airfield for Saigon but it had been the United States Operations Mission (USOM) that had drawn out the process.[14] Williams argued that violating the Geneva Agreements was not the first obstacle; rather, it was the unwillingness of Durbrow and USOM to see the project through. Williams also countered Durbrow's claim that both he and Williams had been asked not to come to the evening meeting between Brucker and Ngô Đình Diệm. Only Durbrow had been asked not to return.[15] Williams decided against accompanying Brucker because he still had to work with Durbrow. Further, Williams indicated that Durbrow's letter neglected to mention the tone at the end of the meeting that resulted in Brucker leaving the Presidential Palace without Durbrow. In Durbrow's account, he never hinted at the embarrassing situation that arose after he used, what Williams described as, inexcusable language in Ngô Đình Diệm's presence. Williams also questioned Durbrow's commitment to maintain MAAG as expressed in his correspondence with Parsons. As Williams asserted in his 1971 memorandum, "I believe that he [Durbrow] was jealous of the high standing of MAAG with the RVN and further he was influenced in his anti–MAAG and anti–RVN feelings by the French Ambassador and his Staff."[16] Williams asserted that Durbrow had worked to decrease MAAG and that he had no interest in maintaining TERM. While Williams' account was just one perspective and was influenced by his poor working relationship with Durbrow, Durbrow's duplicity remained consistent throughout the year regardless of who reported it.

When Williams read Durbrow's January 8 letter to Parsons and Parsons' February 1 response, he forwarded to the ambassador a one-page observation of the exchange. The tone of the memorandum suggests that the relationship between Williams and Durbrow was at a low point. In response to Durbrow's assertion that Brucker had not been well briefed on the MAAG ceiling question, Williams responded that he had and concluded that if the briefing was inadequate, it was because much of the correspondence between Durbrow and the Department of State was not made available. Williams also countered Durbrow's jab at him as the senior military commander influencing Brucker's line of thinking. As the year progressed, it became clear that Williams had little respect for Durbrow's actions as ambassador, while Durbrow liberally used his office and association with Williams to bully, cajole, convince, and encourage the Vietnamese to his line of thinking, which almost always followed that of the Department of State.

The Brucker episode helped to establish a few precedents for 1960. For Ngô Đình Diệm, it reinforced his view that there were individuals in Washington who were favorable to continued U.S.-Vietnamese relations despite repeated concerns expressed by Durbrow. It also exposed the level of divisiveness that existed between the Department of State and Department of Defense which would further intensify as the year progressed. Ngô Đình Diệm did not need an ally who was divided internally at a time when the Vietnamese were facing their greatest threat since 1955. Unfortunately, Ngô Đình Diệm's concern about Durbrow and his control of the embassy staff, coupled with the ambassador's strategy and tactics in conveying his policies to the RVN, also contributed to the tension as Ngô Đình Diệm focused more on the needs of his country than on the internal relationships that existed among the Americans. Ngô Đình Diệm would not cater to Durbrow and, as a result, earned the same scorn and ire that the ambassador had focused upon Williams. Likewise, Durbrow would not deviate from the course that he believed was best for the RVN regardless of Ngô Đình Diệm's obstinance.

On the military front, the condition of the ARVN was also strained. In a January 12 conversation between Ngô Đình Diệm and Williams, the president asked the general what he believed to be the cause of the laxness within ARVN. Because Williams and Ngô Đình Diệm shared each other's confidence, Williams provided a detailed analysis of ARVN's deficiencies. Williams argued, though Ngô Đình Diệm disagreed, that the principle problem with ARVN personnel was the fact that they expected the United States to enter the war if an emergency arose. This allowed many within the military to expend less energy in accomplishing their training and mission than they should have done given the situation. Ngô Đình Diệm argued, however, that it was the fault of the Vietnamese General Staff who did not push their men hard enough. While both men were correct to some extent, Williams' assessment would become truer later in the 1960s. Still, both agreed that the demobilization of seasoned non-commissioned officers because of budgetary constraints had caused a decreased effectiveness of ARVN, while the tendencies to stay out of the field by some officers caused them to lose the effectiveness of the training that they had received.

Williams had also indicated that another problem with the ARVN was that it was under-strength from its authorized level of 150,000 personnel, with many units having only 130 of the 150 men required. Williams was also concerned that the number of reservists trained for 1959, some 7,000, was less than half of the 15,000 planned. He complained that this low number helped to justify the arguments of the Country Team, who believed that Williams' proposal to train 30,000 reservists in 1960 should be reduced to 15,000. Durbrow had also argued that the reservists should be a part of the 150,000 count, in part because the additional expenses would take away from economic development dollars.[17] Since the training of reservists provided the ARVN with some flexibility during times of emergency, the failure to have these men available served as a handicap, as did the failure of the ARVN to train technicians. The RVN had relied too heavily on foreign technicians and, as a result, was not prepared to take over the responsibilities when they left. Williams implored Ngô Đình Diệm to read the training visit and logistical visit reports made available to him by MAAG, to which Ngô Đình Diệm agreed, and he promised to call a meeting of his General Staff and Ministry of Defense to address these discrepancies. This exchange between Ngô Đình Diệm and Williams was indicative of the relationship the two had during Williams' tenure as chief, MAAG, which he had held since 1955. The two men respected one another, and as a result Williams was able to bring up criticisms to Ngô Đình Diệm in a way that did not threaten the president or insult the Vietnamese people. Williams was one of only a few Americans who had mastered this technique, while Durbrow, despite his own self-perception, was not.

Ngô Đình Diệm accepted Williams' remarks and expressed concern. Ngô Đình Diệm had been arguing for some time, based upon intelligence gathered from captured prisoners, that the Việt Cộng were planning to intensify their attacks against Saigon. The event that occurred two weeks following this conversation reinforced the dangerous position of the ARVN. On January 26, four Việt Cộng companies, or approximately 200 men, attacked the 32nd Regiment, 21st ARVN Division, camp in Trảng Sụp, Tây Ninh province, which had approximately 250 to 300 men in residence at the time.[18] The Việt Cộng engaged the ARVN force for an hour and inflicted significant casualties. These numbers included sixty-six soldiers killed or wounded, two barracks and the regimental headquarters destroyed, and the capture a significant number of weapons and ammunition.

The attack, which occurred approximately twenty kilometers from the Vietnamese-Cambodian border, was one more in a series of events that demonstrated the increased Việt Cộng activity and the importance of internal security that would be the focus of the opening months of the lunar New Year. It also exposed some of the problems in defending against the communist insurgency and also confirmed that peaceful coexistence between the RVN and the DRV was not an attainable goal in the near future.[19] It also showed that guerrilla tactics used by the Việt Cộng against the RVN Armed Forces had a few advantages. Because of the size of the ARVN, it was difficult to remain vigilant on a continuous basis.[20] This was especially true as the ARVN trained for an invasion from the North, which required a different organization of military units, strategy, and tactics.

The Việt Cộng, as demonstrated in the January 26 incident, exposed this weakness by attacking at 2:30 a.m. after the troops had been celebrating the New Year. The episode also showed the vulnerability of the ARVN officers who did not have enough experience in fighting, and it demonstrated the necessity of training the ARVN troops to fight by using guerrilla tactics, winning the cooperation of the civilian population, and increasing the role of MAAG in the field. The attack also led to another frank discussion between Williams and Ngô Đình Diệm.[21] During the course of a February 1 evening meeting, the two men reviewed the event. Williams took it upon himself to defend the colonel commanding the 21st ARVN Division who had been replaced as a result of the attack. This move demonstrated one of the many problems plaguing the ARVN. The colonel, who had the full confidence of MAAG, had already been rotated out of the 22nd ARVN Division because of a personality difference with its commander. He was replaced after the Tây Ninh incident in order to save face for the commanding general. Williams suggested that in a time of emergency, it was disheartening to see a career military officer sacrificed for political reasons. Ngô Đình Diệm agreed but also felt compelled to make the move in order to alleviate political concerns within the military. While Williams did not necessarily agree with the decision, he respected Ngô Đình Diệm's reasoning. This was something that Durbrow had difficulty doing.

Williams also took the opportunity of the Tây Ninh incident to review the tactical mistakes of the Vietnamese 32nd Regiment. Again, it was evident from the conversation that Williams and Ngô Đình Diệm understood one another. Williams criticized the sentry posts personnel, which consisted of ten posts and 110 men. He argued that the only way the Việt Cộng could have succeeded in attacking the camp was if the sentries had been asleep, and he maintained that this could not have happened if the officer of the day had made physical inspections of the posts. Williams also noted that the 32nd Regiment erred by allowing its married personnel to sleep with their families. The most significant criticism, however, was the failure of the men to have their weapons with them at the time of the attack. Because they were locked up in the battalion sheds, the initial assault was met without them.[22]

Williams also criticized the delay it took for the 21st ARVN Division to respond to the attack. The action commenced at 2:30 a.m. but the Division did not receive word until 7:38 a.m. and the relief force did not deploy until after 3:00 p.m. By the time it arrived to pursue the Việt Cộng, they had left the area. Ngô Đình Diệm had predicted that Việt Cộng activity would intensify, and recent statistics showed that his concerns were valid. Việt Cộng targeted assassinations (Trụ Giãn) and kidnappings had plagued Ngô Đình Diệm's efforts to pacify the countryside and promote his Agroville, or Garden City, Plan.[23]

Chart 1: The Number of Assassinations and Kidnappings by Months During 1958–1959

Assassinations	Jan.	Feb.	March	April	May	June	July	Aug.	Sept.	Oct.	Nov.	Dec.
1958	10	36	26	17	13	21	11	7	8	15	8	21
1959	10	11	31	13	16	5	16	12	22	29	35	33
Kidnappings												
1958	25	5	43	12	5	15	24	18	24	26	19	20
1959	17	6	21	16	22	15	22	11	34	42	89	48

Source: Durbrow to the Department of State, Telegram 278, "Special Report on Internal Security Situation in Viet-Nam," March 7, 1960, Annex I of Enclosure I, *FRUS, 1958–1960: Volume I: Vietnam*, 317–320.

Further, the boldness of the Tây Ninh attack and the lack of cohesiveness of the ARVN forces was a real problem for the RVN. The Việt Cộng's increased activity was part of a larger effort by the DRV to disrupt the RVN's government and oust Ngô Đình Diệm by the end of the year. Victims of targeted assassination were usually leaders in the hamlets, such as chiefs, educators, and other local authorities, as evidenced by a series of such events at the end of January.[24] American efforts were focused on internal security and the necessity of forcing reform in the Saigon government to make it more palatable to the American people. These efforts were also entrenched in a Cold War mentality that pitted the free, democratic world against communism. Ngô Đình Diệm concentrated on internal security, but he was also concerned with maintaining his position in the South and deflecting the internal dissenters who wished to see his government fail. This conflict in perspective, one that pitted reform against maintaining status even if the objectives were the same, was at the root of the growing problem between Ngô Đình Diệm and the Americans. It would, by the end of the year, result in a major turning point in the Ngô Đình Diệm–American relationship.

The increased activity of the Việt Cộng in South Vietnam elicited a number of responses by the RVN and the United States. For Ngô Đình Diệm, the increased threat in the countryside did not deter his role of being available and accessible to the people as president. In the days leading to the Vietnamese New Year, Ngô Đình Diệm conducted several inspection trips into the countryside to assess rural conditions, inspect youth training, army, and civic action camps, and study the progress in agricultural and infrastructure development.[25] These visits to the countryside occurred in addition to the numerous commitments related to ceremonies, exhibits, and inspection tours within Saigon, all of which were beyond the normal administration of the country. Clearly, Ngô Đình Diệm did not shy away from the people as had been reported and assumed by many who would write, then and after, about the RVN leader. He was doing more than any leader could be expected to accomplish in the midst of an armed insurgency against his government.

South Vietnamese newspapers recognized this while commenting on the increased communist insurgent activities. In a *Cách mạng Quốc gia* editorial, the paper credited the

Ngô Đình Diệm touring the countryside circa 1950s (United States Information Agency, Photograph 55-17194, National Archives and Records Administration, College Park, Maryland).

success of the Saigon government as the explanation for the atrocities: "In the past five years the Việt Cộng have not missed an opportunity to terrorize and murder their compatriots. In their eyes, massacre and sabotage are heroic and patriotic. Worried by the brilliant success of the RVN in improving the peasants' living standards, the Việt Cộng increased their terrorism. But they fail to realize that they have only increased our hatred of them."[26] This sentiment was expressed by most of the Saigon dailies and culminated in an *Ngôn Luận* editorial that called for the National Assembly to outlaw Vietnamese communism in order to end the terrorist attacks, but it failed to have the significant propaganda effect that some of the North Vietnamese papers accomplished.[27] This Vietnamese objective of neutralizing the insurgency was shared by the United States, but, again, this common goal was overshadowed by American politics and diplomacy.

One sign of this, and one of the more significant issues leading into 1960, was the proposed reduction in spending by the Department of Defense for the military budget of the RVN.[28] MAAG had provided Ngô Đình Diệm with guidelines that outlined approximately $169.3 million in spending for the fiscal year. This was significantly lower than the $185

Vietnamese people greet Ngô Đình Diệm, circa 1960s (United States Information Agency, Photograph 55–17197, National Archives and Records Administration, College Park, Maryland).

million requested from Congress but not a significant surprise given the congressional atmosphere of decreasing rather than increasing military spending. Durbrow further reduced the DOD military allotment another $4.3 million by reducing the ARVN budget for pay and allowances, foodstuffs, reserve forces, and new construction. He justified this additional reduction on the assumption that ARVN need not reach its 150,000-man projection nor would the reserve force need to be at the full projected strength.

Durbrow had earlier told Ngô Đình Diệm that the United States would contribute $130 million toward the proposed RVN military budget, but he suggested reducing this amount to $124.4 million, with the remainder to come from customs receipts collected on defense support aid ($26.6 million) and RVN resources ($14.1 million). The lesser amount than the one promised would be explained away by congressional cuts and the Commercial Import Program insistence on the RVN becoming more self-sufficient.[29] Lost perhaps in this assessment was the increasing difficulty of the RVN in stabilizing its economy, especially in a time of increased insurgency made possible by the insertion of DRV personnel. Ngô Đình Diệm later remarked to Williams of the political consequences of a decrease in American aid. He argued that such a reduction provided the North Vietnamese and Việt Cộng with propaganda to show the lack of U.S. support for the RVN. During their conversation, Ngô Đình Diệm argued that the United States should announce an increase in aid, regardless of its final position, in order to garner as much psychological advantage as possible.[30]

Durbrow was cognizant of the significance of the reduced commitment by the United States during this critical time for the Vietnamese, who were struggling to make the Agroville Program functional while combating the policies of Trụ Gian that had grown increasing more effective in eliminating the cadre of younger, effective supporters of the Saigon government. When Ngô Đình Diệm and Durbrow met on February 12, 1960, a few days before Ngô Đình Diệm would leave for a five-day visit to the Federation of Malaya, the ambassador was prepared to justify the reduction in American military spending for Vietnam but was met, instead, with Ngô Đình Diệm offering his assessment on how the ARVN might handle the increased Việt Cộng activity.[31]

Where Durbrow had come ready to use the power of the purse strings to manage the Vietnamese president, Ngô Đình Diệm was entirely focused on defeating the very real threat posed by the possible introduction of the People's Army of Vietnam into the RVN. Ngô Đình Diệm argued that too many ARVN forces were organized in large units, which made it difficult to combat the small-unit Việt Cộng bands roaming through the countryside. Additionally, he lamented the fact that many of his Civil Guard, the force best suited for anti-guerrilla activity, were preoccupied with staff or specialist duties or in static defensive positions. In short, the armed forces of the RVN were not being utilized to their fullest.[32]

During the course of the two-hour conversation, one which it seems was once again dominated by Ngô Đình Diệm, Durbrow complained of his inability to get his points across in the onslaught of Ngô Đình Diệm's monologue.[33] The president concluded that the best strategy to defeat the new Việt Cộng threat was to train the existing security forces in anti-guerrilla tactics and recall to active duty approximately 10,000 military reservists who had prior experience fighting in guerrilla warfare. Ngô Đình Diệm had mentioned this plan to Williams during their February 1 conversation in reference to the attacks at Tây Ninh. During that conversation, Ngô Đình Diệm outlined a plan to recall former NCOs and other enlisted personnel who had been demobilized because of budget constraints. Ngô Đình Diệm used the number 2,500 during this meeting.[34] He planned to attach these additional forces in platoon- or company-size strength to existing Civil Guard and ARVN units as well as selected elements of the Self-Defense Corps. Durbrow was dubious of Ngô Đình Diệm's suggestion for additional troops, in part because he believed there to be sufficient forces available. He also maintained that the suggestion was a ploy to increase U.S. military aid to the RVN for the fiscal year 1960. Again, Durbrow focused on the purse strings and influence while Ngô Đình Diệm was more concerned about internal security.

Ngô Đình Diệm never brought up the question of budget, much to the surprise of Durbrow, who believed that to be the reason for the conversation. Even when Durbrow hinted at his willingness to discuss the issue, Ngô Đình Diệm remained entirely focused on internal security and praise for his vice president, Nguyễn Ngọc Thơ, whom he considered to be "one of the most intelligent and clear thinking of his collaborators."[35] That the two men came to the conversation with the best of the RVN in mind, even if Durbrow lacked confidence in Ngô Đình Diệm's leadership, should not be surprising; that each was focused on different issues speaks loudly to the growing schism that was separating them.

The opening days of the 1960 lunar New Year foreshadowed the events to come that would call into question the American commitment to the RVN, the integrity of that commitment, and the staying power of Ngô Đình Diệm. The RVN was at a critical point in its young life and poised to either be very successful or fall victim to a determined enemy from the North who had allied with a dedicated insurgency in the South. Ngô Đình Diệm still had confidence in his American allies, even if that confidence was beginning to wane with Durbrow. Durbrow, in turn, became more focused on managing Ngô Đình Diệm rather than working with the Saigon government. While both men shared a common goal of an independent and stable RVN, their conflicting methods and philosophies raised tension within the alliance at a time when unity was paramount. The force of personality that each man possessed meant that neither would yield to the other. The result of this clash, within the context of a growing crisis of internal security, a domestic opposition that had the ear of the U.S. embassy staff, and a divided American Country Team in Saigon marked the beginning of the unraveling of the relationship that had existed between the United States and the RVN.

3

Conflicting Personalities and Egos

The issues in the RVN that confronted the Saigon government and the Americans working toward stabilizing the internal security situation were significant and posed a constant danger to the rule of Ngô Đình Diệm. The Year of the Rat would give rise to other items that threatened to distract the Vietnamese and Americans from their focus on the real objectives shared by both groups. A conflict of personalities and egos both within and between the Vietnamese and Americans jeopardized the potential for progress. Within the American camp, individuals emerged in support of the continued rule of Ngô Đình Diệm who battled those advocating a change. Within the former, the secretary of defense's deputy assistant for special operations, Edward Lansdale, joined Williams in defending Ngô Đình Diệm against pressure from the U.S. embassy in Saigon, led primarily by Durbrow.[1]

Lansdale was a strong advocate of a more holistic approach to defending the RVN.[2] In a February 12 letter to Deputy Secretary of Defense C. Douglas Dillon, Lansdale outlined his thoughts on how to help the Vietnamese.[3] He argued that the fundamental problem in the RVN was a political one as well as a military one. Because the United States had advised and helped create the political organizations in the RVN, Lansdale maintained that it was also the responsibility of the United States to help fix the problem. He did not advocate the same reform-minded position as Durbrow, however. He argued in his letter to Dillon that "Vietnam has a strong leader in Ngô Đình Diệm and much of the stability of this new nation came about only through his strong leadership. It would not be wisdom now, at a time of threat, to harass him with ill-conceived political innovations, with demanding compliance under the duress of withdrawing aid, or of derogatory criticism from the sidelines."[4] Lansdale called for sound guidance, understanding, and friendship where Durbrow followed a different approach that sought to correct Ngô Đình Diệm's rule through punishment. The clash between the strategies of Lansdale and Durbrow foreshadowed how Durbrow would handle Ngô Đình Diệm in the Year of the Rat.

Lansdale had some influence in advising Ngô Đình Diệm in internal security. He had always been an advocate of working with Ngô Đình Diệm rather than dictating to him how he should govern his country. This approach led to a series of events which pitted Lansdale against Durbrow; the two men offered different ways to work with the Vietnamese even when they agreed on the nature of the problem. This was seen in the case of U.S. Army Special Forces training the Civil Guard.[5] Durbrow maintained that the American advisers should train the Civil Guard in anti-guerrilla tactics while Lansdale suggested that counter-guerrilla tactics would be more appropriate. What on the surface appeared to be a question of semantics was really a symptom of the larger disagreement in American strategy. For Lansdale, Durbrow's anti-guerrilla operations meant training the Civil Guard to protect the rear areas from Việt Cộng threat. The focus was on missions such as protecting truck convoys from ambush. Lansdale's counter-guerrilla training would allow the Civil Guard to conduct operations against the Việt Cộng. Where Durbrow wanted to apply a passive approach, Lansdale preferred something more active. As Lansdale would assert, "This enemy is 'everywhere,' not just in the rear areas. This was the type of warfare we need to understand more thoroughly than we do today."[6] Ngô Đình Diệm advocated the Lansdale perspective in his conversations with Durbrow. It was not surprising that the division which existed between Ngô Đình Diệm and Durbrow expanded to Lansdale as the year progressed. Durbrow was not willing to share his influence on Ngô Đình Diệm with Lansdale, nor was he willing to concede that Lansdale's approach had a better chance of gaining positive outcomes for the RVN.

When Durbrow, accompanied by U.S. Army command in chief, Pacific, Lieutenant General Isaac D. White, next met with Ngô Đình Diệm on February 27, Ngô Đình Diệm again raised the question of additional American servicemen to help train the Civil Guard and ARVN. The Special Forces personnel would enter the RVN as instructors rather than as advisers and would, in part, come into the country with some type of cover to avoid an adverse reaction by the ICC. Ngô Đình Diệm, however, was more concerned with increasing the number of instructors, which had been planned at only ten, rather than a negative ICC report.

The role the ICC played in Southeast Asia during the year was one of continued frustration for the United States and RVN. Rather than serving as a mechanism to enforce the terms of the Geneva Agreements, it became a vehicle to obscure, or restrict, the movements and jockeying for power of the United States, RVN, DRV, and the Việt Cộng. The DRV flooded the ICC with reports of South Vietnamese violations of the agreements and used these alleged violations as propaganda against Ngô Đình Diệm's rule.[7] There were a number of examples of the DRV's abuse of the ICC violation process. It used the ICC to conceal its own violations by bombarding the organization with alleged South Vietnamese violations so that the ICC members, who were already shorthanded, would never be able to investigate every occurrence.[8]

The propaganda battle, or what would become know as the war for the hearts and minds of the Vietnamese peasants, was evident in South Vietnam in February. The North Vietnamese made it a point to reinterpret the Saigon government's programs in order to criticize the very nature of reform that they tried to accomplish. One example was a project known as the interfamily group program. The concept behind this program was to bring together families living on the same street in order to create a better environment and promote community.[9] The theory behind this type of activity was based in Personalism, which Ngô Đình Diệm and Ngô Đình Nhu had introduced into Vietnamese society as a counterbalance to communism.[10] The interfamily group program united between five to twenty households into one group with a leader selected from that group. Sections would comprise several groups, with a section chief acting as a liaison to the administrative chief of the district. While generating commonality and unity was a major goal of the program, a secondary objective was explaining government policies to the Saigon inhabitants while it also served as a vehicle to enumerate problems and issues generated by the city dwellers.

The South Vietnamese Chinese daily, *Sun Wun Jih Pao*, greeted the program as a counter to the communist commune system and maintained that it would improve individual relations and "develop a spirit of democracy and provide an opportunity for each person to prove his ability."[11] The North Vietnamese used the same program to demonstrate how Ngô Đình Diệm was working toward the suppression of the Vietnamese people. In a February 9 *Voice of Vietnam* commentary titled "No Scheme can Destroy the Patriotism and Unity of the Indomitable People of Saigon-Cholon," the message was clear. It argued that the people in Saigon and Cholon were already united, but that this union was based on its opposition to Ngô Đình Diệm and his policies. It argued that the interfamily group program was nothing more than an extension of earlier Ngô Đình Diệm measures to force the people to spy on one another, denounce their neighbors in order to save themselves, and eliminate what it called the patriotic movement to remove Ngô Đình Diệm from power.[12] Unfortunately, this interpretation was more readily accepted than the former one.

Other Saigon dailies issued a cautious note of the program. *Ngôn Luận* argued that the interfamily groups needed careful study before implementation; the families that were affected had to be told of the benefits of the program not only to ease any anxieties, but also to counter the communist agents in Saigon from using the program against the government.[13] In order for the program to work, the people needed to believe that they had a stake in its realization and a share in its benefits. Failure to allow the people to freely commit to the program would only serve to alienate some of them. This sentiment had some merit and perhaps was a failure of the Saigon government. The concept of the interfamily group was sound, because it worked toward the mobilization of the population for the betterment of the Republic; the execution of the program, however, needed to be sensitive to the people's needs and explained in such a way that those affected could claim ownership over the process. This did not always occur.

The interfamily group program had the potential to be both beneficial and harmful to the RVN. By early March, the program, under the direction of the sub-district chiefs and other local representatives in Saigon, had established over 8,500 family groups in 451 sections of Saigon and Cholon.[14] It offered an opportunity to unite and mobilize the people together toward the common goals of security and stability. However, it operated in a uniquely Vietnamese environment that was riddled with problems inherently counterproductive toward these goals. By May, the program, coupled with the Republican Youth, was hailed as an effective weapon against the communists.[15]

Programs like the interfamily groups were often susceptible to the political intrigue that was never in short supply in the RVN, even when it was not inspired by the North. Throughout Ngô Đình Diệm's tenure in office, he and his closest advisers plotted, schemed, and manipulated the Vietnamese people to gain and retain power. Ngô Đình Diệm was not alone in these political maneuverings, but he was more successful than his detractors. In 1960, political intrigue once again surfaced and, when coupled with the question of Vietnamese internal security, became an area of focus for Durbrow, his cadre, and his Vietnamese counterparts who were either frustrated with Ngô Đình Diệm or had aspirations of political power. One such Vietnamese detractor was Minister of Agriculture Lê Văn Đông who was worried about Ngô Đình Diệm's high-handedness in dealing with the Vietnamese peasants.[16] His chief complaint was that government officials were dictating policy without consulting local leaders and adhering to peasant needs: "Unless the GVN does something to take the peasantry into its confidence," Lê Văn Đông would tell Wolf Ladejinsky, who served as an adviser to Ngô Đình Diệm, "the situation can become quite serious."[17] Lê Văn Đông's concerns were legitimate, as he most likely was worried about the setbacks to the Agroville Program and the seemingly inefficient and allegedly corrupt way it was being developed.[18] As minister of agriculture, Lê Văn Đông was well suited to discuss and criticize this aspect of the Ngô Đình Diệm government.

However, Lê Văn Đông also complained to Ladejinsky that the morale of the ARVN was deteriorating because many of its officers were upset at being passed over for promotion, claiming that officers with less skill but greater influence had received preferential treatment. Lê Văn Đông also cited the recent setbacks against the Việt Cộng at the beginning of the year and low pay as other reasons for the declining state of the armed forces.[19] It was in these criticisms of the ARVN and Ngô Đình Diệm's handling of internal security that Lê Văn Đông hoped to make the greatest impression. Ladejinsky would report that Lê Văn Đông seemed genuinely concerned over the fate of the ARVN and internal security and believed that "unless something was done about it almost immediately the regime would be in serious jeopardy."[20] This warning foreshadowed the tension that would erupt into full-scale violence when, on November 11, 1960, a small number of dissatisfied airborne officers attempted a coup d'etat against Ngô Đình Diệm because they were disgruntled about being passed over for promotion though they argued that their cause was one that called for greater prosecution of the war against the Việt Cộng.

Durbrow, who reported the Lê Văn Đông–Ladejinsky conversation to the Department of State, had a different interpretation of Lê Văn Đông's intentions. For Durbrow, pay was not an issue as the ARVN was the highest-paid force in Asia.[21] He also suspected that Lê Văn Đông's interest about ARVN promotion was because his faction was being overlooked while Ngô Đình Nhu's followers were being promoted. Whatever his motives, Lê Văn Đông was deeply involved in the political intrigue of 1960 and one voice in opposition to the rule of Ngô Đình Diệm that was being heard by the Americans. Another critic of the current Vietnamese situation was Võ Văn Hải, who was chief of Ngô Đình Diệm's private secretariat. Võ Văn Hải's main concern was his belief in the growing corruption of the Cần Lao Party.[22] He complained to Ladejinsky that Ngô Đình Diệm was aware of special government payments received by individuals within the party but did nothing to curb the corruption. While Ladejinsky acknowledged that corruption rumors had been corroborated by other government officials and Vietnamese sympathetic to Ngô Đình Diệm, he questioned whether Ngô Đình Diệm had any direct knowledge of those practices. For many Americans, this practice was anathema to the type of government the United States was trying to create in the RVN.

In commentary on the various conversations by Ladejinsky with Vietnamese concerned about Ngô Đình Diệm, Durbrow reported to the Department of State that Ngô Đình Diệm had not been provided with accurate intelligence of Vietnam's internal security. Durbrow asserted that it was generally agreed that "government officials have failed to speak frankly with Ngô Đình Diệm about the internal security and the basic grumbling of the people but instead told him what they thought he wanted them to hear."[23] Durbrow concluded that this resulted in Ngô Đình Diệm having an unrealistic understanding of Vietnam's internal security status while he dismissed Ngô Đình Diệm's ideas of creating a 20,000-man force to combat insurgency as unwise and desperate. It was unclear how Durbrow had reached the number 20,000 when Ngô Đình Diệm had started with 2,500 then increased it to 10,000, and reverted back to 3,000 to 4,000 before Durbrow's dispatch had been sent. Likewise, Durbrow seemed to discount Williams' value in updating Ngô Đình Diệm even though the general provided memoranda to the ambassador of almost every conversation recorded. In the same dispatch, Durbrow contradicts himself on Ngô Đình Diệm's awareness of what was occurring in the countryside of the RVN.

Durbrow reported that Ngô Đình Diệm understood that many Vietnamese government officials had been too forceful in carrying out their instructions, had ignored the plight of the people in the countryside and had failed to explain government policies. While he concluded that vice president Nguyễn Ngọc Thơ was probably the source of this information, Durbrow maintained that Ngô Đình Diệm was "now getting a more realistic picture of current developments."[24] Durbrow also asserted that Ngô Đình Nhu was causing more harm than good in running what amounted to a parallel government: "Nhu spends practically all his time in his 'ivory tower' in the Palace making his Machiavellian plans of how to control the population, eliminate Sihanouk, or perhaps how to get more income for the Can Lao Party."[25] Durbrow advised easing out Ngô Đình Nhu, in part to have greater access to and influence on Ngô Đình Diệm in the governing of the RVN and encouraging the Vietnamese president to offer both political and economic reform in his country based on Durbrow's American model.

Even if Durbrow was correct in his assessment, his solution offered little hope of resolving the issue when understood from a Vietnamese perspective. Creating a rift between Ngô Đình Diệm and Ngô Đình Nhu would not make the RVN president more malleable. Rather, any American attempt to force a division between the brothers to create leverage would

President Dwight D. Eisenhower with Ngô Đình Nhu and RVN ambassador to the United States Trần Văn Chương, 1957 (photograph 72-2157-2, National Park Service, Dwight D. Eisenhower Presidential Library and Museum).

result in Ngô Đình Diệm trusting his American allies less. The United States did not learn this lesson until after it was too late.

While Durbrow was thorough in his reporting of events that put the Saigon government in a negative light, he failed to pass along to Washington evidence of the government's fight against corruption. In one significant event in early March, the Long An police chief and a Self-Defense Force agent were severely penalized for illegally arresting and torturing innocent peasants. *Cách mạng Quốc gia* concluded in an editorial that the men arrested were "nothing but social ulcers and dangerous viruses that have spoiled society."[26] The officials had done damage while in power and representing the Saigon government, but it was that same government that made sure they were removed and punished. Another case that ended around the same time involved the death sentence of two Civil Guards who took VN$8 million worth of gasoline.[27] These types of men helped to cause discontent in the countryside. Durbrow and his embassy staff seemed to focus on these corrupt individuals as representations of Ngô Đình Diệm rather than allowing for the realization that it was the RVN president who was working to eliminate them from society. However, there was no mention of the mass rallies, such as the 10,000-person one held on April 3 in Xuân Lộc district, Long Khánh province, where protests against communist terrorism and resolutions that supported the government were common.[28]

Similar criticism had been voiced in conversations between Vietnam's urban intelligentsia and American personal. In an earlier February meeting, Theodore J.C. Heavner, the vice consul in Hue, reported a conversation that he had with Phạm Ngọc Vinh, who had been the president of the Thừa Thiên Citizen's Rally before it had merged with the National Revolutionary Movement and had worked with Ngô Đình Diệm's brother Ngô Đình Cẩn to elevate Ngô Đình Diệm over Bảo Đại in 1955.[29] Phạm Ngọc Vinh complained to Heavner that Ngô Đình Cẩn, like his brother, had isolated himself from the people and listened to only those who told him what they believed he wanted to hear. Phạm Ngọc Vinh had been refused an audience with Ngô Đình Cẩn when he wanted to remove himself from Cần Lao Party activities. His criticism was representative of the type passed along to the Americans. On the surface, it seemed valid and significant. The brothers Ngô had increasingly set themselves up as the ruling elite who, in their thirst and drive for power, forgot who assisted them into positions of leadership in the first place; they needed to be checked and reminded of the path toward democracy. The reality was that Phạm Ngọc Vinh had become a part of the opposition that resulted from the development of democratic institutions.

By early March, Durbrow was once again reporting on the failing internal security of the RVN but held muted praise for Ngô Đình Diệm and his government in "showing a reassuring awareness of the gravity of the situation."[30] The embassy did show some concern, however, when the operations of two Saigon dailies, *Tự do* and *Buổi sang*, were suspended because they had been reporting too many of the Việt Cộng atrocities in their papers.[31] The *Vietnam Press* argued that the papers were suspended because they had been publishing stories without verifying their facts. Specifically mentioned was the case of the reports of nine vicious murders of hamlet officials in Vĩnh Long province who had not been attacked. The papers, according to the government, were suspended because their groundless reports were demoralizing the population. For Durbrow and others, it was a question of freedom of the press.[32]

While Durbrow conceded that Ngô Đình Diệm had finally come to realize the seriousness of the situation in the countryside, he concluded that it was Ngô Đình Diệm's policies, coupled with the increased Việt Cộng activity, which played a significant part in the current situation. Durbrow did not report the mass rallies that occurred toward the end of March in sixteen provinces or the March 20 meeting by former members of the Việt Cộng who met in Ba Xuyên and issued a resolution denouncing the communist attempts to overthrow the Saigon government.[33] There were several theories as to why the Việt Cộng had decided to increase its activity at the end of 1959 and, as the Đảng Lao Động Việt Nam (Lao Động Party or Vietnam Workers Party) had announced in May 1959, force the United States to leave Southeast Asia.[34] One explanation was that the increased activity was a part of a larger communist Chinese strategy to intensive confrontation with Asian countries bordering communist ones in the Pacific Rim, while Durbrow suggested that the DRV might also be responding to their inability to disrupt the August 1959 GVN National Assembly elections.

Ngô Đình Diệm believed that the DRV had increased its assassinations and kidnappings to disrupt the Agroville Program, which had been making some progress.[35] While Durbrow did not directly dismiss this claim, he suggested that the Agroville Program was the root cause of peasant dissatisfaction with the GVN. Because the program called for volunteers, or corvée labor, that took the people away from their harvest and livelihood, and local officials used coercion and fear in governing the Agroville, the people were less willing to assist the government in identifying and eliminating the Việt Cộng. The Việt Cộng also used the peasants' disaffection to their advantage through their sustained Trụ Gian program, which had the effect of causing the people to wonder if the GVN could protect them from the Việt Cộng. If the government could not provide that protection, then it made little sense to turn against the Việt Cộng and support a program that appeared not to work.

Durbrow's criticisms were valid, and even Ngô Đình Diệm recognized that the Agroville Program had its shortcomings, though he would continually speak with the Americans about the strategy behind the program and the successful tactics employed during it. As Durbrow would report, Ngô Đình Diệm had begun to replace corrupt and inefficient local officials to regain the confidence of the people as well as slowing the development of future Agroville projects until the abuses of the previous efforts had been analyzed and fixed.[36] However, Durbrow was only half correct in his assessment. The real cause of the failure of the Agroville Program by this point was the inability of the Saigon government to deal with the increased assassinations and kidnappings, which were a direct consequence of the potential success that pacification efforts similar to the Agroville Program might bring to Vietnam. If the Việt Cộng were successful in maintaining fear in the hearts and minds of the peasants and thwarting GVN efforts to secure the countryside, no pacification program would be successful. The problem was not the Agroville Program, though it did serve as the easily recognizable measuring stick for whether internal security was present, but rather the ability of the United States and the RVN to reach an understanding on how the Việt Cộng could be eliminated as a threat to the people.

Not all Agrovilles failed, and Ngô Đình Diệm often highlighted the successful ones when he could, though he did not always find a sympathetic audience. The exception to this was Williams who had a chance to visit the Agrovilles, often referred to by Ngô Đình Diệm as Garden Cities, of Vị Thanh and Hỏa Lựu in Phong Dinh province during a visit to the MAAG detachment at Cần Thơ. On March 15, Ngô Đình Diệm and Williams had a long conversation about these Agrovilles which had reached approximately 1,000 houses and 5,000 inhabitants but were programed for five times that number.[37] Ngô Đình Diệm was very enthusiastic about his Garden Cities, having just visited these two earlier in the week.

Ngô Đình Diệm focused on the new hospitals and schools as the primary reason that the people were so happy with the projects, though he also alluded to the easing of the inferiority of the peasant toward the urban environment as a positive consequence. This urban-versus-rural perspective caused Ngô Đình Diệm some trouble throughout his presidency. Ngô Đình Diệm worked to bridge the gap between the two groups while others exploited the differences to create instability within the countryside. When Williams informed Ngô Đình Diệm that he had visited the same Garden Cities a few days later, Williams remarked how pleased Ngô Đình Diệm was that he had done this.[38] Ngô Đình Diệm's reaction to Williams' visit was more than just a result of the general's affirmation of the project. The fact that Williams visited the very same Garden Cities the two had discussed earlier demonstrated to Ngô Đình Diệm that Williams took him seriously and valued his enthusiasm and analysis of the situation.

The Agroville Program was not Ngô Đình Diệm's only strategy to counter communist insurgents in the countryside. Ngô Đình Diệm had also forcibly called for the creation of a 10,000-man commando force to deal with the increased assassinations and kidnappings as a response to a change in the insurgent tactics. In July 1959, with the August National Assembly elections looming, the GVN began to increase military operations in the Delta region, anticipating that the Việt Cộng would increase its number of assassinations and kidnappings to disrupt the electoral process. The ARVN sweeps were successful in that the elections occurred, but it did force the Việt Cộng to reorganize its troops from smaller bands of three to five men to larger groups ranging from thirty to one hundred men.[39] The Việt Cộng became more successful with these large-unit operations, culminating in the Tây Ninh attack on January 26, 1960.

General Samuel T. Williams (photograph 76–44–1770, U.S. Army, Dwight D. Eisenhower Presidential Library and Museum).

Attacks in the Delta were one of the main reasons Ngô Đình Diệm wanted to create the 10,000-man commando force, organized into 131 companies of fifty men each, though Ngô Đình Diệm had also expressed a real concern for the increased North Vietnamese infiltration into southern Laos.[40] Durbrow had political opposition to such a move, but he also pointedly refuted the military necessity of such a force. In a conversation with Nguyễn Đình Thuận on March 3, which included Daniel Anderson, director of Southeast Asian affairs, Durbrow argued that the 230,000 personnel of the ARVN, Civil Guard and Self-Defense Corps were more than sufficient to carry out the security needs of the RVN. He maintained that the Vietnamese would be better suited to remove ARVN personnel from their training missions to meet the enemy rather than dilute ARVN to form the commando units.[41] Ngô Đình Diệm's original plan called for retired NCOs, who had been placed in that status because of budgetary constraints, to return to form the nucleus of the force. A more tempered, military explanation came from Williams who was concerned that the new force had the potential to be successful if their deployment and mission was well defined, but it would also have the effect of draining away the best of the fighting men from the other ARVN units; Ngô Đình Diệm had planned for volunteers. Williams was also worried that the new companies might not be equipped as they should be in order to fight the enemy. He cited the GVN's inability to obtain the necessary jeeps, radios, and U.S.-made weapons from the USOM for its Civil Guard because it had not provided a plan of action for usage of the equipment that was acceptable to the Americans.

The question of funding for Ngô Đình Diệm's projects was also a tense topic of discussion. For Ngô Đình Diệm, the main obstacle was the USOM who held up funding in order to exert pressure on the RVN to organize its military in a way it had determined. During a March 7 conversation, Ngô Đình Diệm explained his frustration to Williams after the general informed him that USOM had $5 million available to purchase equipment for the Civil Guard even though MAAG had established that it would take $18 million to purchase the equipment necessary to make the Civil Guard effective.[42] In the course of their conversation about the type of equipment that should be prioritized based upon this limited budget, Ngô Đình Diệm complained that USOM had delayed funding for over two years because it wanted the units organized along different lines than the Vietnamese had planned. Ngô Đình Diệm also complained of the Michigan State University Group recommendations, which received the support of USOM, and maintained that the Civil Guard should be formed as rural police or highway patrols. In essence, the struggle between Ngô Đình Diệm and USOM was similar to the one that existed between Lansdale and Durbrow over how best to utilize the Civil Guard.

Ngô Đình Diệm would continue to complain about equipment not reaching the RVN in a timely manner. During several conversations with Williams in March, Ngô Đình Diệm referred to his failure to receive dredging machines that would have allowed him to make canals along the Cambodian and Laotian borders accessible and enabled him to construct a defense road system and airfields near the canals, which would have also greatly improved the security situation.[43] Ngô Đình Diệm also worked with Williams to get additional equipment for the RVN while Williams served as a buffer between the RVN president and Durbrow on how best to ask for and receive this type of aid.[44]

Williams' greatest concern was Ngô Đình Diệm's control over the military. Because the two men understood each other, Williams was able to offer advice to Ngô Đình Diệm without fear of their relationship suffering. Williams pointedly criticized the military professionalism of some of Ngô Đình Diệm's handpicked officers and offered critical observations of the military structure of the ARVN.[45] ARVN forces in the Delta were controlled by each province chief, who was sometimes a military man, but regardless of status, was always under the control of the RVN president. The result was a disconnect between Ngô Đình Diệm and his field commanders and poor operational planning and indecision in the field. Ngô Đình Diệm justified this action because too many of his province chiefs failed to act; he did attempt to rectify the situation by placing military operations in the Delta under the control of one military figure, Colonel Nguyễn Khánh, whom Ngô Đình Diệm would eventually promote to brigadier general.[46] Lansdale also lamented Ngô Đình Diệm's arrangements of personally handling the military operations via his selected province chiefs but understood that factors such as the president's strong personality and the nature of trust between Ngô Đình Diệm and his cadre played a major role. That Lansdale recognized the problem should not be surprising, but he also understood, or at least attempted to understand, the nature of Ngô Đình Diệm's rule during this critical time.[47]

While Williams was not pessimistic about the GVN chances of holding the line against the Việt Cộng, he did address some serious concerns in his March 10 dispatch about the nature of the military organization in the Delta. It was clear that the internal security in the region was on the decline and everything Ngô Đình Diệm had done up to this point had failed to turn the tide, and in some cases, such as certain Agrovilles, had made the situation worse. However, Williams did believe that Nguyễn Khánh might hold the key to a military reversal of fortune should Ngô Đình Diệm give him a free hand. Williams also commented on the growing negative atmosphere between Americans and Vietnamese officials: "I gain the impression that GVN are of ever growing opinion that some Americans are too hide bound, unsympathetic, and unrealistic in their evaluation of GVN acute problems and how they should be solved particularly with funds and equipment."[48] In many respects, Williams was similar to Lansdale to whom the dispatch was addressed. He recognized the shortcomings of the Ngô Đình Diệm government in its military and political struggle against the Việt Cộng, but he chose to work with the Vietnamese, rather than dictate to them, to find solutions to the ever-growing problems. Evidence of this type of relationship was found throughout their working relationship, such as the April 6 meeting during which Ngô Đình Diệm outlined the VC threat as he saw it and its implications toward internal security. Throughout the conversation, even when Ngô Đình Diệm took on the "lecturing" tone that Durbrow found so distasteful, Williams continued to ask questions of the president and listened to his answers. Williams shared information with Ngô Đình Diệm that others might have been reluctant to do and gave Ngô Đình Diệm the respect desired of a president of an independent country.[49] However, Williams in many ways was also a part of the American disease spreading over South Vietnam.

In a March 20 letter to Lieutenant General Samuel L. Myers, assistant deputy chief of army staff for logistics, Williams commented on the problems of forming the 10,000 commandos from a few companies of volunteers of the existing regiments. While Williams did not think that Ngô Đình Diệm was purposely creating the units to garner additional aid from the United States—this was especially true as the Vietnamese planned to form the units with existing equipment—he did believe that the plan would, in the long run, be a detriment to the fight against the Việt Cộng: "This would skim off the cream of officers, NCOs, and privates, I'm doing my best to sabotage the project and may be successful as none of the Corps or Division commanders want to lose these people."[50] When Ngô Đình Diệm offered an outline of the plan to Williams, he suggested bringing retired NCOs back to form the nucleus of the new group. Williams did hold a certain amount of confidence in the Vietnamese president, even if he was bypassed from time to time on issues for which the two did not agree. His rejection of the plan, which had some urgency given the nature of the crisis, could not have settled well with Ngô Đình Diệm, whose list of confidants seemed to be shrinking as the year progressed.[51]

In another instance, during the same April 6 conversation, Williams passed Ngô Đình Diệm confidential information about the internal dynamics of the Country Team in

Vietnam.⁵² Williams assured Ngô Đình Diệm that he supported the president's calls for an increase to the Department of Defense budget for Vietnam. Williams argued that $165 million was not enough to support the 150,000-man armed forces and voiced the concern of the Department of Defense. While this must have been comforting to Ngô Đình Diệm, Williams' next statement most likely added to his suspicion of the American political officers in Vietnam. Williams informed Ngô Đình Diệm that some members of the Country Team, especially Durbrow, might sabotage Ngô Đình Diệm's request for more money by arguing that his calls for 10,000 to 20,000 commandos, equipped with RVN monies, meant that he had enough resources to pursue his plans without an increase in funding.

Williams confirmed that Durbrow had reported to Washington that Ngô Đình Diệm's commandos would place the South Vietnamese military well above the 150,000-man ceiling funded by the Department of Defense. The implication in this admission was that Durbrow was working against Ngô Đình Diệm and doing so in a nefarious way. Ngô Đình Diệm maintained that the commandos would not break the troop ceilings and, in fact, would not exceed 3,000 to 4,000 commandos, and the total troops would still be 3,000 below the troop ceiling. Ngô Đình Diệm informed Williams that, as a result of his inability to raise the desired force, he no longer intended to pursue the commando force. While Williams confided in Ngô Đình Diệm and, in turn, was recipient of Ngô Đình Diệm's trust, the unintended damage of further exposing Durbrow must have reinforced Ngô Đình Diệm's growing doubt of the American diplomat's ability to work with him.

After the Ngô Đình Diệm–Williams exchange, it seemed destined that Durbrow and Ngô Đình Diệm would clash during the Year of the Rat. The first incident occurred on March 10 when the ambassador met with the president before the latter left for a state visit to Malaya.⁵³ When Ngô Đình Diệm informed Durbrow that he had already gathered 4,500 of the 10,000 volunteers needed for the elite commando units to counter the increased Việt Cộng activity, Durbrow reiterated his objection to the plan because of the potential drain caused by removing experienced and dedicated personnel from existing ARVN units. Ngô Đình Diệm, who had already heard this argument from Williams, disagreed with the ambassador's reasoning, trying again to explain the nature of the emergency in the Mekong. In the course of the discussion, Ngô Đình Diệm made additional pleas for more hardware to fight the war, including AD-4 aircraft to replace the older F-8F fighters, alligator amphibian vehicles for greater mobility in the water, automatic weapons and mortars to counter the increasingly better-equipped enemy, and communications equipment which all agreed was essential to the war effort. In his report to Washington, Durbrow concluded that Ngô Đình Diệm was really requesting the materials and additional 10,000 commandos to raise the RVN force level above the 150,000 ceiling established by the United States.

The exchange with Ngô Đình Diệm confirmed that Durbrow treated the situation as such when he questioned where Ngô Đình Diệm expected to get the hardware to equip his commandos given the fact that the U.S. Congress had cut Military Assistance Program (MAP) funding. While Durbrow was correct to assert the potential for the lack of materials available for this project, Ngô Đình Diệm was increasingly frustrated by the ambassador's objections to his plans to win the war. In the course of the conversation, Durbrow told Ngô Đình Diệm that he was not convinced that more large-unit forces were needed to fight the Việt Cộng, as it was more important to win the peasants' confidence within each individual village. While Durbrow was alluding to the Agroville Program, his comments held a key to one of the major differences between the two men. Durbrow wanted to reform political and military programs to win the confidence of the Vietnamese people and improve internal security, while Ngô Đình Diệm wanted to improve internal security by defeating the Việt Cộng and establishing a more permanent government presence in the villages.

Both men had similar goals but held different views on how to achieve them. While admirable, Durbrow also began to show more of his personal distaste for Ngô Đình Diệm's rule: "I felt I had to speak frankly and firmly because [sic] seems clear he moving in all directions without any clear-cut plan to utilize what he has on hand to meet situation and probably hopes use deteriorating internal situation to force U.S. finally agree to his long sought after 170,000 force level."[54] Durbrow believed himself in the position of taking charge of an unruly child who needed the older, experienced hand to guide him rather than an ally to share resources in the fight against a common enemy; this was exactly what Lansdale had warned against earlier in the year. The commander in chief, Pacific Command (CINCPAC), Admiral Harry D. Felt, reaffirmed this position on March 14 maintaining that what Ngô Đình Diệm had planned had not worked for the British in Malaya and called on Washington to resist such requests.[55]

It was ironic that the Vietnamese experts in Washington recognized the same problem of control in the countryside as Ngô Đình Diệm. In a March 18 conference on internal security in Vietnam held at the Pentagon, which included principles from each of the major departments with active interests in the country, they agreed that the Civil Guard was "not capable of coping with the present guerrilla capabilities nor would it develop sufficiently in the foreseeable future to successfully conduct counter-guerrilla operations."[56] The conference offered the familiar refrain that Ngô Đình Diệm had to relinquish greater control to the military and pointed to steps he had already taken with the appointment of Colonel Nguyễn Khánh. The conversation at the Pentagon highlighted an obvious and important point. If the Civil Guard was inadequate, the ARVN involved in large-unit operations, and the Việt Cộng attacking in groups of thirty, fifty, and one hundred, then why were Ngô Đình Diệm's calls for the elite commando units made up of seventy-five-men companies who were well equipped, trained, and motivated rejected by the United States? The suggestion that Ngô Đình Diệm only wanted more American aid without justifying it, and that the plan would dilute the existing officer corps helped to explain the logic behind the American resistance. However, in light of the real and dangerous threat of increased Việt Cộng activity and a fuller appreciation of the significance in Saigon's political intrigue and balance of power, Ngô Đình Diệm's requests were not unreasonable. The obstinate American behavior could do nothing other than frustrate the Vietnamese leader, who was caught between building pressure in the countryside and the political pressure from the U.S. embassy.

The March 18 conference also examined ways to improve the political environment by inserting advisers to create greater efficiency in command and control. The second secretary and political officer in the U.S. embassy in Saigon, Chalmers B. Wood, presented a plan that would insert Third Country personnel, specifically Malayan or Filipino, to serve as advisers at the national level to the ministers of defense and interior. The plan also included advisers at the province level to better coordinate presidential directives. While the plan had merit and there was certainly enough evidence to suggest that the South Vietnamese were losing the countryside to the Việt Cộng in the early months of 1960, the selection of the Malayans offered some insight into the lack of sensitivity to the Vietnamese perspective.[57]

The counter-insurgency plan in Malaya had achieved success, but the transfer of the plan to Vietnam brought with it additional obstacles. The Malayan advisers fought their counter-insurgency under a colonial system, in which the British held total control of the military and civilian decisions. Lansdale argued that transferring the colonial system to Vietnam, which had just ended a similar experience with the French, would not work. The Vietnamese controlled their own military forces, and counter-insurgency operations and would not want to follow the Malayan model of relinquishing control. The adviser scenario might have been practical, but the Americans who were suggesting it demonstrated their failure to understand the difficulties in offering a colonial solution to a Vietnamese problem.

Lansdale argued a similar point to Williams in a later memorandum.[58] He was concerned that the British-Malayan model might not be an effective way of combating the insurgents in Vietnam. He outlined three objections: (1) it did not make sense to hand over American dollars to British experts to advise Ngô Đình Diệm when the Americans had advisers in place; (2) the British experience in Malaya was very different from Vietnam because the Vietnamese were fighting one another while the British-led colonial troops fought against a largely foreign communist force (Chinese nationals) and the internal security concerns were very different at the village level; and (3) the American-Vietnamese relationship in the field had tremendous potential for success while introducing colonial advisers, despite their previous success, had the potential for disaster. Lansdale demonstrated again, in his assessment of the situation, that he was more in tune with the Vietnamese than his political counterparts.

When Ngô Đình Diệm and Durbrow met again, this time in a conversation that included Parsons, Durbrow renewed his frustration with the president, who dominated the three-hour conversation. As with previous interviews, Ngô Đình Diệm lectured the assistant secretary with the background and history of the internal security problems in South Vietnam. He highlighted how the United States had resisted his plans for successful action, and worked against his solutions that were already under consideration by the United States. Of particular note in this conversation with Ngô Đình Diệm was Durbrow's renewed claims that no additional monies were available for South Vietnam and that the United States was doing all it could to support that country. These assertions, however, were in conflict with earlier communications Durbrow received from Richard Usher, the acting director of the Office of Southeast Asian Affairs, who informed the ambassador that $15 million remained in the contingency fund in the Department of Defense and that requests needed to be made before the money was committed elsewhere.[59] Durbrow continued to report that Ngô Đình Diệm was overly optimistic about the support in the countryside and provided an analysis to the ambassador that directly conflicted with information received by the embassy.

While Ngô Đình Diệm and Durbrow butted heads in Vietnam, Nguyễn Đình Thuận visited the United States to discuss areas of mutual concern for the United States and the RVN. On April 4, he and Ambassador Trần Văn Chương visited the State Department.

The difference in perspective and importance between the Vietnamese and Americans was evident here as well. Parsons was the ranking State Department official at the meeting, and he invited Nguyễn Đình Thuận to raise any points he wished to discuss.[60] Nguyễn Đình Thuận dominated his opening remarks around the shrinking American budget for Vietnam, which had declined 38 percent since 1956, and the real negative effect that it was having on the Vietnamese fighting against the communist insurgency. Programs such as the Agrovilles and Youth Movements, both of which were necessary to counter communist efforts in the countryside, were suffering as a result. Nguyễn Đình Thuận also highlighted the use of southern Laos by the communists to wage war against his government as evidence of increased, rather than decreased, assistance by the DRV. For Nguyễn Đình Thuận and his Vietnamese contingent, it was a fight for survival. Parsons countered by bringing up three items of equal importance, in the State Department's way of thinking. The first was the shared concern of internal security, though Parsons also mentioned the issue of Cambodia and the value of foreign exchange. In introducing these topics, Parsons remarked, "We Americans do not like to be talking to the Vietnamese about their relations with Cambodia all the time as though the Cambodians were always right and Viet-Nam was always wrong; but the Vietnamese were the bigger people and the more experienced people." Parsons then went on to discuss the foreign exchange: "we do not normally talk to people about the value of their currency" and added that "we hoped the Vietnamese will talk with the IMF on subject."[61] In both cases, despite his "reluctance" to discuss matters of Vietnam's internal affairs, Parsons did exactly that. The implication of "reluctance" and subsequent discussion of the matters was that the Vietnamese did not fit into the normal way of doing things.

Nguyễn Đình Thuận appeared to be unsettled by the conversation. Regarding the budget, he agreed that it was a major concern but that he was not an expert on fiscal matters. With Cambodia, he indicated that the Vietnamese had planned to send a delegation to Cambodia earlier but was delayed when Ngô Đình Diệm went to Malaya for a state visit. Nguyễn Đình Thuận maintained that he would have gone to Cambodia himself, but that was impossible as he was in Washington.[62] There was no way he could be in two places at once. Interestingly, Nguyễn Đình Thuận's most significant issues were the shrinking budget and Vietnam's fight for survival, while Parsons was concerned with Vietnam's relationship with Cambodia and fiscal matters. The two men were concerned with the same region but were focused on very different matters.[63]

The question of Laos also dominated Nguyễn Đình Thuận during his visit to the United States. In an April 8 meeting with Wood, Deputy Director of the Central Intelligence Agency General Charles P. Cabell, and CIA officers, Nguyễn Đình Thuận brought up Laos and its role in the infiltration of North Vietnamese agents to the South.[64] Nguyễn Đình Thuận saw the situation as critical and believed the southern part of Laos to be in the control of the communists. He dismissed French reports that the troop movement in the region south of Vinh was related to an ARVN division deserting to the North and some of its members returning to the South as a communist smoke screen to mask infiltration. Nguyễn Đình Thuận informed the Americans that the ease by which the northerners conducted this illegal movement of troops was one of the reasons why the Agroville Program was so important to Ngô Đình Diệm and the South's survival. In Nguyễn Đình Thuận's final meeting with Parsons, he reiterated the disastrous consequences of the reduced Department of Defense budget for South Vietnam, only to be told that there were two significant obstacles: corruption within the Cần Lao Party and Ngô Đình Diệm's relationship with the people.[65] Nguyễn Đình Thuận learned that Durbrow had already had a long and serious talk with Ngô Đình Diệm about the former to which Nguyễn Đình Thuận was not privileged; Parsons told him to speak with Durbrow. Nguyễn Đình Thuận denied the latter obstacle, citing various statements by U.S. congressman, and he reminded Parsons of the difficulty of winning over the Vietnamese people, who were both terrorized and rewarded by the insurgents to the point that the psychological damage would take time to rectify.[66] While the Vietnamese encounters in Washington were going less ideally than expected, the same was true in Saigon.

On April 6, as Durbrow was waiting for his instructions to deliver his démarche to Ngô

Đình Diệm, the two men met.⁶⁷ Ngô Đình Diệm offered an overview of the internal security situation from about fifty miles north of Saigon to the Cà Mau Peninsula at the southern tip of the RVN with the implications that the Civil Guard needed to be reinforced to protect the isolated villages in the Mekong Delta. Durbrow agreed that the villages needed to be protected, but he argued that the existing force level of the Civil Guard was adequate for the job. As the conversation concluded, Ngô Đình Diệm informed Durbrow that he had recruited 3,000 commandos and was planning to stop at that number in order to make sure the force level of the Vietnamese armed forces remained under 150,000.⁶⁸

The Durbrow–Ngô Đình Diệm meeting that Parsons' referred to took place on April 7 when the ambassador used the excuse of the possibility of an additional $4.6 million allocation to Vietnam to discuss reports of alleged Cần Lao activities detrimental to the Ngô Đình Diệm government. Durbrow began the meeting by warning Ngô Đình Diệm that additional monies could be forfeited and that it would be difficult to convince Washington to add millions of dollars for Vietnam if the Cần Lao Party was not reformed.⁶⁹ Durbrow told Ngô Đình Diệm he was speaking as a friend, though one might wonder exactly what type of friend would extort concessions in the form of political reforms in order to fund a fight for survival. Durbrow also maintained that he had documented cases. When Ngô Đình Diệm asked for names and details so that he could initiate investigations, Durbrow refused to reply. When Durbrow remained silent, Ngô Đình Diệm suggested that the allegations most likely came from opposition groups, disgruntled businessmen, or communists. Durbrow conceded that this might be true, which would tend to negate the validity of the allegations, but he maintained that the reports of misconduct were persistent and increasing. For Durbrow, the consistent flow of allegations was enough proof that the Cần Lao Party was corrupt, regardless of the source of these complaints. For Ngô Đình Diệm, who had and was given no proof that the allegations came from any other source than the ones told by Durbrow, the quantity and consistency of reports was as meaningless as the origin of them was suspect.

As the conversation continued, Durbrow finally provided some details on the consequences of the corruption, which included lower military morale because of politically motivated promotions, favoritism, the need for bribes to the party to obtain export licenses, and shortages in war-related materials such as rubber tires and charcoal. When Ngô Đình Diệm tried to explain the situation and maintained that the criticisms were unfounded, Durbrow dismissed him. Durbrow's only response was that whether or not the allegations were true, they were being continuously repeated and believed by more and more people. Durbrow told Ngô Đình Diệm that he would have to do something. This was rather ironic as Ngô Đình Diệm began the conversation by asking for names and details so he could investigate and Durbrow refusing to give any names. Durbrow's notes from the meeting suggest that the conversation was civil, though it was clear that Durbrow did not value Ngô Đình Diệm's response. In his communication to the State Department, he put quotes around the word "explanation" when referring to Ngô Đình Diệm's response to the allegations, and he concluded that, "whether Ngô Đình Diệm's explanations are correct or not, and I am inclined believe the party or individuals therein are involved in many shady practices, I was able to let Diem know that we have fairly solid information about these matters."⁷⁰ When Durbrow learned from Wolf Ladejinsky that Ngô Đình Diệm offered the same explanations to him as he did Durbrow, the ambassador's only conclusion was that Ngô Đình Diệm was either "disturbed that either we know too much or he has not been given straight story."⁷¹ Clearly, in the case of Cần Lao Party activities, Durbrow presumed guilt before innocence and wanted to make his point with Ngô Đình Diệm. If he thought that dangling an extra $4.6 million dollars would get Ngô Đình Diệm's attention and force him to act, then the ambassador was truly out of touch with the RVN president's mind-set.[72]

Durbrow might have grown to distrust the rule of Ngô Đình Diệm, but he did understand how Ngô Đình Diệm was ruling his country. When a plan to send young Foreign Service officers to advise the Vietnamese secretaries of defense and interior and serve as a conduit between Ngô Đình Diệm and his province chiefs was introduced, Durbrow was quick to realize that this was not a plausible plan of action. Durbrow did not approve of Ngô Đình Diệm's "'divide and rule' policy of not allowing individual generals or administrative officials to obtain positions of centralized power," but he did have confidence that he could change the president before it was too late.[73] It probably did not help that the National Assembly passed bill number 2/60 as introduced by the second vice chairman of the National Assembly, Cao Văn Trường, which called for drastic governmental actions to halt communist subversion and eliminate communism as an ideology.[74] While Durbrow did not specifically mention the legislation, which harkened back to bill Decree 10/59 it most likely only served to reaffirm Durbrow's position toward Ngô Đình Diệm.[75]

Durbrow's view of the Saigon government did not improve with the RVN action against a series of islands held in dispute with the Cambodians in the Gulf of Thailand.[76] Cambodia and the RVN had been fighting over the islands, usually with words and non-military action, since the end of French rule in Indochina. Ngô Đình Diệm had sent a note on March 9, 1960, asking the royal Cambodian government to relinquish its claims to the islands. The Cambodian reply was, as expected, couched in language that expressed astonishment at the RVN's demands. The RVN responded by sending two naval vessels, loaded with marines, to parade around the islands as a show of force on April 13 and 14.[77] While nothing came of the incident, it did reinforce to Durbrow that the RVN was naïve and reckless in its dealings with Cambodia, which threatened to continue to destabilize the political and military situation in the region. It did not help matters that the most recent action occurred after Nguyễn Đình Thuận had assured the Americans in Washington that the RVN was working to improve its relationship with the Cambodians.

Ngô Đình Diệm was not the only victim of Durbrow's wrath at the beginning of 1960. Williams presented a constant challenge to his authority as ambassador and confidant of Ngô Đình Diệm and was not shy of demonstrating his opposition to some of the president's plans, as witnessed by his efforts to disrupt Ngô Đình Diệm's call for the 10,000-man commando force. It was unclear that Durbrow actually believed Williams to be a challenge to his authority, though their exchange in mid–April certainly showed the inability of the two to see eye-to-eye on the important issue of training and command structure. On April 19, Durbrow complained to Parsons that Williams supported conventional training for the ARVN forces while he saw anti-guerrilla training as more important. Ngô Đình Diệm had made this a point earlier with Durbrow, though the ambassador believed Ngô Đình Diệm to "have been a bit too precipitous in flailing around in all directions because of the stepped-up Việt Cộng guerrilla activities."[78] Durbrow then related a situation that had arisen between the army attaché Colonel Richard Comstock and Colonel Nguyễn Ngọc Khôi, who served as the chief of staff to the deputy secretary of state for national defense, Trần Trung Dũng.

In the course of the conversation, Nguyễn Ngọc Khôi complained that MAAG had dissuaded the ARVN from anti-guerrilla training in two letters dated July 14 and November 10, 1958, to the chief of staff, ARVN. Williams had already sent Durbrow a copy of another document dated September 7, 1958, which called for commando training in Nha Trang and widespread anti-guerrilla training in all of Vietnam's armed forces. This was received on April 6, 1960, and had been unknown to Durbrow as had the two previous 1958 documents. Durbrow questioned Williams on the inconsistencies within the three documents, which seemed to both call for and reject anti-guerrilla training of the ARVN.

At issue as well was the fact that Durbrow was not aware of MAAG planning, and, as ambassador, he believed he should have been involved in all aspects of the military operations. The two clashed when Durbrow confronted Williams on April 12. Williams had not expected to be broadsided by Durbrow and Comstock who had requested to be present at the meeting, and he reacted accordingly. In the follow-up to the clash, which rolled over to the next day with a telephone conversation that ended in less-than-agreeable terms, Durbrow produced a memorandum for Williams' action that he also forwarded to Parsons.[79] The language and tone of that document was similar to Durbrow's handling of Ngô Đình Diệm during his tenure in office. It was full of condescension and veiled accusation of misconduct, misdirection, and incompetence. There was a sense that Durbrow's memorandum to Williams was more for Parsons than the general and served as an attempt to place upon Williams the responsibility of the internal security failure affecting Vietnam at the time.

On April 13, Williams met with Ngô Đình Diệm, during which time the Comstock–Nguyễn Ngọc Khôi controversy was discussed. Williams provided Ngô Đình Diệm with the correspondence and relayed the conversation he had with Durbrow the evening before. According to Williams, Ngô Đình Diệm was "visibly moved but speechless" by the knowledge of the exchange.[80] Ngô Đình Diệm summoned his naval aide to find Nguyễn Ngọc Khôi and Trần Trung Dũng and have them report to him. Clearly embarrassed and disturbed by the situation in which Williams had been placed, Ngô Đình Diệm offered a casual explanation that Nguyễn Ngọc Khôi had probably overheard Trần Trung Dũng say something off the top of his head and had misinterpreted it. Ngô Đình Diệm promised Williams that the two men would provide an explanation of their actions to Williams, though Williams suggested, and Ngô Đình Diệm agreed, that it would be more appropriate for them to explain themselves to Durbrow. While the political dynamics within the Country Team continued to fluctuate and the relationship between Durbrow and Ngô Đình Diệm strained, the same could not be said for the RVN president's relationship with Williams. The two men understood one another, and even if they did not agree on all matters, they had a mutual respect for one another and the role each played in working toward Vietnamese independence, stability, and security.

The tension was also increasing in the countryside, as the insurgents stepped up their activity against the ARVN, and clashes of personality were manifesting themselves. Two camps emerged in the Year of the Rat. The first, headed by Durbrow, sought to lead Ngô Đình Diệm through the impeding crisis by dictating advice and action. Durbrow's confidence in Ngô Đình Diệm was waning. The other camp sought to work with Ngô Đình Diệm by offering advice and action. While this group, led by Williams and Lansdale, did not always agree with the actions of the Saigon government, it was slower to condemn without reasoned thought.

For Ngô Đình Diệm, it was clear that his relationship with Durbrow and the American embassy staff was on the decline. This, however, was only one of the many problems facing the embattled RVN. As spring rolled into summer, Ngô Đình Diệm would face legitimate opposition from within that encouraged Durbrow to continue down the path he had chosen. Lost in this process were the continued protests by thousands of individuals throughout the RVN against the communist activities and in support of Ngô Đình Diệm. Durbrow chose to focus on other demonstrations that were more in line with his thinking.[81]

4

The Caravelle Carnival

The month of April had been a particularly bad one for the RVN. The Việt Cộng had intensified their attacks against in the countryside and had initiated several large-scale, organized attacks against Agrovilles in the south and southwest of the country. The incidents of targeted assassination had reached an all-time monthly high of 224 while the United States estimated that approximately 3,000 irregular troops had been supplemented with 3,000 to 5,000 regular Việt Cộng armed cadres.[1] While Central Vietnam appeared to be quieter than the South, there was still a great concern for the internal security of the country. Just as the military scene seemed to be turning for the worse, a political challenge to Ngô Đình Diệm was issued by a group of Saigon intellectuals and former government officials. This challenge proved to be benign, but the damage done to the credibility of Ngô Đình Diệm within the diplomatic corps in Saigon and specifically with the American embassy personnel caused a further deterioration of the already strained relationship.

On April 26, eighteen members of the Bloc for Liberty and Progress issued a proclamation, known later as the Caravelle Manifesto because it was signed at that famous Saigon hotel, in which they called for reforms within the Ngô Đình Diệm government and paved the way for the possibility of a new government in the RVN. The signatories of the document were either former politicians, many of whom had served under Bảo Đại, or prominent members of the three politico-religious organizations that Ngô Đình Diệm had defeated in 1955.[2] The Caravelle Manifesto represented a legitimate threat to the Saigon government and raised questions that Durbrow had long believed to be valid. The language of the manifesto, in many ways, echoed the communist propaganda that had been directed against Ngô Đình Diệm during his consolidation of power:

> Let us look toward the past, at the time when you were abroad. For eight or nine years, the Vietnamese people suffered many trials due to the war: They passed from French domination to Japanese occupation, from revolution to resistance, from the national imposture behind which hid Communism to a pseudo-independence covering up for colonialism; from terror to terror, from sacrifice to sacrifice—in short, from promise to promise, until finally hope ended in bitter disillusion.[3]

It suggested that Ngô Đình Diệm was not present at a critical time during the Vietnamese struggle for independence and was a usurper who fled the country during its trials only to return after the foreign threat had passed. Ngô Đình Diệm reappeared in time to reassert his form of colonial rule as a puppet to the United States. The document then outlined the people's expectations of Ngô Đình Diệm upon his return:

> Thus, when you were on the point of returning to the country, the people as a whole entertained the hope that it would find again under your guidance the peace that is necessary to give meaning to existence, to reconstruct the destroyed homes, put to the plow again the abandoned lands. The

people hoped no longer to be compelled to pay homage to one regime in the morning and to another at night, not to be the prey of the cruelties and oppression of one faction; no longer to be treated as coolies; no longer to be at the mercy of the monopolies; no longer to have to endure the depredations of corrupt and despotic civil servants. In one word, the people hoped to live in security at last, under a regime which would give them a little bit of justice and liberty. The whole people thought that you would be the man of the situation and that you would implement its hopes.[4]

It was interesting that the eighteen members of the Bloc for Liberty and Progress would have such high expectations for Ngô Đình Diệm while, during his period of consolidation, many of these same men were a part of the politico-religious organizations that were vying for the same position of power or were a part of Vietnam's government that guarded its position against Ngô Đình Diệm carefully.

The manifesto then went on to outline grievances within the political arena, including corruption and continuous arrests of the opposition and a harkening of the days of the politico-religious organizations. The group urged Ngô Đình Diệm to "liberalize the regime, promote democracy, guarantee minimum civil rights, recognize the opposition so as to permit the citizens to express themselves without fear, thus removing grievances and resentments, opposition to which now constitutes for the people their sole reason for existence."[5] The manifesto cautioned Ngô Đình Diệm to reform the army, end the Agroville Program, and abolish the monopolies set up by individuals who were members of the Cần Lao Party.

Throughout the manifesto, the eighteen signatories stated that their aim was to make Ngô Đình Diệm aware of their support for the RVN and the problems they saw in his government that allowed the enemy within an opportunity to multiply. The group concluded that it was their responsibility to "speak the truth, to awaken public opinion, to alert the people, and to unify the opposition so as to point the way."[6] The manifesto, received during a time of internal security crisis and an increasingly distant Durbrow surely had the opposite effect of drawing Ngô Đình Diệm toward compromise and conciliation. If Ngô Đình Diệm was fighting for the survival of the Republic, this intellectual opposition certainly would not have persuaded him to relinquish control during such a critical time.

Ngô Đình Diệm's immediate reaction, and one that he sustained throughout the political life of the Caravelle Group, was to ignore this would-be political opposition party. This decision, however, was not based on Ngô Đình Diệm's insecurity or a desire to eliminate an opposing voice. Rather, he gave little credence to this group of Saigon intellectuals and former Bảo Đại supporters as a reasoned political force who offered constructive suggestions for change during a time of increased communist subversion. Indeed, Ngô Đình Diệm had a precedent with the politico-religious crisis of 1955 when dealing with internal opposition. The main difference in 1960 was a strong communist insurgency that was receiving active and escalating support from the North and an American embassy working actively against him.

The U.S. embassy was well aware of the Caravelle Group and their message when it was finally promulgated on April 26. As early as March 15, army attaché Richard Comstock had been approach by Frank Gonder, owner of the American Trading Company of Vietnam, about the opposition group. Gonder had earned a reputation as one who was anti–Ngô Đình Diệm and anti–Saigon government because he believed that he was being discriminated against when he represented firms who wished to do business with the RVN. He was also well connected to the Saigon intelligentsia that formed the core of the opposition to Ngô Đình Diệm. It was Gonder who had supplied much of the alleged evidence of corruption and malpractice that Scripps-Howard correspondent Albert Colegrove had used in his July 1959 articles on U.S. aid to Vietnam.[7] According to Mendenhall, Gonder had "the reputation of having a not too savory character."[8] In their March 15 meeting, Gonder told Comstock that he had been in contact with the leaders of an opposition group led by Trần Văn Văn, former minister of national economy under Bảo Đại, and Dr. Hồ Văn Nhựt, who was serving as a vice chairman of the Vietnamese Red Cross. Trần Văn Văn provided three charts to Comstock that outlined a provisional government, provisional National Assembly, and details of those individuals and political parties that opposed Ngô Đình Diệm. It was interesting to note that these organizational charts represented a transformation of the governmental structure of the RVN and could have been easily construed as a sign that the Caravelle Group was more interested in a coup'détat than in voicing their opposition to Ngô Đình Diệm's handling of internal security or in establishing a legitimate political party.

When they met again on March 21, Gonder informed Comstock that the group planned to see Ngô Đình Diệm within the next two weeks to deliver notice of the formation of their opposition group and present him with a letter explaining their actions. Gonder assumed the role of liaison with the embassy, with the principle mission of sounding out the embassy's position toward the Saigon government. He was also charged with handling contacts with the international press. Trần Văn Văn, who was joined in the leadership of the group by Phan Khắc Sửu, an oppositionist deputy in the National Assembly, and Trần Văn Đỗ, who had been foreign minister in 1955 and was the brother of Vietnamese ambassador to the United States, Trần Văn Chương and uncle to Madame Ngô Đình Nhu, suggested that at least one Vietnamese newspaper, *Tiếng Chuông*, already supported the objectives and stated goals of the new group. Gonder next met with the group's leadership on April 1 and informed Comstock of their impatience and need for action.

During this meeting, the group expressed a hope of convincing Ngô Đình Diệm to step down from office, and barring that, removing him by force. Gonder claimed to have met an individual who controlled a Hòa Hảo regiment which was based near the Cambodian border. If this report was true, the Hòa Hảo regiment, which represented one of three from the Hòa Hảo, Cao Đài, and Bình Xuyên, was part of a force that numbered over 10,000. Even if Mendenhall dismissed the threat value of the group, this potential force did represent a problem. If the number 10,000 was an overestimation, its position vis-à-vis Cambodia suggested how dangerous the border had become for the internal security of the RVN. When Gonder next met Comstock on April 11, he handed him a copy of the letter the group planned to present Ngô Đình Diệm on April 25. Gonder would later add four additional members to the group: Hồ Viết Điểu, a professor at Saigon University; Trần Văn Hương, secretary of the Vietnamese Red Cross; Lâm Văn Tết, a cultural leader for the three politico-religious organizations; and, Đào Hưng Long, who had been exiled to Madagascar when Ngô Đình Diệm served as the president of the Council of Ministers of Vietnam under Bảo Đại.[9]

In reflecting on the role of Gonder and the oppositionists that would become known as the Caravelle Group, Mendenhall maintained that they were intellectuals who had "resorted to plotting and drawing up charts because, powerless to undertake effective action either overtly or covertly to oppose the GVN, within the restrictive framework of Vietnamese political life, there is little else that they are able to do."[10] Whether this was an assessment based in disgust or lamentation was not clear. Mendenhall then repeated many of the complaints that would form the nucleus of the Caravelle Manifesto as evidence already provided by the embassy, such as alleged corruption by members of Ngô Đình Diệm's family. Like Durbrow, Mendenhall argued that it did not matter whether the accusations were correct because the public perception believed them to be correct. As a result, he agreed with the ambassador that Ngô Đình Diệm needed to accept the issue or suffer the consequences.

Mendenhall provided Durbrow a copy of a manifesto that turned out to be the same document released on April 26 by the Bloc for Liberty and Progress.[11] It also became the foundation of the anti–Ngô Đình Diệm movement spearheaded by the Saigon intelligentsia in the months to follow. Its significance was not lost to those within the Vietnamese community who followed Saigon politics. It was not surprising that Durbrow knew of the document, had it translated, and inadvertently released it. However, the fact that he concluded that the Caravelle Group and its Manifesto were not "sufficiently effective to constitute danger" demonstrated a lack of understanding of the changing dynamics within Saigon. Durbrow informed Washington that the bloc was no different than other organizations that had surfaced and suggested that he not inform Ngô Đình Diệm of its pending announcement.

This stance, while on the surface it seemed reasonable, underpinned the dangerous possibility that Durbrow wanted to allow the group to have the element of surprise for maximum public affect. In the same cable to Washington in which he informed the State Department of the manifesto, Durbrow also provided a built-in excuse should it become known that the embassy withheld vital information from Ngô Đình Diệm.[12] He suggested telling the RVN president, should a leak occur, that this opposition group was no different than what other organizations had brought to the embassy and that Durbrow had already offered a blanket warning to Ngô Đình Diệm that followed the intelligentsia line of thinking. Durbrow recommended telling Ngô Đình Diệm that the embassy dismissed the significance of the Caravelle Group and its manifesto.

If Durbrow firmly believed that the Caravelle Manifesto was benign, then it was curious that he had fabricated a justification for withholding the information from Ngô Đình Diệm and passed along that strategy to Washington. Another possibility that better fit Durbrow's actions was that he subscribed to the basic tenets of the document and saw this new organization as an opportunity to work toward diminishing the RVN president's influence and make him more malleable to American advice. It did not seem likely that Durbrow placed any great faith in Trần Văn Văn, Hồ Văn Nhựt, Phan Khắc Sửu, or Trần Văn Đỗ, nor had he any respect for Frank Gonder. He, however, was cognizant of the internal security situation and empathetic to those Vietnamese who found Ngô Đình Diệm frustrating to deal with on a daily basis.

The Caravelle Manifesto reaffirmed for Durbrow many of the reports that he and his embassy staff had received in the months leading up to its promulgation, even though some within the embassy argued that the situation in the central region of the RVN was less serious than the Saigon area and the Mekong Delta.[13] A March visit to that area by embassy and USOM staff revealed that internal security had been relatively achieved even if there were still signs of Việt Cộng activity near the border with Cambodia. The group was impressed with the officials it met, noting specifically their competence, level of education, and administrative experience. The group also highlighted the improvements in economy and infrastructure, including roads that were built solely by the Vietnamese with Western equipment. While there was some concern about the lack of sympathy exhibited to the Montagnard population, there were indications that the officials in the various provinces understood the necessity of working with the ethnic tribes and were making progress, albeit slowly, to improve the conditions of the people. The group, which had provided very little notice of its intentions or itinerary, was well treated and experienced a favorable trip that was contradictory to the reports received in the South. The lack of planning with the Saigon government was significant, as it was argued that good receptions and visible, productive examples of Vietnamese progress were often pre-arranged by the government in order to provide a better image of what was occurring than was the real case.

This observation, forwarded by Mendenhall to the Department of State on April 1, served in direct contradiction to other reports making their way to Washington. In most circles, the deteriorating internal security in Vietnam was the principle subject of dispatches.[14] In the weeks leading to the manifesto, Americans reporting from London, France, and within Southeast Asia commented on how critical the situation had become. On April 6, *Réalités Cambodgiennes* printed a "confidential column" which suggested that the internal security had deteriorated so much in the RVN that the U.S. had ordered its citizens in the countryside to return to Saigon and remain there until otherwise instructed.[15] Durbrow did not believe the United States should respond directly to the Phnom Penh claim, but he did think it wise to inform the government that no order had been issued. While this passive approach might have been diplomatically wise, a stronger rapprochement would have signaled to the Saigon government greater support for its situation.

Likewise, Durbrow had been focused on alleged corruption within the Cần Lao Party since an April 6 meeting with Ngô Đình Diệm during which he confronted the president with the assertion without providing the names of the individual accused or his sources. Durbrow's version of this meeting reached Parsons, who relayed it back to Nguyễn Đình Thuận during his visit to Washington earlier in the month. The meeting, which Durbrow deemed a success because he was able to forcibly impress upon Ngô Đình Diệm the seriousness of the allegations, whether they were true or not, set up the conditions to more readily accept the Caravelle Manifesto even if the group was not deemed noteworthy. Durbrow used the April 6 meeting to relay his concerns to Ngô Đình Diệm but would refer to that meeting frequently as he approached Vice President Nguyễn Ngọc Thơ and Nguyễn Đình Thuận.[16]

Durbrow's efforts to communicate his concerns to the vice president and secretary of state for the presidency offered two alternative perspectives. Assuming that Durbrow had Ngô Đình Diệm and the RVN's best interests in mind, his approach to the second- and third-most powerful men in the country represented an attempt to relay the seriousness of his concerns and work with all interested parties to reach a satisfactory resolution on the issue of corruption within the Cần Lao Party. However, Durbrow's earlier actions and his immediate future directives suggest that he approached the two men, not to seek greater consensus, but because he had grown frustrated with Ngô Đình Diệm's unwillingness to submit to his calls for greater action without providing vital information to confirm the allegations.

Durbrow's perception of his meetings with Nguyễn Đình Thuận and Nguyễn Ngọc Thơ suggest that he believed both men to be sympathetic with his concerns about corruption and willing to help alleviate the problem but unable to act out against Ngô Đình Diệm or his family. As Durbrow would comment in an April 28 dispatch regarding his conversation with Nguyễn Ngọc Thơ, "He added that unfortunately he could do little about these activities himself but expressed the hope that maybe the frank conversations I had had with Diem and Thuan would do some good. He gave the impression, however, that he was not too hopeful."[17]

The conversations these Vietnamese leaders had with Williams offered a different perspective. Where Durbrow interpreted the Vietnamese response as sympathetic, perhaps because that was what he desired, Williams would learn that the Vietnamese were embarrassed and in some cases angered by the continued allegations.

This was not to suggest that some type of corruption was unknown to the Vietnamese. Rather, they had been engaged in fighting corruption within the RVN since its inception, and there were several high-profile cases on which they could report success. Part of the frustration for Ngô Đình Diệm and his supporters, who were continually bombarded with reports of corruption that were given credence by the embassy, was the source of these allegations. Gonder had been an active rabble-rouser while French businessmen and intellectuals seemed to have the ear of the embassy, as evidenced by the April 20 and April 21 memorandum of conversations with Dr. Jacques M. May received by the embassy and forwarded to Washington.[18] May had been a doctor of Medicine in Hanoi during the Second World War and was well respected by his students, many of whom most likely left the North during Operation Exodus because of their close connections with the French.[19] These former students reported to May many of the same complaints that had been filed by the embassy. Durbrow and Director of the USOM Arthur Gardiner found the evidence convincing despite the fact that there was no indication of who the Vietnamese offering the analysis were or what political position they held. May's Vietnamese were considered reliable and therefore credible. As a result, Durbrow used that data to reinforce his own conviction that Ngô Đình Diệm was becoming increasingly isolated by his family and no longer had the support of the military or the people in the countryside.

Durbrow was not content to stand aside and let Ngô Đình Diệm continue down a path that he had already determined would lead to failure. While one might not question the good intentions of this strategy and the real possibility that Durbrow was correct in doing so, he took a real gamble in alienating Ngô Đình Diệm from the U.S. embassy as well as Washington. The Manifesto marked a critical time for the RVN as internal politics threatened to erupt into chaos and further intensify the crisis that had begun with the failure at Tây Ninh in January.

Within a few months, the Caravelle Manifesto seemed to have run its course despite the dire warnings of individuals, both Vietnamese and foreign, who argued that the internal security situation had deteriorated rapidly throughout the RVN. The Saigon government chose to ignore the Bloc for Liberty and Progress and its initial foray into the political scene. It also refrained from responding to its April 30 press conference. The opposition group seemed to be unable to garner too much support from outside the capital, though Durbrow would inform the Department of State that "word of its action spread rapidly by word of mouth through Saigon."[20] Durbrow may have been referring to the diplomatic corps in Saigon, as he or his staff had been continually approached by others to gauge U.S. reaction to the Caravelle Group and determine the level of American support toward Ngô Đình Diệm.[21]

Ngô Đình Diệm maintained, in a conversation with Williams, that the group's influence in Saigon was even less than Durbrow had indicated.[22] He argued that the April 30 press conference was designed to coincide with the planned May Day union demonstrations the next day. Ngô Đình Diệm argued that the Caravelle Group had sought to take over the demonstrations and use the May Day rallies as proof that their position was supported by the people. When the three trade unions petitioned for permission to parade, Ngô Đình

Diệm had initially thought to reject the request. He was persuaded by Ngô Đình Nhu to grant permission, who then informed the unions of the Caravelle Group's intentions. After the trade unions learned of these developments, they decided not to march and, instead, held their rallies in their meeting halls around the city. There was no indication in the records on how Durbrow responded to the failure of the Caravelle Group to bring home their point.[23]

By May 10, the Bloc for Liberty and Progress had still not been able to register as a political group, but not because of any obstacles established by Ngô Đình Diệm. The group seemed to be disorganized, as the press noted, and lacked strong leadership.[24] On May 7, *Sài Gòn Mới* issued a condemnation of the group, who had "plotted to lure local intellectuals into approving their so-called 'democratic' motion to the government."[25] In another editorial, *Cách mạng Quốc gia* criticized the "elite and intellectuals" for their wait-and-see attitudes while *Sài Gòn Mới* issued another salvo against those who argued that there were parallels between the Caravelle Group motives and the events within the Republic of Korea. These two papers, both of which serve as a voice of the groups that supported Ngô Đình Diệm, represented, unofficially, the position of the Saigon government. They would continue to put pressure on the Caravelle Group until the episode waned.[26]

The Caravelle Group and its manifesto did not entirely disappear as the summer began in earnest. It continued to play a role in the thinking of both Americans and Vietnamese, usually indirectly, as a precedent for exposing the allegedly corrupt nature of the Saigon government, but also directly as was the case with a June 17 mimeographed statement purportedly emanating from the group's leaders. The document, supposedly released by Trần Văn Văn, Phan Khắc Sửu, and Trần Văn Tuyên, responded to a number of alleged accusations that had been leveled against the three men.[27] The document, which Durbrow and the British believed had been the product of the director of the Office of Political and Social Studies, Trần Kim Tuyến, offered a series of statements based on rumors that had been spread among the people in Saigon.[28] The answers to these statements were designed to refute the claims put forward but were done so in a clumsy way that often implied even greater problematic issues than the ones they were trying to refute. If Durbrow was correct, and it seems reasonable to assume that he was given the educational level of the Caravelle Group leaders, the mimeographed statement was really nothing more than a parting shot by the government against the group that had attempted to destabilize Saigon politics. It was significant that the Saigon government attempted to further discredit the group even after it had been proven to be ineffective and had failed to garner popular support. The Caravelle Group never amounted to a real threat, but it did bother Ngô Đình Diệm and his supporters at a critical time in the history of their Republic.

The Caravelle Manifesto represented an internal threat to the Saigon government that complemented the external threat posed by the Việt Cộng. It was not too surprising that Ngô Đình Diệm chose to ignore it, nor was it unexpected that the American embassy offered too much commentary on the group which had as its liaison Frank Gonder. If the Caravelle Group succeeded in making an impact on Saigon politics, Durbrow could always point to its manifesto as a warning Ngô Đình Diệm should have heeded. If it did not accomplish anything of substance, then Durbrow would not be connected with the failed enterprise. Either way, the embassy held the initiative on how it would organize its position within Saigon politics. Regardless of the public persona, Durbrow, the embassy, and the Department of State expressed continued skepticism about Ngô Đình Diệm's rule, which set up another confrontation with Williams, MAAG, and the Department of Defense. While this was a conflict based on personality, power, and control, it had as its common theme what appeared to be a deteriorating situation in the RVN. At the same time as the Caravelle Manifesto, other events in the RVN significantly affected the Vietnamese relationship with the Americans.

An April 21 memorandum for Eisenhower prepared by Laurin B. Askew, the officer in charge of Cambodian affairs, emphasized the increased intensity of communist insurgent activity that was sponsored by Hanoi.[29] This memorandum described Ngô Đình Diệm as seriously concerned with the new level of violence and characterized him as working with U.S. officials to improve the efficiency of the RVN's counter-insurgency strategy while lamenting the failure of the International Supervisory and Control Commission to investigate Saigon claims of violations. Durbrow had sent a similar telegram two days earlier which did not boast of Ngô Đình Diệm but did focus on improving the Civil Guard to deal with the increased insurgent violence. Askew and Durbrow agreed on the changing dynamics of Vietnam's military situation, which were moving toward a critical stage, but they differed on where to focus. Just as the manifesto focused on the failure of Ngô Đình Diệm to deal with the situation, so too would Durbrow, by his absence of praise for Ngô Đình Diệm as seen with the Cambodia desk, indicate that a change was needed to save the situation.

In the same telegram, Durbrow also resisted requests by Ngô Đình Diệm to bring Lansdale to Vietnam to provide advice and assistance to deal with the situation. The relationship between Durbrow and Lansdale was strained and would further deteriorate as the Year of the Rat continued. Lansdale, who had a history with Ngô Đình Diệm and had earned the trust of the RVN president, represented a threat to the influence that Durbrow worked to gain in Saigon.[30] In many respects, Durbrow worked as hard to keep Lansdale out of Vietnam as he did trying to manipulate Saigon politics and Ngô Đình Diệm's vision for the RVN.

A few days before the announcement of the Caravelle Manifesto, the Vietnamese counselor to their embassy in Washington, Nguyễn Duy Liên, called at the Department of State with a request from Ngô Đình Diệm to have Lansdale visit Saigon and provide consultation on how to deal with the increased communist insurgent activity.[31] When Durbrow received word of this request, his reaction was not surprising. In addition to being bypassed as the principle American representative to the RVN and learning of the request after the fact, Durbrow saw no positives in the visit as it related to his strategy in dealing with Ngô Đình Diệm.

In rejecting the Lansdale visit, Durbrow offered two justifications for his position. He believed that Lansdale was too well known in Vietnam and would serve as a lightning rod for anti–American propaganda from Hanoi, which had been highly critical of the increased U.S. effort in the RVN. He also suggested that Lansdale's visit was not necessary, as the RVN had just received three British experts from Malaya. Durbrow concluded that Ngô Đình Diệm's request was merely an attempt at "groping in all directions to get 'best advice' instead of taking appropriate action of means at his disposal to ameliorate [the] situation."[32] Durbrow also questioned Lansdale's qualifications: "As far as I aware Lansdale is not an expert [on] anti-guerrilla activities."[33] Durbrow conceded that if Ngô Đình Diệm needed to be satiated, it would be best to avoid Lansdale. He maintained that Lansdale's profile was too public while his qualifications were questionable. Instead, Durbrow suggested that the best experts in anti-guerrilla tactics be sent to Vietnam on temporary duty. It was clear that Durbrow saw this as a concession to appease Ngô Đình Diệm, as one might quiet an unruly child with a distraction, rather than as a necessity to avert what was clearly becoming a critical situation in the RVN. Durbrow ignored or refused to accept that it was Lansdale's trust that made him the right candidate to consult with the Vietnamese president regardless of his qualifications or personality.

Durbrow's position was not lost on Ngô Đình Diệm, which was perhaps why he circumvented the diplomatic process, but also on Lansdale who worked from within Washington as an advocate for the embattled RVN president. On April 25, Lansdale forwarded a memorandum on Third Country doctrine as it related to the internal security of Vietnam to the secretary to the General Staff of the U.S. Army, Major General Charles H. Bonesteel, in which he attacked Durbrow's position regarding counter-insurgency.[34] After a subtle jab at Durbrow that implied he had not been as forthright as he should have been regarding U.S. efforts of introducing Third Country counter-insurgency advisers, in this case British officers who were headquartered in Malaya, Lansdale offered to fill in the "curious gaps in some American reports from Vietnam."[35] There was no question as to who had provided these curious gaps.

Lansdale continued his memorandum by criticizing the idea of relying on British officers for the program even though Ngô Đình Diệm had requested three of them to visit Vietnam after his trip to Malaya. It became clear that the British model in Malaya did not transfer to the RVN. Additionally, Lansdale reported that the Vietnamese officers who interacted with the British had found their advice lacking and not applicable to the situation in the Mekong Delta, nor had the Vietnamese forgotten the less-than-professional reception by the British when they had visited Malaya and were told that the Vietnamese were less capable when compared to other Asian troops. From the Vietnamese perspective, the British model was impractical while the British attitude was too similar to the old French colonial position.

Just as Durbrow worked to keep Lansdale out of Vietnam, Lansdale targeted Durbrow's position as it related to Ngô Đình Diệm and his attempts to force the RVN president to conform to his position regarding reforms in politics, the economy, society, and diplomacy. In this struggle of personalities, which complemented the similar personality skirmish between Ngô Đình Diệm and Durbrow, Lansdale had a willing ally in Williams. On April 30, Lansdale brought Williams up to date on the continuing saga regarding his proposed visit to Saigon.[36] Lansdale essentially requested Williams' assistance in getting approval to visit Vietnam even though he claimed to be "damn tired and worn out."[37] Williams replied nine days later. In it, he confirmed the general attitude that the U.S. embassy personnel had toward Lansdale: "You are considered a bad fellow because of your prior close association with Diem!"[38] It was clear to Williams and those outside the American embassy in Saigon that Lansdale was not welcomed in the RVN by Durbrow or the Department of State. When Williams met with Ngô Đình Diệm in the evening of May 9, the Lansdale controversy was one of the first items on the agenda. Both maintained that they were at a loss as to why the request was rejected though it seemed fairly clear to each man that Durbrow had played a significant role in the refusal.[39]

Williams shared with Lansdale his growing frustration with Durbrow as it related to handling Ngô Đình Diệm. He went against Durbrow and, as a result, had to endure criticisms directed against him. In one case, Williams received a written reprimand for informing Ngô Đình Diệm that the United States had approved the transfer of 5,000 Thompson submachine guns to the Civil Guard. Durbrow argued that Ngô Đình Diệm should not have been informed. Rather, the weapons could have been mentioned but withheld until the embassy received a greater political benefit. Where Durbrow was constantly thinking about ways to hold political leverage over Ngô Đình Diệm to force him against his will toward the embassy position, Williams focused on what was right for the RVN: "My only defense," Williams told Lansdale in a May 9 letter, "was that I'd gotten the weapons to help the poorly equipped C.G. and not for a political hammer."[40] These conflicting strategies of how best to work with Ngô Đình Diệm highlighted the tense relationship between Durbrow and Williams which extended to Lansdale and the Department of Defense and Department of State.

In another example, Williams explained his opposition to efforts by Durbrow and Mendenhall to reduce the U.S. budget for the RVN from the absolute minimum of $169.1 million set by Williams to $165 million. The result was that the embassy's new numbers supported a Vietnamese Armed Forces of 143,000, which was a number 7,000 below the number the U.S. had promised to maintain. To make up for this difference, Durbrow suggested the deactivation of field command, corps, and division headquarters. When Durbrow expected Williams to go along with his pressure to deactivate these units, Williams disappointed him by rejecting the idea even though Durbrow had counted on his support. As a result, Williams would incur the wrath of Durbrow until he left the RVN in September 1960, including a written requirement from Durbrow penned in "poisonous language" requiring a report on U.S. efforts in training the Vietnamese since 1956.[41]

The situation became so strained that even Ngô Đình Diệm sensed the internal discord among the Americans. During an RVN visit by Admiral Felix B. Stump, former commander in chief, Pacific, and his wife, during which they dined with Ngô Đình Diệm in Dalat, the RVN president appealed to the admiral to intervene in the dispute so that Williams would not be sacked. He told Stump that "the embassy people were out to get General Williams."[42] Ngô Đình Diệm understood the internal dynamics within the American community in Vietnam, which was probably another reason he wanted Lansdale with him. It seemed to be getting more and more difficult to work with the Americans, and concern that his closest confidant in Saigon was being targeted did little to bolster his confidence.

The strained relationship between Ngô Đình Diệm, Lansdale, and Williams on one side and Durbrow, his embassy staff, and various members of the State Department on the other intensified in the weeks following the Caravelle Manifesto. In addition to his attempt to block Lansdale from returning to the RVN in order to advise Ngô Đình Diệm, at the latter's request Durbrow also worked his angle with Washington to authorize his tactics of pressure-for-progress stake against the RVN president. On May 3, Durbrow sent a telegram to Washington that outlined a series of events that demonstrated how out of control Ngô Đình Diệm had become in his rule of South Vietnam. Included in his message to the State Department was the alleged backing by Saigon of the Free Khmer Radio, a group dedicated to the overthrow of Norodom Sihanouk in Cambodia and the furnishing of weapons to the followers of Sam Sary who used the weapons to raid the city of Pailin across the border from the RVN.[43] Durbrow was also concerned with the Saigon position vis-à-vis some islands in the Gulf of Thailand, for which both the Vietnamese and Cambodians had laid claim, as well as continued allegations of corruption against the Cần Lao Party.

While Durbrow did note that Ngô Đình Nhu was most likely the lead instigator of the "unfavorable developments," he was critical of Ngô Đình Diệm for failing to acknowledge his brother's faults and refusing to act. Durbrow called for "drastic means to bring him to his senses."[44] Before offering some suggestions of what drastic means entailed, Durbrow offered the observation that Ngô Đình Diệm was simply unwilling to listen to anything

Durbrow told him regarding these issues. While the record does not reflect complete obstinacy by the RVN president, it was easy to see how Durbrow perceived this given his established position against Ngô Đình Diệm. Add to this the encouragement from the Saigon intelligentsia and Ngô Đình Diệm's insistence on doing what he believed best for his country regardless of the musings of the U.S. ambassador, and Durbrow's position becomes clearer. Nonetheless, as Durbrow would conclude, "since our previous efforts to persuade Diem to see the evils of his ways have been too little or no avail and brother Nhu seems to be riding even higher, I have given considerable thought about what positive and fairly drastic action we should take to make our efforts more effective."[45] Durbrow was clearly targeting Ngô Đình Diệm to either force him into submission or cause his removal from power so that someone more malleable to the ambassador could be set up in his place.

Durbrow suggested that he be instructed to discuss with Ngô Đình Diệm the stepped-up insurgent activity and possible American responses to the crisis, the inefficiency of Ngô Đình Diệm's use of U.S. aid, the corrupt practices of the Cần Lao Party, and the anti–Khmer action and rhetoric originating from Saigon. He requested instructions that would allow him to tell Ngô Đình Diệm that unless the Vietnamese were able to convince the embassy that they were committed to rectifying these problems, the United States, through Durbrow, would withhold all extra equipment promised to the RVN. Durbrow maintained that his ultimatum, which he labeled a calculated risk, was the only way the United States would be able to force Ngô Đình Diệm to come to his senses.

The State Department's response, under the authorship of Chalmers B. Wood, the former second secretary and political officer in the U.S. embassy in Saigon under Durbrow and then-current officer in charge of Vietnam affairs, and director of the Office of Southeast Asian Affairs, Daniel Anderson, occurred within a day of its receipt.[46] The response, which was not sent, gave Durbrow free rein to do as he had asked, but it needed approval from the Office of the Assistant Secretary of Defense (International Security Affairs). The Department of State's approval of the draconian request did not escape the notice of Lansdale who immediately worked to unravel this potential disaster. Durbrow's request to withhold aid against the increased insurgent threat and Wood and Anderson's quick response brought and intensified the Durbrow, Lansdale, and Williams debate to Washington. For five days, the State Department and Defense Department clashed over the appropriate response. Lansdale worked from within Washington to make sure that Durbrow was not provided the instructions that would allow him to manipulate Ngô Đình Diệm. Elements in the State Department, whose ties and loyalties to Durbrow were clear, pushed the anti–Ngô Đình Diệm line.

While the Department of Defense continued to serve as an obstacle to Durbrow's plan to force Ngô Đình Diệm into submission, the Department of State rallied to the ambassador's call. In response to Durbrow's request, Parsons sent a telegram indicating that he would contact the Vietnamese ambassador to the United States, Trần Văn Chương, even though he was seldom used for such things. Parsons suggested that notifying Trần Văn Chương would have the added value of a "'shock effect' as well as demonstrate to Diem that you [Durbrow] are not alone."[47] While Parsons set to work on Trần Văn Chương, he also informed Durbrow that the director of the Office of Southeast Asian Affairs, Kenneth Young, had impressed upon Nguyễn Đình Thuận the seriousness of the U.S. concern. As Parsons would relay to Durbrow, Young told Nguyễn Đình Thuận that the RVN "should listen to us as we had had great experience in seeing consequences which followed when populace in Asian country subject to Communist infiltration became disaffected with its leaders."[48] While this may have been true, what Parsons and Young did not convey was that the United States might have seen the consequences, but Nguyễn Đình Thuận and Ngô Đình Diệm were experiencing the potential of not only those consequences but the unintended consequences of following American advice. Young might have been offering what he thought was good advice, but it lacked the necessary perspective that influenced Vietnamese decision making.

Another scenario that had the backing of the Department of State and U.S. embassy in Saigon was the perceived parallel situation that was occurring in the Republic of Korea. In response to the March 15, 1960, national elections in which incumbent president Syngman Rhee won a significant victory, students in the city of Masan initiated a series of protests against the election results. This led to violence and further protesting. On April 19, South Korean students began demonstrating against the government, which responded with force. On April 25, the students were joined by faculty and others, and demonstrations spread beyond Seoul. Syngman Rhee resigned on April 26, effectively ending the First Republic.[49] When Ngô Đình Diệm was queried about the situation in the Republic of Korea with hints that he must be careful not to follow the same path, the Vietnamese president dismissed the suggestion, arguing that Syngman Rhee was senile and that the two situations were not the same. Ngô Đình Diệm maintained that the Caravelle Group was a relic of the old French colonial regime.[50]

While Ngô Đình Diệm might not have had the data to assess the mental capacity of the South Korean president, it was true that the situations were different. It was here that the United States kept making the same mistake of trying to group together all situations that were Asian. Just as the Malayan emergency had characteristics that made it unique to Malaya, so did the situation in the Republic of Korea. The RVN was its own country, and while many Americans tried to connect it to the Asian world as one might connect the United Kingdom to Europe, the commonalities broke down rather quickly. The Vietnamese press was not very sympathetic with Syngman Rhee either. A *Dân chúng* editorial on April 27 argued that if the Korean election had been fair and the people's political rights had been respected, then violence would never have occurred. Another editorial in the same paper the next day called upon the Democratic Party to retain Syngman Rhee in order to maintain coordination among the anti-communist elements in the country. Other Saigon newspapers followed a similar, albeit less direct, vein, though a *Tin Mới* editorial asserted that the Republic of Korea incident provided a valuable lesson for the RVN, in that "the only way to win the people's hearts in the anticommunist struggle is to sincerely implement genuine democratic freedom."[51] *Tiếng Chuông* argued that the cases between the RVN and the Republic of Korea were similar but not identical and that individuals who drew comparisons needed to be careful.[52]

While Durbrow waited for the Department of State to respond to his request to step up the pressure against Ngô Đình Diệm, the deliberations in Washington intensified. At one meeting, on May 5, Chalmers Wood, Deputy Assistant Secretary of Defense for International Security Affairs Robert Knight, and Lieutenant Colonel Joseph Flesch, who represented the Far East region for international security affairs, met to discuss withholding emergency military equipment from the RVN.[53] Wood repeated Durbrow's claims, suggesting that they had been supported by Williams, and argued that such action might make it more difficult for Ngô Đình Diệm to fight the Việt Cộng but less important than the growing rift between the RVN and Cambodia. Knight countered with Lansdale's objections, highlighting the question of integrity and the timing of the threat when Việt Cộng activity was on the rise. Wood concluded the meeting with the weak argument that the RVN could not remain independent if it continued to harass the Cambodians, who would then open their borders to the Việt Cộng. What Wood did not realize or failed to appreciate was the fact that the Việt Cộng was already in the border region using the neutrality of Cambodia to its advantage. Williams, Lansdale, and the Vietnamese were well aware of this fact, which was why Durbrow's request came as such a shock.

Meanwhile, Durbrow received confirmation of his impressions of Ngô Đình Diệm from the French ambassador to the RVN, Roger Lalouette, who seemed to have nothing positive to say about the Vietnamese. The Federal Republic of Germany ambassador to the RVN, Baron Von Wendland, also passed similar negative information and lamented the inability of Germany to economically exploit the lumber industry in the RVN because of the Cần Lao Party.[54] Durbrow's confidence in the matter was also bolstered by Wolf Ladejinsky, who argued that Ngô Đình Diệm was "unrealistically optimistic and stubborn about recent developments" and "blindly convinced" that the RVN was defeating the Việt Cộng.[55] Durbrow seemed ready to report any conversation that backed his initial assertion while ignoring or editorializing individuals who offered a different point of view. One such example was Durbrow's report of a conversation with Major Trần Cửu Thiên, chief of Phong Dinh province.[56] Durbrow argued that the major was one of the most egotistical men he had ever met and concluded that his accomplishments were nothing more than boasts. Durbrow visited the Vị Thanh–Hỏa Lựu Agroville on April 30, which had been constructed under Trần Cửu Thiên's supervision.[57] This Agroville had served as a model for the program which had developed in the RVN. This was the same Agroville that had been the center of conversation between Ngô Đình Diệm and Williams on March 15 and that Williams had visited a few days later. The difference of perception between Durbrow and Williams was pronounced. While supporters of Durbrow maintained that Williams was myopic in his praise, it was just as easy to make the argument that Durbrow focused on the negative in his analysis. If Durbrow did not want the Agroville Program to succeed, there was no way he could have accepted its success at the hands of Trần Cửu Thiên, nor could he have acknowledged the positive work being done.

On May 9, Durbrow finally received a response to his request to use aid as a leverage to affect policy change, but it was not the one for which he had hoped.[58] Drafted by Wood and Deputy Assistant Secretary of State for Far East Affairs John Steeves, and signed by Secretary of State Christian Herter, Durbrow's new instructions allowed him to approach Ngô Đình Diệm about the issues brought up in his May 3 telegraph with the exception of the threat to withhold additional aid. Durbrow won a partial victory and went to see Ngô Đình Diệm on May 13.[59] The tone of the meeting had already been pre-determined by an earlier May 11 session which included Williams and Ladejinsky. In that meeting, Ngô Đình Diệm pointedly praised Williams for his efforts in front of Durbrow to show his support for the general, whom he believed was being targeted for removal by the embassy. Ngô Đình Diệm also was extremely critical of Durbrow throughout the conversation, though in hushed tones because he was in front of the other men.[60]

After discussing a number of minor issues and reviewing the internal security situation, Ngô Đình Diệm called in his secretary, Võ Văn Hải, who delivered a series of transcripts of press dispatches related to a May 2, 1960, incident along the RVN-Cambodia border. Ngô Đình Diệm asserted that Durbrow had been the source for the dispatches and that the information was basically false. Major John Dolan, who authored the meeting minutes, recorded

Durbrow as answering the charges "in soft conciliatory tones that could not be heard by all those present."[61] However, after a few minutes, it appeared that Durbrow conceded the point, to which Ngô Đình Diệm responded, "Well, it's about time that you recognized the facts." What followed was a silence described by Dolan as awesome, which emphasized the importance of Ngô Đình Diệm's point. While Ngô Đình Diệm might have believed that he had finally gotten through to Durbrow on the Cambodian issue, Durbrow's May 13 response suggested that the ambassador was merely playing the part of a diplomat and had not undergone any significant transformation.

In his thirty-minute meeting with Ngô Đình Diệm on May 13, Durbrow offered his list of grievances as instructions from Washington. This was done to add importance to the oral message but also allowed Durbrow to imply that his position was not isolated and included important members of the U.S. government. Durbrow read his "instructions" from a page that had been translated into French.

Durbrow's perception of the meeting varied from that of Ngô Đình Diệm. Durbrow reported that Ngô Đình Diệm remained grave but calm until Durbrow mentioned corruption within the Cần Lao Party. While Ngô Đình Diệm let the ambassador finish reading his written "instructions," Durbrow remarked that Ngô Đình Diệm had become agitated and responded to the oral condemnation by telling him that he was hurt that the U.S. preferred to report and repeat false rumors about Sam Sary and the RVN involvement in support of the Free Khmer Movement and, in Durbrow's words, irritable when the Cần Lao Party's alleged corruption was discussed. In a later conversation between Williams and Nguyễn Đình Thuận, the latter observed that the episode had made Ngô Đình Diệm "white with anger."[62] The official RVN reply to Durbrow's démarche was received on June 20. In it, Trần Văn Chương indicated that Ngô Đình Diệm had expressed profound indignation to the Americans giving credence to the rumors that resulted in the meeting, arguing that the Cần Lao Party had never asked for or received U.S. aid, that the RVN was working hard to improve its relations with Cambodia, and that it did not support Sam Sary or other Khmer rebels.[63] Whether angered or expressing profound indignation, it was clear that Ngô Đình Diệm marked this series of meetings as a turning point in his relationship with the U.S. embassy.

Perhaps the greatest source of ire for Ngô Đình Diệm in his May 13 meeting with Durbrow was the allegations of corruption within the Cần Lao Party. While there were indications that members of the party had used their positions of influence for questionable purposes, which was something Ngô Đình Diệm vehemently opposed, the approach that Durbrow took in confronting Ngô Đình Diệm about the allegations did more to harm their relationship and made it less likely that the embassy could effect positive change for the Saigon government.

Durbrow brought up the issue of corruption within the Cần Lao Party on several occasions during the Year of the Rat. Like the exchange that transpired on May 13, most of the conversations began with Durbrow bringing up the topic and demanding, to varying degrees, that Ngô Đình Diệm fix the problem. When this line of approach was used on May 13, Ngô Đình Diệm was agitated for a few reasons. First, he reiterated that one of the missions of the Cần Lao Party was to root out corruption and that they had been successful in several high-profile cases, most recently with the Hiệp Hòa sugar refinery. Second, Ngô Đình Diệm was dismayed that Durbrow and his staff gave credence to rumors and stories of corruption emanating from disgruntled businessmen and outspoken critics of the Saigon government. Finally, Ngô Đình Diệm repeatedly asked for U.S. assistance in rooting out corruption and implored Durbrow to provide specific information to him or members of his cabinet so that they could investigate the claims and rectify any injustice. Taken in context, Ngô Đình Diệm's points were reasonable and did show a real concern for the need to eliminate corrupt practices within the RVN.

Durbrow's perspective was different. Throughout the year and during his tenure as ambassador, he seemed to be more willing to listen to and accept the claims of corruption within the Cần Lao Party and Saigon government. While it seemed reasonable to assume that Durbrow did not directly implicate Ngô Đình Diệm in these corrupt practices, he did fault the RVN president for failing to address the issue as Durbrow believed it needed to be in order to find resolution. In Durbrow's worldview, Ngô Đình Diệm's inaction was reason enough for the United States to discontinue its support for the current government and find a suitable replacement. Pronouncements like the Caravelle Manifesto only served to reaffirm Durbrow's position even if the group's leadership was weak, while events later in the year confirmed, in his eyes, that the ambassador was correct and Ngô Đình Diệm had lost his effectiveness.

Even when Durbrow conceded a point to Ngô Đình Diệm on the issue of corruption, he did it in a way that negated any opportunity for positive effect. During the May 13 meeting, Ngô Đình Diệm lamented the fact that the United States believed rumors that connected the Cần Lao Party with a questionable case involving the procurement of an import license for flour.[64] Durbrow's reply did not defend against Ngô Đình Diệm's point but, rather, argued that it did not matter if the rumor was true or not because many people believed it to be true. While Ngô Đình Diệm's reply to the revelation was to repeat the unfortunate circumstance that led to the United States believing that a connection existed, it must have been maddening to hear from the U.S. ambassador that the truth in the case was irrelevant when compared to the perception.

Ngô Đình Diệm, in defending his country against a real threat from the North and working to build up the country from within to provide for his people, was working in absolutes. The truth did matter to him; it was more important than perception.[65] Ngô Đình Diệm believed that perception could be altered over the long term so long as the proper course was maintained. Durbrow, who had been in Vietnam for only a few years and most likely knew he would not be in Saigon for the long term, was more concerned with perception. This notion pervades his discussions with Ngô Đình Diệm and was frequently mentioned in his reports to Washington. For Durbrow, it mattered how Ngô Đình Diệm was viewed within the confines of Washington and Saigon and how that view projected into the international community. As such, perception often outweighed the reality of the situation. When Ngô Đình Diệm refused to become intertwined in this scheme and failed to show proper deference to Durbrow as he tried to guide him rather than work with him, the ambassador increased his efforts to isolate Ngô Đình Diệm from Washington until he came around to his way of thinking. If that did not work, Durbrow was prepared to go one step further.

As Durbrow was delivering his instructions to Ngô Đình Diệm without the ultimatum but still with the desired effect of putting Ngô Đình Diệm into his place, his allies in the State Department continued to undermine the Lansdale visit to Saigon. A meeting between Deputy Secretary of Defense James Dillon, whom Lansdale had kept informed; Robert Knight; Deputy Assistant Secretary of State for Far East Affairs John Steeves; and Chalmers Wood examined the prospects for a temporary-duty assignment for Lansdale. While Dillon, who was the principle representative for Defense, defended the idea of the Lansdale visit and believed it would not create complications as outlined by Durbrow, Steeves objected.[66]

Steeves argued that there was evidence from senior military officers who had served with Lansdale during the Saigon Military Mission period who maintained that he was difficult to get along with and was not a team player. More important, Steeves explained that the State Department and, though not mentioned specifically, the embassy "were putting very heavy pressure on Diem and that if we acceded to his request to send someone to whom he could unburden himself, some of those necessary pressures would be diminished."[67] Whether this type of diplomacy had been successful in the past was irrelevant when one considered the RVN. Ngô Đình Diệm was not a weak leader and would not succumb to pressure or school-yard bullying. As Trần Văn Chương had explained to Dillon, the situation in 1960 was similar to that of the early days of Ngô Đình Diệm's rise to power in 1954. Ngô Đình Diệm had felt alone and isolated then and had come to rely on Lansdale whom he considered a friend and confidant.[68] This isolation had returned in 1960 with the increased tension created by the U.S. embassy staff, the rising internal dissent, and more ambitious insurgent activity. Lansdale's visit was important to Ngô Đình Diệm; Durbrow's blocking of the visit thus became another indicator to Ngô Đình Diệm that the ambassador was trying to force him to take a direction with which he was not in agreement or entirely comfortable.

One of the consequences of the meeting was a compromise in which Lansdale would be granted a sixty-day temporary-duty assignment but also be under the direct control of Durbrow. On May 17, Durbrow reluctantly agreed to the compromise because of Ngô Đình Diệm's insistence and his failure to sway the RVN president to reform.[69] Durbrow could not help, however, reiterating the conditions and questioning Lansdale's usefulness. He consented to the arrangement if Lansdale was fully briefed and instructed, was under the ambassador's control, cooperated fully and openly, and reported accurately to Durbrow his conversations with Ngô Đình Diệm. In addition, Durbrow's telegram suggested that Lansdale's knowledge of Vietnam was outdated, relying on a 1956 perspective, and therefore was likely to be ineffective. Clearly, Durbrow did not know or failed to understand that Lansdale had been in contact with Williams as well as Vietnamese who had traveled to the United States.[70] It was supremely arrogant to assume, as Durbrow did in the telegram, that Lansdale needed to learn Durbrow's Vietnam before he could be effective, but it should not be surprising. Durbrow treated Ngô Đình Diệm the same way when offering his advice on how his country should be governed.

As Durbrow penned his telegram, Williams sent another letter to Lansdale that provided an overview perspective of what had transpired in Saigon in the days since the Caravelle Manifesto.[71] With regard to the Durbrow telegram of May that requested authorization to threaten Ngô Đình Diệm by withholding additional equipment, Williams learned, much to his surprise, that his name had appeared on the document as agreeing to the plan. It was not until May 14 that Williams learned of this duplicity. As he would tell Lansdale, "This could have been an honest error but I do not believe so."[72] By this time, however, the ultimatum had been diluted so Williams did not press the matter.

He was more concerned with the atmosphere within the U.S. embassy in Saigon. His version of the conversation between Ngô Đình Diệm and Durbrow on May 13, as told by Nguyễn Đình Thuận, was different than the version Durbrow relayed to Washington. More important, Durbrow had indicated that he had read from a French translation of the instructions received from Washington in his telegram to the State Department but failed to leave a copy of that document with Ngô Đình Diệm, as was custom. When Ngô Đình Diệm sent Nguyễn Đình Thuận to get a copy, he was denied. While this made Nguyễn Đình Thuận a little worried, implying that Durbrow might have gone beyond his instructions, it was later events that perplexed Williams.

At the May 17 Country Team meeting in Saigon, Durbrow told the group that the head of various missions had asked him if the United States was looking for a replacement for Ngô Đình Diệm, speculating that word of his May 13 meeting had leaked. While Williams questioned who would ask such a dangerous question, he did concede that it created an opportunity to instill doubt about the Saigon government. As he would tell Lansdale, "What the hell. Is this a one man campaign to ruin Diem? Why? Personal hate?"[73] Williams was also surprised when Durbrow asked him at the same meeting if he thought ARVN commander Dương Văn Minh was being groomed to replace Ngô Đình Diệm. Williams had to ask him to repeat the question because he was so taken aback and wondered in his letter to Lansdale if Durbrow understood the nature of the rumors that would originate from such a statement as well as the possible consequences to Dương Văn Minh if such rumors reached Ngô Đình Diệm and he believed them. For Williams, Durbrow was playing a dangerous game with the Saigon government leadership that was driven by ego and a personality clash. The relationship between Williams and Durbrow had deteriorated past the point of no return. The only thing keeping the relationship professional was Williams' impending retirement and Durbrow longing for that day.

Durbrow believed that the rumors regarding American support for a replacement to Ngô Đình Diệm were a result of information about his April 6 meeting being leaked to the diplomatic corps in Saigon and the situation in the Republic of Korea. On May 10, Durbrow had been approached by the Indonesian consul general, Basri Haznam, at a social gathering and was asked if the United States was looking for "another Diem."[74] At the same party, Durbrow received similar questions from the Thai ambassador and the officer in charge of the Indian consulate general and would later be approached by the Dutch. Durbrow assumed that it was his "hard hitting recent approaches to Diem" that led to the series of questions rather than a product of the ever rumor-filled Saigon.

While the political intrigue with Saigon intensified, its counterpart in Washington ebbed.[75] The controversy surrounding the Lansdale visit was resolved on May 19. In a telephone conversation between Parsons and Knight, the two representatives of the Department of State and Department of Defense finalized the rejection of Ngô Đình Diệm's request. Parsons explained that the request could not be honored because it undermined the U.S. effort to force Ngô Đình Diệm into line with the American position in Southeast Asia: "It would seem, moreover, to be both strange and not useful from the standpoint of our prestige and influence to reward recalcitrance by acceding to this unusual request."[76] Parsons did not explain how the request was unusual and even argued that Durbrow had not been the one to block the visit. Parsons' recounting of the telephone conversation did not reveal Knight's response to this revelation, though Knight did make it clear that the Pentagon would not push the matter if the State Department opposed the visit even if it disagreed with its reasoning, which had been "prejudiced a bit by certain old scars at the working level in the State Department."[77] Durbrow, backed by the Department of State, had won a victory of sorts.

The Lansdale episode helped to further fracture the working relationship between the

Department of State and Department of Defense over Vietnam that had already been exacerbated by the dispute between Durbrow and Williams. Williams had expressed severe reservations about Durbrow's actions in the days following the Caravelle Manifesto. In addition to preparing for his impeding departure in advance of his retirement, Williams was also bogged down by an inquiry from Senator Mike Mansfield (R–Montana) who was the chairman of the sub-committee on State Department Organization and Public Affairs within the Senate Foreign Relations Committee. Mansfield had made inquiries regarding the MAAG use of personnel through the Temporary Equipment Recovery Mission and whether these men violated the U.S. observance of the 1954 Geneva Agreements. At the same time, Williams had also finalized preparations of a significant memorandum on the training of the RVN Armed Forces that had been requested by Durbrow before the Caravelle Manifesto was announced.[78]

Durbrow's relationship with Williams had never been cordial, while the ambassador's efforts to have the general removed as chief, MAAG, intensified around the time of the Caravelle Manifesto. The State Department position, as outlined by Parsons, was to allow Williams' tenure of office to end normally rather than make an issue of it. The State Department had already successfully blocked Lansdale's visit and had made strides to dominate America's Vietnam policy in Washington though Parsons would confide to Durbrow that members of the State Department involved in Vietnam Affairs were annoyed that the Department of Defense had not consulted them when they decided upon Williams' replacement, Lieutenant General Lionel C. McGarr. Parsons also relayed to Durbrow the plan to make sure McGarr was properly briefed and counseled, "in a manner which may help him to be a better team member than General Williams was and especially to appreciate the principle that he must be subject to your direction."[79] Fresh off of the victory over the Lansdale Affair, the Department of State and Durbrow worked to exploit their leverage in Vietnam to ensure control over the direction of American policy and aid to that country.

Parsons was not the only one attempting to influence McGarr before he arrived in the RVN. Lansdale also worked from the Department of Defense to ensure that the General understood the situation as he understood it.[80] Lansdale used a June 21 letter to Williams to ask that the general return to Washington when Durbrow was schedule to be there and consider extending his time in the RVN beyond his retirement date. There was some concern that Durbrow's perspective, as the on-site expert, would persuade those in Washington who, as Lansdale described, were "nice people and not used to the sort of things which I suspect will be pulled by some folks who are emotionally involved in thinking that you and Diem and other like you are a bunch of bums who need a come-uppance."[81] In this assessment, Lansdale, who was in Washington, was correct. The force of Durbrow, with the might of the Department of State behind him, would be difficult to counter without Williams at Lansdale's side.

Williams would respond a week later that he did not want to come back to Washington to battle Durbrow, nor was he interested in extending his stay in Vietnam which was in its fifth year. He acknowledged, as Lansdale had indicated, that the State Department was running the show. Williams saw no reason why he "should be thrown to the lions."[82] Even as Williams acknowledged that Durbrow had won on the political scene, he did not ignore the many examples of American personnel who assessed Ngô Đình Diệm's actions based on their perception of their own self-importance rather than on the reality of their limited knowledge of Vietnam, its history, and people.

One such example occurred on June 24 when Ngô Đình Diệm and Nguyễn Đình Thuận met with the USOM's acting director, Donald Coster, and the chief of public safety, Frank Walton.[83] Ngô Đình Diệm held the two men for a five-hour conversation in which they had hoped to only discuss the Civil Guard. Instead, Ngô Đình Diệm used the time to explain not only the background history of the Civil Guard and its many problems but also such items as the lack of U.S. support for non-military improvement projects such as Agrovilles, his hatred of the French, the importance of roads, a history of his time in power, political opposition groups, and security.[84] Coster and Walker concluded that Ngô Đình Diệm's mannerisms and language indicated that he was concerned: "Diem gave the very definite impression that he is worried about his position," they maintained, "and that he was making an all-out effort to convince us that he had everything under control."[85] From their perspective, one that dismissed Ngô Đình Diệm's point of view and enhanced their own importance, this analysis might seem reasonable. For Williams, who had spoken to Nguyễn Đình Thuận and had joked about the length of the meeting, their report simply confirmed to him that the USOM men did not understand Ngô Đình Diệm or Vietnam. As Nguyễn Đình Thuận would confide to Williams, Ngô Đình Diệm kept them for five hours because he believed that neither man understood Vietnam, its history, and the history of the Civil Guard. Ngô Đình Diệm felt obligated to go into such detail to both educate the Americans and reinforce the seriousness of the situation.[86] This difference of perspective would continue to plague Ngô Đình Diệm, whose monologues were not taken in the positive, educational vein in which they were delivered. Instead, the Americans believed that Ngô Đình Diệm lectured them to avoid confronting the problems facing his country. His actions were interpreted as obstinacy and aloofness, which when coupled with time, caused many who interacted with Ngô Đình Diệm to turn against him.

The period directly after the Caravelle Manifesto marked an important time in Ngô Đình Diệm's rule in the RVN. The opposition group did not have the leadership or popular support to offer a legitimate challenge to Ngô Đình Diệm's rule but the promulgation of its manifesto reinforced to Durbrow and the Department of State that Ngô Đình Diệm was losing control of his country and the sympathy of the Vietnamese people. This notion, reinforced by the Saigon diplomatic corps, when coupled with the ongoing controversy with Cambodia led Durbrow to request authority to act beyond his normal charge, so that he could apply the pressure he felt necessary to make Ngô Đình Diệm change. When this did not work, Durbrow stepped up the pressure by working against the request to have Lansdale visit. These actions, taken together, changed the tone in Saigon as Ngô Đình Diệm became more politically uncertain with his American allies and Durbrow continued on the offensive.

5

The French Connection

With the Caravelle Manifesto and Lansdale visit resolved, albeit not forgotten, the summer months continued to offer intrigue and duplicity. Durbrow had not scored his initial victory against Ngô Đình Diệm after the Department of State denied him his request to use the leverage of military aid to force submission. He did win his victory to keep Lansdale out of the country, however, and that allowed him to continue to work within the system to exert his power and influence over the diplomatic corps and within the Saigon government. Durbrow and his embassy staff found willing allies in the French who continued to provide the façade of support toward Ngô Đình Diệm but worked to undercut international confidence in the RVN president by undermining those who were most loyal to him.

At the end of April, Lalouette met with Durbrow before his departure to France for a month visit during which the French would reevaluate their position toward the Saigon government and the RVN.[1] During their conversation, Lalouette briefed Durbrow on his most recent conversation with Ngô Đình Diệm. While Ngô Đình Diệm focused on recent ARVN victories against the Việt Cộng in the U Minh forest, Lalouette directed the conversation toward the Caravelle Group as a viable opposition party. When confronted, Ngô Đình Diệm repeated his refrain about Trần Văn Văn having no political backing, dismissing them as opportunists who had formally collaborated with Bảo Đại. Lalouette did not comment on the obvious connection between Bảo Đại and the French and the implications of collaboration with French colonialism, though he did remark to Durbrow that Ngô Đình Diệm had made it perfectly clear that he was, "not prepared to recognize any legal opposition."[2] While Durbrow conceded to Ngô Đình Diệm that the group did not have any real political backing, he did agree with Lalouette that it would have been better had the president acknowledged the group and met with them. This does seem a curious suggestion as Durbrow had originally argued in his correspondence to Washington that the group was not politically viable. Throughout the conversation, Lalouette seemed to be testing Durbrow's position toward the Saigon government given the Caravelle Manifesto and the Republic of Korea incident. It seemed clear that Lalouette represented a French position that would continue to support Ngô Đình Diệm so long as he had the backing of the United States but would change as soon as there was a shift in American thinking.

The French ambassador continued to discuss the internal security situation with Durbrow, remarking that Ngô Đình Diệm seemed to understand how perilous it was in the countryside. Ironically, a Mendenhall report on internal security that was issued in July indicated that the Saigon government and military had made inroads on the security issues during the month of May. While the number of clashes between RVN security forces and Việt Cộng increased in April, Mendenhall maintained that the increase was more a result of activity on the RVN side who had initiated a series of offensive actions to drive the Việt Cộng from some of their traditional safe havens.³ The U Minh operation was one of the largest during the month, but there were also other operations throughout the south and southwest. Only one Agroville had been overrun, while no large-scale plantation attacks had occurred. The number of targeted assassinations and kidnappings had also decreased. While Mendenhall could not refrain from suggesting that the decreased numbers of incidents might have been a product of the Việt Cộng deescalating their activity in order not to alienate the people, the fact remained that the Việt Cộng did not take advantage of two May opportunities, May 1 (May Day) or May 19 (Hồ Chí Minh's birth date), two attacks that would have been appropriate. Additionally, the Vietnamese military was progressing with its commando training program, and newer equipment was reaching the security forces. May was an improvement over April but still not enough to satisfy those who carried a disposition to oppose anything positive in the RVN.⁴

Lalouette continued to lament the actions of the Cần Lao Party under the leadership of Ngô Đình Cẩn and the National Revolutionary Movement under Ngô Đình Nhu. To Durbrow's credit, he maintained in his official correspondence to the Department of State the U.S. position of continued backing of the Saigon government, even though Lalouette provided several openings for the American ambassador to voice his opinion. Privately, however, it seemed that the two diplomats shared a confidence that did not always find its way into the diplomatic messages headed for Washington or Paris.

Durbrow continued to receive affirmation of his stance in early June as various members of Ngô Đình Diệm's cabinet approached the embassy staff. On June 1, Minister of Agriculture Lê Văn Đồng spoke with Mendenhall at a dinner at the latter's house in which he lamented the internal security situation.⁵ The minister had been an outspoken critic of Ngô Đình Diệm for some time as evidenced by his earlier criticism of the government in March. Most of his criticisms stemmed from the same source, and as a result it really was up to the embassy staff to determine how and what it should report to Washington. Durbrow, through Mendenhall at times, seemed determined to report this type of meeting in full whenever possible.

While Lalouette and Durbrow developed a common stratagem to deal with Ngô Đình Diệm, the French were also hard at work pushing forward their agenda in Washington. On the same day as the meeting in Saigon, Etienne Manac'h, director of Asian Affairs in the French Ministry of Foreign Affairs, met with Parsons, Anderson, and Wood.⁶ Manac'h's purpose was to update the Americans on the French reassessment of Ngô Đình Diệm and its RVN policy. He began by highlighting the seriousness of the internal security situation and alluded to the Caravelle Group as liberal opposition to the Saigon government. Manac'h maintained that the French supported Ngô Đình Diệm even if his political strategy was flawed and asserted that the popular support for the government might falter if the "iron corset" was removed.⁷ It seems likely that the timing of these two approaches to American officials involved in the decision-making process in the RVN was planned. The French were foremost interested to understand American thinking about Ngô Đình Diệm given the Caravelle Manifesto and the situation in the Republic of Korea. However, the French were also keen on inserting their influence on the U.S. decision makers in order to extract a foreign policy closer to their own.

While the French plotted with the Department of State and U.S. embassy, Ngô Đình Diệm was focused on improving the military and dealing with the internal security situation.⁸ Earlier, on May 18, Ngô Đình Diệm issued a challenge to the media at a press conference at

Bình Tuy.⁹ He called upon the press to criticize government officials when they abused their power. Essentially, he called for investigative reporting to expose corruption.

The Saigon press did take up the call of Ngô Đình Diệm to criticize governmental officials who had abused their power. While Ngô Đình Diệm's challenge was not the beginning of the press's attempts to expose corruption, it was significant given Durbrow's repeated comments about Ngô Đình Diệm's lack of concern. On May 21, *Dân chúng* issued an editorial that demanded a thorough investigation of the national lottery which had been under critical examination because of allegations that tickets were being sold on the black market.¹⁰ On June 7, *Sài Gòn Mới* called for mobile investigation teams to go out to certain provinces in order to listen to the people's complaints and aspirations: "Only in this way can the government clean up the administrative machinery of all-levels."¹¹ Both newspapers, as well as others, heeded Ngô Đình Diệm's call.

A day earlier, *Dân chúng* issued an editorial that lamented the lack of press in the countryside and criticized the only source of news for the peasants, the government paper. It called for local papers to educate the rural population and improve their political knowledge while also serving as a check against authoritarianism and corruption.¹² Continuing to take up the challenge of Ngô Đình Diệm, a June 28 editorial in *Tin Mới* argued that despite the government's efforts, "oppression of people, misappropriation of public funds, abuse of power, and so forth still are prevalent."¹³ It argued that the government needed to be stronger in its response to corruption but also called upon the people and press to help in the process. On July 29, *Dân chúng* praised the land-reform program but urged the government to push forward a housing-reform policy that would end exploitation and oppression of Saigon residents by house owners and landowners.¹⁴ The reaction of the press was not reported by the embassy nor was Ngô Đình Diệm's call to action. Instead, the focus was on internal security, other internal political developments, and negative observations by disgruntled Vietnamese.

On June 2, Ngô Đình Diệm met with Williams before the latter went to Hawaii for a two-week trip. Ngô Đình Diệm focused on four items: the military academy in Dalat and its need for qualified instructors; the successful completion of the Coll de Bai, a fifty-kilometer road between Danang and Hue; the development of the University in Hue; and the success of the 5th ARVN Regiment against the Việt Cộng in the U Minh forest.¹⁵ These topics shared the common trait of internal security. While Ngô Đình Diệm did discuss some of the opposition to his policies related to the above, he made an interesting observation that did not reach the American embassy.

During a part of the conversation in which Ngô Đình Diệm acknowledged criticism from within his inner circle, he mentioned indirectly individuals who opposed his government like those who formed the Caravelle Group. These critics, as Ngô Đình Diệm described them, suggested that individuals within the Saigon government were profiting from the war and that the government needed to curb this corruption and give the money directly to the people. However, as Ngô Đình Diệm pointed out, government officials were making far less money than the ones who criticized. While the opposition argued that the government officials took their money abroad, Ngô Đình Diệm maintained that it was the individuals who brought up the charges who had applied for visas to establish residency elsewhere. In many respects, Ngô Đình Diệm was correct, though the reporting from the American press and American embassy failed to make these connections. However, corruption with the Saigon government, regardless of its source or stature, was enough to hamper the reputation of Ngô Đình Diệm and provided further justification for Durbrow's criticism of his rule.

Another major move made by Ngô Đình Diệm occurred near the end of May when he removed the eight police commissioners in the arrondissements of Saigon.[16] These men had been members of the Bình Xuyên when it held power during Bảo Đại's rule and had received the support of the French. While they had turned against the Bình Xuyên and had thus gained Ngô Đình Diệm's trust, he argued that they had become too stagnant and susceptible to corruption. Colleagues of the eight men, many of whom owed their loyalty to the commissioners, maintained that Ngô Đình Diệm had made the move to insert members of the National Revolutionary Movement into these positions of power even though three of the commissioners were transferred to other arrondissements in Saigon. The argument that they had become susceptible to corruption and that junior officers needed an opportunity to hone their skills was not as heavily reported as the NRM connection. That five of the new commissioners were reportedly members of the Cần Lao Party did not help the Vietnamese cause for the Americans.[17]

A *Tiếng Chuông* editorial on May 28, after the Saigon police chiefs were installed into their positions, focused on the real concerns of the people. The paper implored the new police chiefs "to eliminate those bad and undesirable elements in their organizations whose cruel and impolite attitude toward the people has alienated the affections of the masses."[18] While the concern of the Saigon intellectuals was power, the people were more interested in justice. *Ngôn Luận* followed a similar line of reasoning as *Tiếng Chuông*. It argued that the new police commissioners had a unique opportunity to change the tone in Saigon. The new commissioners and their assistants met with the minister for the interior Lam Lê Trinh during which the minister called upon the law enforcement organization to learn from the examples of the Republic of Korea and Turkey.[19] Lam Lê Trinh argued that it was "better to educate and explain than to impose punishment" on lawbreakers to make them better citizens of the Republic.

The continued rumor mongering within the Saigon diplomatic corps and the extracurricular French activities continued to focus on an American effort to remove Ngô Đình Diệm or members of his family from the government.[20] These private conversations and Saigon intrigue reached Ngô Đình Diệm who decided to respond in June. On June 10, Ladejinsky reported a conversation with Ngô Đình Diệm in which the president lamented the American position vis-à-vis the Caravelle Group.[21] While Ngô Đình Diệm focused on Frank Gonder as the main instigator, he believed that Gonder had the backing of the embassy. Ladejinsky reiterated to Ngô Đình Diệm that Gonder did not have the confidence of the embassy. While Ngô Đình Diệm might have found this reassuring, it seems likely that Gonder did have willing co-conspirators within the foreign press corps. Media personnel approached the embassy staff several times to confirm the position of the Caravelle Group and, in the process, repeated Gonder's line.

Coster also was questioned by Nguyễn Đình Thuận about U.S. policy based on the rumors floating around Saigon. Like Ladejinsky, Coster attempted to ease the concern of the Saigon government officials, though Nguyễn Đình Thuận was particularly concerned about reports of a MAAG officer criticizing Ngô Đình Diệm in public, inferring that he should be replaced like Syngman Rhee had been in the Republic of Korea. Ngô Đình Diệm would also comment to Williams about the MAAG officer during their June 15 conversation upon Williams' return to the RVN after his vacation.[22] Durbrow also met with Nguyễn Đình Thuận after learning of Coster's conversation in order to reassure the secretary of state for the presidency. The rumors spreading throughout Saigon had an effect on Ngô Đình Diệm, who clearly saw Durbrow as a threat despite what he reported to Washington. There was a deliberate attack, justified or not, against Ngô Đình Diệm and his family that involved the Americans, some of whom were directly connected to the assault while others played an indirect but still significant role.

One particularly involved American was Theodore Heavner, the consul in Hue, who produced a series of reports that were sent to Durbrow that underscored the corrupt practices of Ngô Đình Cẩn and generally undermined the Saigon government's claims that Central Vietnam was more secure than the South. On June 22, Heavner reported the remarks of Nguyễn Văn Bưu, who was closely connected to Ngô Đình Cẩn and the Cần Lao Party.[23] Nguyễn Văn Bưu was involved in the shrimp and cinnamon trade and brother of the Quảng Trị province chief Nguyễn Văn Đông who was related to Ngô Đình Diệm by marriage. Because of his political and economic connections, Heavner placed a great deal of faith in Nguyễn Văn Bưu who spent most of his remarks criticizing the internal security situation in Central Vietnam, Ngô Đình Nhu's Republican Youth in which he drew a parallel to the Nazi SS in Germany during the 1930s, and Ngô Đình Diệm's choice of ministers. He also claimed that the Saigon government was filled with communists. Nguyễn Văn Bưu offered his remarks for public consumption though he did not reveal that he was also in conflict, as was Ngô Đình Cẩn, with Ngô Đình Nhu. Whether Nguyễn Văn Bưu's comments were motivated by real concern for the RVN or as a means to gain leverage against Ngô Đình Nhu are uncertain. What was clear was that Heavner's report was fully read in Washington and added to the growing list of concerns that members of the Department of State had for Ngô Đình Diệm and his RVN. There was no indication that the U.S. embassy queried Ngô Đình Diệm on Nguyễn Văn Bưu's analysis, though it might have made the reporting a little more balanced.

Another individual who seemed to be become more and more frustrated with Ngô Đình Diệm was Wolf Ladejinsky, who served as an adviser to the president. During a June 28 meeting on the issue of rice paddy value in which Ladejinsky repeated the often-heard argument that the Saigon government needed to increase the price it was paying for rice paddy land, Ladejinsky maintained that the low price being paid had caused a certain amount of discontent that was making it more difficult to garner popular support for the government. Ngô Đình Diệm responded, as Durbrow would convey to Washington, that he would "take no such action until 'peasants were starving.'"[24] Durbrow recommended that Ladejinsky continue to repeat his argument to Ngô Đình Diệm, as the RVN president appeared to be concerned about the subject of peasant discontent and was weakening against the constant barrage by Ladejinsky and others. While Durbrow's perspective might be correct, it was equally possible that Ngô Đình Diệm had grown tired of discussing this problem which was of greater concern to the Americans than himself. This does not discount the negativity emanating from the countryside; rather, it suggests that Ngô Đình Diệm was more willing to force sacrifice for the long-term security of the peasants than the American officials who continually placed perception of the situation on equal footing with the reality of the situation.

As the summer months continued, Durbrow continued to report on the growing schisms within the Saigon government. Already discussed by the ambassador was the split between Ngô Đình Nhu and Ngô Đình Cẩn, though to what degree this division existed can only be surmised by the American perspective. Durbrow had earlier discussed the potential misgivings of Vice President Nguyễn Ngọc Thơ and, as a result of a series of encounters culminating in a July 6 meeting, reported that the vice president had become reluctant to speak with Americans because of Ngô Đình Diệm's critical position taken toward him and his possible contact with the Caravelle Group leaders.²⁵ Durbrow reported that Nguyễn Ngọc Thơ's uneasiness matched the recent apprehension of Ngô Đình Diệm and Nguyễn Đình Thuận. Though Durbrow did not directly credit himself as the source of this uneasiness, he must have realized that his actions during the year had caused an inordinate amount of tension between the embassy and the Saigon government.

Durbrow continued to receive and pass along reports of Ngô Đình Diệm's problems based on others' experiences or observations whenever the opportunity arose. Ngô Đình Diệm did make Durbrow's job easier with a series of decrees passed in early July. These decrees, laws 3/60 and 4/60 fixed a tax on beer and soft drinks.²⁶ This move was not popular among the Saigon intellectuals and others who had the ear of the U.S. embassy. On July 7, Ngô Đình Diệm broadcast his "Double-Seven Day" address that marked his sixth year since coming into power.²⁷

In the speech, he outlined what he considered the real problems for the RVN: the double pressure of internal and external factors that sought to overthrow the Republic. There was no mention of the United States or its efforts to assist the country or any specific discussion of his policies. This led to Durbrow sending two dispatches to Washington on July 14.²⁸ The first item included a discussion with Professor Joseph Zasloff who offered a critical appraisal of the Agroville at Tân Lược in Vĩnh Long province, arguing that the process of building the Agroville, which included forced labor without pay, had caused more discontent than any benefits that the people could derive from the facility.²⁹ The second dispatch focused on a conversation with Ngô Đình Luyện, brother of Ngô Đình Diệm and the Vietnamese ambassador to the United King-

Ngô Đình Diệm addresses a "peace fair," circa 1950s (United States Information Agency–Saigon, Photograph 55-222, National Archives and Records Administration, College Park, Maryland).

dom. Durbrow remarked in his dispatch to the Department of State that he was favorably impressed with Ngô Đình Luyện who had offered a position closer to Durbrow's than Ngô Đình Diệm. Durbrow suggested that the United States' work to replace Ngô Đình Nhu with Ngô Đình Luyện would help "in overcoming the increasing loss of prestige of the Diem regime."³⁰ This was an interesting observation as Durbrow had been keen to eliminate the Ngô family influence on the RVN president. It seems that Durbrow was willing to make an exception for Ngô Đình Luyện so long as he adhered to Durbrow's way of thinking.³¹

The internal dynamics of American reporting to Washington continued to serve as a cause for concern to Ngô Đình Diệm, but he was also focused on the military situation within the RVN. Ngô Đình Diệm, who seemed more relaxed with Williams, informed the general on July 25 that he planned to maintain the initiative after his May victories.³² Two significant changes were the creation of a National Security Council that would help to centralize the Vietnamese intelligence agencies and provide more efficient use of resources to combat the Việt Cộng and the reorganization of the 1st and 5th Military Regions. The reorganization was evidence that Ngô Đình Diệm understood the strengths and weaknesses of the military officers serving under him. In the case of the 1st Military Region reshuffling, which involved annexing the provinces of Tây Ninh, Bình Dương, and Biên Hòa to the Capital Military Region, it meant recognition that the commander of the 1st Military Region was unable to handle such a large area. A division of the 5th Military Region into two zones with the addition of two deputies under General Nguyễn Khánh strengthened a military command that was already doing well but was still embattled by the enemy. During the same meeting, Williams offered his criticism of the commando training that had begun earlier in the spring.

Just as Ngô Đình Diệm focused on the moves made to improve the internal security situation, Williams offered a series of suggestions to improve the training program which was suffering from a 30 percent failure rate. Williams recommended that those who failed the commando training be reassigned away from their commando units but not released from military service as had been suggested by General Tôn Thất Đính.[33] This suggestion would deny those who had purposely failed the program in order to be released from military service. Williams also stressed the importance of a strong officer corps and the training of Vietnamese instructors to keep the commando schools progressing. Ngô Đình Diệm accepted his criticism and moved to enact Williams' ideas. However, Ngô Đình Diệm did remarked to Williams that one cause of the high rate of failure was due in part to the fact that the inhabitants of the central region of Vietnam were soft, lazy, and had no endurance. Williams did not offer a rejoinder.

Durbrow was also concerned about the commando training, but his focus, at the time of the Williams–Ngô Đình Diệm conversation, was whether the commandos violated the 150,000-man ceiling that the United States supported. As of June 16, there were 143,618 regular soldiers in the Vietnamese armed forces and 8,360 commandos, which brought the total to 151,978. In a July 1 telegram to Washington, Durbrow complained of this number as well as the excess of Civil Guard personnel above the 50,000 ceiling established by the United States. He suggested that he should be allowed to let the Saigon government know that International Cooperation Administration–financed deliveries might have to be held up if the Civil Guard level did not return to the 50,000 level, though he did concede that it did not matter how one counted the commandos so long as the personal ceilings were maintained.[34]

Another move to improve the internal security situation came from Madame Ngô Đình Nhu. Following up on her conversation with Durbrow in which she outlined plans for a new women's movement, Madame Nhu presided over two regional meetings of what would become the Women's Solidarity Movement.[35] Over 1,000 women attended the two meetings on July 13 at Cần Thơ and July 21 in Saigon during which the organization's objectives were discussed. The Women's Solidarity Movement, like the Agroville and Republican Youth programs, was designed to mobilize the population during a time of crisis to ensure that basic services and needs did not go unattended. Mendenhall, who reported on the meetings to Washington, focused his comments not on the objectives or benefits of the organization but, rather, on Madame Nhu's comments that the new group would not receive financial backing from the Saigon government. He concluded that this ploy was an attempt by Madame Nhu to counter rumors about her involvement in corrupt financial practices. Again, rather than focusing on the potential positives from this new Vietnamese effort, the Americans in Saigon concentrated on the possibility of negatives.

One of the issues that frustrated Ngô Đình Diệm in dealing with his critics was their unwillingness to examine the internal security problem in person. This disappointment extended to not only Americans but also Vietnamese. As early as March, there had been calls for members of the National Assembly to take advantage of their recess to visit the countryside. *Dân chúng* called upon the officials to go to the rural areas and participate in community development projects, inform the people about the government services available, and inquire from the people what they needed. The paper concluded, "Only in this way can the government understand their problems and adopt practical measures to alleviate their suffering."[36] On March 8, Ngô Đình Nhu praised a group of 160 civil servants from Saigon who had volunteered to work in the provinces. Ngô Đình Nhu reminded the group that they were the vanguards of a revolutionary republican movement and, as such, had certain responsibilities which included informing the people of the ideas of law and more rational working methods. These men and women represented the Saigon government, but in Ngô Đình Nhu's view, they also represented the leadership of a new Vietnam.[37]

The focus of Americans and Vietnamese in the RVN was temporarily diverted when, on August 9, the commander of the Second Paratroop Battalion of the Lao National Army, Captain Kong Le, initiated a coup d'état in Laos. Kong Le took over Vientiane at a time when the Lao Cabinet convened in Luang Prabang, the royal capital, to work on the arrangements for the state funeral of King Savang Vatthana who had died the previous October.[38] At a mass rally in Vientiane the same day, Kong Le justified his actions. At the heart of his argument was the continuation of the Laotian Civil War that had pitted the royal government forces against the communist insurgents, the Pathet Lao. Kong Le argued that "the civil war has continued to expand because of foreign intervention and the attempt of some political parties to 'enjoy the fruits of labor of others.'"[39] Kong Le called for the end of the Laotian internal conflict, government corruption, and a move toward international neutrality.

The Vietnamese press reaction to the overthrow remained cautious as the events unfolded. *Ah Chau Jih Pao* believed that both sides were committed to a peaceful resolution to the crisis that appeared to be internal rather than external.[40] As negotiation seemed to fail, *Dân chúng* commented that the Laotian crisis was tantamount to the Berlin of Asia that pitted the Free World against the Communist World.[41] The immediate crisis did resolve itself on August 16 when Kong Le received guarantees from King Sri Savang Vatthana; General Ouane Rattikone, the spokesperson for the old government; and Premier Prince Somsanith that a new government would be formed. This was done at the end of the month with Souvanna Phouma serving as the prime minister and Phoumi Nosavan serving as the deputy prime minister.[42] While the immediate crisis had been averted, the new coalition government remained fragile and would not survive the year. This was not lost on the Vietnamese press as expressed by editorials in *Tin Mới* and *Dân chúng*.[43]

As the events in Laos commenced and unfolded, members of the RVN government continued to meet with Americans to express their position on the issues directly affecting them. On August 1, the president of the National Assembly, Trương Vĩnh Lê, and five of his fellow members met with Wood and Parsons during a trip to Washington.[44] During the course of the meeting, Trương Vĩnh Lê maintained that the government had made tremendous progress in the past three months due largely to increased cooperation from the rural population. The group emphasized the significance of the Agroville Program in helping to improve security in the countryside, though Trương Vĩnh Lê acknowledge that, at the beginning, the Saigon government had done a poor job explaining the nature and significance of the program to the people. Statistics provided by the USOM Public Safety Division for the first six months of 1960 confirmed their assertions, though Durbrow was dubious of the numbers.[45] In opening the National Assembly on April 4, Trương Vĩnh Lê had made similar statements about the Agrovilles, arguing that "the bright successes of our national policy have incited the Viet Cong to multiply their attempts at sabotage and destruction in remote villages."[46] Parsons did not speak directly to the Vietnamese comments but did acknowledge Trương Vĩnh Lê's observations and offered encouragement to his people's struggle. The view of the Vietnamese delegation was immediately challenged by Phan Khắc Sửu and Trần Văn Văn in the name of the Freedom and Progress Bloc.[47]

In a letter to Ngô Đình Diệm, acquired by a member of the United States Information Service, the two men called for an immediate stop to the Agroville Program. They argued that the people who were involved in the construction of the Agrovilles were suffering from lack of proper food, shelter, and medical care. The two leaders of the Caravelle Group maintained, as Durbrow would report, that the practice of corvée labor and the destruction of their old homes, while preaching Personalism, had created a situation in which the people could no longer tell the difference between that philosophy and communism. Durbrow reported the criticism of the Agroville Program but also acknowledged that the Saigon government had slowed down the building of the Garden Cities and had taken steps to inform the people about why they were being resettled to cut down on the frustration and anger associated with forced relocation. Another letter, written by Phan Quang Đán who had been denied his seat in the August 1959 National Assembly election, also condemned Ngô Đình Diệm and countered the positive report of the Vietnamese who visited with Parsons and Wood.[48] This new round of public internal dissent coupled with news from the U.S. embassy in London of a possible coup d'état attempt against Ngô Đình Diệm by a member of the trade union group planned for August 21 again raised the level of concern emanating from the U.S. embassy in Saigon.

Ngô Đình Diệm was able to explain the latest coup d'état attempt to Durbrow on August 22.[49] Counter-intelligence agents had been aware of the possible action earlier in the week and had arrested thirteen individuals who had been organizing the anti-government demonstrations.[50] The group had planned to take advantage of students and taxicab workers. Ngô Đình Diệm argued that the former were ready to criticize the government after receiving their results on baccalaureate examinations while the latter would be willing to participate because of higher gas prices. Durbrow found neither explanation reasonable and specifically connected Ngô Đình Diệm's explanation for the taxicab drivers as a protest against the United States for having taken petroleum products off the aid-financed list. Durbrow's comments to Washington in his August 22 report of their conversation suggested that he was more inclined to believe that these groups would be likely to protest the government not because of American action but because of real discontent within Saigon.[51]

While Durbrow might have been dubious about Ngô Đình Diệm's explanations, he was quick to point out the times when the Vietnamese president followed his advice. On August 25, Durbrow offered a laundry list of events and activities initiated by Ngô Đình Diệm to improve his political position and the internal security situation in the countryside.[52] While Durbrow did not directly state it, he implied that these Vietnamese actions were made possible, in part, because of his démarches over the past few months. Still, Durbrow was not willing to let praise of Ngô Đình Diệm's actions go without some word of caution or frustration. A day after sending his airgram, Durbrow offered a summary of an August 16 meeting with Ngô Đình Diệm that included the assistant secretary of defense Franklin Lincoln.[53] Durbrow complained of Ngô Đình Diệm's attempts to reintroduce the need to increase the armed forces by 20,000 men to 170,000 even though he had made it clear on numerous occasions that the U.S. embassy did not support the request. Durbrow did concede to Ngô Đình Diệm's point of increasing the number of U.S. trainers for the Civil Guard but halved the number requested. For Durbrow, fifty trainers were all that the Vietnamese needed. This assessment was made at the same time Durbrow reported that the number of clashes between the Việt Cộng and RVN forces had reached an all-time high of 351 for the month of July. Durbrow acknowledged a decrease in incidents in the Mekong Delta but pointed to increased activity to the north and east of Saigon as evidence that the situation was still dire.[54]

Earlier, Durbrow forwarded a recurring complaint by Nguyễn Đình Thuận about the Vietnamese need for additional piasters for the 1960 military budget.[55] Durbrow consented to supplying the needed money and recommended that it be offered without conditions because of the internal security situation. Even as Durbrow recognized that the Americans, in Vietnamese eyes, had been slow to respond to Vietnamese needs, he still jockeyed for position to influence Ngô Đình Diệm. Saigon politics and Durbrow's duplicity toward Ngô Đình Diệm continued into the month of September, though Durbrow was not alone. Despite standing orders by the ambassador to avoid Vietnamese dissidents and the appearance of taking sides, embassy staffers continued to do so. In mid–August, Mendenhall met with Nguyễn Phương Thiệp, the secretary general of the National Assembly, who relayed information on what he saw as the "demoralization of political life" in the RVN.[56] On September 1, Chalmers Wood met with Nguyễn Văn Thời, the former secretary of state for land reform, who had resigned from Ngô Đình Diệm's government in 1956 after a falling out with the president.[57] While Nguyễn Văn Thời did not criticize the Saigon government, he did assert to Wood that the population was dissatisfied with it and the government needed to respond soon. Wood reported in his memorandum of the conversation all of the proper statements that should have been issued by the embassy regarding U.S. support for Ngô Đình Diệm. This gave the appearance of no impropriety, though the meeting did confirm that American personnel in Saigon were meeting with individuals who were known opponents of the government.

The French were also involved during the month, with Lalouette continuing to try to guide Durbrow in Saigon and working on the American personnel in the U.S. embassy in Paris. Lalouette met with Durbrow and the British Ambassador H.A.F. Hohler on September 1 during which he informed the two that Ngô Đình Diệm was planning to organize a National Security Council but had decided not to reorganize his government as the French had suggested. During the course of their luncheon, Lalouette maintained that Ngô Đình Diệm planned to include non-government officials in the new council, including the former secretary to Bảo Đại, Nguyễn Duy Quang, who currently served as the assistant director of the General Directorate of Re-Education Center for Political Prisoners under the minister of the interior and Nguyễn Xuân Chữ, the head of the Cancer Research Institute and also an ally of the Đại Việt Quốc dân Đảng.[58] Lalouette could not confirm his information, and Durbrow rightly guessed that the French statement was more designed to guide the Americans into accepting the idea in order to pressure Ngô Đình Diệm and his supporters.

Insertion into the Saigon government of these types of men would benefit the French and increase their influence over Ngô Đình Diệm. A September 2 meeting between U.S. ambassador to France Amory Houghton and Henri Roux, the French acting director of political affairs, reaffirmed France's desire to support Ngô Đình Diệm and commented on his many good qualities but then qualified his statements with the notion that Ngô Đình Diệm needed to provide more room in his government for non-communist opponents.[59] Roux suggested that Ngô Đình Diệm was becoming more authoritarian by not allowing other individuals into power. When Houghton saw Etienne Manac'h on September 7, the French director of Asian affairs argued that Ngô Đình Diệm was facing his most challenging trial to date because of the increasing opposition from the peasants, intellectuals, and the ARVN.[60]

Durbrow's telegram from Saigon did reaffirm Manac'h's perspective. A September 3 telegram to Washington reported on the ambush of two province chiefs in late August in the Mekong Delta, with Durbrow commentary reinforcing the hazards of traveling on the roads south of the Mỹ Thuận ferry over the Mekong River.[61] On September 5, Durbrow sent a lengthy telegram to Washington in which he outlined the major groups in Vietnam that might incite a demonstration in the RVN which would lead to anti–Ngô Đình Diệm activities.[62] In examining the peasants, communists, trade unions, students, Catholic refugees, opposition groups, politico-religious organizations, police, Civil Guard, and the ARVN, Durbrow concluded that the trade unions offered the greatest threat to incite demonstrations that would, most likely, be exploited by the communists. Durbrow concluded that there was a real possibility of demonstrations against the Saigon government if Trần Quốc Bửu and the minister of agriculture Lê Văn Đông decided that benefits of such action outweighed the risk of communist exploitation. Throughout the telegram, Durbrow seems to go beyond the objective observations of an ambassador reporting on the internal situation of the country under his charge. There was a sense that Durbrow was predicting action based upon his views toward Ngô Đình Diệm which had been confirmed by the French.

If this had been the case, Durbrow worked hard at the end of September to avoid this connection. During this period, the French had been pushing for tripartite talks about the RVN and the rule of Ngô Đình Diệm. Durbrow refrained from supporting the meetings, in agreement with the Department of State, because of the pessimistic attitude of the French, especially Lalouette. Durbrow told Hohler that Ngô Đình Diệm's anti–French attitude required avoiding the appearance of either joint talks with the British or tripartite discussions with both the British and French.[63] It was possible that Durbrow had Ngô Đình Diệm's best interests in mind when making this assessment; it was more likely that he did not want to relinquish his perceived influence on the RVN president to the French or British.

Durbrow followed up his telegram on September 16 with another message to the Department of State in which he further outlined his thinking.[64] In this latest version of his assessment, Durbrow argued that Ngô Đình Diệm was faced with two real dangers, one of which was the possibility of demonstrations while the other related to how the communists could exploit the demonstrations and force a coup d'état. Durbrow offered several suggestions to avert this potential disaster, including the removal of Ngô Đình Nhu and Madame Nhu and the head of the secret intelligence service, Trần Kim Tuyến.[65] Durbrow also wanted a reorganization of the cabinet, the disbandment of the Cần Lao Party, greater authority for the National Assembly, full financial disclosure for government official, and a series of economic reforms. In short, everything that the French had called for over the past few months and that Durbrow had publicly shied away from in his correspondence with Washington was on the list, as were the concerns of the Vietnamese with which he and Mendenhall had conversed since the beginning of the year. Ironically, Durbrow followed up his latest scheme the next day with a note to Washington in which he cautioned against engaging with the French in a comprehensive study on the political situation in the RVN.[66]

Lansdale was quick to pick up the problems with Durbrow's telegram and responded to it in his own September 20 memorandum to Rear Admiral Edward O'Donnell, the regional director, Far East, in the Office of the Assistant Secretary of Defense for International Security Affairs.[67] As only Lansdale seemed to be capable of doing when issues related to the RVN surfaced, he asked the obvious questions of what next. Lansdale did agree with some of the points put forward by Durbrow, such as the transfer of Vice President Nguyễn Ngọc Thơ to the Ministry of the Interior and appointment of Nguyễn Đình Thuận as minister of national defense, but he was highly skeptical of the idea of replacing Ngô Đình Nhu and the transfer of Trần Kim Tuyến. Lansdale dismissed the notion of adding new cabinet members from the opposition, the exposure of the Cần Lao Party membership, and the increased charge of the National Assembly as American ideas that were conceived without consideration to the realities of Vietnam. He was especially critical of Durbrow and the idea that he could communicate these American concerns to Ngô Đình Diệm: "in view of our spotty record of understanding past problems in Vietnam and of Ambassador Durbrow's past expressed emotions, which caused mistrust by top leaders in Vietnam, I am most dubious that Durbrow will be able to achieve the 'frank and friendly talk' he proposes to hold."[68] Lansdale's concerns were more than just a response to Durbrow trying to block his return to the RVN. He was legitimately worried that Durbrow was working to influence a change in the Saigon government that would isolate, or even possibly eliminate, Ngô Đình Diệm from power.

Whether Durbrow's actions represented a real attempt at duplicity or a simple change of opinion remains difficult to assess, though his actions, when taken together, must have surely caused some concern within the Saigon government. In the meanwhile, the French continued to press the Americans on the issue of Ngô Đình Diệm. On September 20, the French Indochina section chief of the Quai d'Orsay, Jean Brèthes, reported to Houghton that the situation in Cochin China (Mekong Delta) was particularly bad.[69] Brethes also confirmed reports that Ngô Đình Diệm was in discussions with former Bảo Đại cabinet members, though the Americans continued to find skepticism in these stories.

Around the same time, word began to reach the U.S. embassy in Saigon that Ngô Đình Diệm was worried about stories that involved his family and began to inquire about their validity. In a dinner affair in mid–September, S.S. Ansari, Indian delegate to the International Control Commission, had a candid discussion with Ngô Đình Diệm in the presence of Ngô Đình Nhu and Nguyễn Đình Thuận. In the course of the conversation, Ngô Đình Diệm asked Ansari about what he had heard related to the RVN. Ansari told them that there were many stories about corruption and that they involved Ngô Đình Nhu. Ngô Đình Diệm's response was that he had also heard the stories and told him that if they turned out to be true he would hang his brother in front of the palace.[70] This was more than just an idle threat, though it seems reasonable to assume that Ngô Đình Diệm's punishment would have fallen short of the death penalty. Ngô Đình Diệm was an ardent nationalist who believed in the RVN. The Saigon government had been harsh on those involved in corruption, though no family member associated with Ngô Đình Diệm was targeted.

A few days later, Ngô Đình Diệm asked George Calfo, an American businessman who worked for the American Trading Company, whether anyone from his family had tried to extract bribes from his organization for contracts.[71] When Calfo tried to deflect the question, Ngô Đình Diệm forced the issue. Calfo told the RVN president that his firm had been approached by individuals who said they represented the family but after some checking it became clear that not all of them did. Francis Cunningham, who wrote up the report of the conversation to Washington, commented that this left the implication that some of the individuals did represent the family, though it could have easily meant that Calfo's team had not been able to identify the individuals' position. Nonetheless, it was significant that Ngô Đình Diệm was keenly interested in rooting out corruption from within his family.

The situation in the RVN by the end of September was still fluid as Ngô Đình Diệm continued to work toward solutions to his internal security problem. He met obstacles when trying to push forward his commando project and faced resistance to the Agroville Program. The emerging crisis in Laos also caused concern for the Saigon government and served to highlight the real vulnerabilities for the RVN in its fight against the Việt Cộng and DRV as well as its desire to become the stabilizing element in Southeast Asia. However, a significant concern for Ngô Đình Diệm was the role and actions of Durbrow, who seemed to provide a different message in public and private. While Lansdale continued to be a friend, even if he was barred from Vietnam, Ngô Đình Diệm's trust in Durbrow waned as the ambassador continued to work toward increasing his influence and control over the Saigon government.

6

The Turning of the Screw

At the end of August, Williams rotated out of his position as chief, MAAG. The move was expected though Durbrow did not necessarily find the replacement to his liking. The arrival of General Lionel McGarr started another round of conflicts between the Department of Defense and the Department of State as individuals from each area worked to influence McGarr toward their line of thinking. At the same time, a Special National Intelligence Estimate (SNIE) was being prepared that would result in more tension between representatives of the Department of State and the Department of Defense.

On August 23, the Central Intelligence Agency and the intelligence organizations of the Departments of State, the Army, the Navy, the Air Force, and the Joint Chiefs of Staff (JCS) submitted SNIE 63.1–60 titled *Short-Term Trends in South Vietnam*.[1] The SNIE concluded that the situation in the RVN had seriously deteriorated within the first six months of 1960. It highlighted internal, urban dissent, most likely a reference to the Caravelle Manifesto, as well as governmental concern in Saigon for the direction that Ngô Đình Diệm had taken to combat the increased Việt Cộng activity. The SNIE also asserted that Ngô Đình Diệm needed to take action to avert a real crisis: "If Diem is not able to alter recent trends and the situation deteriorates substantially, it is possible during the period of this estimate that the government will lose control over much of the countryside and a political crisis will ensue."[2] The SNIE offered a pessimistic appraisal of the situation in the RVN that reflected the growing concern of the U.S. embassy and Department of State as well as the French position and those Vietnamese who had access to the American diplomats in Saigon.

Concern about the SNIE emerged as it was being prepared. Lansdale was one of the more outspoken who called for a reasoned, more objective appraisal.[3] Lansdale was troubled by assertions emanating from the National Board of Estimates that concluded the RVN problem was due to increased guerrilla action and terrorism by the Việt Cộng and poor administration by a willful Ngô Đình Diệm. Lansdale cautioned against this type of analysis though he agreed that a crisis was looming in the RVN. In reference to Durbrow and the embassy staff, Lansdale maintained that "there are and have been a number of U.S. observers in Vietnam who seem to be subjectively emotional about Diem and the military and apparently permit this bias to color and guide their reporting."[4] The episodes with Durbrow over Lansdale's proposed visit and his correspondence with Williams and the Vietnamese who held his confidence was more than enough evidence for Lansdale to come to this conclusion.

Lansdale also asserted that the Việt Cộng were more than just a group of guerrilla fighters lurking in the swamps and jungles of Southeast Asia. Lansdale offered a more vivid image of the enemy who was skilled, organized, and dedicated. He accurately maintained that the

Việt Cộng, who had had more than a decade to hone their talents against the French, worked to exploit the discontent of the Saigon intellectuals and opposition groups to their own advantage. Lansdale also suggested that the Việt Cộng worked hard on the image they portrayed to the West as a small ragtag group of fighters in order to demoralize their opponent when they intensified their efforts. Lansdale called on Sherman Kent, chairman of the National Board of Estimates, to consider firsthand accounts of Americans, Vietnamese, and others who had actually gone into the countryside and had communicated and observed the people. He suggested that this type of data provided a very different RVN than the one commonly described. Lansdale continued to champion Ngô Đình Diệm against a Washington establishment that seemed to increasingly move against him.

On August 10, as Lansdale considered his response to the Kent memorandum, the two men met and discussed the RVN. The next day, Lansdale provided a lengthy memorandum to McGarr in which he offered written answers to many of the questions that were asked at that meeting.[5] Lansdale provided McGarr his considerable experience and observations of the RVN and all of its nuances. He repeated many of the points that he had been arguing were necessary to understand the Vietnamese. Lansdale was particularly tactful in cautioning McGarr not to get sucked into the politics and intrigue that seemed to capture the imagination and ambitions of some Americans. In many ways, Lansdale was working hard to mentor McGarr to replace Williams and put him in a position to be as knowledgeable as possible but also as sympathetic to Ngô Đình Diệm as both he and Williams had been. Lansdale knew that Durbrow would work to influence McGarr to his line of thinking and strove to avoid that possibility.

As a result of the SNIE and the concern it raised among members of the Department of Defense, a special meeting of the Collateral Activities Coordinating Group was called for September 14. This included one member from the MAAG, Vietnam, present for a September 7 meeting that would consider a recommended course of action. As a result, on September 2, the JCS delivered a telegram to McGarr in which it asked for a list of recommendations to improve the situation in the RVN. McGarr responded to the JCS request by developing with his senior staff a long position paper. This paper called for an increase of the ARVN force levels from 150,000 to 170,000, a transfer of the Civil Guard from the Ministry of the Interior to the Ministry of Defense, MAAG training of the Civil Guard to include the forty additional advisers already agreed to during Williams' tenure, the distribution of small arms and ammunition to the Civil Guard with logistical support, and a $20 million increase in assistance.[6]

McGarr presented this paper to Durbrow late in the afternoon on September 2 to which the ambassador responded that the list of suggestions went against three years of policy and planning conducted by the embassy.[7] Durbrow, however, agreed to present it to the Country Team on September 4. He explained to Parsons that the paper was less a result of the actual situation in Vietnam and more a response to the pent-up frustration of the American military that was released with the arrival of a new chief, MAAG. Durbrow did acknowledge, however, that McGarr seemed more flexible than Williams. Durbrow seemed to dismiss the actual content of the position paper as a reflection of the military thinking that occurred as a result of the situation in the RVN. The ideas of the paper were not created in haste nor were they an attempt to relieve frustration. Rather, the position paper was a methodical examination of the real issues facing the RVN. Again, Durbrow chose to report the political and personality perspective rather than the concrete, military reality facing Ngô Đình Diệm.

In Durbrow's review of the MAAG position, he argued that the 20,000 extra men, something he had opposed on numerous occasions, was really a result of the failure of MAAG to adequately train the existing seven ARVN divisions.[8] Durbrow wasted no effort in criticizing Williams' leadership and plan. At no time did Durbrow acknowledge the difficulties of training troops while they were involved in major operations against the Việt Cộng. Durbrow also failed to acknowledge the actual state of the Vietnamese military in 1956 and 1957, when it had recently been under French control and was without an adequate officer corps. To suggest that Williams missed an opportunity to train troops during the quiet times was to acknowledge a real lack of understanding of how one develops an effective fighting force. Further into Durbrow's recollection of the events of early September was evidence, again, of his impatience with the military position: "The rather naïve MAAG point of view boils down to this: Diem is in trouble, he is facing approximately 5,000 well-trained communist guerrilla cadre, and, therefore, he needs more aid. If we only give him more dollars, he can more easily build up his forces to face the threat, and by giving him this extra dollar aid we will convince him we are backing him to the hilt."[9] Durbrow's explanation failed to mention that Williams, in addition to calling for additional assistance, was more concerned with Durbrow's recommendation to cut existing aid at a time of crisis. Williams was at odds with Durbrow's propensity to use American aid as leverage against Ngô Đình Diệm, who was an American ally, to gain political, economic, social, or diplomatic concessions sought by the embassy.

Durbrow's position with the new MAAG chief was guarded but optimistic.[10] He still believed he could control events and force the military into agreeing with his plans to mentor Ngô Đình Diệm in the American ways. As Durbrow would assert to Parsons, "Our main problem is not to pamper Diem by giving him more security forces with which to beat people into line but to give him sufficient forces, i.e., a fully-trained Civil Guard to handle the security problem, and bring all other pressures on him to take essential steps which will win over the populations by other methods than sheer force."[11] For an ambassador who had stated publicly and privately so many times in the months preceding this exchange that he fully supported Ngô Đình Diệm, these remarks revealed the true Durbrow. He saw himself as the father of a pampered child who needed discipline and guidance so that he would not make the same mistake over and over again. This strategy was not the most appropriate to follow, as Lansdale, Williams, and others maintained, with the leader of a free country that was your ally.[12]

As the drama surrounding McGarr continued, Ngô Đình Diệm prepared for his annual State of the Union message. On October 3, 1960, he delivered it at the opening of the second session of the National Assembly. The speech was remarkable for two reasons. It highlighted the real advances that the RVN had made under Ngô Đình Diệm's presidency, and it failed to identify, save two brief references, South Vietnam's one major ally, the United States, in its struggle against the internal and external communist threat. The main theme of the speech revolved around the following ideas asserted by Ngô Đình Diệm: "In our national struggle for existence and liberty, we have come out of an area of shadow and uncertainty. However, the road is still long and difficult on account of the aggressive policy of the communist imperialism, and out of the complex factors we face in a world in full evolution."[13] Ngô Đình Diệm sought to inspire the Vietnamese people toward completion of the Republic and its ideals. Durbrow and the French, however, chose to listen to the speech differently because of their predisposition to criticize.

The speech marked the beginning of a significant turning point in the Ngô Đình Diệm–United States relationship, one that had been plagued by the soured relationship between Ngô Đình Diệm and Durbrow. When South Vietnam should have been celebrating some of its remarkable achievements in its brief six years of existence, it instead was struggling with its ally and a growing communist insurgency that threatened to undo all that had been accomplished. While not mentioning the strained association between the United States and South Vietnam, Ngô Đình Diệm did foreshadow this significant turning point, one that would culminate in an attempted coup d'état against the first president of the RVN and an unexpected response by Durbrow and the U.S. embassy.

Of the many advances during the Ngô Đình Diệm era, agrarian reform was one of the more successful. Even if the Agroville Program had failed to achieve its desired results, Ngô Đình Diệm had made good on many of his promises to the people. By the time of Ngô Đình Diệm's speech, the RVN had redistributed 457,149 hectares of land to 122,802 tenant families. Ngô Đình Diệm asserted that this reform ended the inequalities of land distribution and in doing so offered "a new life to the peasants by providing them with a minimum property which is a guarantee for their democratic liberties."[14] In addition to the redistribution of land, Ngô Đình Diệm's Agricultural Development Center's reclaimed 101,500 hectares, which allowed for the resettlement of 50,700 people.[15] While Ngô Đình Diệm's claims might have been a bit premature, the land redistribution program was an attempted step in the right direction.

The Agroville Program, which was also criticized for its poor implementation, progressed until its August suspension for new villages. Agrovilles were designed to improve the lives of the people by offering them the benefits that South Vietnam's urban population enjoyed while at the same time protecting them from subversive elements within the country. The government had completed seventeen of nineteen planned Agrovilles by the opening of the National Assembly, creating an atmosphere that Ngô Đình Diệm hoped would allow the people to "realize their own capacity of achieving important works, which so far only the State or big companies had been able to undertake."[16] Even if the Agroville Program was flawed, the basic underlying concept behind the movement was sound. The Agroville Program sought to inspire the people to make a difference. Organizations such as the Republican Youth, which had reached a membership of over 1,300,000 members, and other organizations with a combined membership of 680,000 created the possibility of real change. The South Vietnamese people with, and then without, the aid of the government were the ones who needed to effect permanent change.

Ngô Đình Diệm's agrarian reforms, in addition to redistributing the land, also had the effect of increasing that land's production. The amount of rice grown in South Vietnam increased by over 1,000,000 tons from the year before to reach a level of 5,380,000 tons, which created a surplus of 400,000 tons.[17] While Ngô Đình Diệm highlighted this remarkable increase, he also recognized that the Vietnamese farmer did not always benefit in direct proportion to the effort put into his fields. A depression of prices in the international rice market, which he blamed on communist countries dumping their surplus into the marketplace, and speculation of middlemen had negated some of the benefits of this increased production. Still, the increase in rice production was joined by other advances such as the growth in the textile industry and marked improvement in South Vietnam's sugar, paper mills, sawmills, glass, and cement industries. Despite the communist surge at the end of 1959 and into 1960, South Vietnam continued to make progress in becoming a viable economic asset in the community of international countries.

The RVN's progress was also marked by the expansion of its infrastructure, seen best in the creation of new roads and highways that linked the nation. New waterways, such as the forty-four-kilometer Động Tiên Canal also improved transportation as well as making it possible to cultivate over 50,000 hectares of land that had been previously under-utilized. Ngô Đình Diệm also praised the continued progress of the trans–Vietnam railway. This infrastructure not only helped South Vietnam's industry but also its communication and ultimately played a role in its defense against internal and external communist threats.

It should not be surprising that a State of the Union, as this speech has been characterized, was filled with the positives of the previous year. Indeed, Ngô Đình Diệm's speech followed a very familiar pattern. One thing missing, however, was multiple direct references to the United States and its role in helping the South Vietnamese achieve their results. The United States was mentioned in passing during Ngô Đình Diệm's discussion of the construction of a national telephone network and the anti-malaria campaign. The United States was indirectly referred to early in the speech when Ngô Đình Diệm asserted that South Vietnam's progress was all the more remarkable when one considered that its foreign aid had been reduced from U.S. $300 million in 1955 to U.S. $150 million in 1960. While this public pronouncement and his neglect of the Americans in the speech clearly indicated that Ngô Đình Diệm wanted to highlight what the RVN had accomplished rather than remind the people, and his critics, of the extent of American involvement in their country, it also was indicative of the acerbic feeling Ngô Đình Diệm must have felt as he dealt with Durbrow on a day-to-day basis.

The Saigon press was quick to offer the National Assembly advice on its priorities for its second regular session. A *Tự do* editorial called for the body to focus on the 1961 national budget but also to remember the significance of communist terrorism in the RVN.[18] *Tự do* maintained that the National Assembly needed to form a special committee to study the security situation and offer solutions to the problems of internal security. This would allow the Saigon government to formulate a plan to resolve the crisis. *Dân chúng* also offered instruction for the National Assembly though it focused on a housing reform bill that would protect families who lived on rented land who had been exploited and oppressed.[19] These types of calls for action contradicted the Durbrow position that the press was too passive and that the National Assembly only received its directives from Ngô Đình Diệm.

Durbrow's first reaction to Ngô Đình Diệm's speech to the National Assembly occurred at lunch with Lalouette and Hohler the same day.[20] All three of the ambassadors were disappointed with the RVN president's remarks and lamented the fact that he did not seem to take into account the need to find political solutions to the Việt Cộng problem. Both Hohler and Lalouette expressed concern that Ngô Đình Diệm had not mentioned foreign aid. While Durbrow did not inform Washington that he agreed, his airgram suggested it as he referred to Ngô Đình Diệm's remarks on foreign aid as taking a potshot at the U.S. cut in its aid level. Durbrow's observations of the lunch meeting and the speech to the National Assembly were also designed to reinforce his request for the measures asked for in his September 16 telegram. Durbrow's version of the lunchtime discussion, in which he "relayed" the other ambassador's concerns, followed the earlier telegram's points. Essentially, Durbrow was informing Washington that he was not the only one to share these concerns even if he had stated earlier that the United States should try to distance itself from the French because of Ngô Đình Diệm's anti–French remarks. Durbrow was using the French and British ambassadors to justify his position and receive authorization for another one of his "frank" talks with Ngô Đình Diệm. He continued to push for this authorization for the rest of the week.[21]

If Durbrow had any doubts as to how the Vietnamese would react to his proposed démarche, an October 13 editorial in the *Times of Vietnam* titled "The Suspension of U.S. Military Aid to Laos" should have served as a guide.[22] The editorial speculated on the reasons for the U.S. decision to cut aid to Laos following the two-month crisis that country had faced after Kong Le's coup d'état. While the editorial had no sympathy for the Laotian decision to negotiate with the Pathet Lao or open diplomatic ties with the Soviet Union, it did find fault with the United States for its action: "We find it equally hard to sympathize with a big nation punishing a small one in such a harsh manner for having strayed off its approved course." As the *Times of Vietnam* continued its discussion of U.S.-Laotian relations, they had an uncanny similarity to U.S.-RVN relations: "If the cause for the aid suspension has been the new Laotian policy, there is no valid reason for abruptly cutting off aid which had loudly been proclaimed as 'granted' without any strings attached." Even as Durbrow was preparing his démarche, it was clear that the Vietnamese position would not be conducive to the American demands.

The United States continued the policy of carrot-and-stick diplomacy that Durbrow had been employing for some time. Because Ngô Đình Diệm had acknowledged some errors in his policies during the speech, both Ladejinsky and South Vietnamese vice president Nguyễn Ngọc Thơ encouraged Durbrow to once again request that Ngô Đình Diệm make substantive changes in his government.[23] The primary objective of change for Durbrow was to call for the removal of Ngô Đình Nhu, Madame Nhu and Trần Kim Tuyến, but he was also to suggest reforms in the South Vietnamese government to eliminate corruption. Durbrow was to recommend that the National Assembly be given broader powers to investigate alleged government corruption as well as to establish precedents for public behavior of government officials and the power to force individuals to disclose finances.[24] Durbrow was also to compel Ngô Đình Diệm to reduce press censorship by allowing the media to police itself, offer more control of the villages back to the villagers, and change the implementation of the Agroville Program in order to appease the growing criticism that it had generated.[25]

The approach Durbrow was to take was one in which he offered praise and encouragement first before demanding reform. Both in Washington and at the American embassy in Saigon, the objective was to push for these reforms and convince Ngô Đình Diệm of the need for change before he delivered his Independence Day speech on October 26. Durbrow met with Ngô Đình Diệm and Nguyễn Đình Thuận on October 14 to offer the carrot-and-stick message.[26] One such carrot was an Eisenhower letter to Ngô Đình Diệm issued before the October 26 speech that praised the South Vietnamese president for all he had done in his five years in office. The Department of State believed that this letter would offset some of the "strong and rather unpalatable suggestions to President Diem regarding measures which were felt to be necessary if his government were to retain its popular support and put down the Communist guerrillas."[27] Another carrot, in the form of a new proposal for the Civil Guard, for which Ngô Đình Diệm had been pushing, was also well received. Ngô Đình Diệm and Durbrow had been sparring on whether American aid should be focused toward training and equipping more in the Civil Guard to combat the growing insurgency or whether resources should be utilized to increase the RVN's armed forces by 20,000 troops. Durbrow was an advocate of focusing on the Civil Guard, as he believed Ngô Đình Diệm was not conducting a realistic strategy to win the hearts and minds of the Vietnamese people; the Civil

Guard had the best chance to do so, while Ngô Đình Diệm pushed for the 20,000 combat troops in anticipation of increased insurgent activity and continued North Vietnamese interference in South Vietnam and in Laos. The instability in Laos after the August coup d'état did little to bolster the confidence of the Saigon government. Were Laos to fall to the communists or continue to deteriorate, Ngô Đình Diệm feared for the northern section of his country, which would be surrounded by the enemy. Durbrow offered a compromise on the two issues even though he was firmly opposed to the 20,000-man increase.

Believing himself on firm ground, Durbrow asked to speak with Ngô Đình Diệm alone and then read the fourteen-page document agreed to by the Department of State. Playing the part of the reluctant messenger, Durbrow apologized profusely when he arrived at the part that called for the removal of Ngô Đình Nhu, Madame Nhu, and Trần Kim Tuyến. Durbrow offered his recognition of the value of Ngô Đình Nhu and Trần Kim Tuyến to Ngô Đình Diệm in his struggle to mobilize the people toward an independent state in the face of communist aggression but offered the observation, again with apologies, that they had become a negative force in his administration: "whether based on fact or not, this criticism has reached a point that question is no longer whether these allegations are true or not. The fact that more and more people are believing them is seriously damaging the prestige of the government."[28] Again, Ngô Đình Diệm must have had mixed emotions at the American position that seemed to favor perception over reality when it came to assessing him. Even if Durbrow designed his position as to not directly confront and embarrass Ngô Đình Nhu and his cohort, this diplomatic move was a poor substitute for an honest, direct approach as had been the practice of Lansdale, Williams, and McGarr.

Ngô Đình Diệm remained quiet after the delivery of the paper related to Ngô Đình Nhu, Madame Nhu, and Trần Kim Tuyến, though he did interject at times during Durbrow's reading of the other reforms to remind the ambassador that it was difficult to find qualified people to replace members of his cabinet who were not carrying out their responsibilities. Durbrow had been instructed, at this point, not to offer the names of individuals, some of whom formed the opposition, that the United States believed to be suitable replacements. Durbrow appeared surprised that Ngô Đình Diệm had taken the criticism better than expected. While no record exists of Ngô Đình Diệm's immediate reaction to what must have appeared to be a rather forceful power play, Ngô Đình Diệm did let his feelings show during a follow-up meeting with Parsons on October 18. Rather than reforming his cabinet, Ngô Đình Diệm offered only a minor concession of eliminating the Ministry of Information in order to consolidate it with civic action and youth organizations under the president. In direct reply to the fourteen-page paper on reform, Ngô Đình Diệm openly criticized the opposition who he argued had taken no real risks in the struggle for independence.[29] Implied in this reference was the observation that critics of his policy and advocates for changed needed to act rather than speak in order to gain legitimacy. Ngô Đình Diệm also criticized his Saigon bureaucrats who had failed to answer the call of securing more volunteers to go out into the countryside to improve the administration of his policies. It was fair to assume that Ngô Đình Diệm would have little use for his Saigon critics if they failed to act on the problems they were so quick to bring to the attention of anyone who would listen. Ngô Đình Diệm must certainly have known that these critics found willing ears in many individuals in the U.S. embassy.[30]

Finally, in direct reference to Ngô Đình Nhu, Madame Nhu, and Trần Kim Tuyến issue, Ngô Đình Diệm spent a good deal of the one-hour conversation praising Ngô Đình

Nhu who had become indispensable in the organization of South Vietnam's trade union and the elimination of communist infiltration into the labor movement as well as the efforts to mobilize the Republican Youth and other grassroots associations.[31] Durbrow's attitude toward Ngô Đình Diệm's response regarding Ngô Đình Nhu was indicative of his feelings toward the Ngô family and Ngô Đình Diệm's rule in South Vietnam: "Whether Nhu is doing a good job or not, the antagonism toward him has so increased in the last year that he has become the symbol that represents all the bad and corrupt things in the country. Whether he is the sinister figure he is reputed to be or not, is, as I have said beside the point, the sad fact is that more and more people think that he is."[32] It might have been beside the point for Durbrow, the intellectual and labor critics in the urban centers in South Vietnam, and some officials in Washington, all of whom wanted to see some major restructuring within the government of the RVN and saw Nhu as a significant obstacle, but for Ngô Đình Diệm it was the issue. He did not believe Nhu was performing badly, nor did he think that his most trusted confidant should be replaced to appease a group of intellectuals who discussed and debated strategy, tactics, and political philosophy from the safety of the city. Whether, in the long run, Ngô Đình Diệm was wrong not to kowtow to the urban elite and Durbrow's embassy seemed a moot point given the deterioration within South Vietnam and the Ngô Đình Diệm presidency in the years to come. Without the backing of the American embassy and the Department of State, which would be made very clear in the next few weeks, Ngô Đình Diệm was already ruling on borrowed time.

Durbrow was obviously pleased with his performance. He had been jockeying for position for some time and, as his personality dictated, had satisfied his need to assert his influence and authority on Ngô Đình Diệm regardless of whether it was necessary or effective. Durbrow quickly informed Hohler and the Australian ambassador to the RVN, William Douglas Forsyth, of his "frank" talk, though, as he informed Washington, he asked these men not to discuss his conversation with Lalouette to whom he provided a sanitized version.[33] The French continued to push the United States to pressure Ngô Đình Diệm, as was relayed to Durbrow, and their position was not too far from the one advocated by the ambassador.[34]

In the weeks that followed the October 14 exchange, Ngô Đình Diệm did make some efforts at reform.[35] On October 18, he announced four cabinet changes, three of which were significant posts, with individuals who had Durbrow's approval and provided some optimism that the National Assembly would have the opportunity for increased power. The secretary of state for justice, Nguyễn Văn Sỹ, was replaced by Nguyễn Văn Lương, who was a magistrate, while the commissioner general for land development, Bùi Văn Lương, replaced Secretary of State for Interior Lam Lê Trinh. Secretary of State to the Presidency Nguyễn Đình Thuận added the position of assistant defense secretary to his portfolio when Trần Trung Dũng was reassigned. The Ministry of Information was also converted into a Directorate General and was later occupied by Trần Văn Dĩnh, the former consul general of Vietnam to Rangoon as a result of Presidential Decision No. 225.[36] Ngô Đình Diệm also received some good news on the international front when Rufino Laspiur presented his credentials as a minister plenipotentiary on October 20. Laspiur became the first diplomatic representative from Argentina.[37]

The reshuffling of the cabinet did satisfy some Vietnamese. Đặng Độc Khối, the chargé d'affaires ad interim in the RVN embassy in Thailand met with Ben Dixon, the liaison officer to the Economic Commission to Asia and the Far East, soon after the announcement and discussed a number of issues.[38] Đặng Độc Khối asserted that the new ministers, who had a history of disagreeing with Ngô Đình Diệm on certain matters in the past, represented a "healthy sign" that the Saigon government was moving in the right direction. Durbrow was also pleased by "his effect" on Ngô Đình Diệm and advocated continuing to push this new direction. As a "pat on the back," Durbrow suggested that Eisenhower's letter would serve as the proper response to Ngô Đình Diệm's recent moves.[39] Durbrow's tone continued to be one of the patient father trying to guide his good-intentioned but misdirected son. It was not an attitude that worked well with Ngô Đình Diệm and only reinforced the strain that existed between the two men.

An October 24 press conference by Lê Trọng Quát, who held the chairmanship of the Socialist Union Group in the National Assembly, also indicated that Ngô Đình Diệm was closer to relaxing price controls on agricultural goods and, more important, reaffirming freedom of the press. Lê Trọng Quát announced that the Socialist Union Group was preparing a draft on freedom of the press because, even though the RVN Constitution stated that the press was free, it never defined the freedom or the role of the press.[40] Lê Trọng Quát maintained that the resolution would intertwine the freedom of the press with the press's responsibilities to the nation that was under siege by the communist insurgents. The American embassy affirmed Lê Trọng Quát's assertions about the press, and the director of the Vietnam Press Nguyễn Thái confirmed that Nhu also supported a new statue in the National Assembly, even though it would not be put in place until after the April 1961 elections. The new measure gave Durbrow pause for hope that he had finally persuaded Ngô Đình Diệm to move in the right direction. Durbrow was confident, but he still held on to the possibility that Ngô Đình Diệm would not make any real dramatic changes as Durbrow had advised. Durbrow made it a point to inform Washington that Ngô Đình Diệm had gone out of his way to praise his brother, Ngô Đình Nhu, on multiple occasions. Durbrow attributed this to the effectiveness of his "frank" talk, though it was more likely that Ngô Đình Diệm was trying to educate the American ambassador of the usefulness of a man upon whom he was deeply reliant and who was the focus of, in his mind, unfounded criticism.[41]

Across the ocean, the Vietnamese ambassador to the United States, Trần Văn Chương, tried to direct attention about Vietnam toward the Cold War struggle. In an interview, Trần Văn Chương argued that neutrality in Vietnam or in any country in the region was not an option, especially after the communist takeover in China.[42] Trần Văn Chương's goal was to reassert the importance of Vietnam in American Cold War diplomacy. The people of the United States, its representatives abroad, and its leadership needed to be less concerned with price controls or the level of authority within the National Assembly and more worried about supporting the non-communist government in Saigon.

On October 26, Ngô Đình Diệm delivered his National Day address. It was the fifth anniversary of the RVN and his rise to power.[43] In the speech, Ngô Đình Diệm praised the Vietnamese people for their work and achievements for the Republic in a time of unrest caused by the Việt Cộng: "While we devote ourselves to the development of the country, they think only of its destruction; while we work to raise the people's living standards, they surrender themselves to pilfering and racketeering."[44] Ngô Đình Diệm focused more on the communist insurgency and announced plans to intensify pacification and security measures coupled with economic and social development. In the order of the day to the armed forces, Ngô Đình Diệm reminded the troops of their noble mission and sacrifice: "Your heroic behaviour is an example which galvanizes and stimulates the whole population in the struggle against the Communist pirates as well as in the building of a new life featuring liberty and prosperity with the view toward achieving the reunification of the country."[45] National Day was intended to revitalize the people to the cause of the Republic and remind them as well as the military of the struggle in which they were engaged. There were celebrations throughout the country as well as in the Vietnamese communities in Cambodia and Laos. It was also a time for South Vietnam's major ally, the United States, to reaffirm its support for the non-communist Republic.[46]

Such celebrations were marred by continued reports coming from the embassy in Saigon and the consulate in Hue. On November 3, the American vice consul in Hue, Thomas Barnes, forwarded to Washington three memoranda of conversations from Vietnamese who criticized the Saigon government for corruption and Ngô Đình Diệm for favoritism.[47] The three conversations, which took place in the last half of October, were forwarded as a sampling of the Vietnamese mind on the rule of Ngô Đình Diệm despite the fact that one of the individuals spoke better French than Vietnamese, one had been repeatedly passed up for promotion, and the final was one whose family had left North Vietnam during the exodus following the 1954 Geneva Agreements because of his family's French association. If these three truly represented a sample of the growing voice of opposition, then they also confirmed that that voice had been in opposition to Ngô Đình Diệm since his first days in office because they had lost, or failed to gain, the power and influence that they had come to expect. The French had also used the occasion to pass along to the Department of State a series of documents that criticized Ngô Đình Diệm and his recent moves as "too little too late."[48] This report contradicted a November 3 airgram from Mendenhall that argued Ngô Đình Diệm was becoming more aware of his political position and had made efforts to correct it based, in part, on Durbrow's October 14 démarche.[49]

There were some positives in the days that followed the speech, however. On November 3, Trần Văn Chương and Vance Brand, managing director of the Development Loan Fund, agreed to a US$17.5 million loan to finance foreign exchange to improve the water supply in Saigon.[50] The project would allow 480,000 cubic meters of water to reach Saigon from the Đồng Nai River to increase the daily yield from its 1960 rate of 158,000 cubic meters. The agreement was important for the Vietnamese as Saigon continued to be a growing urban center and the demands on the water supply were increasingly heavy.

Internally, the National Assembly began to exert the authority that Durbrow had pushed and Ngô Đình Diệm concurred was necessary. On November 5, three drafts concerning freedom and the status of the press were submitted to the National Assembly Intercommittee for Information, Justice, and Internal Affairs for consideration and debate.[51] The three drafts, registered as 7/11, 23/11, and 28/11 were presented by Phan Khắc Sửu (Saigon Fourth Constituency), Lê Trọng Quát (Social Union Group), and Ngô Hữu Thời (Bình Lớn Second Constituency). As these documents were received, the National Assembly in a plenary session adopted resolution 7/60 which called on the government to "apply all emergency measures to protect the people's lives, check outlawed Communists and overt Communist attempts at aggression."[52] The document also urged the government to mobilize the popular forces and support the armed forces to secure the countryside. Several thousand people took part in demonstrations against the Việt Cộng throughout South Vietnam, denouncing their activities and expressing loyalty toward Ngô Đình Diệm. One demonstration in Phú Yên province ended with the surrender of sixty-one Việt Cộng.[53] Durbrow also had a very positive experience during a trip to Kontom, Pleiku, and Qui Nhơn in which he had high praise for General Tôn Thất Đính, commander of the II Corps.[54]

Finally, on the economic scene, it appeared that the good news of the beginning of the year had continued despite the internal security crisis and the American aid cuts. On November 9, the National Assembly approved the report of the Budget and Accounting Committee on the national budget for the fiscal year ending in September 1960.[55] The report showed an increase of direct and indirect taxes as well as of the sources of revenue. The total increase was expected to be VN$436 million.

The two speeches given by Ngô Đình Diệm in October, the recent moves by the Saigon government to adhere to some of the advice provided by Durbrow, and the economic news should have been an opportunity for the United States and RVN to reevaluate their relationship in a positive way. The internal security situation was still critical and indicators showed that the Việt Cộng were increasing, rather than decreasing, their efforts, while a small cadre of internal dissenters continued to complain to the Americans about Ngô Đình Diệm and his family. Still, the RVN was healthy despite these worries. The positive reevaluation, however, was not to occur as the events of November 11 unfolded. Rather than offering reinforcement to Ngô Đình Diệm, Durbrow used the event to continue his "frank" talk and defined the episode not as it really was but rather as an indication that he was right about the path Ngô Đình Diệm had taken and, as a result, that he deserved what he had received. The U.S.-RVN relations after November 11 would never be the same.

7

Turning Points: The November 1960 Coup d'État Attempt

At some time after 3:00 a.m. on November 11, a group of dissatisfied ARVN paratroopers and other units attempted a coup d'état against Ngô Đình Diệm.[1] While the coup d'état was unexpected and took Durbrow by surprise, American reaction to the event caused a further erosion of the already fragile relationship between Ngô Đình Diệm and Durbrow. Durbrow first heard word of a potential coup d'état after a telephone conversation with William Colby, the CIA station chief but officially the political officer and first secretary to the U.S. embassy, shortly before the gunfire commenced. Colby informed Durbrow that a coup d'état was in the making and would probably be initiated by 6:00 a.m. The attack began sooner than expected when elements of the Vietnamese Airborne Brigade attempted to capture key military and political centers in Saigon and Biên Hòa.

Earlier, the coup d'état leaders met at midnight of November 10 at the Airborne Brigade headquarters to launch the attack between 3:00 and 3:30 am.[2] The 1st Airborne Battalion (709 men) and 3rd Airborne Battalion (728 men) were ordered to neutralize or take the ARVN headquarters, Tân Sơn Nhứt Airbase, the Saigon radio station, the Presidential Palace, the National Assembly building, and police and Sûreté headquarters while the 8th Airborne Battalion (680 men) was divided into company strength and ordered to cut the roads to the south, denying the troops loyal to Ngô Đình Diệm in the 5th Military Region from coming to his rescue. The 5th Airborne Battalion (722 men), which was stationed in Thủ Đức, approximately seventeen kilometers north of Saigon and near the Saigon River, had the mission of cutting the roads to the north of the city as well as seizing the approximately forty tanks at the Thủ Đức school and securing the Phú Lợi Brigade stationed there.

The commandant of the Thủ Đức school, General Lê Văn Nghiệm, refused to release the tanks, and rather than fighting their way in, the 5th Airborne Battalion continued on its mission to cut the road between Thủ Đức and Saigon. The 6th Airborne Battalion (735 men), which was stationed in Vũng Tàu to the southeast of Saigon, was supposed to move to Biên Hòa, neutralize the airfield, and stop the Vietnamese air force from entering the fray. It was delayed at Bà Rịa by elements of the 12th ARVN Infantry Regiment, which allowed the commander of the 7th ARVN Division to reinforce Biên Hòa. When the two forces met, the commander of the 7th ARVN Division invited his rebel counterpart to lunch to discuss the matter, during which time his ARVN units surrounded the airborne battalion. The airborne battalion surrendered rather than engage the superior force. The situation in

Saigon was not as pleasant or successful for the coup d'état plotters in part because Ngô Đình Diệm had been forewarned about the attempt.[3]

As the fighting commenced, American embassy officials made their way to the embassy as soon as they considered it safe. During the early morning, there was confusion as to what exactly was taking place with the exception of Colby, who had been forewarned, and Mendenhall who, after being awoken by a friend about twenty minutes after it had begun, watched and listened to the attack. In response to his wife's concern that it was a communist attack, Mendenhall commented that it was a non-communist attempt to overthrow Ngô Đình Diệm. There was no evidence that Mendenhall knew of the attack beforehand or he would not have been so unprepared for the events that followed, but his assuredness that it was a coup d'état attempt when all others were taken by surprise suggests that he was rather omniscient or lucky in his assessment.[4]

The initial assault in Saigon lasted approximately one hour, with evidence of heavy weapons and small-caliber fire on both sides. The sporadic firing lasted until approximately 8:30 am.[5] About forty men from the 1st Airborne Battalion with explosives, grenades, machine guns, and small-caliber weapons attacked the Presidential Palace guard between 3:15 and 3:30 a.m. for approximately seventy-five minutes.[6] The Presidential Security Guard thwarted the initial attempt, losing their captain, Hoàng Đình Tú, to a wound after the first fifteen minutes of fighting. Shortly after Captain Phạm Văn Bàng assumed command of the defenses, General Nguyễn Khánh arrived at the gate of the Palace, identified himself, and climbed over the fence to help protect the President and coordinate a response.[7] At approximately 5:50 a.m. Durbrow received word from *Time* correspondent James Wilde that Lieutenant Colonel Vương Văn Đông, a commander for one of the paratrooper battalions, was taking credit for the event. Vương Văn Đông had informed Wilde that he was in control of the airport, Presidential Palace and other key objectives, including the radio station. A call from Colby at 6:20 a.m. confirmed that the Palace was still in the hands of troops loyal to Ngô Đình Diệm, and Radio Saigon began broadcasting music at 6:15 a.m. indicating that it had not yet been seized. Vương Văn Đông was a part of the coup d'état, but he was not in control.[8]

The situation was also becoming clearer around this time as the embassy had finally made contact with Nguyễn Đình Thuận who informed the Americans that he was free of the rebels and that Ngô Đình Diệm, to whom he had spoken fifteen minutes earlier, was safe at the Presidential Palace. He, however, still did not have a clear picture as to what was occurring.[9] Forty minutes later, Nguyễn Đình Thuận telephoned the embassy to let the Americans know that an attempt to take him at his home had failed. He confirmed that the rebels had seized Tân Sơn Nhứt and the military radio system, but that it had not seized Radio Saigon. Nguyễn Đình Thuận reported that roadblocks had been set up on the roads leading into Saigon and that there were also rumors of the establishment of military committees who supported the coup d'état in Dalat, Biên Hòa, and Vũng Tàu.[10] As Nguyễn Đình Thuận reported this information to Ngô Đình Diệm, Radio Saigon began to repeatedly broadcast Ngô Đình Diệm's voice stating that a coup d'état had been attempted and calling for loyal troops to come to his aid.[11] The embassy did observe RVN naval personnel and gunboats cruising up and down the Saigon River during the day, but these military units took no action for or against the coup d'état.[12]

At some point in the morning, most likely before 9:45 a.m. Ngô Đình Diệm was able to pass an urgent message to the Belgium Reverend Raymond J. De Jaeger, the general representative of the Free Pacific Association, Far East Area, requesting that the United States send in marines to protect its citizens and property as well as to secure the airport from the rebels.[13] De Jaeger, who had in the past acted as an unofficial contact with Ngô Đình Diệm and the local Chinese community, agreed to send the message. Durbrow, who received the plea after the airport had already been secured by the rebels and at that point had received no reports of injuries to American personnel or threats to their property, chose to ignore the request.[14] This was the first of many actions by Durbrow which foretold of the shift in the American embassy's policy toward Ngô Đình Diệm.

Because of the physical position of his home near the Presidential Palace, Colby had a clear view of the fighting and was, or had assets who were, well connected with both sides in the conflict.[15] He reported at around 7:00 a.m. that the fighting was still heavy at the Palace, with rebels lodged in the guardhouses at the front of the premises and loyal troops attempting to repel them. Two armored units with approximately twenty-four armored cars under the command of Lieutenant Colonel Nguyễn Văn Thiện and a Major Boi arrived at around 7:30 a.m. to take up positions on the Palace grounds, which helped to stabilize the forward area while, at the rear of the Palace, Lieutenant Colonel Lê Quang Tung, whose troops were outnumbered, failed to remove the rebels.[16] As a result, he sent for reinforcements from Biên Hòa. Shortly after the Colby update, the CIA station received a call from Saigon lawyer Hoàng Cơ Thụy in which he asserted that the coup d'état was 80 percent successful and would most likely be complete within an hour after the Presidential Palace capitulated.[17] Hoàng Cơ Thụy, who was connected though not a signer of the Caravelle Manifesto, was the uncle of Lieutenant Colonel Vương Văn Đông. The CIA station also reported that there was some indication that the communist insurgency had been involved in the event when a rumor of a Việt Cộng attack at the ARVN camp on the outskirts of Saigon was received. The extent of communist involvement proved to be an exaggeration, though Ngô Đình Diệm would claim that the attempted coup d'état was communist inspired.[18]

Early on, it was clear that the attempted coup d'état was not communist inspired or directed.[19] Vietnamese officers loyal to Ngô Đình Diệm, but not engaged in the conflict, were treated with respect by their counterparts. However, many of the paratroopers involved in the incident had not really understood their role, or had been tricked into attacking. Francis Cunningham reported that his neighbor, a Vietnamese air force lieutenant who was sequestered by paratroopers at Tân Sơn Nhứt, told him after the coup d'état that they had been informed that Ngô Đình Diệm was under attack by communists and believed they had been sent to rescue him.[20] Ngô Đình Diệm offered a similar explanation to Durbrow in a conversation after the attempted coup d'état on November 14. This explanation did not entirely convince the embassy staff.

The Vietnamese marines in Saigon divided their loyalties between the two opposing forces. At 9:30 a.m. those loyal to Ngô Đình Diệm, approximately two companies under the acting commanding officer of the National Navy, Commander Hồ Tấn Quyền, joined the Presidential Palace Guard protecting Ngô Đình Diệm and shored up defenses until further reinforcements arrived.[21] Another two companies of marines joined with the airborne battalion. The embassy air attaché, Lieutenant Colonel Butler Toland, reported that, with the exception of the Presidential Palace and the marine-navy section of the main military installation, the paratroopers controlled all the major targets. The national police had been isolated, and its chief was in the custody of the paratroopers.[22] Reports from the Australian military attaché indicated that the rebels had penetrated the Presidential Palace walls while the British military attaché observed that no ARVN forces were coming to the aid of Ngô Đình Diệm. It was the considered opinion of Toland that the coup d'état had been well executed with a well-armed force and a flawless strategy. Toland went on to conclude that Ngô Đình Diệm would either surrender to the coup d'état leaders or commit suicide before the next day, though at this early point in the event, it was unknown whether Ngô Đình Diệm was dead, alive, captured, or mounting a counterattack.[23]

Toland also reported that the Saigon civilians were going about their daily business and that the initial reaction to the coup d'état attempt was positive, with the hope that the rebels would be successful. Elsewhere in Saigon, throughout the coup d'état attempt, the situation appeared normal. Newspapers appeared around noon, the city's utility services remained working, and most market and shop areas away from the Presidential Palace were free of disturbance, though the streets were unusually vacant. The seemingly apathetic response by the Saigon residents and lack of loyal response by the national police and navy led the CIA station to conclude early on that the coup d'état was gaining ground.[24]

However, the situation continued to remain fluid and confused. The airborne units were using heavy weapons on vehicles while the Palace troops responded with small-arms fire. Ngô Đình Diệm broadcast a radio message to the rebel troops in which he explained that they had been duped into this treasonous action by junior officers. By this time, Ngô Đình Diệm had been broadcasting an appeal every three minutes on the radio for troops loyal to the government to come to his aid.[25] He called on Colonel Trần Thiện Khiêm, the commanding officer of the 5th Military Region, to send men and tanks to Phú Lâm, in Cholon, and wait for further orders.[26] Meanwhile, the air attaché reported at 9:30 a.m. that ARVN troops sent to engage the rebels at the Palace had ended up joining the rebels, while reports from the police station still indicated heavy fighting rather than occupation by the rebels. Durbrow learned at 10:30 a.m. that the heavy fighting had stopped and that the rebels had given Ngô Đình Diệm until 11:00 a.m. to surrender.[27]

Durbrow reported at 10:50 a.m. that General Lê Văn Ty and Colonel Nguyễn Chánh Thi had control of the Palace and were entering to talk with Ngô Đình Diệm. Around the same time, Radio Saigon returned to the air with an "Order of the Day of the Revolutionary Council," which stated that it had succeeded in its revolution against Ngô Đình Diệm and called upon the people to remain calm. Both messages proved to be premature.[28]

Around noon, embassy officials witnessed four airplanes flying over the Presidential Palace dropping leaflets that called upon the rebels not to fire into the Palace grounds.[29] As the leaflets fell to the ground, a Radio Saigon broadcast by the coup d'état's Revolutionary Committee outlined the goals of the day's action. The rebels, who were believed to be led by General Phạm Xuân Chiểu, General Lê Văn Kim, Colonel Nguyễn Chánh Thi, the previously mention Vương Văn Đông, and Hoàng Cơ Thụy, called for the

1. Removal of Ngô Đình Diệm because he was so unpopular and proved to be an ineffective leader against the Việt Cộng while he in office.
2. Uniting the people to fight Việt Cộng.
3. Gradual increase of democratic liberties such as press freedom.
4. End of corruption and increasing access to economic benefits.
5. Holding of free elections and the end of the provisional government when the situation stabilized.[30]

It was later confirmed that the rebel leaders included Lieutenant Colonel Vương Văn Đông and Hoàng Cơ Thụy as well as Lieutenant Colonel Nguyễn Triệu Hồng and Phạm Văn Liễu, and Nguyễn Văn Lợi and Major Nguyễn Văn Lộc. Colonel Nguyễn Chánh Thi was not one of the principals in the operation but was forced into participation after the attempt to overthrow Ngô Đình Diệm began.[31]

The situation was still unstable after the broadcasts. Reports came into the embassy that the command of the Capital Military Region, General Thái Quang Hoàng, and chief of staff of the South Vietnamese Joint General Staff, General Lê Văn Ty, were under arrest and being used by Colonel Nguyễn Chánh Thi to negotiate with Ngô Đình Diệm at the Presidential Palace.[32] This did not bode well for Ngô Đình Diệm, nor did the thinking of Durbrow who was inclined to believe that the ultimate aim of the plotters was not the elimination of Ngô Đình Diệm but a unified government that was more effective in fighting the communist insurgency in South Vietnam. If this turned out to be the case, Durbrow expressed a hope in a 3:00 p.m. telegram to Washington that Ngô Đình Diệm might agree to most of the demands in the radio broadcast to end the violence in Saigon. As Durbrow, with the support of the Saigon intelligentsia, had been pushing Ngô Đình Diệm for these reforms, the attempted coup d'état served as another opportunity to strong-arm Ngô Đình Diệm into reform.[33] Durbrow, with the concurrence of McGarr, did agree not to act as mediators to any negotiations that took place as a result of the events of the day. While Durbrow might have tacitly supported the published aims of the Revolutionary Committee, he was enough of a career diplomat and professional not to publicly support the group without instructions from Washington.[34]

It was fair to assume that the events of the day were confused and that the American personnel in Saigon were doing all that they could to get a clear idea of what had transpired. Even if the civilian populations outside of the affected areas went about their business and the streets were, for the most part, deserted, American officials, rightly so, took extreme caution to make their way to the embassy. Durbrow did not arrive at the embassy until after 12:00 p.m. and Mendenhall shortly thereafter. Colby, who lived near the main entrance to the Presidential Palace, remained in place during the early part of the day to report on the fighting taking place around him. After Durbrow arrived at the embassy and received updates from his personnel and presumably had access to the Australian, British, and Vietnamese reports arriving at a steady flow, he must have had an idea of the status of the coup d'état. If this is a reasonable assumption, Durbrow's first conversation with Ngô Đình Diệm after the start of the coup d'état is significant and insightful.

At some point in the early afternoon, most likely before 2:00 p.m. Ngô Đình Diệm finally was able to contact Durbrow at the embassy. Durbrow had no recollection that he ever spoke to Ngô Đình Diệm, and no record of the telephone conversation survived the event, though Mendenhall and Colby remembered the conversation.[35] Durbrow did recall speaking to Generals Dương Văn Minh and Nguyễn Khánh as well as Nguyễn Đình Thuận. While Durbrow forgot what would become a significant event during the American experience in Vietnam or feigned lack of memory, unfortunately it is lost as all the principal participants are gone. Mendenhall later recalled the telephone conversation during which Durbrow failed to offer support for Ngô Đình Diệm. According to Mendenhall, Durbrow urged Ngô Đình Diệm to accept a compromise with the rebels so as to not jeopardize their common struggle against the communist insurgency.[36] At the time, Mendenhall agreed with Durbrow that the U.S. embassy should remain uncommitted during the coup d'état, as it was not clear who would come out ahead at the end of the day. Both Mendenhall and Durbrow believed that the rebels had a better chance if the reports coming into the embassy were correct. Mendenhall marked this moment as the beginning of the end of the relationship between president and ambassador.

Colby had a slightly different memory of the conversation. He recalled Durbrow offering no support or encouragement for Ngô Đình Diệm and his government during this most critical time: "This isn't our coup and this isn't our government. And so, no we're not 100 percent in support of Diem in this fight. Diem took that as a total washing of hands."[37] It did not help matters that the embassy had personnel at the rebel headquarters assessing the situation or that McGarr had been visited by rebel leaders at his home, a fact that Ngô Đình Diệm must have surely been aware of during his conversation with Durbrow. During the attempted coup d'état, Colby was one of the better-informed individuals within the American embassy. He was in contact with Ngô Đình Nhu throughout the day, offering him as much support as the ambassador would allow, a fact that Colby seemed to think Ngô Đình Nhu understood. It is remarkable that the Ngô Đình Diệm–Durbrow conversation has failed to elicit more examination in the post–Ngô Đình Diệm, post–Vietnam War era, as it served as a catalyst for the deteriorating relationship between Ngô Đình Diệm and the American embassy that would ultimately end with the assassination of Ngô Đình Diệm and Ngô Đình Nhu on November 1, 1963.

Ngô Đình Diệm had every reason to be distrustful of Durbrow and his staff after the coup d'état attempt. He had been fighting a dual war since his ascension to power five years earlier, with an ally that was now non-committal in the defense of his leadership and his country. He had established a relationship with Durbrow, which was in its fourth year, even if was showing signs of wear and fragmentation over the previous twelve months. As president of the RVN, Ngô Đình Diệm did have the right to a certain expectation, despite wavering American faith in his leadership, of a commitment by the United States and its main representative to show some support for the embattled leader of a country who was engaged in a struggle against a communist insurgency from within and a growing communist threat from the North. Even if Ngô Đình Diệm had made some mistakes in the past, Durbrow made a fatal error in not voicing his support for the president during the height of the crisis. Durbrow's actions in the immediate aftermath of the coup d'état would be no better.

The situation in Saigon began to change after the telephone conversation. Word reached the embassy that troops loyal to Ngô Đình Diệm were heading toward Saigon and would reach the city before the rebels had a chance to take over the Presidential Palace and capture Ngô Đình Diệm. Approximately seven battalions under the command of Trần Thiện Khiêm, who had heard Ngô Đình Diệm's earlier appeal, and a Lieutenant Colonel Bùi arrived at An Lộc from the Cần Thơ region and organized for an assault on the city if needed, while at a little after 2:10 p.m. Nguyễn Đình Thuận informed Durbrow that armored units from Mỹ Tho, under the command of Major Lâm Quang Thơ, were on the outskirts of Cholon and that two battalions, also from Mỹ Tho, were expected before 3:00 p.m. From the afternoon and through the night, troops loyal to Ngô Đình Diệm responded to his radio appeal.[38] While the 2nd Military Region did not send units, it remained loyal to the president. In the 4th Military Region, students from the NCO academy and units stationed at the Headquarters of the Vietnamese Military Academy in Dalat were sent to Saigon. The commanding officers also appeared to remain loyal to Ngô Đình Diệm throughout the crisis. In the 1st Military Region, at least two battalions left War Zone D to travel to the southwest toward

Saigon while at least seven ranger companies from Tây Ninh joined units from Biên Hòa in the Capital Military Region to converge on the capital. Trần Thiện Khiêm, who had been specifically mentioned in Ngô Đình Diệm's initial radio appeal, led at least four ARVN battalions, two marine battalions, one tank company, field artillery, and some ranger units to relieve his besieged president. His arrival in the morning of November 12 would be a significant turning point in the coup d'état attempt. Overall, Ngô Đình Diệm and his loyal followers would have battalions and units from the 2nd, 5th, 8th, and 21st ARVN divisions. Ultimately, this show of loyal force, with its quick, efficient response, would be enough to carry the day.[39]

Even though Durbrow remarked years after the incident and in some cables during the coup d'état that it was not his place to interfere in the internal situation on November 11, he did tell Nguyễn Đình Thuận several times during the telephone call that he hoped the troops would not engage the rebels surrounding the Presidential Palace, as that would lead to civil war and an advantage for the communist insurgents. Durbrow envisioned Ngô Đình Diệm and the proclaimed Revolutionary Committee compromising. While he did not specifically suggest that Ngô Đình Diệm relinquish power, there was certainly a feeling in the embassy that Ngô Đình Diệm needed to make concessions to the coup d'état planners, who still seemed to have the upper hand. Durbrow informed Nguyễn Đình Thuận that, as the secretary of state for the presidency, he should let his boss know that the United States Marines would not be arriving, nor did Durbrow have any intention to request their presence.[40] Ngô Đình Diệm was on his own. Parsons's response to Durbrow's telegram informing him of his position was to suggest that Vice President Nguyễn Ngọc Thơ would be a logical person to replace Ngô Đình Diệm because of his experience but also because he had not been closely associated with the activities of Ngô Đình Diệm and Ngô Đình Nhu.[41]

Durbrow and Nguyễn Đình Thuận would speak again thirty minutes later.[42] At that time, Durbrow learned that Ngô Đình Diệm and the Revolutionary Committee had begun negotiations around 2:00 p.m. at the Presidential Palace. The rebels were offering Ngô Đình Diệm the position of supreme adviser, which amounted to little more than an honorary title. The new RVN government would consist of members of the Revolutionary Committee and senior paratrooper officers involved in the coup d'état. Nguyễn Đình Thuận, who had received most of this information and instructions from Ngô Đình Nhu, encouraged Durbrow or McGarr to push the Revolutionary Committee to keep Ngô Đình Diệm because of his stature in South Vietnam and the world. Durbrow reaffirmed that Ngô Đình Diệm was the president, but he again urged compromise between Ngô Đình Diệm and the Revolutionary Committee so that the two could maintain a united front against the Việt Cộng. After the Ngô Đình Diệm–Durbrow telephone conversation and the affirmation that the United States would not intervene with marines or pressure, Ngô Đình Diệm and Ngô Đình Nhu, through Nguyễn Đình Thuận, must have questioned the motives of Durbrow and the embassy during the crisis, which was still very far from resolution.

Nguyễn Đình Thuận called again ten minutes later to let Durbrow know that he had passed Durbrow's message to Ngô Đình Nhu.[43] Ngô Đình Nhu again called for the United States to support Ngô Đình Diệm because of his prestige and let Durbrow know that the only rebel demand at that time was that Ngô Đình Diệm become the supreme adviser. Durbrow's only comment was that if the Revolutionary Committee contacted him, he would find out what other demands they might have, and he again asserted that a strong compromise was needed.[44] Durbrow did not have to wait long to hear from members of the Revolutionary

Committee. At 3:00 p.m. McGarr telephoned the embassy and informed Durbrow that representatives of the Revolutionary Committee and members of the press were at his home. Durbrow instructed McGarr to inform the rebels that the U.S. representatives could not offer them any advice or interfere in this internal matter; he did hope that the rebels kept Ngô Đình Diệm and placed him in an active role because of his prestige around the world.[45] For someone who had repeatedly stated that he was not going to become involved in the event, his statement seemed a little like advice and suggested that his assessment of the attempted coup d'état was favorably inclined toward the people at McGarr's residence.

During the course of the conversation, the 2nd Armored Regiment, which was loyal to Ngô Đình Diệm, arrived from Mỹ Tho and reinforced the defenders around the Presidential Palace. The armored section from Budang, which was attempting to join the government forces led by Major Đỗ Văn Điền, the provincial chief of Phước Long, was ambushed by Việt Cộng forces. This was one of the few instances where the Việt Cộng directly played a role in the events of November 11, though the Việt Cộng force, which had been operating on Route 14, was quickly dispersed. Near the time of the ambush, another two companies of marines joined the defenders at the Presidential Palace, which was now a formidable force.[46]

By 5:00 p.m. the fighting had calmed down significantly, though troops within the city and on its outskirts were posed to attack the Presidential Palace or launch a counterattack designed to eliminate the coup d'état attempt. Fifteen minutes later, McGarr telephoned Durbrow at the embassy to let him know that the talks at the Palace had concluded with Ngô Đình Diệm considering his options. In fact, Ngô Đình Diệm had been buying time throughout the day and prolonging the negotiations at every chance. He and Ngô Đình Nhu understood that the attempted coup d'état had come very close to succeeding in the early hours and that the government had not had appropriate contingency plans for such an event. Most likely, Ngô Đình Diệm also expected a greater degree of support from Durbrow and the Americans.

At 5:30 p.m. Radio Saigon broadcast another announcement from the Revolutionary Council in which it stated that Ngô Đình Diệm had surrendered and that all of the Vietnamese generals supported the coup d'état. This was done even while troops loyal to Ngô Đình Diệm moved toward Saigon. The Presidential Guard was augmented by seven ranger companies under the command of Major Lư Đình Sơn, commander of the 1st Ranger Battalion, from Tây Ninh at 7:45 p.m. The unit took up position outside of the Presidential Palace and began the process of securing the area around the scene of the day's most intense fighting.[47] Meanwhile, negotiations at the Palace had reached a standstill as some of the rebels continued to demand the removal of Ngô Đình Diệm from power and were in no mood to compromise.

At the request of the rebels, Durbrow consented to allow McGarr to accompany Vương Văn Đông to the Presidential Palace to negotiate. McGarr's presence was designed to ensure that Vương Văn Đông would not be harmed. As it turned out, Vương Văn Đông had already arranged for safe conduct to the Palace, but McGarr ended up going with him anyway. As the day closed, the embassy received word that General Lê Văn Ty had been broadcasting a message claiming that Ngô Đình Diệm had relinquished power and handed over the government to him and eighteen other military and civilian leaders. Nguyễn Đình Thuận, however, dispelled that rumor at 10:00 p.m. in a call to the embassy, suggesting that General Lê Văn Ty was not a part of the coup d'état attempt. Later, Ngô Đình Diệm revealed that General Lê Văn Ty had been captured, as had his press secretary Võ Văn Hải.[48]

As night settled and the situation in Saigon calmed, the embassy staff sorted out the fact from fiction and reassessed the situation.[49] It learned that the attempted coup d'état had been initiated by junior officers within the airborne brigade led by Vương Văn Đông who publically agreed that they were dissatisfied by the lack of progress against the increased Việt Cộng activity and the political infighting within the military. Another argument, that they had been angered into action by the failure to be promoted as was the custom during the October 26 Independence Day celebrations, emerged later. There had always been some form of resentment in the RVN armed forces that could have been exacerbated by the actions of Ngô Đình Nhu and other pro–Ngô Đình Diệm elements within the government. What was striking to the embassy officials was that there were no confirmed big names involved in the incident.

Of particular interest was Major General Dương Văn Minh, commander of the Field Command Headquarters, ARVN, who garnered much respect and influence throughout military circles in Vietnam. General Dương Văn Minh was a very popular leader who, after his house had been surrounded by paratroopers on November 11, had been allowed to travel through the ranks in civilian clothes without incident.[50] He did not commit himself during the events of November 11 as he would three years later, though he did have a reputation as being pro–Ngô Đình Diệm and pro–American at the time. With his refusal to act one way or the other, many senior officers, including two corps commanders, I Corps commander, General Trần Văn Đôn and General Tôn Thất Đính, did not act.

Brigadier General Nguyễn Khánh, who had played a key role earlier in the year, remained on Ngô Đình Diệm's side throughout the coup d'état. The senior officers in South Vietnam were not going to join the rebels unless there was a real chance at success with minimal risk and maximum benefit to the people. While Durbrow may have been inclined to see a change in South Vietnam and certainly did offer Ngô Đình Diệm pause for reconsideration of the extent of American support for his government, he was a skilled enough diplomat to realize that the coup d'état could never succeed without senior military leadership.

Nonetheless, a 10:30 p.m. assessment from the CIA indicated that Colonel Nguyễn Chánh Thi and the Revolutionary Committee had gained a concession from Ngô Đình Diệm in which the president would accept titular power as head of state while the real authority would rest with a military junta. From Nguyễn Chánh Thi's conversation with the CIA personnel, Ngô Đình Diệm was willing to concede power if it meant that his family would receive safe conduct out of the country.[51] The CIA telephone conversation was confirmed by a looped Saigon Radio broadcast between 10:30 p.m. and 11:15 p.m. in which General Lê Văn Ty announced that he and Ngô Đình Diệm had agreed to suppress the government during negotiations with the Revolutionary Committee, entrusted ARVN with the formation of a provisional government, and called for a cease-fire on both sides in order to deny the communist forces the opportunity to take advantage of the situation.[52] While General Lê Văn Ty might have been used by the rebel leaders to gain some military legitimacy and his full support for the attempted coup d'état was not evident, the agreement seemed genuine and meant a significant shift in the leadership of the RVN. Immediately after this message, a second announcement called on the people of Saigon to rally in front of the Presidential Palace in the morning to show their support for ARVN and to "rejoice over the overthrow of Diem's totalitarian regime, and to express our unity in fighting communism."[53] This theme was repeated a few times in the broadcast, which called for all civil servants, work and business men, intellectuals, students, and children to join in the demonstration.[54]

By the time of the broadcast of the two messages, the streets of Saigon were calm even though the second message foreshadowed a potential confrontation at the site of the most intense fighting of the day should Ngô Đình Diệm hold out for the night and receive the reinforcements he had been calling for since the early morning hours.[55]

There is no record of how Ngô Đình Diệm felt during the night, though he did recall being in direct negotiations with the rebels for that time. He must have felt some satisfaction with the messages received at the Presidential Palace of the reinforcements arriving in Saigon. Trần Thiện Khiêm had amassed a significant force by the morning of November 12, including the 2nd Marine Battalion, one battalion of the 2nd Infantry Regiment, two battalions of the 21st ARVN Division, two battalions of the 10th Infantry Regiment, and two batteries of 105 mm howitzers. Additional battalions from the 5th ARVN and 7th ARVN Divisions were also making their way toward Saigon.[56] Some of the rebel officers did not fare as well. A CIA assessment confirmed that by 11:00 p.m. some of these officers at the General Staff Headquarters were jittery and drunk; Colonel Vương Văn Đông and Generals Lê Văn Ty and Phạm Xuân Chiểu were arguing, and a pitched battle in the 6th Police District in Cholon indicated that Ngô Đình Diệm still had loyal troops available helped to keep the rebels off balance.

Durbrow received confirmation of this suspicion of dissent within the rebel camp with a 3:00 a.m. November 12, telephone conversation with Ngô Đình Diệm's private secretary, Võ Văn Hải. Durbrow believed Võ Văn Hải to be a captive of the rebels at Tân Sơn Nhứt and suspected that he was prompted to make the call at gunpoint.[57] He requested Durbrow to contact Ngô Đình Diệm and encourage him to surrender and leave the country. If Ngô Đình Diệm refused, Võ Văn Hải informed the ambassador that the rebels would use heavy artillery on the Presidential Palace. As it turned out, Võ Văn Hải had asked Nguyễn Đình Thuận what he should do when the coup d'état attempt began and took it upon himself to go to Nguyễn Chánh Thi to try to defuse the situation. After the fact, it was Võ Văn Hải who was often seen as the voice of reason who dissuaded the rebels from engaging in more bloodshed than had been committed.[58] In an interview in 1984, Durbrow recalled responding to this request with a defiant refusal and stated his unquestioned loyalty to Ngô Đình Diệm. He let Võ Văn Hải know that the embassy had no confidence in the rebels.[59] Whether Durbrow did this because he believed it, knew that even though Võ Văn Hải was a captive he was still Ngô Đình Diệm's confidant, or understood that the coup d'état had now failed is not clear. There are no other records of the conversation or reaction to this proclamation, and unlike the telephone call to Ngô Đình Diệm earlier on November 11, which Durbrow could not remember, there were no witness statements. This exchange would be the last for a very confused and involved twenty-hour period. As the dawn of November 12 arrived, the events would become even more interesting.

As the sun rose, General Lê Văn Nghiêm and his 7th ARVN Division arrived from the 1st Military Region and joined with troops under the command of Colonel Nguyễn Văn Chuân, Colonel Huỳnh Công Tịnh, Lieutenant Colonel Huỳnh Văn Cao, and Majors Nguyễn Minh Mẫn and Đỗ Văn Điển. These troops were prepared to dislodge the rebels from the areas that had been captured on the previous day.[60] Before they could begin, at approximately 6:20 a.m. on November 12, a tape-recorded message with Ngô Đình Diệm's voice was broadcast. He announced the abolishment of the government and requested the military to set up a provisional government until he and the Revolutionary Committee formed a coalition government. Ngô Đình Diệm also ordered the troops loyal to him to cease their fire to prevent further bloodshed.[61] To punctuate this rather shocking announcement, heavy gun and mortar fire directed toward the Presidential Palace began and lasted for approximately ten minutes, followed by less intense gunfire for another twenty minutes and sporadic weapons fire afterward. McGarr received a status update from Major Lư Đình Sơn who had set up his command post in front of McGarr's house. He advised the MAAG chief that he and Trần Thiện Khiêm would be entering the center of the city momentarily to complete their surrounding of the rebel parachutists.[62]

The outbreak of fighting at 6:20 a.m. would later be confirmed as the final pitched battle of the three airborne companies between the Presidential Palace and the Catholic church down Norodom Avenue who surrendered to the newly arrived ARVN troops.[63] The embassy was made aware of the broadcast soon after it began, and Durbrow, along with a few of his staff, went to the building's balcony to observe the exchange. Viewing the city and the situation from the height of the balcony, Durbrow probably felt a sense of accomplishment with the Ngô Đình Diệm announcement. Notwithstanding the brief exchange of gunfire, he was very interested in preventing a bloodbath on the streets of Saigon. He desired an end to the coup d'état, which might have resulted in a civil war that would have distracted resources from the fight against the communist insurgency. He also accomplished, so he believed, the objective of lessening, if not eliminating, the power of Ngô Đình Diệm, who he maintained no longer served the best interests of the United States in South Vietnam. The moment, as the sun rose on a new day in Saigon, was broken when a bullet from below ricocheted against the building and hit an embassy officer near Durbrow. Later, Durbrow would discover that Ngô Đình Diệm was not about to go quietly.[64]

At 7:00 a.m. Dr. Phan Quang Đán broadcast a radio message as the political commissioner of the Revolutionary Committee. He condemned Ngô Đình Diệm and his rule over the past six years and called upon the people to tear down government slogans and replace them with ones from the Revolutionary Committee.[65] At about the same time, Durbrow learned of the details of the agreement between Ngô Đình Diệm and the Revolutionary Committee.[66] Ngô Đình Diệm would continue to serve as head of state but would be stripped of any real power. General Lê Văn Ty would become the prime minister while several generals, selected it seemed by Vương Văn Đông, would form the government. Additionally, the Revolutionary Committee would continue to exist. Durbrow sought instructions on what he should do in his 7:00 a.m. telegram to the Department of State, though he favored recognition for two reasons. First, he believed that rapid action would convince the new government of continued American support and keep it away from moving toward neutrality in the fight against communism, and second, it would convince the communist insurgents that the crisis was over and any advantage they might have gained from it was now lost. Durbrow offered wording for Department of State approval that recognized the change in government and encouraged Washington to issue a public statement quickly. It seems curious that Durbrow would use the argument of quick recognition to avoid a neutral government when one of the main justifications for the coup d'état was Ngô Đình Diệm's lack of progress against the communist insurgency.

Ninety minutes later the situation once again shifted as word reached the embassy that an element of the 5th ARVN Division had reached Saigon, reinforcing those units who had remained loyal to Ngô Đình Diệm. These troops then confronted approximately two companies of rebel paratroopers and took their surrender without much effort. This had been the source of noise heard at the embassy and the reason the embassy staff had exposed itself on the balcony. The coup d'état that seemed to have resolved itself was now just as volatile as it had been thirty hours earlier when word first reached Durbrow that the Ngô Đình Diệm government was in trouble.

A McGarr update to Admiral Felt confirmed that gunfire had resumed near the Presidential Palace around 6:30 a.m. followed by a response to the broadcast appeal for a demonstration the night before. A crowd had gathered in front of the Presidential Palace, carrying banners that called for the overthrow of Ngô Đình Diệm.[67] At approximately 8:35 a.m. the marines protecting Ngô Đình Diệm opened fired on the demonstrators, killing as many as four and wounding twice that number.[68] The crowd, which some believed had been encouraged by communist insurgents within their ranks and had been carrying signs that read "Down with Diem," fell apart.[69] After the confrontation outside of the Presidential Palace, Durbrow decided that he needed to speak with Ngô Đình Diệm directly and forcefully. At 9:20 a.m. they talked by telephone for ten minutes with Durbrow starting the conversation by expressing his growing concern for the morning's fighting, after a peaceful night and an end to what the ambassador thought was the significant violence of the event. Durbrow expressed his fear that the abortive coup d'état would end in a bloodbath and provide the Việt Cộng with yet another opportunity to exploit the situation.[70] He asserted to the still beleaguered but more hopeful president that he had worked through the night to dissuade the rebels from doing the very thing that he suspected Ngô Đình Diệm had just done: escalate the conflict to the point of creating an unstable situation to the advantage of the communist insurgents. Around the same time, the Saigon Radio station was reoccupied by Major Nguyễn Minh Mẫn, commander of the 1st Military Zone, who was loyal to Ngô Đình Diệm.[71]

Ngô Đình Diệm's private reaction to Durbrow is not known, though it might have been a mixture of relief and anger. That Durbrow had worked toward a peaceful resolution to the situation through negotiations would have been well received by Ngô Đình Diệm given their conversation the previous day. Ngô Đình Diệm must have felt some relief that Durbrow had not publicly sided with the coup d'état leaders even if he suspected that Durbrow had very different private feelings. Still, he could not have been pleased with Durbrow's concern for the safety of the individuals who carried signs calling for the removal of the president from power. After the tumultuous events of the previous day, Ngô Đình Diệm must have had some distress regarding Durbrow's lack of interest in Ngô Đình Diệm and his family's welfare or the fact that Durbrow was, in his own words, extremely perturbed that Ngô Đình Diệm had announced an agreement with the rebels and then violated that agreement by ushering in troops loyal to the government that very morning.[72] Ngô Đình Diệm had been fighting for his life as well as his position within a government that he had led for five years. To what extent Durbrow's comments rankled the president is unknown, but it surely must have been insulting to be chided for breaking a tentative agreement with a group of traitors to your country by an outside observer and principle representative of your primary ally, especially as Durbrow seemed more interested in exerting influence in the day-to-day operations of the government and conduct of the war rather than demonstrating good faith as a friend and ally.[73]

Ngô Đình Diệm was also fortunate not to have known Parsons' reply to Durbrow's message to Washington in relation to the conversation that occurred between Ngô Đình Diệm and Durbrow. Parsons instructed Durbrow to reinforce to Ngô Đình Diệm the confidence the United States had in the Saigon government but also warned him not to seek retribution. Parsons argued that the episode confirmed "a serious lack of support among military and other elements for many aspects of the government's policies" and was focused on members of Ngô Đình Diệm's family.[74] Parsons then instructed Durbrow to reinforce the points of the October 14 démarche as confirmation that Ngô Đình Diệm needed to listen to Durbrow as a trusted ally rather than dismiss the ambassador's ideas.

After what must have been a very stressful thirty hours, Ngô Đình Diệm did not react negatively to Durbrow's comments, or Durbrow chose not to report the reaction to the Department of State. Instead, Ngô Đình Diệm explained to the ambassador that the morning's events were caused by the rebel leaders who, in his mind, had broken the agreement brokered through the night by allowing the demonstration to occur in the first place. While the demonstrators had not been directed by the communists, as South Vietnamese officials had first announced, Ngô Đình Diệm maintained that his military reaction to the demonstration was appropriate and justified. Nonetheless, Ngô Đình Diệm concluded his conversation with Durbrow by agreeing that further violence needed to be avoided in order to regain his prestige internally and continue it abroad. A bloodbath would serve no purpose; Ngô Đình Diệm reassured Durbrow that it was not a part of his plan or an objective in the days to come.

After the night's events and morning demonstrations, enough time had passed for reinforcements loyal to the president to arrive and organize. Trần Thiện Khiêm led elements of the 21st ARVN Division as well as armor and field artillery into Saigon. Before engaging the rebels, he sent an L-17 transport over Saigon to drop pamphlets in the area occupied by the rebel paratroopers and over the site of the morning's demonstrations.[75] The pamphlet was clear on the strength of Trần Thiện Khiêm's force and appealed to the common sense of the Saigon population. The pamphlet explained that the rebel paratroopers had already begun to surrender and give their support to Ngô Đình Diệm. It asserted that Colonel Nguyễn Chánh Thi and Major Ngô Xuân Soạn were taking money from the communists and old colonialists still in Vietnam—both of whom were anti–Ngô Đình Diệm. The pamphlet finally appealed to the soldiers to return to the government, protect the homeland, and preserve the Republic. It offered forgiveness by Ngô Đình Diệm if this was done in a reasonable time and without additional bloodshed.[76] The pamphlet and Trần Thiện Khiêm's show of force proved to be very persuasive.

Reports had already been confirmed regarding the surrender of the two companies of paratroopers, and at 10:15 a.m. Radio Vietnam broadcast that it was now in the hands ARVN paratroopers from the 1st Military Region who were loyal to Ngô Đình Diệm.[77] Major Nguyễn Minh Mẫn, commander of the paratroopers, reported that the radio station was retaken without serious opposition and that his troops recovered 300 weapons, including machine guns and mortars in the process.[78] Nguyễn Khánh also reported the same to McGarr and reaffirmed that there would be no additional bloodshed as a result of the abortive coup d'état.

By 11:20 a.m. government troops added the Office of the Police and Sûreté, the Great Market, the Tea Dan Gardens, and the central police building to the list of objectives recaptured from the rebels.[79] There was every reason to believe that the attempted coup d'état was over by this point. A MAAG officer, dressed in civilian clothes, reported to McGarr regarding his tour of downtown Saigon by foot as he observed the area that had been the scene of heavy fighting the day before.[80] He remarked on how calm the situation was with the men from the 5th ARVN Division who mingled with the civilians and read the leaflets that had been distributed throughout the morning.[81] Even though armor had been deployed in front of the Palace, as well as marines in the strength of at least two battalions, there was little tension in the air. The MAAG officer spoke with the marine commander who told him that he did not want to see bloodshed because he had many paratrooper friends. In fact, the marines and paratroopers were seen fraternizing everywhere.

Another MAAG officer reported that men from the 5th ARVN and 7th ARVN were standing in groups at key points throughout Saigon while one company of the 7th ARVN was moving back to its original position north of the city. ARVN troops had already reoccupied their headquarters around 2:00 p.m. and word reached McGarr that Tân Sơn Nhứt would reopen for business by 6:00 p.m. on November 13.[82] There is very little evidence to suggest that the bloodbath Durbrow had feared and expected was in the minds of the troops or Ngô Đình Diệm, who was more worried about seizing the treasonous junior officers who had never amounted to anything positive before the coup d'état. In Ngô Đình Diệm's mind, they were to blame for the troubles of November 11 and would have been culpable had the Việt Cộng taken advantage of the situation.[83] Durbrow's concern, however, was shared by several in Washington who drew up contingency plans in case Ngô Đình Diệm appeared to be headed toward a bloodbath.[84]

Before the ARVN troops retook Tân Sơn Nhứt, Captain Phan Phụng Tiên, the commander of the 1st Transportation Squadron stationed at the airfield, took off in a C-47 aircraft heading west, presumably toward Phnom Penh, Cambodia.[85] A MAAG air force adviser reported nearly two and a half hours later that the aircraft had aboard it Colonel Nguyễn Chánh Thi, Lieutenant Colonel Vương Văn Đông, and Major Ngô Xuân Soạn, who were now considered the three principals in the coup d'état attempt.[86] It would be learned later that Major Ngô Xuân Soạn, who had been commander of the 5th Airborne Battalion, was murdered when he refused to join the coup d'état and was not aboard the aircraft, though General Thái Quang Hoàng, who had been taken as a hostage, was aboard.[87] Other rumors circulated around Saigon about the fate of the rebel leaders, ranging from their escaping aboard a C-47 to Nha Trang, Vientiane, or Bangkok, to being captured and executed. Reports also came into the U.S. embassy that Trần Văn Văn, Trần Văn Đỗ, Phan Khắc Sửu and Phan Huy Quát, former members of the Caravelle Group and opponents to Ngô Đình Diệm, had been arrested.[88] While there was no evidence that the Americans aided in the escape of the three paratrooper officers and the others aboard the C-47, they did depart on an American aircraft flown by a Vietnamese pilot with training by an American officer, from a unit that had been significantly advised by the United States. It would have been folly for Durbrow or any other American representative to aid in the escape, but in these confused days, perception and reality often became blurred. The rebel leaders were the target of Ngô Đình Diệm's wrath; Durbrow had advised against retribution because it would damage Ngô Đình Diệm's prestige and destabilize the unity of anti-communist forces, and the three had escaped justice. Ngô Đình Diệm most certainly could not have been pleased.

Nonetheless, Ngô Đình Diệm via Nguyễn Đình Thuận, made a radio announcement at some time before 6:00 p.m. offering forgiveness to those military personnel involved in the coup d'état.[89] Trương Vĩnh Lê, president of the National Assembly, then called for a special session at 6:30 p.m. to discuss and, after a minute of silence for the fallen loyal combatants, pass two resolutions. In the first resolution, 8/60, the assembly reaffirmed its total confidence for Ngô Đình Diệm and the anti-communist cause, while the second resolution, 9/60, not only praised the ARVN soldiers but also the civilians who had come to the aid of Ngô Đình Diệm during the crisis.[90] Finally, at 6:00 p.m. nearly thirty-nine hours after the coup d'état had begun, Ngô Đình Diệm broadcast a radio message confirming that the paratroopers had been duped into action by Colonel Nguyễn Chánh Thi, Vương Văn Đông, and Major Ngô Xuân Soạn but had failed in their attempt.[91] He still did not know of Ngô Xuân Soạn's earlier sacrifice. Ngô Đình Diệm explained in the message that he had tried to compromise with the rebels in order to avoid bloodshed but was forced to authorize a counter-coup on the morning of November 12 because "of the continuous perfidy of the rebels who were guilty of many criminal abuses especially that of making the paratroopers believe that they immediately had to come to the rescue of the President of the Republic betrayed by his personal guard."[92] The November 1960 coup d'état attempt was finally over.

In the post–coup d'état analysis, McGarr gave the commanders of the 1st, 5th, and Capital Military Regions high marks on their efficiency in bringing troops loyal to Ngô Đình Diệm into Saigon to confront the rebels. He was of the opinion that this level of professionalism turned the day toward Ngô Đình Diệm.[93] Rather than hurting Ngô Đình Diệm's prestige, McGarr concluded that the outcome of the coup d'état strengthened Ngô Đình Diệm's position militarily but also politically as a result of the military and civilian support he received on November 11 and 12. McGarr confirmed that, by November 13, loyal troops engaged in suppressing the attempted coup d'état had returned to their posts to continue the fight against the Việt Cộng.

As the situation normalized, Durbrow made an appointment to speak with Ngô Đình Diệm on November 14.[94] After the obligatory congratulations on the outcome of the crisis and relief that Ngô Đình Diệm and his family were safe, Durbrow came around to the primary reason for his visit: he wanted Ngô Đình Diệm to refrain from retaliating against those individuals who had plotted his overthrow and wanted him out of the country, presumably alive. Durbrow argued that retaliation was not necessary because the coup d'état leaders were anti-communist. Forgiveness was the preferred response to the event; Durbrow argued that Ngô Đình Diệm's leniency to the rebels would increase his prestige in Vietnam and throughout the world. For Durbrow, violence would aid the communist insurgency by destabilizing the unity of the anti-communist forces. There is no indication, in the written records, of the inherent contradictions of Durbrow's assertion. To ask Ngô Đình Diệm not to think about doing what was clearly the goal of the rebels was either naïve or diplomatically calculating. Whether Ngô Đình Diệm picked up on Durbrow's duplicity or simply chose to ignore it is open to interpretation. He did thank the ambassador for his well wishes and then reiterated that the paratroopers had been tricked into action. Ngô Đình Diệm blamed the leadership and not "his children," as he referred to the troops.[95]

Ngô Đình Diệm expressed no inclination to forgive or be lenient to Lieutenant Colonel Vương Văn Đông or Nguyễn Chánh Thi, both of whom had already earned poor reputations before the events of November 11. Ngô Đình Diệm considered Vương Văn Đông a troublemaker while Nguyễn Chánh Thi was unbalanced. Each, Ngô Đình Diệm asserted, had married women who had clearly been under the influence of the French; he observed that they were often seen dancing with French officers in public.[96] Ngô Đình Diệm refused to reveal the status of either Vương Văn Đông or Nguyễn Chánh Thi, despite Durbrow's attempts at finding out if they had been arrested. The ambassador continued to push for leniency. Ngô Đình Diệm did not specifically give in, though he stated that only a few would be punished; he mentioned the Saigon lawyer Hoàng Cơ Thụy by name. Because Ngô Đình Diệm appeared to be in a relaxed, happy mood, Durbrow did not press the matter, nor did he choose to bring up the reforms that he had suggest were necessary for the Ngô Đình Diệm government to survive during his October 14 frank conversation with the president. This was perhaps a wise decision, as the ambassador's favor was at a very low point.

Many in Washington and Saigon tried to draw lessons from these turbulent days in November. For Ngô Đình Diệm, the decision was whether he could continue to trust the Americans on whom he had relied for several years and still maintain the degree of independence he needed and desired to govern his country. For the America officials, the debate was whether Ngô Đình Diệm had overstayed his welcome as the leader of the RVN or would see the attempted coup d'état as a wake-up call to the real need for reforms in his government and begin listening to Durbrow and his followers in the American embassy in Saigon. The final option was a realization that Ngô Đình Diệm was a permanent fixture in South Vietnam and the change needed was the American ambassador who after more than three years of continuous service had exerted as much influence as he possibly could and perhaps had come to the end of his usefulness as the principal representative of the United States, its policies, and a five-year relationship that had achieved some success but still found itself fighting in this small country in Southeast Asia. In the period of transition at the end of the Eisenhower administration and the beginning of the Kennedy presidency, much would occur in Vietnam that would help to settle the debate.

8

After the Coup d'État: Saigon Responds

The mass demonstration called for by the rebels on the morning of November 12 prompted the Ngô Đình Diệm government to call for its own demonstration of solidarity for the morning of November 13. As early at 6:30 a.m. people began to gather in front of the National Assembly for the march to the Presidential Palace to deliver a manifesto in support of Ngô Đình Diệm and offer speeches of praise for the ARVN troops who had averted the crisis and remained loyal.[1] By 8:00 a.m. the crowd had grown to an impressive size, appeared to be well organized, and had a peaceful, celebratory feel to it. A MAAG officer observed the event that included an honor guard of army, navy, and marine personnel as well as significant involvement from the Civil Guard and the Republican Youth who carried banners praising Ngô Đình Diệm and thanking the loyal troops.

At the National Assembly the demonstrators, which also included members of the National Revolutionary Movement Civil Service League, the Christian Labor Confederation, the National Revolutionary Movement, the Students' Federation, the Workers' Union Confederation, Catholic and Buddhist associations, the Socialist Party, the Labour Union, the Society for the Study of Confucius, and the Anti-Communist Peoples' League, signed resolutions that called for them to "close their ranks behind the enlightened and virtuous leader of the nation" and support Ngô Đình Diệm and the Personalist revolution.[2] The military side of the parade consisted primarily of units from the 5th, 7th, and 21st ARVN Divisions, marines, and the psychological warfare battalion followed a route from the National Assembly to the Presidential Palace some four blocks away, the streets lined with the people of Saigon cheering them forward. Around 10:00 a.m. the Palace gates were opened and the demonstrators moved onto the grounds. After calling for Ngô Đình Diệm, who appeared at one of the Palace balconies with Vice President Nguyễn Ngọc Thơ, Trương Vĩnh Lê, and other National Assemblymen, the demonstrators presented the resolutions and manifesto to the president, who acknowledged the support by waving to his people. The demonstration was much more impressive than the attempt the previous day, even though each had about the same amount of time to prepare and organize. Beneath this show of solidarity, there continued to be unrest in Saigon and discussions between the Vietnamese and Americans as the next few days would show.

The consequences of the coup d'état for South Vietnamese–American relations was foreshadowed by a Lansdale memorandum to Deputy Secretary of Defense James H. Douglas.[3] Lansdale warned Douglas that Ngô Đình Diệm would treat the 1960 coup d'état attempt with reference to the November 1954 attempted coup d'état. In 1954, the leaders of that

Ngô Đình Diệm with members of the Civil Guard at a Denunciation of Communism event, circa 1950s (United States Information Agency–Saigon, Photograph 61-11032, National Archives and Records Administration, College Park, Maryland).

attempt went unpunished and were culpable in the politico-religious crisis of March–April 1955. Lansdale did not believe Ngô Đình Diệm would make the same mistake in 1960. Of greater concern for Lansdale was the action of Durbrow during the crisis. It was Durbrow who had suggested that Ngô Đình Diệm give in to the rebel demands to avoid bloodshed or compromise for the greater good. Lansdale correctly assessed that Ngô Đình Diệm would see Durbrow's actions as evidence that he was listening to, or influenced by, the wrong people in Saigon.

Essentially, Ngô Đình Diệm believed Durbrow as too prone to believe and accept the arguments of his opponents while dismissing the RVN position. In other words, Durbrow had outlived his usefulness. Lansdale did not entirely blame Durbrow, suggesting that the Southeast Asia desk at the State Department had engaged in a policy that negatively influenced Ngô Đình Diệm and gave Durbrow instructions that encouraged him to proceed down his chosen path. Lansdale once again implored Douglas to use his influence to ensure that the American personnel involved in Vietnam took the time to understand the people. Implied in this message was the argument that U.S. initiatives based exclusively on American ideals, political philosophy, or personality without due consideration for the complexities of Vietnamese culture, society, or personality would fail to succeed and only result in a further drifting apart of the two allies.

A further indication that the post–coup d'état relationship was souring came from Jerome T. French, an Office of Special Operations officer who toured South Vietnam between November 14 and November 17.[4] In a report to Lansdale, French observed deteriorating conditions in Saigon, resulting from rumors of U.S. involvement in the events of November 11. In his conversations with key personnel in Saigon, he experienced "bitterness, dissension, and further demoralization which it appears will result and which was affecting even some who are instrumental in saving the day."[5] Coupled with the disintegration of U.S. influence and the general malaise were the real concern of increased Việt Cộng activity and the under-estimation of their strength.

Not too long after the opening battles of November 11, a group of Saigon citizens made up of political, military, and confessional leaders as well as professional organizations took it upon themselves to organize and aid those troops loyal to Ngô Đình Diệm.[6] Trương Công Cửu, dean of the faculty of pedagogy at the University of Saigon and first vice president of the National Assembly, led the People's Counter-Coup d'État Committee whose principle objectives were to supply information in the form of pamphlets and leaflets to the people of Saigon, including the rebel paratroopers with appeals to end the action, warnings of loyal troops converging on Saigon, and reaffirmation of support for the Saigon government.[7] In this objective, the committee was aided by the ARVN who provided trucks that allowed it to distribute information more quickly. Committee members also played an instrumental role in guiding loyal troops through the Saigon streets once they arrived at the city. This allowed for a more efficient deployment of force as well as a quicker response to the critical situation around the Presidential Palace. As the coup d'état progressed through the night of November 11, committee members interacted with the rebel paratroopers to explain how the military had been tricked into action by their officers. In many respects, the work of these Saigon residents helped to defuse the potential bloodbath that might have occurred during the November 12 morning demonstration organized by the Revolutionary Committee. At no time did Durbrow recognize the work of these individuals who shared, and were probably more effective in accomplishing, his goal of avoiding additional bloodshed.

Around noon on November 12, the committee distributed a leaflet titled "People's Revolutionary Committee against Rebellion." As its title suggested, it offered a counter-argument to the Revolutionary Committee established by the rebels during the coup d'état. The leaflet harkened back to the period of 1954 to 1955 when the Vietnamese were fighting communists, colonialists, and imperialists and the outlook was in doubt. Implied in the message was that Ngô Đình Diệm had united the people to get them to the point they were at in 1960. The leaflet argued that it was the Việt Cộng who threatened the stability of the RVN through its terrorism and assassination. In assessing the events of November 11, it concluded that the rebels had been encouraged by the colonialists of old to satisfy their political aims and leave the people at the mercy of the communists: "All of the people must continue the spirit of the People's Revolution of 1954–1955 in order to unmask any cunning against the country and always support the president, our only leader."[8] The leaflet suggested that Ngô Đình Diệm had refocused some of his animosity from the rebels toward the Americans. The People's Counter-Coup d'État Committee's purpose was not to divide the people of Saigon; it desired to bring them together as demonstrated by a call for the people of Saigon and around the country to hoist flags to show their united sentiment against the abortive rebellion on

November 13.⁹ This group was also instrumental in helping to organize the counter-demonstration on November 13 that supported the continued rule of Ngô Đình Diệm.

On November 14, a group of prominent Vietnamese representing some of the more significant political and popular organizations in Saigon met to form the People's Committee against Communists and Rebels.¹⁰ This new committee took over from the People's Counter–Coup d'État Committee, which had dissolved earlier in the day due to the fact that it had existed only to aid the troops loyal to Ngô Đình Diệm and to work to unite the people in Saigon against the rebels. The new People's Committee was also chaired by Trương Công Cửu. In addition to prominent members in Saigon society, the committee also included many officers who had fought on November 11–12, though the organization would be criticized by the individuals that Ngô Đình Diệm had labeled the intellectuals and demagogues as a group of officers who felt remorse and perhaps fear that they had not been more active against the coup d'état.¹¹

The primary goal of the People's Committee against Communists and Rebels was to promote a better understanding between the people of Saigon and the ARVN and improve morale. The committee soon extended upon its original mandate by distributing a leaflet that would sour American-Vietnamese relations. The leaflet, titled "People's Committee against Rebels and Communists," confirmed that Ngô Đình Diệm, Ngô Đình Nhu, and Trần Kim Tuyến had decided that the Americans were more involved in the events of November 11 and 12 than initially suspected. This leaflet specifically mentioned the colonialists and imperialists by name—the United States, Britain, and France—and asserted that the rebels had received support from them.¹² The leaflet then maintained that though the plot had failed, the colonialists and imperialists continued to malign the Ngô Đình Diệm government and the ARVN victory by giving a prejudiced interpretation of the events. This leaflet coincided with a press conference by Cao Xuân Vỹ who, as he dissolved the People's Counter–Coup d'État Committee, implying that the United States was behind the coup d'état attempt.¹³

Durbrow found this new leaflet disturbing because of the reference to the United States as a colonial or imperial power as well as its confirmation to the growing conviction that Ngô Đình Diệm, Ngô Đình Nhu, and Trần Kim Tuyến placed increasing blame on the Americans, who failed to back the government completely in the crisis. Durbrow suggested that this strategy was a result of either a concerted plan to shift the ire of the Vietnamese people away from Ngô Đình Diệm's rule and toward the West or was a preemptive move by Ngô Đình Diệm to make it more difficult for Durbrow and the Americans to continue their pressure on the South Vietnamese leader to make significant reforms in his government.¹⁴

Durbrow concluded that even if neither of his theories was correct, the pamphlet suggested that Ngô Đình Nhu and Trần Kim Tuyến were using this avenue to express their displeasure at the United States for not completely backing Ngô Đình Diệm. Durbrow, or any other American in Vietnam, should not have been surprised by the reaction. Ngô Đình Diệm, Ngô Đình Nhu, and Trần Kim Tuyến knew that the United States had positioned people at the rebel headquarters, and Durbrow's November 11 conversation with Ngô Đình Diệm had been less than encouraging in offering American assistance. With bullets flying, Ngô Đình Diệm had expected support from Durbrow but received instead a noncommitment, a refusal to bring in the U.S. Marines, a lecture after the fact on how Ngô Đình Diệm needed to respond to the rebels, and a scolding for breaking his word to those whose actions were unequivocally treasonous.

The People's Committee against Communists and Rebels, inclined to stir up trouble with the United States, called on Ngô Đình Diệm to enact harsh measures against those who had instigated, and encouraged or profited by, the abortive coup d'état.[15] The committee took it upon themselves to single out the Saigon newspapers who had reported favorably toward the rebels on November 11 and 12. Two newspaper offices, *Dân chúng* and *Tin Mới*, were ransacked because they had published distorted news on the coup d'état, while three other Saigon newspapers, *Chuông Mai*, *Buổi sang*, and *Sài Gòn Mới*, were severely damaged for similar reasons.[16] The director general of information, Trần Văn Thọ, authorized the sealing of the offices of *Dân chúng* and *Tin Mới* to prevent further damage.[17] Each had requested that the seal be broken, but neither was allowed to reopen by Nguyễn Đình Thuận's November 17 press conference, which provided evidence for the foreign press to accuse the secretary of state for the presidency of violating the freedom of the press and pursuing a policy of censorship. All of the other Saigon newspapers had returned to publishing stories that praised the government and criticized the rebel leaders. *Tự do* reported that the quick collapse of the rebellion, isolated as it was, was a clear sign that Ngô Đình Diệm enjoyed widespread popular support.[18]

Another source of tension between the Americans and Vietnamese was the presence of American personnel at the rebel headquarters during the course of the coup d'état attempt. There was no denying that Americans had been seen with the rebel leaders, and even if their actions were those of observers or listeners, it was difficult to explain to the Ngô family, whose members were on edge after November 11. During the day of November 11, Lieutenant Colonel Vương Văn Đông went to McGarr's house to provide an overview of the coup d'état objectives and then asked him to accompany him to the Presidential Palace to guarantee safe passage while he negotiated with Ngô Đình Diệm.[19] McGarr was politically astute enough to realize that accompanying Vương Văn Đông to the Presidential Palace would be interpreted as de facto recognition of the coup d'état attempt. After November 11, Ngô Đình Nhu learned that a CIA operative had been in contact with the some of the civilian coup d'état plotters. When confronted with this fact, Colby tried to deflect the criticism, but Ngô Đình Nhu would not be distracted.[20] Ngô Đình Nhu had the American removed from Vietnam by sending a letter to the operative, allegedly from the rebel leaders, that threatened the man and his family because the promise of support that he had offered never materialized. Colby, faced with a fait accompli, removed the operative and his family and then informed Ngô Đình Nhu of his actions.[21]

While Colby acted properly and his men never supported the coup d'état, his actions in protecting his agent and family certainly would have confirmed to Ngô Đình Nhu that the Americans were more involved in the November 11 events than previously suspected. In a Vietnamese atmosphere charged with suspicion, distrust, anxiety, and fear, the fact that Colby had sent his man to observe rather than to act became irrelevant. It only confirmed to the Ngô family that the Americans were not as they appeared. Trust, once suspected or lost, was a difficult thing to regain. The appearance of betrayal, true or false, became unforgivable.

In the evening of November 14, Durbrow and McGarr met with American reporters who were covering Vietnam and were available at that time in Saigon. Durbrow provided a brief synopsis of the conference in two telegrams to the State Department.[22] In the first telegram, Durbrow insisted that no embarrassing questions were asked while he asserted in the second, "In answer to a point-blank question I replied that I was 'happy that President

Diem had successfully resisted the coup.'"[23] Neither statement was entirely true. Durbrow certainly did indicate that he was pleased that Ngô Đình Diệm had succeeded and might have thought none of the questions were embarrassing, but his comments throughout the meeting give a very different impression.

If the questions proved not to be embarrassing, the answers must be considered provocative to the Vietnamese loyal to Ngô Đình Diệm. Throughout the press conference, which Durbrow insisted remain off the record, he appeared to lament the fact that the rebels held an advantageous position around the Presidential Palace on the morning of November 11 but never pressed the issue. This allowed Trần Thiện Khiêm to arrive from the 5th Military Region with his armor and ARVN troops. In one instance, Durbrow remarked, "But the thing I still don't understand myself, why with three battalions or whatever they had surrounding if not practically surrounding completely the palace, they did not finish off the job before all of these other troops got here."[24] Durbrow would return to this theme several times in the interview.

Later in the press conference, Durbrow bemoaned the fact that the paratroopers who had maintained their position throughout the night at the Presidential Palace had failed to defend themselves when the counter-attack began after the morning demonstrations on November 12. While Durbrow complimented Ngô Đình Diệm as "playing his cards extremely well," he once again offered a glimpse into his real thoughts: "I still say that I don't know why they did not try to take the palace and storm it then."[25] After McGarr answered some questions about Colonel Vương Văn Đông and their meeting on November 11, Durbrow cast aspersions on the official statement of the RVN that the paratroopers had been tricked into attacking the Presidential Palace to rescue Ngô Đình Diệm from an attempted communist takeover. He received affirmation by Stanley Karnow, one of the reporters present at the press conference, who would later comment in one of his questions that the idea that the paratroopers were tricked did not hold water because he had had a conversation with several paratrooper officers about that very issue.

Apparently it did not occur to Karnow at the time that the leaders of the abortive coup d'état were the ones doing the tricking rather than being tricked and Karnow was one of their victims. While Durbrow was pleased to hear this, evidently he too did not make the distinction between officer as leaders and troops as followers, he continued to voice this recurring theme: "I don't know whether that's true or not, but the thing [is], as I've said before, I do not understand why the devil they didn't storm the palace and get it over with."[26] As the press conference progressed, it turned more into a bull session, with reporters offering theories and bringing in their own sources, not always confirmed, which helped to drive the discussion.

Two such examples have bearing on how Durbrow reconciled the failure of the rebels with the great need of reform within the Ngô Đình Diệm government. The first had to do with the mass demonstration scheduled by the rebels for November 12.[27] When the radio broadcast went out on the night of November 11, Durbrow expected that many more Vietnamese would respond than the estimated 3,000 to 4,000 who showed up in the morning. This suggested to Durbrow that maybe Ngô Đình Diệm had more support than previously suspected. The reporters helped to ease Durbrow's mind that there was widespread discontent with Ngô Đình Diệm in Saigon by offering the theory that no sensible person would have taken to the streets that morning after the day of gunfire. When McGarr interjected that the streets between MAAG headquarters and his house were normal, *New York Times* foreign correspondent Jacques Nevard responded that sensible people would avoid the square in front of the Presidential Palace. This begged the question as to how insensible the 3,000-plus demonstrators were that did congregate on that morning, though Nevard dismissed them as pleasure seekers and concluded that the demonstration would have been much more successful had it been given time to develop. This might be true, but using the same logic, the coup d'état would have been successful had Ngô Đình Diệm surrendered or forsaken the five years he had given to the RVN for the benefit of disgruntled junior officers, foreign correspondents, and the Saigon intelligentsia who believed that they understood what was best for Vietnam based on their vast intimate knowledge of the country, its people, and culture.

The other scenario played out in the press conference after the interview process turned into an exchange of information was the fact that the coup d'état attempt was not targeted at the removal of Ngô Đình Diệm but at the elimination of the influence of Ngô Đình Diệm's brothers and his closest advisers. This might have helped to explain why the rebels did not finish the attack on the Presidential Palace the morning of November 11, to which Durbrow had constantly referred. If Ngô Đình Diệm was not the target, then why shed blood to capture him? It did not help the Karnow thesis that the paratroopers were not tricked into action by being told that Ngô Đình Diệm was in danger. If Vương Văn Đông or Nguyễn Chánh Thi were sincere in their objectives, as outlined to Karnow—removing Ngô Đình Diệm from power and placing him in a titular head-of-state position—then there was no reason that the paratroopers surrounding the Presidential Palace should have stopped, especially when there were an estimated twenty-nine of the Palace Guard left. It also does not explain why the paratroopers allowed the two companies of marines to enter the grounds unmolested to take up defensive positions that would hold the rebel paratroopers at bay. If anything, the off-the-record press conference–bull session signified the dissatisfaction that Durbrow and the foreign correspondents had with the Saigon government and demonstrated the limited perspective they were willing to grant Ngô Đình Diệm when exposing their inconsistencies, intuitive counter-arguments, or unsubstantiated facts they brought with them to the attempted coup d'état or took away after it failed.

While public demonstrations of Vietnamese support for Ngô Đình Diệm pervaded throughout the city, much of what private American citizens had to say helped the embassy staff confirm the Durbrow position, though in each case these individuals had a personal grievance against the Vietnamese or Ngô Đình Diệm's government that affected their work in South Vietnam and certainly would have influenced their observations. This did not seem to matter to the embassy personnel who looked for confirmation of Ngô Đình Diệm's shortcomings rather than reconciling their differences with the leader of the RVN. On November 14, embassy counselor Francis Cunningham received the Reverend John S. Sawin at his home on the advice of the U.S. embassy air attaché Lieutenant Colonel Butler Toland. Sawin had been in Vietnam for a number of years on a religious mission. He had experienced some difficulty with the Vietnamese Catholic priests in Cholon, where he was situated, who were also firm supporters of Ngô Đình Diệm. The priests were, as he put it, "quite unable to repent, and that when they had made mistakes they never admitted them and kept on asserting that they had been right."[28] Sawin's frustration with the Vietnamese was very similar to many Americans who spent time in Vietnam. The clash of culture and stubborn resistance on both sides often resulted in lamentation and bitterness.

Sawin informed Cunningham that the Vietnamese around his mission were very pleased with the early results of the coup d'état attempt and were glad to see the government fall.

When Sawin pursued this line of questioning, he learned that the real animosity was toward Ngô Đình Nhu, Madame Nhu, and Bishop Ngô Đình Thục, the older brother of Ngô Đình Diệm. Sawin also passed along an assertion that there was a strong feeling against Ngô Đình Cẩn, younger brother of Ngô Đình Diệm, who operated out of Central Vietnam, though he did not elaborate on his source for this information. Finally, Sawin observed that Ngô Đình Diệm would believe that, since he had been able to put down the November 11 attack, he was popular and had been governing correctly, just as Saigon Catholic priests never admitted their errors. Sawin's position in Saigon and perceived intimate knowledge of the local scene gave him credibility with Cunningham and the American embassy staff, which then reaffirmed to Durbrow the stubborn nature of Ngô Đình Diệm's resistance to change and failure as a leader to accept what Durbrow believed to be very sound counsel.

In a November 16 conversation between Mendenhall and Trần Văn Lắm, member of the National Assembly, the question of Ngô Đình Nhu and Madame Nhu again surfaced. Trần Văn Lắm was very critical of Madame Nhu, who he argued alienated Vietnamese women "because of her European education and modernism, and also alienates others by the way she handles herself."[29] Ngô Đình Nhu, on the other hand, while not a real politician, was crucial to Ngô Đình Diệm in handling southern politics, just as Ngô Đình Cẩn was vital for central politics. That same evening, Cunningham dined with the influential businessman and active member in the Vietnamese-American Association, Trần Đình An.[30] Before the food had reached the table, Trần Đình An expressed his concern for Ngô Đình Diệm and whether he would learn the right lessons from the coup d'état attempt. Trần Đình An believed that Ngô Đình Diệm "had been blinded by his entourage." In this case, Ngô Đình Nhu and Ngô Đình Cẩn were the ones who negatively influenced the president. American civilians in Saigon reinforced the anti–Ngô Đình Diệm feelings.

Dr. Luther Allen, a visiting professor from the University of Massachusetts who was housed at the University of Saigon, lashed out at the "autocratic president" in a November 15 *New York Times* editorial. He sympathized with the paratroopers who revolted "to force a change in Diem's dictatorial ways, which they charged were costing him popular support in the fight against mounting communist infiltration of South Vietnam."[31] Allen also lamented the fact that the abortive coup d'état killed 400 of Vietnam's best fighting soldiers and allowed the Việt Cộng to take advantage of the situation. Allen reported that his sources would not give up the fight against the Vietnamese dictator: "In whispers, Diem's disgruntled subjects predicted that another revolt was only a matter of time."[32] Of course, hindsight showed that a few of Allen's assertions, if not his final prediction, turned out to be false. The total number of servicemen wounded during the uprising was 214, while 54 civilians sought assistance at either the Cộng Hòa or Bình Dân hospital in Saigon.[33]

Allen was not the lone civilian to question Ngô Đình Diệm's right to rule. After the incident, American officials questioned their Vietnamese, French, and American contacts within Saigon to get a sense of the nature of the coup d'état. There was near consensus that the fall of the government had the tacit support of the citizens, though they continued to support Ngô Đình Diệm and hoped that the change of government would force Ngô Đình Diệm to confront those family members who surrounded and insulated the president.[34] Some elements of the educated Vietnamese society offered an alternative scenario for the coup d'état. University of Saigon professor Nguyễn Đình Hoà suggested that Ngô Đình Diệm orchestrated the event to demonstrate the loyalty of the people and armed forces to himself and to expose those in opposition to his continued rule.[35] This was not a plausible explanation, but it did give a sense of the limits to which the opposition would go to damage Ngô Đình Diệm's reputation and rule.

There was little question that the confused events surrounding the coup d'état and Vietnamese reaction to perceived American involvement helped to shape the events to come. Regardless of how Ngô Đình Diệm's brothers were viewed by the Vietnamese and American civilians in Saigon, their names appeared in most of the reporting that entered the embassy in the days following November 11. It did not take too much of a leap of faith to associate Ngô Đình Nhu and Ngô Đình Cẩn with the discontent that was under the surface in the major cities, as perceived by Durbrow and his staff, and it was easy for the American embassy to interpret Ngô Đình Diệm's nepotism as a sign that his rule in the RVN was at an end.

Durbrow was also very concerned about the reports coming from the Committee against Communists and Rebels, which had implicated the United States in the abortive coup d'état. He met with Nguyễn Đình Thuận on November 16 to discuss the matter and urged him to avoid trying to place the blame on others when the real cause was internal.[36] Durbrow also took the opportunity to reinforce the idea that Ngô Đình Diệm needed to be lenient with the rebels. Nguyễn Đình Thuận did not agree with Durbrow's statement, though he did concur with the idea that some reforms were needed to ensure that the lessons learned from the recent events were not lost. Durbrow would later report to Washington that "some hotheaded pro–Diem, probably Cần Lao, younger officials" were trying to distract attention away from the real causes of the abortive coup d'état, which he diagnosed as Ngô Đình Diệm.[37] This would be a recurring theme for Durbrow for the next few weeks.

At a November 17 press conference between Nguyễn Đình Thuận and members of the international press corps, the level of distrust and discord between those loyal to Ngô Đình Diệm and their American counterparts was finally publicly exposed.[38] The exchange also confirmed the level of animosity that now existed between the Saigon government and the American press.[39] The first question asked by the press was whether there had been any foreign intervention in the event of November 11. Nguyễn Đình Thuận responded simply and succinctly, "To our knowledge no foreign government has intervened in this attempted coup d'état."[40] Based on material and memoirs available for the four days following the event, it was clear that some Vietnamese within Ngô Đình Diệm's circle believed that the United States had failed to live up to its obligations as an ally and friend. Ngô Đình Diệm, however, denied the point when confronted by Durbrow following the press conference. The reporters present at the press conference, however, would not be satisfied with Nguyễn Đình Thuận's initial response, asking two more times immediately following the initial answer: once by rewording the question and the other time by introducing one of the leaflets drawn up by the People's Committee against the Communists and Rebels, which specifically pointed to the United States, France, and Britain.[41]

At first Nguyễn Đình Thuận repeated his response but then added, "I also wish to say that during these last months this government has been subjected to a systematic campaign of disparagement and some foreigners have echoed this campaign. And we do think that those foreigners are more or less responsible for the Vietnamese blood, which has been shed. If they were writers I would say that the fountain pen has been somewhat involved with the blood which has been shed here."[42] Nguyễn Đình Thuận then attempted to deflect the value of the leaflet by stating that it had not been printed by the committee but rather by the communists to cause discontent between the Vietnamese and Americans.

When countered with the statement that one of the correspondents had telephoned the committee office and confirmed that they had printed it, Nguyễn Đình Thuận, caught in a potentially embarrassing situation, asked for the name of the person who answered the telephone. He did not receive an answer, but in a follow-up question he was asked to further elaborate on an earlier statement that there had been a systematic campaign of disparagement driven by the media toward the Ngô Đình Diệm government. It was clear that Nguyễn Đình Thuận was losing control of the situation at the press conference. When he was questioned about government-sponsored reporters' stories, he replied, "On your side, you have to fulfill your duty, which is how to pass your cable through, and, on our side, we have to do our duty, too, as a government; that is, to prevent what we think might harm us."[43] It was clear by the end of the press conference that Nguyễn Đình Thuận believed that the American press, under the guidance or influence of American embassy officials, was the root cause of the coup d'état attempt. He represented the Saigon government's thinking at the time.

Nguyễn Đình Thuận ended the press conference by thanking the British and French press corps for their attempts at objectivity toward the Vietnamese. There was no mention of the American reporters. It was from this episode that the Saigon government's relationship with the American press turned. It had been negative up to this point; now it would be negative and targeted toward creating the conditions for a significant policy shift in Vietnam. The conflict that ensued, as Ngô Đình Diệm moved further away from American advice, relying more upon his own and his family, led the United States down a slippery slope to its inevitable and disadvantageous conclusion: the assassination of Ngô Đình Diệm and new, more intense American involvement in Vietnam.

As the press conference reached its end, McGarr received an urgent summons to meet with Ngô Đình Diệm. Ngô Đình Diệm had never made such a request in that manner before, so McGarr went immediately to the Presidential Palace with the expectation that his interpreter would follow. He was shown in upon arrival to speak with what was a clearly troubled president. As Ngô Đình Diệm was without an interpreter as well, the president spoke in English to the general, something he had never done up to that point in their three-month acquaintance. Ngô Đình Diệm felt the need to assure McGarr that he harbored no ill will toward the United States and wanted him to know that he had been very pleased with the support he had received from MAAG, from Lieutenant General John W. O'Daniel in 1954 to 1955 and Williams from 1955 to 1960, and especially including McGarr, who Ngô Đình Diệm believed had been a constant source of support in the troubling days of November.

Implied at that point, and later elaborated upon, was the lack of support Ngô Đình Diệm had received from other Americans, both civilians and within the embassy.[44] Ngô Đình Diệm was emphatic that he was not anti–American, though he was deeply troubled by the "campaign of disparagement" conducted by foreigners, including Americans and especially correspondents. He was also bothered by the fact that word had reached him that some Americans had also expressed regret that the coup d'état had not been successful. If Ngô Đình Diệm was merely echoing Nguyễn Đình Thuận's remarks at the press conference, he did want to assure McGarr that MAAG still had his confidence.

As the two continued their discussion, Ngô Đình Diệm asked that McGarr help his colleagues understand the value of not only listening to the "demagogues and rumor mongers" in Saigon but also the government. It seemed reasonable that government reports and evidence on the course of the war, the state of the union, and the progress toward significant reforms should be considered and regarded just as significantly as those coming from the opposition. To reinforce this obvious double standard, Ngô Đình Diệm questioned the loyalty and value of those "intellectuals and demagogues" in Saigon who criticized his government and demanded reforms but failed to offer any reliable or feasible solutions.[45] Ngô Đình Diệm believed he had a sympathetic colleague in McGarr, and it was reasonable to suggest that his respect for MAAG was not seriously diminished by the events of November 11 and 12. The same cannot be said for the diplomatic side of the American effort in the RVN.

Comments written on the McGarr–Ngô Đình Diệm memorandum of conversation that reached the embassy confirmed Ngô Đình Diệm's suspicion that the American embassy was not as sensitive. Handwritten notes, most likely from Mendenhall, on the copy of the memorandum of conversation McGarr sent to Durbrow suggest the state of animosity that had developed between the American diplomatic corps and the Ngô Đình Diệm government. Near the spot that Ngô Đình Diệm asked that government reports be given credence, Mendenhall wrote, "There is no question that more and more VN'ese are against entourage, arbitrary gov't, lack of coordinated effort against V.C., lack of some press freedom, corruption and arbitrary action by GVN functionaries. Does Diem have any dope to refute this?"[46] It would be easy to state that one was innocent until proven guilty unless that individual dared to go against the Americans, but Ngô Đình Diệm, Nguyễn Đình Thuận, and other Vietnamese officials had addressed these issues. The fact that the people of Saigon failed to support the coup d'état on the morning of November 12 or anywhere in South Vietnam should have given some pause to the assertion that the Vietnamese people were against Ngô Đình Diệm. While it was true that there were elements within Vietnamese society who did oppose Ngô Đình Diệm and his family, these individuals generally were ones who lived in the larger urban areas, had had the prospects for their future advancement stymied by the current Saigon government, or wished to govern the country, or parts of it, themselves for their own personal gain.

In short, Ngô Đình Diệm was correct to label them intellectuals and demagogues who were more apt to criticize than act; they were individuals who believed in the power of the word rather than force of the deed. That Ngô Đình Diệm did not give them credence, offer them concessions during a time of war, or bow down to the inevitability of their intellectual prowess was testament to his fortitude and ability to lead a country in difficult times. Mendenhall's comment, "Look in the mirror, Diem," next to the section where the president complains of his critics as being irresponsible was ironic, as it really foreshadowed what Mendenhall, Cunningham, and Durbrow should have been doing as they attempted to unite and concentrate their support for a major shift in American foreign policy away from the Ngô Đình Diệm government should he fail to significantly reform his administration within the year.[47]

Durbrow also kept up the pressure against Ngô Đình Diệm with his reporting of a conversation with Trần Văn Dĩnh, who had just been replaced as director of general information because of health reasons. Trần Văn Dĩnh spoke very critically of Ngô Đình Diệm and argued that Ngô Đình Nhu and Madame Nhu had to go. He confirmed many of the suspicions that Durbrow had maintained and offered credence to his view that Ngô Đình Diệm needed another "frank" talk.[48] Durbrow, however, believed that, since he had already given Ngô Đình Diệm two such talks, it was better that he waited. Instead, he worked to unify the message to Ngô Đình Diệm with the ambassadors of Britain, France, Australia, the Republic of Korea, and Japan. The basic thrust of the message was to be lenient with the rebels, initiate reforms, and get rid of Ngô Đình Nhu and Madame Nhu.[49] Essentially, Durbrow was expanding his organization of the diplomatic corps in Saigon against Ngô Đình Diệm to continue to apply pressure against the RVN president who was now embattled from within and without. Coupled with his work on the foreign press corps, Durbrow was slowly working to isolate Ngô Đình Diệm, whom he increasingly believed had run his course in the RVN.[50]

While the American embassy in Saigon rallied around the time-for-a-change banner, if not the Ngô-Đình-Diệm-has-to-go flag, officials in Washington were also assessing the fallout of the abortive coup d'état. Trần Văn Chương met with Parsons in Washington soon after the Nguyễn Đình Thuận press conference. Following the standard State Department line, Parsons offered his relief that Ngô Đình Diệm had survived the attempted coup d'état but expressed concern over the developments after November 11, with a specific mention of the People's Committee against Rebels and Communists leaflet accusing the United States of supporting the rebels. Parsons repeated to Trần Văn Chương what Durbrow had told him about the events and expressed his concern for the pamphlets: "It is strange to see such language employed against foreigners, especially those who have tried to help the regime."[51] While Parsons reassured Trần Văn Chương, who was father-in-law to Ngô Đình Nhu and therefore well connected with the Ngô family, that the United States did not believe the People's Committee against Communists and Rebels represented official Vietnamese policy, rumors that the leaflets had been passed out from the back of army trucks as well as the fact that someone in Vietnam would have had to approve the message was still disconcerting.

Parsons then commented on Nguyễn Đình Thuận's remarks about the campaign of disparagement and the fact that the Saigon government had not denounced it, finishing his views on the topic by reiterating that "any comments that we have made about certain problems faced by the GVN have always been made privately to high GVN officials and there has been no campaign of disparagement."[52] While this might have been true from Parsons' perspective as he looked to the events in Vietnam from Washington and relied on his ambassador for guidance and information, the same could not be said for those individuals in the RVN who, through a sympathetic ear or musing with reporters, gave almost daily reminders to Ngô Đình Diệm, his family, and supporters that America's diplomatic representatives in Saigon did not see eye-to-eye with the government.

Trần Văn Chương did not have a prepared answer to Parsons, though he promised to report their conversation to Saigon as soon as he could. As the meeting closed, the ambassador gave Parsons and Chalmers B. Wood, who was also in attendance, a copy of a *Le Monde Diplomatique* article, which had been written before November 11 and suggested that the United States supported the possibility of a coup d'état in Vietnam. Both Parsons and Wood denied the allegation. The article may not have been true, but in the environment of distrust and discord that emerged after the attempted coup d'état, any piece of evidence against the United States was seriously considered by the Vietnamese.

The division that existed between Durbrow and Ngô Đình Diệm could not be easily fixed, and Durbrow did not work on modifying his behavior to become a more trusted American representative in the RVN. His actions after the coup d'état might be explained by increased frustration in dealing with Ngô Đình Diệm or Durbrow's inability to shape Ngô Đình Diệm into the leader that he believed would become a more effective ally to the United States. It was possible that the three and a half years in Saigon had finally caught up with the ambassador, who had never spent so long in one post. Certainly, the leaflets of the People's Committee against the Communists and Rebels exposed a sensitive area for Durbrow even if it was not completely accurate, whereas his self-imposed isolation from Ngô Đình Diệm and McGarr's increased influence with the president must have played a role in the psyche of this proud and, up to this point, accomplish diplomat. Nonetheless, Durbrow's actions in his consultation and advice to Washington and his interaction with his fellow chiefs of mission in Saigon demonstrated the actions of a man who no longer served a useful role in the RVN. In many respects, he did more to harm the situation than help it.

Soon after the stabilization of the situation in Saigon, the State Department sent a draft congratulatory message from Eisenhower to Ngô Đình Diệm that expressed approval of his actions during the attempted coup d'état and encouraged American support for the Ngô Đình Diệm government in the months to come.[53] Durbrow, who had been asked to approve the message before it was sent, declined to do so for three reasons. First, he did not think Eisenhower should associate himself with Ngô Đình Diệm until the Vietnamese president had demonstrated a willingness to initiate reforms, or as he put it, grasped and heeded the lessons of the coup d'état, which Durbrow understood as a warning that the people of South Vietnam were frustrated and fed up with Ngô Đình Diệm's autocratic rule, of which the coup d'état was the first overt warning. Durbrow did not want Eisenhower to be connected with the ruthless, stubborn Ngô Đình Diệm who he believed was leading his country down a path of failure. Durbrow also was inclined to reject the congratulatory message because of the leaflets associated with the People's Committee against the Communists and Rebels, which had specifically mentioned the United States as an imperialistic and colonial power who had encouraged the rebels.

Second, Durbrow believed that an Eisenhower note would contradict and undermine the approach he had taken in the days following November 11 and 12 of using the event to force reforms. Finally, Durbrow believed that a presidential communication expressing support for Ngô Đình Diệm and encouragement as he led the Vietnamese people could potentially conflict with the position Durbrow believed the United States would have to take in the coming months. What was lost in the Durbrow reply to the State Department draft was the psychological effect the absence of a message from the president of the United States might have on the embattled leader of the RVN. Where Durbrow most likely maintained that the message would be a reward to Ngô Đình Diệm at a time that the ambassador believed him to be less than worthy, its absence also had the effect of confirming to Ngô Đình Diệm and his brothers that the possibility of American interests, if not actual encouragement, for the coup d'état now played a role in the American-Vietnamese relationship.

As Durbrow transmitted his recommendations against the Eisenhower letter, he also began rallying the chiefs of mission in Saigon toward his position in an attempt to consolidate a united front of international support for reforms in the Saigon government. Durbrow had meetings with British ambassador Roderick W. Parkes, French ambassador Roger Lalouette, Australian ambassador William Forsyth, Republic of Korean ambassador General Choi Duk Shin, and the Japanese ambassador, as well as the chairman of the International Supervisory and Control Commission, Gopala Menon of India. He reported a consensus of the chiefs of mission, which included a shared view on no retribution against the coup d'état plotters, pushing Ngô Đình Diệm to use the occasion to act as a statesmen, and agreement that Ngô Đình Nhu and Madame Nhu had to leave the government but that the timing was not yet right.[54] As such, Durbrow urged his fellow diplomats to push Ngô Đình Diệm as he had been doing in order to achieve some results. Durbrow worried that their failure to get through to Ngô Đình Diệm might result in his following the hard-liners in Vietnam, represented by the People's Committee against Communists and Rebels.

Durbrow had every reason to fear that Ngô Đình Diệm was moving in the wrong direction; he had received confirming reports that both Ngô Đình Diệm and Ngô Đình Nhu were upset by American press accounts of the Saigon government and stories that called for the removal of Ngô Đình Nhu. Durbrow recommended that the United States not pressure Ngô Đình Diệm, for fear that it would push him closer to the position of the People's Committee against Communists and Rebels.[55] In the same breath, however, Durbrow maintained the position that if Ngô Đình Diệm did not begin serious reforms, then the United States must deliver an ultimatum to Ngô Đình Diệm to get rid of Ngô Đình Nhu and his wife or face a situation where the entire American policy in Vietnam would be reconsidered.

In what was clearly a contradiction of his earlier statement about not applying pressure, Durbrow outlined what he thought his instructions should be when talking next to Ngô Đình Diệm. First, Durbrow maintained that he should take the position that the United States was considering the request for the 20,000-man addition, but it would never act without the transfer of Ngô Đình Nhu. Durbrow would not mention Ngô Đình Nhu by name, but he would specifically refer to their October 14 conversation, during which he had suggested that Ngô Đình Nhu was a problem and might need to be transferred overseas. In Durbrow's reasoning, "to give him more force before he has taken drastic action in the political, psychological, social and economic fields would not rectify the situation."[56] The State Department, removed from the intensity of the Saigon situation, did not succumb to Durbrow's point of view, instructing the ambassador to speak to Ngô Đình Diệm in a relaxed tone, express his gratitude that the coup d'état had failed, and encourage him to announce the moderate reforms already agreed to in principle.[57]

The reforms in question, according to Nguyễn Đình Thuận who relayed them to an embassy officer on a strictly personal and confidential basis included the establishment of a National Economic Council charged with assessing the various sectors of the Vietnamese economy and offering advice to the government.[58] They also included greater freedom of the press, which had been introduced to the National Assembly before November 11, so long as it did not promote the communist position, as well as expanding the authority of the National Assembly in overseeing governmental department budgets. There would also be a reorganization of the ministries and changes in the cabinet. Finally, and most important to the war effort, the government acknowledged the need to place the Civil Guard under the Ministry of Defense in order to reorganize, train, and equip it. The final reform was not totally complete as province chiefs still had access to the Civil Guard, but the coordination between the commanders of the military regions and the Civil Guard did increase.

McGarr's conversation with Ngô Đình Diệm marked another rift that had developed as a result of the November 11 events, though in this case it involved a split on the American side. For some time, Durbrow and his principle supporters in the embassy had caused other Americans as well as Vietnamese to question their effectiveness and practice of trying to place what amounted to an ultimatum on Ngô Đình Diệm to reform his government. Earlier in the year, Lansdale had cautioned that to be effective in Saigon, you had to talk with Ngô Đình Diệm rather than talk to him, but Durbrow never managed that skill, preferring instead to conduct a series of frank discussions. Members of the Saigon government had already questioned Durbrow's conduct during the coup d'état attempt. In Washington, approximately a week after the event, the rift in American thinking divided roughly along a military–diplomatic split became more pronounced.

A State Department–JCS meeting on November 18 confirmed the differences of opinion.[59] Chief of Staff of the Army General Lyman Louis Lemnitzer indicated that he was concerned by the strength of Durbrow's messages from November 11 and 12 that stressed the need to avoid bloodshed and, as such, promoted a mentality of compromise for Ngô Đình Diệm during a time of armed treason. Lemnitzer argued that Ngô Đình Diệm had to act decisively, which meant that he could not have possibly avoided the loss of life: "We are against bloodshed as much as anyone but when you have rebellious forces against you, you have to act forcibly and not restrain your friends."[60] This position was a reasonable one even if it was discouraged by Durbrow, who believed that Ngô Đình Diệm did not have the right to react in such a way to those who opposed him.

Deputy Assistant Secretary of Defense for International Security Affairs Robert H. Knight, in his attempt to defend Durbrow's action, under-represented the nature of the abortive coup d'état by suggesting that it was only three companies of rebel paratroopers rather than the whole airborne brigade plus the two companies of marines and other troops.[61] Deputy Under-Secretary of State for Political Affairs Livingston Merchant did not believe Durbrow was trying to weaken Ngô Đình Diệm's position by his actions, but Merchant did not have the full records and most likely would not have called out his State Department colleagues as easily as had Lemnitzer. Lemnitzer was approaching the situation as an outsider and made what was a very practical observation. While he might not have had the experience of living in Vietnam or the interaction with Ngô Đình Diệm as had Durbrow, his conclusions did have a level of common sense to them. One does not try to dictate how an ally should respond during a time of internal crisis if that advice does not offer full, unwavering support and allow for some flexibility, depending upon the local conditions, to guide the action. Others, who had as much experience in Vietnam as Durbrow, shared Lemnitzer's commonsense approach. As each side began to express their view, the rift widened.

Lansdale had been in contact with McGarr through November, and the two shared much information about the military situation in Vietnam, often without informing Durbrow or the embassy. The McGarr/Lansdale conflict with Durbrow and his team stemmed from the disagreement about the 20,000-man increase for the RVN's armed forces. Toward the end of November, the Department of Defense suggested that Lansdale travel to Vietnam as part of a larger trip to Southeast Asia to appraise the situation and make recommendations for Department of Defense action.[62] Durbrow believed a visit to Saigon was in order despite the public objections Hanoi would offer to the international media outlets, provided Lansdale did two things: follow the Department of State's instructions and cooperate fully and openly with Durbrow. Durbrow expected Lansdale to report to him after speaking with Ngô Đình Diệm and stressed that Lansdale needed to help him persuade Ngô Đình Diệm to make political, economic, and military reforms.[63] This, in itself, was a little condescending as the suggestion that Lansdale was the loose cannon reminded one of Mendenhall's comments on the McGarr November 17 memorandum of conversation with Ngô Đình Diệm in which Mendenhall mused that Ngô Đình Diệm should look in the mirror. While Durbrow concurred with the Lansdale trip, he did so despite the fact that he believed that Lansdale had already acted improperly. Durbrow believed that Lansdale had sent Jerome French, a member of the Office of the Assistant to the Secretary of Defense for Special Operations, to Saigon immediately after the coup d'état attempt to serve as his source on the ground. While in Saigon, Durbrow claimed that French, who subsequently traveled throughout the city, dismissed his military escort officer at one point and made several unscheduled visits to the Vietnamese, including Nguyễn Đình Thuận and Võ Văn Hải. Durbrow argued that French was not authorized to speak to these Vietnamese and was only in the city to discuss the military situation with MAAG officers. Durbrow also complained that French made no effort to contact the embassy to report these contacts or his mission. Implied by Durbrow was the assertion that Lansdale, through his proxy French, had worked to undermine the plans Durbrow and his staff had been formulating for the RVN and especially their efforts to force Ngô Đình Diệm to concede to political, economic, military, and other reforms that Durbrow believed necessary if South Vietnam was to survive. The Lansdale mission, so Durbrow assumed, would have the same objectives just without the proxy.

As soon as Lansdale received word of Durbrow's communication with the State Department, he wrote to Parsons with his version of the events.[64] Lansdale was stunned by Durbrow's implied criticisms as French, who had been attending SEATO's committee of security experts meeting in Bangkok was asked to visit Saigon as well as Manila, Okinawa, and CINC-PAC to discuss Department of Defense issues. On his way to Saigon, French's plane had been diverted to Phnom Penh because the coup d'état was in progress. He returned to Bangkok after checking in with the embassy and took the first Air France flight to Saigon on November 14. Thus, French's visit to Saigon had been planned and not a result of the coup d'état. Lansdale did not deny that French met with several Vietnamese, but their encounters were not in an official capacity. He had been very close friends with Nguyễn Đình Thuận and Võ Văn Hải before the trip. French did report his findings to Lansdale, who, in turn, transmitted that information to the Secretary of Defense, Thomas Gates, as well as Knight. As Lansdale would comment to Parsons, the subject of the discussions did not warrant official notification to the embassy. Lansdale also informed Parsons that French had no military escort officer in Saigon, which made it rather difficult to respond to the accusation that he dismissed him.

Durbrow's version of the events, especially with the dismissal of the escort, gave the impression that French had something to hide. Without the officer and that action, it lessened the intrigue. Lansdale might have been playing with the truth in his letter to Parsons, since it was difficult to believe French would not have discussed the specifics or consequences of the events of November 11 and 12 with Nguyễn Đình Thuận and Võ Văn Hải, as they were as close as Lansdale suggested. Later, French would confirm that he had discussions related to family but also touched on the abortive coup d'état and its effects for the RVN.[65] In French's first report to Lansdale on November 17, he suggested ending his Southeast Asian trip immediately because of the deteriorating conditions in South Vietnam to which Lansdale concurred. This assessment might have been reached through his discussions with MAAG officers even though evidence suggested that the Việt Cộng did not take advantage of the attempted coup d'état to increase their activity. It was safe to make the assumption that French's conversations with Nguyễn Đình Thuận and Võ Văn Hải went beyond keeping in touch with old friends on family news as Lansdale suggested, but Durbrow's implied fear that French had undermined the embassy went too far.[66]

About a week later, French would confirm the timeline of his adventure to Saigon and weigh in on the Vietnamese contact issue and his failure to report to the embassy. Both Nguyễn Đình Thuận and Võ Văn Hải did provide French with information about the coup d'état attempt and its effects on South Vietnam's internal security as well as their assessment of Việt Cộng activity. While French did not report the conversation to the embassy, he did inform McGarr about the non-personal parts of the conversations. A copy of the encounter with Nguyễn Đình Thuận and Võ Văn Hải, though their names are not specifically mentioned, and French's observations on the situation in Vietnam after the coup d'état were transmitted to Parsons on December 6.

French's observations, which were formulated by his Vietnam experience and personal connections, echo the commonsense pattern established by Lemnitzer in his outsider-looking-in comments earlier. The dissatisfaction within the Saigon community did exist—even Ngô Đình Diệm admitted as such—though French believed that discord had been strengthened by the inability to improve Vietnam's internal security and the constant flow of rumors and hearsay. According to French, Ngô Đình Diệm had lost his connection to the people of Saigon, though, as had been reported through other sources, Ngô Đình Nhu and Ngô Đình Cẩn were becoming the focal point for the discontentment. For Nguyễn Đình Thuận and Võ Văn Hải, the main problem for Ngô Đình Diệm was the political intrigue and appearance of arbitrary action by the Saigon government. Both men called for reform, but neither believed that this reform or the fight against the communist threat could be accomplished without Ngô Đình Diệm. What was significant in French's observations and was also confirmation of the American split was his assessment of Durbrow and his staff:

> Unfortunately it would appear that many people in the U.S. community in Saigon have forfeited their ability to render a constructive influence on the Vietnamese Government by short-sighted and ill-conceived words and actions during and immediately following the Coup attempt. These people, apparently victims of rumors and their own bias against Diem, were quick to assume the Coup attempt was a popular movement and Diem would be toppled. Their expressions of sympathy for the rebel cause, both during and after the Coup attempt, have been extremely damaging to U.S. interests in Vietnam.[67]

The same could be said for the People's Committee against Communists and Rebels. Durbrow and his supporters on the Country Team chose only to focus on the negative aspects of the group. They did not report such stories as the one that appeared on November 25, which disavowed any connection between the committee and posters placed throughout Saigon that denounced individuals allegedly associated with the abortive coup d'état.[68] There was no reporting from the embassy that discussed the over $1,750,000 piasters (U.S. $50,000) raised by the group, which went to the families of the killed and wounded during the November 11–12 period. Other events by the committee, such as the organization of entertainment programs for military units in remote places and the sponsorship of certain units also received no attention from the U.S. embassy. Durbrow, Mendenhall, and their members of the Country Team chose to report only the negative while, at the same time, expressing their sympathy and support for Ngô Đình Diệm. This duplicity would not go unnoticed.

Only McGarr had access to, and the confidence of, Ngô Đình Diệm in the immediate aftermath of the attempted coup d'état. As such, according to French who was representative of the military side of this debate, the only way the Americans could regain Ngô Đình Diệm's trust and convince him that the United States was sincere in its commitment as an ally to the RVN was to approve the 20,000-man addition to the armed forces, provide the much needed H-34 helicopters, and increase the number of special forces advisers to combat the Việt Cộng in the countryside. Vietnam had to be given a high priority because of the real threat that existed before November 11 and the emergency that emerged afterward.

It was not until November 26 that Durbrow next met with Ngô Đình Diệm.[69] Durbrow believed that Ngô Đình Diệm had purposely kept the ambassador away, postponing a November 22 meeting in order to punish Durbrow for purportedly supporting the coup d'état attempt. Ngô Đình Diệm had claimed to be sick, which Durbrow concluded was nothing more than an amateur attempt at diplomatic isolation. When he discovered that Ngô Đình Diệm had actually been sick, he was forced to admit that he had been incorrect. Durbrow believed Ngô Đình Diệm was playing the same diplomatic and political game that he had been practicing; Ngô Đình Diệm simply had an inflamed throat.

Durbrow opened their discussion, as he had been instructed, by once again congratulating him on surviving the events of November 11 and 12 and limiting the bloodshed. He then brought up reforms. The two discussed the nature of reform. Ngô Đình Diệm believed it was most important to help the villagers by actually doing something for them. He had ordered his ministries to send their best people to the villages, including recent graduates of medical programs. Ngô Đình Diệm complained, as he had done before with both Durbrow and McGarr, that too many in Saigon criticized his government, made speeches about helping the peasants, but ended up doing nothing constructive. Ngô Đình Diệm was correct in pointing out that too many bureaucrats enjoyed living in Saigon and the other big cities in South Vietnam and did not want to sacrifice their standard of living by moving to the countryside. When Durbrow questioned Ngô Đình Diệm on elections at the district, province, and national levels for the National Economic Council, Ngô Đình Diệm returned to his theme of strengthening the village-level governance first before real progress could be achieved at a higher level. The only election Ngô Đình Diệm had planned was to add younger members to the village councils in order for the youth to gain a voice in the village. This was hardly the degree of reform that Durbrow had envisioned.

The two then reviewed Ngô Đình Diệm's expected decree that shifted training and equipment procurement of the Civil Guard from the Ministry of the Interior to the Ministry of Defense. Durbrow worried that the decree would not go far enough in removing the Interior's control over the individual units, which also made it difficult for the United States to provide MAP equipment to it. The Civil Guard was an integral part of the network of units protecting the villages from the Việt Cộng. It required MAP equipment, but it also needed to have better coordination with the ARVN commanders. In Durbrow's mind, the conversation was encouraging, especially given recent events, as it provided evidence that Ngô Đình Diệm understood the importance of the village in the battle against the communist insurgency, though he did question exactly how the Civil Guard would reorganize under the decree and remained unsure whether these reforms would be implemented in time or be effective in the overall battle. On November 22, Decision No. 272-NV placed the Civil Guard temporarily under the responsibility of the Ministry of Defense, allowing this ministry to reorganize, train, and equip the Civil Guard.[70]

The days following the abortive coup d'état were troubling for the Vietnamese and Americans, albeit for different reasons. For Durbrow and the embassy, there was a great concern that Ngô Đình Diệm would lash out against those who had conspired against him. When this did not occur, the Americans maintained the message but also returned to the themes of reform, corruption, and the elimination of Ngô Đình Nhu and Madame Nhu. The Vietnamese responded through the actions of the People's Committee against Communists and Rebels as Ngô Đình Diệm worked to return his Republic back to the right path. While Ngô Đình Diệm did not directly and publicly support the People's Committee against

Communists and Rebels, it was clear that he supported and was likely helping to direct its frustration against those who had either directly or indirectly supported the abortive coup d'état. He continued to maintain his relationship with McGarr and MAAG, but the events of November 11 and the week that followed made reconciliation with Durbrow and his cohorts almost impossible.

9

Returning to Normality

With Saigon calm, the People's Committee against Communists and Rebels all but dissolved, and the abortive coup d'état receded from the headlines, the United States and RVN returned to the important matters at hand as the Year of the Rat came to a close.[1] Of primary importance to Ngô Đình Diệm was the need to increase the ARVN to 170,000 men in order to better combat the Việt Cộng threat in the RVN. The 20,000-man addition had been a priority for the RVN for more than a few years, but for the United States, specifically Durbrow and his Department of State, it was not seen as a necessity but rather as an incentive to induce reforms from the Saigon government or a clumsy attempt by Ngô Đình Diệm to garner more aid from the United States.

When queried by Ngô Đình Diệm about the proposed increase to ARVN, Durbrow chose to focus on reforms to liberalize Vietnamese society and its government.[2] Ngô Đình Diệm became annoyed with this exchange. The RVN was at war, and as such, certain conditions needed to be understood. Ngô Đình Diệm saw little difference between his actions and those of Franklin Roosevelt during the Second World War. That Durbrow failed to make this connection, at least to Ngô Đình Diệm's satisfaction, when other world leaders acknowledged it, resulted in increased tension between the president and the lead representative of the United States in Vietnam.

For Ngô Đình Diệm, the Americans did not understand the situation in Vietnam, and it seemed to him that Durbrow toyed with the Vietnamese in a dangerous game of diplomatic carrot and stick. Conversely, Durbrow and other American decision makers remained skeptical of Ngô Đình Diệm's growing insistence that his strategies and tactics be employed. As a result, the question again resurfaced as to whether the president should continue in office.

In late October 1960, MAAG formulated a plan to deal with the insurgency problem.[3] The plan generated much discussion in Washington and Saigon among military and diplomatic circles, with Durbrow and McGarr at opposite ends. Durbrow had called for the plan earlier in the year in part to embarrass Williams and keep him busy and out of the way as he neared his departure date from Saigon. With the attempted coup d'état, much of the discussion on the MAAG plan was delayed until after normalcy returned to Saigon and was diverted while Durbrow was engaged in his frank talks with Ngô Đình Diệm and organizing the Saigon diplomatic corps to push for reforms. It would not be until the end of November that the MAAG plan returned as the focus of American efforts. By this time, the military–diplomatic split that had transpired as a result of the American response to the abortive coup d'état had already been established. The debate on the MAAG plan reaffirmed the American difference of opinion on what to do in South Vietnam and highlighted the disparity of view on Ngô Đình Diệm as the Vietnamese president.

The original October 27 MAAG report was a response to several factors that had occurred in South Vietnam from 1959, including the Agroville Program, the increase in Việt Cộng activity, and the introduction of McGarr to the position of chief of MAAG, Saigon. The main purpose of the document was to outline a counter-insurgency plan that both the United States and RVN could follow to achieve maximum effect. The report helped to identify Vietnamese needs that would, in turn, allow American assistance to be more effective. Of particular concern for MAAG was the increased nature of Việt Cộng activity, which included armed propaganda, taxation of Vietnamese peasants, kidnapping and murder of village and hamlet officials, ambushes, and more bold attacks against Agrovilles and military outposts.

The report's recommendations of an increase in the Civil Guard, increased intelligence at the village level, and more effective psychological warfare were all mentioned as vital. From these objectives, MAAG, with the concurrence of Ngô Đình Diệm and the Vietnamese military, agreed that an increase in the armed forces of 20,000 men plus a reorganization of the Civil Guard under the Ministry of Defense, and the establishment of a strong intelligence infrastructure, were keys to turning the situation around.

Durbrow provided his comments on the MAAG plan to Parsons on November 8, just three days before the attempted coup d'état.[4] While he concurred with the MAAG plan in most of its recommendations, he disagreed with the idea of increasing the armed forces by 20,000 men. Durbrow did not dispute the need for a larger security force or a centralized intelligence agency that worked at the village level, but he maintained that these needs could be met by increasing the training of the Civil Guard. Durbrow did not believe that South Vietnam would effectively utilize the additional troops, because Ngô Đình Diệm had failed, in his eyes, to use the security forces at his disposal in an efficient manner. Thus Durbrow argued that better use of existing resources was preferable to adding to the inefficient system. Additionally, Durbrow asserted that an approval of the 20,000-man increase would reaffirm to Ngô Đình Diệm that the only way to defeat the Việt Cộng was by force. Durbrow believed that force had to be accompanied by political, social, and economic reforms coupled with psychological operations designed to win the people to the government's side.

The combination of military and non-military efforts to defeat the enemy and win over the population was a sound idea, though it did not take into account the importance of strength as a rule in Vietnamese society. Strong emperors and territorial leaders in Vietnam's 2,000-plus-year history marked the periods of expansion, prosperity, and stability. This perspective on strength made it paramount for the Vietnamese government to rule from a strong position. As a result, political, social, and economic reforms or psychological operations would not be effective unless the communist insurgency was made impotent. This meant that the armed forces had to have a constant presence in the countryside, as a show of strength, to combat the Việt Cộng. The RVN armed forces needed more men to accomplish this goal. A reform movement without this military strength or the defeat of the Việt Cộng would be perceived as a weakness even if, in Western terms, it were not viewed as such. Durbrow's plan to use the 20,000-man increase as a club to force Ngô Đình Diệm into these reforms would do nothing more than push the president further away from his American allies.

Durbrow offered two alternatives to the 20,000-man increase. The first was the reorganization of the ARVN away from a corps model and toward smaller units operating in equal numbers to the Việt Cộng units and fighting a guerrilla-type war. Elimination of the corps, which had been the original plan for the ARVN because of the fear of a conventional attack across the 17th parallel at the DMZ, would free up trained individuals who had been assigned staff duty with corps and other headquarter units. This was something that Ngô Đình Diệm had called for at the beginning of the year. Durbrow indicated that both Ngô Đình Diệm and Nguyễn Đình Thuận had complained of the over-staffing within the ARVN, while Nguyễn Đình Thuận provided Durbrow with a study that showed that 3,000 men would become available if corps and division headquarters were eliminated. Durbrow argued that this option might be used to fulfill a significant number of the 20,000-man increase proposed by MAAG. He also advocated spending American dollars on training, advising, and equipping the Civil Guard to take over some of the static duties of the ARVN.

MAAG was already involved in improving 32,000 of the 54,000 Civil Guard that existed. Rather than add 20,000 troops to the payroll, Durbrow suggested that MAAG train all 54,000 of the Civil Guard. As these troops already had some training and cohesion as units, it would take considerably less time to improve the lot than the two years MAAG estimated it would take to bring the armed forces up from 150,000 to 170,000. Durbrow did not forward his comments to McGarr because Admiral Felt canceled his trip to Saigon, which had been scheduled to begin on November 11. Before McGarr could respond, the abortive coup d'état occurred and the debate on the MAAG report was delayed. When the discussions on the report resurfaced, the atmosphere in Saigon had changed dramatically.

McGarr responded to Durbrow's comments on the MAAG report in an undated paper probably written around November 20 or 21. In it, McGarr and his MAAG advisers agreed that the best way to defeat the increased Việt Cộng activity was a coordinated plan of increased military, political, social, economic, and psychological assets.[5] While the Việt Cộng had to be defeated, MAAG acknowledged the necessity of winning over the population. The two objectives were intertwined; the successful completion of one made it possible to achieve the other. As such, both had to be aggressively pursued rather than using one to force Ngô Đình Diệm to do the other as Durbrow had suggested before November 11.

McGarr argued that the 20,000-man increase in strength for the armed forces would accomplish several goals: It would allow for the real possibility of rotation of troops away from the battlefield. MAAG had observed the problems in morale and unit cohesion that were a result of being in the field too long and away from family or the opportunities for rest and recuperation. Not only would an increase in the troop level help to alleviate this problem, but it would also allow for greater training opportunities for the ARVN units. The increase would also help with the surveillance of the difficult terrain throughout Vietnam and along its long border and coastline. The physical space, coupled with rugged terrain, demanded a larger force. In addition to surveillance, the additional troops would improve intelligence capabilities by adding assets in the field and an organized intelligence-gathering unit. These troops were also necessary to operate and maintain the additional H-34 helicopters needed in the counter-insurgency effort to provide the advantage of air mobility as well as close air support. Finally, these new troops would aid in correcting the differences in logistics present in the armed forces and act as a deterrent against increased Việt Cộng activities.

McGarr concurred with eliminating the headquarters of the military regions and the field command, per Durbrow's recommendation, but he did not think that the number of personnel who would be freed for action was significant. He also stressed the importance of adequate training for the Civil Guard as well as equipping it to perform its function. MAAG believed the new troops and improved training and equipment of the Vietnamese forces could be completed in eighteen months rather than the originally stated two years. McGarr agreed that these reasons alone were enough to approve the increase, though such a commitment by the United States would also have the effect of showing Ngô Đình Diệm the extent of American support for his government and improve its bargaining position as the diplomats pushed for political, social, and economic reforms to help win the hearts and minds of the people. McGarr argued against making the troop increase a significant bargaining chip for the United States. Any delay in increasing the armed forces or improving the Civil Guard would have lasting effects in all aspects of South Vietnam's internal security and could, he warned, result in a situation from which the United States would not be able to extradite itself or save the RVN from a communist takeover.

In his November 21 letter to Admiral Felt, McGarr enclosed a copy of the MAAG comments handed to Durbrow.[6] McGarr emphasized the need to approve the increase even though he and Durbrow did not agree. Because of the disagreement between the military and diplomats in Saigon, McGarr believed that the decision would have to be made in Washington between the Department of State and the Department of Defense. He did warn Felt that Ngô Đình Diệm had repeatedly called for the increase and would most likely proceed with or without American assistance as he had done earlier when he wanted to expand the ranger units and did so in March. McGarr argued that "a prompt decision favoring the force increase would permit the MAAG to condition the approval of the increase on the establishment of proper type units and proper utilization of all forces available."[7] Essentially, McGarr argued that not only was the force needed, but also the United States would be better served to initiate the process rather than have to respond to Ngô Đình Diệm who already understood the importance of the increased number of troops to South Vietnam and would act on his own if necessary.

Durbrow's response to the MAAG comment and the Felt letter occurred nine days later in a letter to Parsons.[8] He continued to voice his opposition to the increase. He did not think that the reforms Ngô Đình Diệm or Nguyễn Đình Thuận had revealed to him earlier were significant enough to make a difference, nor did he think that the reforms would provide the catalyst necessary to reverse the anti–Ngô Đình Diệm feeling in South Vietnam. Durbrow never reported the mass demonstrations for Ngô Đình Diệm and the Republic throughout South Vietnam after the abortive coup d'état, preferring instead to rely on American and Vietnamese intellectuals who had made contact with himself, Mendenhall, and Cunningham. Durbrow, in his letter to Parsons, reaffirmed his belief that the only way to make Ngô Đình Diệm begin the necessary reforms was to hold back the one thing he needed and wanted—the 20,000-man increase. Durbrow mentioned that the force would have no value unless the reforms were initiated. For Durbrow, the two American objectives were not intertwined. The troop increase would not bring about the reforms or victory. Only reforms, before the increase, would make the extra commitment of resources worthwhile. Holding back the troops that Ngô Đình Diệm and MAAG believed were essential to fighting the communist insurgency in order to force Ngô Đình Diệm's hand was a dangerous gamble, but it was also indicative of how Durbrow viewed his relationship with the president of the RVN.

Durbrow's position represented a strategy of failure in the volatile Saigon atmosphere with an increased communist insurgency determined to overthrow the legitimate leader of South Vietnam. In Vietnam, Ngô Đình Diệm was also making moves to highlight the need to increase the 150,000-man ARVN ceiling. On November 22, he issued a presidential decree that suspended the discharge of reserve officers and non-commissioned officers while also recalling those who had been recently discharged.[9] The Vietnamese justification for this move was the 1,475 officer and 4,354 NCO shortfall in the ARVN based upon a 150,000-man force. Durbrow, however, believed that Ngô Đình Diệm was angling to get his additional 20,000 men and that this decree was designed to help justify the increase. While this might have been true, it was also a reality that the RVN was under an increased threat from the Việt Cộng, who would soon be making an even stronger move to overthrow the Saigon government. Ngô Đình Diệm also issued a decree that transferred the responsibility for training and equipping the Civil Guard to the Ministry of Defense from the Ministry of the Interior.[10]

The JCS agreed with the MAAG report on the need to increase the air mobility requirements for the ARVN. A memorandum from Vice Chief of Staff for the U.S. Air Force General Curtis E. LeMay to Secretary Gates recommended that the Department of the Army provide eleven H-34 helicopters with ground-support equipment and spare parts.[11] The helicopters had been another point of difference between the diplomats and the military personnel in Saigon. Durbrow did not feel that Ngô Đình Diệm deserved the reward or that his armed forces would be able to utilize the equipment properly. Helicopters did not equate to reform. When Eisenhower received a special note from the Department of Defense on the deteriorating conditions in Southeast Asia, he penciled in the comment, "If we do—then now!"[12] It appeared that round one had gone to McGarr.

On November 23, the USS *Card* arrived in Saigon with seven AD-6 Skyraider aircraft to replace some of the older F-8F fighter aircraft that the Vietnamese air force had been using. This version of the single-engine, propeller-driven Douglas Aircraft Corporation Skyraider aircraft, developed originally as a carrier-based fighter bomber, would prove to be an effective weapon for the South Vietnamese as well as the United States later in the war as it developed into the A-1 Skyraider.[13] The same day, the United States transferred its chaser USS *Anacortes* (PC 1569) to the South Vietnamese navy in a ceremony in Seattle. The ship, which would operate under Lieutenant Trịnh Xuân Phong, was renamed VNS *Vân Đồn*, when it was officially commissioned in the Vietnamese navy on March 24, 1961.[14] As the American military exerted its influence in Southeast Asia, Durbrow organized a counter-action to emphasize the importance of diplomacy and reform.

Because Durbrow's moves since the abortive coup d'état continued to apply pressure on the Vietnamese, it should not have been surprising that Ngô Đình Diệm and Ngô Đình Nhu would react in a more formal setting. Abandoning leaflets and public committees, both men complained to British ambassador to the RVN Henry Hohler on November 28 about the United States, knowing that their words would reach Durbrow.[15] They argued that the Americans in Vietnam did not understand them, citing the futile efforts of Nguyễn Đình Thuận earlier in the year when he was in Washington trying to garner more military aid, while Ngô Đình Diệm asserted that the U.S. would abandon the RVN just as it had abandoned China a little over ten years earlier. When questioned by Hohler, both men refocused their anger toward the American press who had been printing stories based on rumors.

It is clear that neither Ngô Đình Diệm nor Ngô Đình Diệm Nhu were comfortable with American influence in the RVN while both wanted to move forward with more American aid that was not encumbered by unnecessary or controversial demands. In another instance, Nguyễn Đình Thuận offered a sarcastic comment to the director of USOM, Arthur

Gardiner, on the American suggestion that if the RVN wanted to temporarily end conscription, it would have to pay for the cost. Durbrow reported to Washington that Nguyễn Đình Thuận remarked to Ngô Đình Diệm, "This was the first time we have ever received authorization to spend our own money."[16] In the post–abortive coup d'état atmosphere, tensions still ran high.

Ironically, the South Vietnamese were trying to mend relations with the foreign and Vietnamese reporters by creating a more open relationship. In a December 3 press conference, General Director of Information Trần Văn Thọ implored the media to share in the burden of responsibility to defend human liberty.[17] *Cách mạng Quốc gia* had already set a recent precedent with a December 1 editorial that blamed government personnel who had remained aloof from the people and failed to motivate them toward the goals of the Republic as a reason why the communists had been so successful to that point.[18] Nguyễn Ngọc Thơ, who had recently assumed the position of general director of information, argued that his primary objective was "to fight Communism as it encroaches upon the dignity of the human being and on the progress of the masses."[19] In fulfilling this goal, Nguyễn Ngọc Thơ agreed to meet with the newsmen every week and forewarned of some major reforms within the government that would be announced soon.

In another attempt to improve relations with the media, the Saigon government announced on December 9 that it would create an Information Office to assist both the foreign and Vietnamese press.[20] Nguyễn Ngọc Thơ called for the new office to help disseminate information from the government but also to serve as a resource for reporters to ensure that their queries would be answered correctly and quickly. In this vein, the Radio Broadcasting Service was also integrated into the Information Office. Nguyễn Ngọc Thơ believed this office was important given the fact that the Việt Cộng were very successful in taking advantage of any errors in reporting.

Saigon would also see the creation of three new Vietnamese-language dailies by the end of December, bringing its total up to twenty-three.[21] The *Sài Gòn Mai*, edited by Ngô Quận, a retired army captain and former editor within the Defense Ministry; Dương Chí Sanh's *Sài Gòn Thời Báo*, who was in a leadership position in the National Revolutionary Movement; and *Đồng Nai*, directed by National Assemblyman for the Socialist Alliance Huỳnh Thành Vị, joined the twenty other dailies in Saigon. Additionally, the Saigon government announced that the National Press Club would be run by newspapermen rather than the government. This move was seen by many as a step toward a more liberalized Vietnamese press.[22] While the Saigon government worked to improve its situation along the lines suggested by the Americans, the test of wills between Durbrow and McGarr continued.

Durbrow did not give in to the MAAG report because he was convinced that the United States, that is to say Durbrow, would lose its position in guiding Ngô Đình Diệm. The 20,000-man debate was a real opportunity to force Ngô Đình Diệm to conform to Durbrow's way of thinking. In a December 4 telegram to Washington, Durbrow continued his line of reasoning.[23] While he acknowledged that the Việt Cộng activity had diminished since November 11, he believed it to be a lull before the storm rather than a benefit of the armed forces being on full alert and active throughout the countryside. Durbrow even conceded that the reforms promised by Ngô Đình Diệm, Ngô Đình Nhu, and Nguyễn Đình Thuận were of the right quality even if he still feared that the reforms might end up being nothing more than reforms on the surface with little or no substance. Durbrow was even forced to admit that Ngô Đình Diệm, after three weeks, had not taken the vengeful approach he feared would materialize after the abortive coup d'état, though he did repeat the assertions received from the Saigon elite and intellectuals that actions of the People's Committee against Rebels and Communists were unfortunate. The only mention of the money distributed by the committee or the countless hours of morale boosting and comfort given to the wounded soldiers and the families of victims of the events in November was buried in the WEEKA No. 48 for November 26.[24] The committee was not perfect, but it was not a group of vigilantes as characterized by some of the reports received at the embassy and passed on to Washington.

Durbrow refused to move beyond the resentment of Ngô Đình Diệm and Ngô Đình Nhu for the ambassador's failure to fully back the president during the crisis and dismissed the real anxiety that Ngô Đình Diệm must have felt in the strained relationship with America's top representative to his country. He continued to lament that the rebels had not finished the job in the early hours of November 11, though he never directly reported this to Washington. Instead, Durbrow mocked Ngô Đình Diệm's "miracle theory" for surviving the coup d'état and the president's refusal to admit that the rebels could have captured or killed him when only approximately thirty Presidential Guard remained after the initial attack. Never did Durbrow acknowledge the quick response of the armed forces to Ngô Đình Diệm's defense as a basis for their loyalty nor the fact that once the paratroopers learned that they had been tricked they stopped fighting, which indicated that the military either supported him or were disciplined and intelligent enough to realize the nature of command.

Durbrow continued to maintain that a general malaise existed in the RVN aimed primarily against Ngô Đình Diệm's family and advisers but including the president, who did not seem able or willing to rein them in. There was concern from some Vietnamese circles as well as from personnel within the U.S. embassy in Saigon about the status of Dr. Phan Quang Đán, Dr. Phan Huy Quát, and Phan Khắc Sửu, all of whom had been arrested in connection with their involvement in the abortive coup d'état.[25] While Phan Khắc Sửu and Phan Huy Quát had been released, Phan Quang Đán was still missing.[26] Mendenhall used the status of these three men to bring home the point that the Saigon government still had legitimate opposition and had treated that opposition harshly.[27] This reinforced Durbrow's point about the unsettled nature of Saigon politics. Just below the surface, he warned, "there is much talk about another coup unless Ngô Đình Diệm relaxes some control, puts in effective reforms, takes more effective action to fight [the] VC and give protection to [the] population."[28] This position countered a report from Bangkok in which the chargé d'affaires of the Vietnamese embassy, Đặng Độc Khối, told United Nations Economic Commission for Asia and the Far East representative Ben Dixon that the situation in the RVN was improving after the abortive coup d'état and that the Saigon government had moderated its position to get itself back on track.[29]

It also contradicted a *Voice of the Republic of Vietnam* broadcast at the end of November which claimed that the RVN had no legitimate opposition that provided a positive counterposition to the Saigon government. The opposition, the broadcast concluded, consisted of intellectuals, the rich, and former members of the Bảo Đại regime who were only interested in self-promotion rather than the advancement of the Republic.[30] Durbrow, when reporting on his Vietnamese contacts, continued to focus on the negative, highlighting discontent, corruption, and misguided policy.[31] Mendenhall was also hard at work in providing reports back to Washington that reaffirmed the idea that Ngô Đình Diệm, even if he was the only choice available, was not working to improve the country as the Americans believed necessary.³²

Mendenhall authored a series of dispatches to the Department of State that warned of Vietnamese discontent and countered the few positive reports that made their way to Washington. On December 22 and 23, he sent a memorandum of conversation with a prominent Vietnamese businessman and a member of the National Assembly that warned of a dire future.³³ In the case of the former, the criticism against Ngô Đình Diệm resulted from the Saigon government pressuring him in his financial dealings. While Mendenhall viewed the businessman's warnings as bordering on desperation because of his financial status, he did conclude that this attitude was a direct result of the way that the Saigon government and Ngô Đình Diệm's family had closed in on him. In the case of the latter, Nguyễn Phương Thiệp, who had served as the secretary general of the National Assembly until October 1960, argued that Ngô Đình Diệm's prestige had suffered greatly since the events of November 11 and 12. According to Mendenhall, Nguyễn Phương Thiệp urged the United States to use its assistance as leverage against Ngô Đình Diệm to force him to reform his government.

Durbrow added to this barrage of dispatches with his own on December 28 when he reported a conversation with the Chinese ambassador to the RVN, Yuen Tse Kien, in which the ambassador "volunteered" a comment to Durbrow that asserted that Ngô Đình Diệm needed to initiate reforms if he was to be successful.³⁴ While Mendenhall seemed to be garnering evidence of the hopelessness of continuing to support Ngô Đình Diệm, Durbrow continued to oppose the one thing that the MAAG had recommended and Ngô Đình Diệm had been adamant about receiving: the additional 20,000 men for the armed forces that would have gone a long way in rectifying his final two requirements for Ngô Đình Diệm to maintain his control.

Durbrow also warned that a coup d'état was imminent if Ngô Đình Diệm continued to fail in controlling the actions of those anti–American organizations like the People's Committee against Rebels and Communists. He argued that Ngô Đình Diệm, bolstered by his success of defeating the anti-communists coup d'état and spurred by the People's Committee, would have no incentive to make the necessary reforms, which would lead to Ngô Đình Diệm's critics becoming more frustrated, seeking American aid to effect changes and, failing at that, moving toward a more neutralist position, which would severely damage the American effort to stem the communist tide in Vietnam and, as a consequence, in Laos and Cambodia.

For Durbrow, Ngô Đình Diệm's obstinacy could mean the beginning of the falling dominoes so feared during the Eisenhower presidency. The Department of State responded to the Durbrow telegram on December 9 in a message, cleared by Parsons, in which he instructed Durbrow not to connect reforms with the authorization for the troop increase.³⁵ The telegram argued that Washington should base any troop increase on merit and as a result of the internal security conditions in South Vietnam. Durbrow was to inform Ngô Đình Diệm that the United States was considering the troop increase in Washington but that he could not predict how it would turn out. He was to warn Ngô Đình Diệm not to proceed with the increase on his own but was also instructed not to tie in reforms to the 20,000-man debate.

The nature of these instructions suggested that the Durbrow–McGarr debate had transferred to Washington. Taking up the argument for Durbrow was the director of the Office of Southeast Asian Affairs in the Department of State, Daniel Anderson, who reported his conversation with Livingston Merchant, undersecretary of state for political affairs, to Parsons.[36] Merchant and Anderson echoed Durbrow's concerns about Ngô Đình Diệm and his inability to make any progress in real reforms. They concurred that "now is not the time to distract Diem from the problems he must solve soon by dangling hopes of a major force increase which he is likely to regard as a panacea."[37] Instead, the two recommended that Durbrow suggest to Ngô Đình Diệm that, rather than a 20,000-man increase, the Saigon government with United States assistance increase training and equip all of the 54,000 Civil Guard and the 47,000 Self-Defense Corps who were already operating at the village level.[38] At the same time, the United States could concentrate its efforts on fixing South Vietnam's infrastructure in the contested areas to improve lines of communication and mobility. Essentially, they forwarded Durbrow's solution to the problems in the RVN, which then became the Department of State's position.

Chalmers B. Wood had added his voice earlier to the Durbrow camp on December 2 by reaffirming that the Department of State not become involved in issuing statements of support for Ngô Đình Diệm because of his resentment of Americans after November 11.[39] Wood asserted that it was difficult to understand why Ngô Đình Diệm was resentful toward the United States but conceded that it was probably a result of Durbrow not providing enough support during the abortive coup d'état, opting instead to stop Ngô Đình Diệm from retaliating against the rebels and providing an opportunity for the Việt Cộng. Essentially, Wood followed the Durbrow reasoning in his telegrams to the Department of State. As a result, Wood argued against bringing in Trần Văn Chương to offer a statement of support for Ngô Đình Diệm.

He reasoned that since Parsons had already indicated America's continued support for the president and Durbrow had repeatedly expressed the United States' position that it was glad Ngô Đình Diệm had resisted the rebels with minimum bloodshed, there was no need to provide further proof of American support. Wood represented many within the Department of State who lacked the understanding of what had transpired in the RVN and the devastating effect it had on Ngô Đình Diệm. With the absence of the Eisenhower letter and a refusal to communicate to Ngô Đình Diệm's ambassador in the United States, the Department of State was sending a message, intended or not, to Ngô Đình Diệm that there was a question of its support for his continued rule in Vietnam.

When Durbrow met with Ngô Đình Diệm on December 14, he did so with the instructions referenced in his telegram that outlined their conversation.[40] In the course of the discussion, Ngô Đình Diệm again justified the need for the troops, referencing the intelligence reports of the build-up of North Vietnamese troops above the 17th parallel, though when pressed he conceded that large-scale guerrilla attacks were a more pressing issue. Ngô Đình Diệm stressed the need for these troops to allow the Civil Guard the time and opportunity to rotate away from their station to train and reequip. Durbrow responded that the troops necessary to allow this to happen would take a considerable amount of time to get into place. While the two positions shared a common goal, neither could convince the other on which would achieve victory. Ngô Đình Diệm again argued that he could not protect the countryside without additional troops, which would make it difficult to implement new programs and reforms. He maintained that he was working toward military reforms in command and control and Civil Guard training but that it was imperative that he have the additional 20,000 men in order to meet any unexpected contingency.

The debate on the 20,000-man increase was interrupted on December 8 when Pope

John XXIII created a hierarchy in the RVN by establishing three ecclesiastical provinces with seats in Hanoi, Hue, and Saigon.[41] Joseph-Marie Trinh Nhu Khue was named the archbishop of the Hanoi archdiocese, Pierre Ngô Đình Thục was named the archbishop of the Hue archdiocese, and Paul Nguyễn Văn Bình was named the archbishop of the Saigon archdiocese. Catholics in Vietnam were overwhelmingly supportive of the move, which occurred on the Day of the Immaculate Conception and helped to promote a sense of pride for those within and outside of the Church.[42] On December 18, the Vietnamese Catholics held a Thanksgiving service to celebrate Pope John XXIII's actions and confirm the RVN's Catholic's loyalty to the Holy See and its commitments to fight against atheistic Communism. Ngô Đình Diệm, Nguyễn Ngọc Thơ, and Trương Vĩnh Lê were in attendance.[43]

The RVN also received praise from NBC correspondent James Robinson who visited Kiến Hòa province within the 5th Military Region. For a period of five days, Robinson and his photographer Grant Wolfkill reviewed the ARVN, Civil Guard, and the Self-Defense Corps in operations against the Việt Cộng. Robinson had nothing but praise for the Vietnamese troops and their relationship with the people while he characterized the Việt Cộng as poorly armed and increasingly isolated from the people because of their strategy of terrorism. Robinson informed the embassy that his film footage reflected "the real story of Viet-Nam, found in the provinces rather than in Saigon, and which the GVN should tell to the rest of the world."[44] Mendenhall, in reporting to Washington, welcomed the NBC story but argued that the embassy needed to move cautiously in advancing the story as part of a larger reflection of the RVN until it could garner further evidence. Essentially, Mendenhall was not convinced by Robinson's reporting from the countryside because it did not match his vision from Saigon.

The fracture in American policy was also experienced within the military, specifically with the proposed Lansdale trip that Durbrow had questioned earlier. The Department of State planned the trip to be a quiet one lasting for seven to ten days and during a time that Durbrow was in country. Parsons wanted to use Lansdale's visit to encourage Ngô Đình Diệm to follow Durbrow's advice and provide the Department of State with his personal assessment of the situation in Vietnam.[45] Admiral Felt informed Lansdale that his primary mission in his visit to Vietnam would not be gathering intelligence on the security situation but rather to use his influence to convince Ngô Đình Diệm to initiate Durbrow's plans for reform. Felt instructed Lansdale to go to Vietnam and "work with Diem as a trusted confidante and try to get him to change some of his fixations."[46]

This was a very different objective than what Lansdale had proposed as a result of Jerome French's assessment. Lansdale believed it critical to go to South Vietnam to speak with Ngô Đình Diệm about the internal security situation, obtain firsthand information on what was actually happening, and assess whether Durbrow's plan was impractical.[47] Lansdale informed Deputy Secretary of Defense C. Douglas Dillon of Felt's instructions and asked for clarification. He argued that the twofold mission of using his close association with Ngô Đình Diệm to understand what the South Vietnam president was thinking and to help where needed was essential given the level of instability emanating from Saigon. Dillon, agreeing with Lansdale, informed Felt of the decision and affirmed that Lansdale would work closely with Durbrow and McGarr and share his findings with Felt, Dillon, and Gates.[48] While the controversy surrounding the Lansdale visit continued to simmer, Washington worked to resolve the impasse between its military and diplomatic representatives in Saigon.

Durbrow received instructions from acting Secretary of State John M. Steeves, who served as the deputy assistant secretary for Far East affairs, on December 16 on how to proceed with Ngô Đình Diệm based on the October 14 démarche.[49] Steeves instructed Durbrow to push liberalization of the Saigon government's policies rather than internal reform. This liberalization included several of the items Ngô Đình Diệm had already announced such as the National Economic Council and village council elections, freeing up the press, coming to terms with the foreign correspondents, and increasing the responsibility of the National Assembly. Durbrow was to apply pressure for completion of these items rather than demanding any additional far-reaching internal reforms. The Department of State believed that a strategy which selected the most important and accepted items to Ngô Đình Diệm would pave the way for better relations. A few weeks later, Steeves followed up with a personal letter to Durbrow.

In it, he offered a slightly different viewpoint, one that was more closely aligned with Durbrow's thinking at the time.[50] Steeves argued that the two main issues in Vietnam, the insurgency fight and winning the support of the people for the government, were intertwined. While the military supported Ngô Đình Diệm and believed, according to Steeves, that all of his problems would disappear once the insurgents were eliminated, others, such as Durbrow, maintained that Vietnam needed a more responsive government in order to fix its problems. Steeves and Parsons saw the issues as "two sides of the same coin."[51] The United States had to continue to pursue both issues vigorously in order to save Ngô Đình Diệm and the Vietnamese people. Steeves confirmed that Durbrow had his and Parsons' support against the 20,000-man increase while Durbrow's justifications for opposition remained solid. None believed Ngô Đình Diệm was using his existing forces effectively, and all believed the Civil Guard would be a more effective weapon in the fight against the insurgents. They did not want Ngô Đình Diệm to become too reliant on force to solve his problems rather than reform to win over the people.

Durbrow and Ngô Đình Diệm finally met on December 23 in a rather one-sided one-hour-and-forty-five-minute conversation that focused on the 20,000-man issue.[52] Durbrow followed the instructions outlined by Steeves, though he did not directly refer to the October 14 démarche, as one of the major points in it was the removal or transfer of Ngô Đình Nhu. Durbrow had hoped for a better meeting with Ngô Đình Diệm, who he felt was distant though pleasant. When Durbrow reminded Ngô Đình Diệm of the arrival of the AD-6 aircraft to replace the F-8F and the pending arrival of eleven additional H-34 helicopters, Ngô Đình Diệm did not offer his thanks or even comment on what Durbrow surely believed deserved some type of recognition. Durbrow noted Ngô Đình Diệm's lack of appreciation in his report to Washington. Ngô Đình Diệm focused on the 20,000-man increase and the viciousness of the foreign press—this time he singled out the French—then tried to explain to Durbrow all of the successes the RVN had achieved in his nearly six years in office.

Ngô Đình Diệm was frustrated by the failure of the United States to push forward with the troop increase, especially as it had the support of McGarr and MAAG. He was also bothered by the division in his country and the inability of the foreign correspondents to distinguish the difference between fact and propaganda. He argued that these correspondents reported from the broadcasts of Radio Hanoi and listened to disgruntled Vietnamese elites and intellectuals "who do not pay their taxes and then blame the government for not doing enough for the people."[53] Ngô Đình Diệm echoed the Vietnamese press, or perhaps the other way around, during this time period. A good example of this was a *Tiếng Chuông* editorial on December 22 which charged that French and American reporters had "shown themselves unworthy of their information mission because they continue to distort the truth concerning the November 11 events in the capital city. They have intentionally seen facts in a subjective manner and distorted the truth for commercial purposes."[54] In the weeks after the abortive coup d'état, Ngô Đình Diệm clearly had felt the strain of leadership. He was being attacked at home and abroad for not doing enough, by the people who worked to ensure that the implementation of his plan would not occur.

Ngô Đình Diệm did begin to act on his own, as was predicted and feared by McGarr. He announced a call-up of reservists and former ARVN soldiers to fill the ranks of the armed forces and increased the size of the Civil Guard by 10,000.[55] Durbrow also learned from Ngô Đình Nhu and Nguyễn Đình Thuận that Ngô Đình Diệm appeared more and more reluctant to initiate any reforms until the Việt Cộng had been effectively contained. The RVN also worked to further publicize the violations by the DRV of the 1954 Geneva Agreements. Three complaints were lodged in the first half of December that were centered around the establishment of a North Vietnamese airlift in Laos and the movement of communist insurgents in the Kontom-Pleiku area.[56] Whether it was the pleasant, albeit negative, atmosphere in the December 23 meeting, the announcement of the 10,000 additional Civil Guard troops, or Ngô Đình Diệm's call-up of the reserves, Durbrow had finally had enough as 1960 drew to a close.

In a Department of State circular sent on December 19, all Far East ambassadors or principal officers were asked to submit to Washington a "think piece" or "year-end review" that explained the current situation in their country, described how that situation fit into American foreign policy, and offered recommendations for future action. Durbrow submitted his report on December 24, the day after his meeting with Ngô Đình Diệm.[57] His succinct report of the state of the RVN was filled with warnings of what might occur in the future. Durbrow maintained that Ngô Đình Diệm was failing because of the political discontent and dissatisfaction that permeated the country; it was as bad as Durbrow had ever seen and comparable to 1954.

Toward the end of his summary, Durbrow argued that unless change occurred, it was likely that Ngô Đình Diệm would be removed from power, either peacefully or by force. As such, the United States needed to begin the process of searching for a new leader of the RVN so that when the removal of Ngô Đình Diệm occurred, a smooth transition would result.[58] Parsons' response to Durbrow's telegrams was to offer him and his staff high praise for their "excellent and realistic analysis."[59] He instructed Durbrow to ease up on pressuring for liberalization and urged that future analysis that involved a discussion of a change in leadership in the RVN be kept at the highest classification with a limited distribution.

Durbrow may have made his comment after reading a recent CIA information report that, as a direct results of the abortive coup d'état, demonstrated the real need of the United States to reassess the political leadership in the RVN in the event of the overthrow or death of Ngô Đình Diệm.[60] Ngô Đình Diệm had survived several attempts at his demise since returning to the political scene in 1954. He had proven himself to be very resilient, but the abortive coup d'état and the upcoming elections in April 1961 begged for a CIA survey of alternative leaders. One of the remarkable conclusions in the lengthy report was the lack of real leadership available to take over for Ngô Đình Diệm should he be forced out of office.

Within the army, Generals Lê Văn Ty, Dương Văn Minh, Nguyễn Khánh, Trần Văn Đôn, Thái Quang Hoàng, and Tôn Thất Đính were mentioned. Lê Văn Ty was dismissed as he did not have enough presence to force others to his will. Both Nguyễn Khánh and

Trần Văn Đôn were respected and had acted forcefully during November 11 and 12, while Thái Quang Hoàng and Tôn Thất Đính were also too loyal to Ngô Đình Diệm to be considered likely candidates for a future coup d'etat. Dương Văn Minh, who had the support of the vice president, Nguyễn Ngọc Thơ, and was popular with the ARVN, seemed a likely candidate, but he had played too much of a "wait-and-see" game during the abortive coup d'état and did not appear to want the job. There were no other officers of prominence who seemed willing to act after the failed rebellion; none were so anti–Ngô Đình Diệm as to risk another failure and its consequences, nor were there any who could muster enough support to make the venture practical.

Within the existing Saigon government, the CIA identified several individuals who it believed could assume a prominent political position in a new government without Ngô Đình Diệm. The primary figure was Vice President Nguyễn Ngọc Thơ, who had a right to the position through the Vietnamese Constitution. Nguyễn Ngọc Thơ had already distanced himself from Ngô Đình Diệm and his advisers and had indicated that, as a result, he would not seek reelection in the April 1961 election. Nguyễn Ngọc Thơ and Ngô Đình Nhu did not get along, which did raise the reputation of the vice president within American and Saigon intellectual circles, but he did not distinguish himself during the November crisis, suggesting that he would not be a likely candidate to lead a revolt.

The CIA report offered Nguyễn Ngọc Thơ as a figurehead in the government in the event of an army coup d'état. This was something that was on Mendenhall's mind as he read the report, as his comments in the margin indicated. Mendenhall maintained that the United States should support Nguyễn Ngọc Thơ if he had the backing of Dương Văn Minh, Brigadier General Lê Văn Kim who was the commander of the military academy at Dalat, or Trần Văn Đôn.[61] Other existing government officials included the president of the National Assembly, Trương Vĩnh Lê, though he seemed to lack the ambition or support to be a real threat. Nguyễn Đình Thuận, as secretary of state and assistant secretary of defense, was also mentioned, but his support came mainly from Ngô Đình Diệm and Ngô Đình Nhu. He would not be expected to lead a revolt, though he was considered a good compromise candidate. While other names were mentioned, none seemed to possess the popular appeal or strength of character to replace Ngô Đình Diệm. The other Ngô brothers were also considered, but their rise to power would only come with the natural demise of the president.

Within the political opposition, Phan Quang Đán, who was secretary general of the Ministry of Foreign Affairs, and National Assembly member Phan Khắc Sửu headed the list. Phan Quang Đán, even though he was the primary political opposition to Ngô Đình Diệm, had ended any chance he had at replacing the president because he had fully endorsed the rebels. Phan Khắc Sửu, who was also one of the leading members of the Caravellists, had the same problem as Phan Quang Đán. Like Hoàng Cơ Thụy, who was also considered, Phan Khắc Sửu was still in hiding. Phan Khắc Sửu did have the support of the Buddhists and some members of the Cao Đài, according to Nguyễn Van Thọ, a dentist and husband of National Assembly member Pauline Tho.[62] As a result of their actions during November 11 and 12, none of these oppositionist leaders seemed a likely candidate to overthrow Ngô Đình Diệm. Other oppositionist groups, like the Đại Việt Party, might consolidate power if Ngô Đình Diệm were removed, while those who had been in exile or resided overseas offered no real chance as alternatives for Ngô Đình Diệm.

Political groups, such as the Cần Lao Party, the Hòa Hảo, Cao Đài, and Bình Xuyên, were either too loyal to Ngô Đình Diệm as in the case of the former or too weak and disorganized to mount a real challenge as were the latter. The one religious organization, the Catholic Church, supported Ngô Đình Diệm and fell under the nominal leadership of Nguyễn Văn Cẩn. Catholics would not overthrow Ngô Đình Diệm, though they would represent a formidable bloc should Ngô Đình Diệm be removed from power.

The CIA report concluded that the removal of Ngô Đình Diệm, by force or naturally, would result in a power struggle among the many groups represented in the study. In the period between Ngô Đình Diệm's removal and the consolidation of a new government, whether it followed the constitutional process or was a radical departure from the existing succession of power already established, would result in a period of time during which the communist insurgency would strengthen and consolidate its position in the countryside. The CIA analysis further warned that the April 1961 election would be a critical point in the young RVN's history, as it could result in the legal removal of Ngô Đình Diệm, a popular uprising, or armed revolt if the democratic process was ignored. For Durbrow, the report was further confirmation that reforms in South Vietnam were essential to the country's future survival as well as for the continuation of Ngô Đình Diệm's rule.

Durbrow's December 24 report, which may have been informed by the CIA, forced McGarr to respond once he had seen Durbrow's comments about continuing the search for alternatives to Ngô Đình Diệm. In a separate telegram to Felt, McGarr argued that Ngô Đình Diệm had to be given the resources he needed in order to solve the two problems in Vietnam. Once this was completed, liberalization of policy could proceed. After meeting with McGarr on December 21 and Ngô Đình Diệm on December 23, Durbrow offered a new position on the 20,000-man increase. He asserted that Ngô Đình Diệm was not going to change his mind and that if he turned out to be correct, he needed the 20,000-man increase to survive. Certainly, there were indications within Vietnam and Laos that the Việt Cộng had stepped up their activities.[63] Because of these factors, Durbrow withdrew his opposition to the 20,000-man increase, though he reaffirmed that the United States had to continue pressing Ngô Đình Diệm for reforms in his government. Perhaps one factor not widely discussed was evidence that the Soviet Union was present in Laos and had been delivering materials using IL-14 transport along the DRV-Laotian border.[64] Durbrow was an old hand with the Soviet Union, having been stationed there as counselor of embassy and deputy chief of mission in Moscow in 1946 to 1948, and the evidence of Soviet involvement might have made a real difference in his approach to Ngô Đình Diệm.

While unknown to the Americans and some within Saigon, December 20 marked a significant turning point in the war when individuals representing various groups in the RVN met in Tây Ninh province and formed the National Liberation Front of South Vietnam.[65] The organization, which had its origins at the Third National Congress in Hanoi in September 1960, offered a ten-point program designed to rally the Vietnamese people against Ngô Đình Diệm and the Americans.[66] While the National Liberation Front would not begin to influence Vietnamese politics until after the April 1961 election, it did foreshadow the new focus and intensity of the organized opposition to Ngô Đình Diệm and his Republic.[67]

As the American military and diplomatic representatives debated the military situation in the RVN and, internally, discussed the alternatives for 1961, the Vietnamese continued the process of governance and working toward the stabilization of the Republic. The National Assembly debated its national budget for the fiscal year 1961 during December.[68] On December 13, the budget was introduced at a total amount of VN$14,985,000,000, which was a decrease of VN$229 million from the 1960 budget. The budget was designed, as outlined by the president of the Budgetary and Finance Committee, Hạ Như Chi, to fund the three principles of the Republic—Personalism, community development, and collective progress—while at the same time increasing the South Vietnamese military struggle against the communist insurgents.[69]

The National Assembly also discussed the creation of the Constitutional Court in December.[70] The Constitutional Court was charged with determining the constitutionality of laws, decrees, and regulations emanating from the Saigon government. Draft 33/11 organized and outlined the functions of the court and its relationship to the president of the Republic. According to article 86 of the draft, the president of the RVN appointed the president of the court with the agreement of the National Assembly. The president also appointed four of the magistrates, while the National Assembly voted in four of the jurists. Critics pointed out that this would mean that Ngô Đình Diệm had control of the court since at least five of the appointees would be his men, though the creation of this institution was important in the development of South Vietnam and a part of the liberalization movement that Durbrow and the Americans had been pushing.

Draft 33/11 caused an intense debate within the National Assembly. One particular source of contention was article 8 that outlined immunity for the court members.[71] The article stated that members of the Constitutional Court could not be arrested or tried without the consent of two-thirds of the members of the court unless they were caught in the act. Some National Assembly members argued that the article was contradictory to the Constitution of the RVN as well as incomplete in creating a procedure by which one could be arrested and tried and specifying who was entitled to take that action. There were also no provisions for high treason and national security cases. The assemblymen Cao Văn Trường, Hạ Như Chi, and Nguyễn Văn Liên were able to amend article 8 to address their concerns, which did suggest that the Saigon government was not trying to push through a court that would answer directly to it but one that would serve the Vietnamese people and the Republic.

On December 21, the National Assembly endorsed the final articles of Draft No. 33/11 as well as amendments introduced by the Justice and Legislation Committees.[72] The Constitutional Court would decide on matters of constitutionality of a law or decree as well as administrative regulations. What is of particular significance was that all petitioners and court proceedings would be held in public. Cameras would be present in the courtroom, providing full access to the Vietnamese people, thus eliminating another of the criticisms of Ngô Đình Diệm's detractors. Ngô Đình Diệm promulgated the Law 7/60 on December 23 that created the Constitutional Court from thirty articles of Draft No. 33/11.[73]

During discussions of the national budget and after endorsing the Constitutional Court, assemblymen formed a Justice and Interior Joint Committee to examine the election procedures for the April 9, 1961, event. Led by the leader of the Socialist Union Group, Lê Trọng Quát, the committee consisted of seven assemblymen.[74] The National Assembly voted on the election laws after three sessions of discussion, issuing Draft No. 34/11.[75] The first fifteen articles of the draft set out the procedures for timing and eligibility for the elections and the candidates, adhering to the RVN's Constitution. Articles 16 through 23 outlined the conditions and procedures for the actual campaigning leading up to April 9, while articles 23 through 43 summarized how and where polling would be conducted, the control of the actual votes from casting to counting, and the penalties (a sentence of five to twenty years of hard labor) for those who created obstacles to the process. Article 24 enumerated the value of direct and secret ballots by universal suffrage, while other articles outlined the procedures for irregularities in voting or complaints of the process by candidates, which would come under the auspices of the first president of the Court of Cassation and all of the advisers of the newly formed Constitutional Court. With the Constitution Court created, the budget set, and the election laws established, the National Assembly ended its second ordinary session on December 31.[76]

The end of the year was marked by the National Assembly advances in democracy but was also tempered by the harsh realities of the situation in the RVN. The *Vietnam Press* revealed in its evening edition on December 31 the discovery of approximately 1,000 human skulls and skeletons that had been removed from three wells in Trung Lập village, Củ Chi district, Bình Dương province, which is located about fourteen kilometers to the northeast of Củ Chi.[77] The remains were from an incident that occurred in 1947 when a group of Cao Đài followers were murdered by Việt Minh soldiers because of their religious beliefs and failure to support the communist insurgency against the French and Bảo Đại. Two witnesses, still alive in 1960, recalled the event during which the insurgents ordered the villagers to the wells, masqueraded as an altar, to relinquish their religion and pledge loyalty to the new Vietnam. The soldiers then forcibly tied the villagers together in pairs, decapitated the Cao Đài, and threw their bodies into the wells. This event, which had occurred more than a dozen years before, was a sobering reminder of the plight of the Vietnamese and the long road ahead.

10

A New Year with an Old Problem

As 1961 began, Durbrow made some attempts to mend the break with Ngô Đình Diệm. His acquiescence to the increase in the Armed Forces made an impact, but the actions within the U.S. embassy would make a still greater statement on how the American diplomats in Saigon would be received. Durbrow started the rebuilding of the relationship by sending Ngô Đình Diệm a birthday greeting on January 3.[1] Durbrow reminded Ngô Đình Diệm of his four-year association with the RVN in his letter that marked the celebration of Ngô Đình Diệm's sixtieth birthday. He maintained that it had been his privilege to witness Ngô Đình Diệm's success economically, politically, and militarily in the face of such great odds, concluding that he and the United States would continue to work with the South Vietnamese to achieve their national goal of independence, free from communist interference. There were other ceremonies to mark Ngô Đình Diệm's sixtieth birthday, including a service at the Saigon Basilica and a 6,000-member parade from the Republican Youth who marched from Thống Nhứt Boulevard to the grounds of the Presidential Palace to proclaim their loyalty to Ngô Đình Diệm.[2]

Durbrow continued the public relations push to win back Ngô Đình Diệm the next day when he was a part of the entourage that presented Ngô Đình Diệm with a Paul Revere silver bowl from Boston mayor John F. Collins and the people of that city in recognition of Ngô Đình Diệm's efforts to preserve freedom in the face of communist aggression.[3] Whether Ngô Đình Diệm reacted to the Durbrow overtures is not known. Durbrow's effort was one among many hundred that occurred during the week. Much had transpired in the last two months of 1960, and two specific events would demand the attention of most Americans involved in the Vietnam decision-making process in the opening weeks of 1961: Lansdale's visit to Vietnam and the release of the Country Team study.

Lansdale's trip had been contested by Durbrow in November, and attempts were made by Parsons and Felt in December to control his actions while in Vietnam. From January 2 through January 14, Lansdale made his long-anticipated visit to the RVN, and the Country Team Staff Committee in Saigon, headed by Mendenhall, transmitted its *Basic Counterinsurgency Plan for Viet Nam* for consideration. These two events marked another change in U.S.-Vietnamese relations and, when coupled with a new administration eager to prove itself in the area of foreign policy, offered a real chance for success. The concern in Washington and Saigon was whether this change would be sustained and if it would rectify the negativism that had resulted from the American diplomatic response to the events of November 11 and 12, 1960.

The January 4 draft of the counter-insurgency plan was notable for a few items that carried over from the previous year.[4] The principle agencies involved in its development,

MAAG, USOM, the United States Information Service (USIS), and the embassy in Saigon, had worked hard at a compromise position. That Mendenhall chaired the Country Team Staff Committee also ensured that Durbrow's concerns for Ngô Đình Diệm's rule would dominate the basic plan narrative, which offered a rather bleak view of the situation in South Vietnam. It focused on the political discontent harbored toward Ngô Đình Diệm, Ngô Đình Nhu, and Madame Nhu as well as Ngô Đình Diệm's leadership ability, though it conceded that he, at that time, offered the best hope in defeating the Việt Cộng. Overall, the basic plan suggested that Vietnam would be one of the most difficult challenges for the new Kennedy administration. The nature of the challenge was confirmed by Lansdale in his January 17 report in which he argued that the situation in the RVN had reached a critical level. For Lansdale, Vietnam was an active battleground in the Cold War and needed to be treated as such.[5]

Lansdale submitted his report to the secretary and deputy secretary of defense.[6] His conclusions did cause a stir in Washington and set in motion the Kennedy administration decisions for 1961. During his visit, Lansdale had been surprised how advanced the communist insurgency was in achieving its objectives of controlling South Vietnam. He predicted that the Vietnamese people, should their reaction to the threat not vary significantly, would be powerless to stop the Việt Cộng. The U.S. personnel in Vietnam would also be unable, he warned, to fix the situation unless they changed their ways and proceeded with some "sensitive understanding and wisdom." Lansdale predicted that the RVN's loss would be a major blow to American prestige and influence and stave off future support from allies in the region and within the emerging post-colonial world. A loss would demonstrate that the United States did not stay true to its friends when the situation became difficult. He concluded that Vietnam was not lost, "but it would require a changed U.S. attitude, plenty of hard work and patience, and a new spirit by the Vietnamese."[7] These remarks were sobering to members of the new Kennedy administration who would read the report and use it as a foundation for its foreign policy decisions in Southeast Asia, especially when the Eisenhower administration officials singled out Laos, and not the RVN, as the most significant hot spot in Southeast Asia and the one country that needed all of America's interest and resources.[8]

As Lansdale outlined the conditions in the RVN, he maintained that Ngô Đình Diệm was the only one who had the experience and ability to govern the country through what Lansdale believed would be a very turbulent time. He warned that another coup d'état attempt might occur, as his conversations and contacts during the trip confirmed that many "highly selfish and mediocre people" had focused their attention on replacing Ngô Đình Diệm after November 11 and still believed it possible given the atmosphere of distrust and discontent among the Saigon elite and intellectuals as well as in the American embassy. Lansdale argued that the United States needed to make it clear to Ngô Đình Diệm and to the local elite that the United States supported Ngô Đình Diệm as the leader of the RVN. The first few pages of Lansdale's report managed to catch the attention of many of the new faces in Washington. His recommendations also inspired a revisit to American diplomacy in Southeast Asia, to the president of the RVN, and to America's top diplomat in that country.

Lansdale offered several observations that tied in to his recommendations for future American action in Southeast Asia. He maintained that there was a real problem with American leadership in South Vietnam with the exception of McGarr and Colby. Indeed, Ngô Đình Diệm confided in Lansdale that some Americans had attacked him as much as the communists, and as a result, according to Lansdale, Ngô Đình Diệm had begun to insulate himself from all criticism. He suggested that some Americans spent too much time and energy on the internal politics of Saigon and less on the Việt Cộng threat. While not mentioned specifically, memorandums of conversation that survived the period pointed to Mendenhall and Cunningham among the leaders in the embassy who were engaged with various members of the Saigon elite and intellectuals, as was Durbrow, who not only relied on their counsel but also had established a strong position against Ngô Đình Diệm's rule. These individuals, Lansdale claimed, where subconsciously involved in a policy of defeat for the RVN, which severely hampered American efforts to assist Ngô Đình Diệm and his government in their struggle.

Lansdale recommended that Durbrow be transferred immediately from Saigon: "He has been in the 'forest of tigers' which is Vietnam for nearly four years now and I doubt that he himself realizes how tired he has become or how close his is to individual trees in this big wood."[9] From Lansdale's conversations during his trip, he reasserted that Durbrow did not realize how out of favor he was with the Saigon government or the extent to which Ngô Đình Diệm and his closest advisers believed that Durbrow sympathized with the November 11 coup d'état leaders. Lansdale called for a new ambassador to be in place a few weeks before the April 1961 elections and to have him operate in what he considered to be an emergency situation:

> When there is an emergency, the wise thing to do is to pick the best people you have, people who are experienced in dealing with this precise type of emergency, and send them to the spot with orders to remedy the situation. When you get the people in position and free them to work, you should back them up in every practical way you can. The real decisions will be made in daily actions in Vietnam, not in Washington. That's why the best are needed on the spot.[10]

These best and brightest, to borrow the phrase, needed to understand Asia and Asians, according to Lansdale. They had to have a strong desire to help the people of Vietnam and be "willing to risk their lives for the ideals of freedom." Lansdale believed that the next ambassador should focus on political operations with the goal of laying the foundations of a Vietnamese-style democracy. He did not think the individual should be military oriented and argued that MAAG needed to be given more leeway and greater flexibility for involvement in the field with their Vietnamese counterparts. MAAG should control the military threat while the new ambassador took care of politics. In what may have been a slap in the face to Durbrow, Mendenhall, and Cunningham, Lansdale maintained that the next ambassador "must not be a 'clever' type who is out to gain a reputation as a 'manipulator' or a word-smith who is more concerned about the way his reports will look in Washington than in implementing U.S. policy in Vietnam."[11] In addition to relieving Durbrow, Lansdale also called for the ouster of USOM director Arthur Gardiner, who also seemed to have spent too much time in Southeast Asia.

Lansdale's evaluation of Ngô Đình Diệm was one of the most penetrating pieces of analysis in the report. Few Americans had the background experience with Ngô Đình Diệm, and even fewer approached the level of respect and admiration that Ngô Đình Diệm held for the American. As Lansdale put it, "President Diem and I are friends. Also, he is a man who put other Vietnamese friends of mine in jail or exiled them. It is hardly a blind friendship."[12] Lansdale's first meeting with Ngô Đình Diệm in many respects demonstrated his understanding of the Vietnamese. Ngô Đình Diệm approached the conversation cautiously, expecting Lansdale to pursue the internal-reforms argument put forth by Durbrow and the other American visitors to Saigon. Instead, Lansdale discussed the long association that the two men had shared. Lansdale reported that Ngô Đình Diệm expressed a desire to share some of the burden of leadership, a point for which his critics had argued vehemently, but he found it difficult to do so because of the lack of talent in South Vietnam. This conversation seemed to confirm the December 1960 CIA report on alternative leadership for the RVN.

Ngô Đình Diệm already over-burdened Nguyễn Đình Thuận because he was talented but did not think that Vice President Nguyễn Ngọc Thơ or Director General of the Budget and Foreign Aid Vũ Văn Thái were capable of more than they currently handled. Because Ngô Đình Diệm believed he had to keep these men in office so as not to confirm American rumors that he was a despot, he ended up with a greater share of the burden than he desired. Ngô Đình Diệm had communicated this to Durbrow several times in 1960, but it took Lansdale's confirmation for it to take hold. Lansdale did comment on the effects of Ngô Đình Nhu who he argued had screened his brother more than Ngô Đình Diệm realized, but also conceded that Ngô Đình Diệm was remarkably well versed on the situation in the RVN, both good and bad. Ngô Đình Diệm was not isolated as many in the American press or Saigon intelligentsia had argued.

Lansdale also concluded that many of the people who spoke with Ngô Đình Diệm, and Durbrow needed to top that list though he was not specifically mentioned at this point, had little empathy and in some cases contempt for the president. The American diplomats in Washington had failed to treat Ngô Đình Diệm fairly during the abortive coup d'état, focusing on the potential causes of the event rather than how Ngô Đình Diệm might have reacted, as anyone would, to the fact that there were people trying to kill him. A friend and ally would be more concerned with this rather than trying to push through reforms. Lansdale maintained that Ngô Đình Diệm had gone through much in the past two months and had experienced more criticism and opposition in the previous five years than most normally faced in a lifetime. Rather than take a "holier than thou" attitude, Lansdale called for the next ambassador to "have the good sense to see him [Ngô Đình Diệm] as a human being who has been through a lot of hell for years—and not as an opponent to be beaten to his knees."[13] The American policy in Vietnam needed to change, and the United States had to admit that it was a part of the problem rather than just blaming the situation on Ngô Đình Diệm. It is interesting to note that a week before the meetings, Cunningham had reported on a conversation with Lê Trung Nghĩa, who was a businessman in Saigon and a supporter of Ngô Đình Diệm. It was one of the very few times that the American embassy recorded a memorandum of conversation in support of Ngô Đình Diệm.[14]

Lansdale lamented that American policy had created too many Aaron Burrs and Alexander Hamiltons, and not enough George Washingtons, Thomas Jeffersons, or Thomas Paines, in South Vietnam. While that might not have been the intent, it was the consequence of five years of mentoring, assistance, and financial assistance. Only an American who understood the Vietnamese people, history, and culture and was willing to work with the existing Vietnamese leadership had a chance to correct the problems and fix the future course of that country.

Within Vietnamese society, Lansdale observed what Ngô Đình Diệm had complained about to Durbrow and others. The talent level simply was not advanced enough for Ngô Đình Diệm to loosen some of his control to individuals. Lansdale met with oppositionists who eagerly criticized the president but failed to offer alternatives to Ngô Đình Diệm's plans or leadership. Criticism was easy, but solutions to problems were harder to come by, especially during a time of war. Lansdale called for the U.S. representatives to bring the opposition together to offer an effective platform for change rather than allow the groups to voice their criticism without backing it up with some type of action. If done properly and with respect for the current government, it might help in creating a few more Washingtons, Jeffersons, and Paines.

The Lansdale report was reviewed in Washington and eventually discussed with the *Basic Counterinsurgency Plan for Viet Nam* on January 28 by the White House.[15] Lansdale and Parsons were also in attendance to brief the president on each report. After Parsons' briefing, Kennedy asked the question that had been on Durbrow and the State Department's mind since Ngô Đình Diệm requested the additional troops: how could additional forces that would not be ready for one or two years make a difference in South Vietnam if the situation there was as critical as had been reported? Kennedy also wondered aloud if it was necessary to have 170,000 in the armed forces if there were only 10,000 Việt Cộng operating in South Vietnam. These questions demonstrated how new Kennedy was to the Vietnam scene even if he had been a member of the American Friends of Vietnam as the junior senator from Massachusetts and was counted as one of the informed in the 1950s Congress.[16]

Parsons patiently explained that the armed forces strength was necessary to counter the PAVN units that were estimated at 300,000 strong; he also indicated that because MAAG had already begun training the Civil Guard, the two-year timetable had started. The communist insurgency was also widespread and determined, which required many more troops to combat it than the Việt Cộng actually put into the field at any given time. Satisfied, Kennedy asked Lansdale to review his findings. Lansdale outlined his report and emphasized the good relations that Ngô Đình Diệm shared with MAAG and the CIA and the poor relationship the embassy and Foreign Service officers had cultivated as a result of their inability to communicate with Ngô Đình Diệm and their extra-curricular activities immediately following the abortive coup d'état. Kennedy quickly picked up on Lansdale's line of argument, asking if he should send a message to Ngô Đình Diệm, to which Lansdale immediately agreed.

The new secretary of state, Dean Rusk, already had a draft letter ready in response to Ngô Đình Diệm's congratulatory message after the November election and offered to send it back for redrafting, with the issue of raising morale addressed in the revision. Much had changed in the last two months as Durbrow blocked Eisenhower's offer of a letter, which would have confirmed American support for Ngô Đình Diệm after November 11 and 12, because it would have decreased the ambassador's leverage with Ngô Đình Diệm. Lansdale ensured that this obstacle was removed in the new administration. Perhaps sensing the direction the conversation was going, Rusk interjected that Durbrow had done a credible job in balancing the difficult position of supporting Ngô Đình Diệm and pushing through reforms to help the Saigon government and Vietnamese people survive. Having praised Durbrow, Rusk suggested, following the Lansdale report, that the ambassador should be relieved; it was now time for a change.

During the course of the discussion, Kennedy asked Lansdale to tell him what needed to be done in 1961 in order to thwart the Việt Cộng. Lansdale offered three requirements. First, the American personnel in Vietnam, especially on the diplomatic side, needed to change their attitude to include a will to win and a commitment to get closer to the Vietnamese.[17] Lansdale then argued that the Vietnamese needed to act quickly and decisively with the encouragement of the Americans and, finally, that Ngô Đình Diệm needed to be

President John F. Kennedy's March 22, 1961, press conference, Accession Number: ST-69-1-61 Cecil Stoughton (White House Photographs, John F. Kennedy Presidential Library and Museum, Boston).

convinced to let his opposition come together in the open to voice their complaints publicly rather than allowing them to plot individually in private. Lansdale reiterated that Ngô Đình Diệm believed, falsely or not, that some of the embassy staff were too close to those who had tried to overthrow him. As Lansdale could not dissuade Ngô Đình Diệm of this notion, it was unlikely that any other Americans could influence Ngô Đình Diệm to move away from this position.

During the evening of January 28, Parsons and Rusk met to discuss the day's events.[18] Rusk wanted some further clarification on Lansdale and the Vietnam situation. Parsons not surprisingly characterized Lansdale as a "lone wolf and operator" who was not a team player and had resented the embassy staff's position vis-à-vis Ngô Đình Diệm, but he maintained that Durbrow was tired and needed to be removed, while Wolf Ladejinsky was frustrated and ready to quit.[19] The main problem, according to Parsons, was that Ngô Đình Diệm did not listen to sound American advice. He credited Durbrow with saving Ngô Đình Diệm's life during the night of November 11–12 and keeping Ngô Đình Diệm from causing a bloodbath after the rebel forces had been suppressed. Given the nature of the evidence, both assertions seem far fetched.

Rusk then asked about the Lansdale report and Ngô Đình Diệm's feelings toward the United States after the attempted coup d'état. Parsons criticized Lansdale for focusing too much on what the United States needed to do rather than what the Vietnamese should accomplish. That statement alone told much about the position of the State Department professionals who were handling Southeast Asia. It was expected that the Vietnamese should conform to American policy and advice because the United States knew better and was providing the money. That Lansdale had the nerve to offer the opposite was anathema to entrenched American diplomacy. While Parsons conceded that they might have pushed Ngô Đình Diệm too far with the calls for liberalization so soon after the attempted coup d'état, it did not excuse Ngô Đình Diệm of his action. Parsons maintained that Ngô Đình Diệm was respected but not popular and that his respect was waning. Of course, Parsons did not experience the mass rallies in support of Ngô Đình Diệm in November and was never informed of them by his ambassador on the spot.

As a result of the January 28 meeting, Kennedy authorized an addition of U.S. $28.4 million to increase the Vietnamese armed forces by 20,000 and U.S. $12.7 million to improve the quality of the Civil Guard.[20] When Durbrow learned later, on February 13, through McGarr that the money would not be available, he complained to Washington. It was particularly embarrassing as he had spoken to Ngô Đình Diệm earlier in the morning confirming that the United States was ready to fund the addition to the Armed Forces and the Civil Guard.[21]

Soon after Lansdale briefed the president, he wrote Ngô Đình Diệm a letter thanking him for his courtesy during the trip to Vietnam and began to implement what he thought was one of the more important recommendations in his report.[22] Lansdale did this without approval, which perhaps confirmed some of Parsons' characterization, though he did offer his advice to Ngô Đình Diệm as a friend and confidant rather than as an official representative of the United States. Lansdale called upon Ngô Đình Diệm to announce a reorganization of the Saigon government to quell those critics who had argued that Ngô Đình Diệm took too much of a role in governance. After the announcement, Lansdale recommended that Ngô Đình Diệm bring together the military commanders and province chiefs of the 1st and 5th Military Regions to get an honest assessment of what was happening in these areas. Lansdale was in Vietnam in 1955 when Ngô Đình Diệm did something very similar to this, and he believed Ngô Đình Diệm would get similar results in 1961, even if he heard things that were not positive or contradicted reports he had been receiving. Lansdale recommended that McGarr and Colby be invited to the conference—there was no mention of Durbrow, Mendenhall, or Cunningham.

Lansdale then consulted Ngô Đình Diệm to bring in the opposition, especially the younger crowd to work with them in understanding the differences in their respective political philosophies. He cautioned against repressive action that might divide the people, instead encouraging him to be passionate about his vision for the RVN as he had done with Lansdale in 1955. Lansdale believed in Ngô Đình Diệm's leadership and knew that he had to show the same passion he had shown for his country and his people to those who had been critical of his policies. His critics might still oppose Ngô Đình Diệm's rule, but they would, so Lansdale hoped, respect Ngô Đình Diệm's goals and objectives for the RVN. Lansdale's long letter was full of praise, cautious advice, and affirmation of America's support for Ngô Đình Diệm and the RVN. He understood the fragile nature of Ngô Đình Diệm's psyche as well as the importance of actively engaging the opposition in an open dialogue rather than allowing them to continue their behind-the-scenes conspiracies that would only destabilize the country. Lansdale believed that another coup d'état was a real possibility and wanted to prevent it.[23]

While Lansdale was working the Ngô Đình Diệm and Washington angle, Durbrow continued to exert his influence on the discussions in Washington from his senior position in Saigon. Durbrow concurred with Lansdale that the United States needed to make a statement in support of Ngô Đình Diệm, especially with the new administration in place.[24] However, Durbrow had two points of contention with such a January 1961 statement from Kennedy. First, Durbrow argued that a statement of support before the April 1961 elections might lead some to speculate that the United States supported Ngô Đình Diệm in the election. This would allow critics of the U.S. presence in Vietnam to argue that the Americans were putting pressure on the Vietnamese for favorable results for Ngô Đình Diệm. Second, Durbrow argued that because he had been instructed to put pressure on Ngô Đình Diệm to liberalize his government and had not seen any real results, a statement of support might allow Ngô Đình Diệm an opportunity to procrastinate further. If U.S. pressure to initiate reforms in the RVN eased, Ngô Đình Diệm would not react as quickly as Durbrow wanted. This was the same line of reasoning that Durbrow had employed in November after the abortive coup d'état. Durbrow reiterated his position that only reforms would reverse the negative trends in South Vietnam and avert a Việt Cộng victory. Durbrow suggested that Kennedy issue a statement, but he cautioned that it be guarded in its praise and focus only on past achievements.

Durbrow was reassured that Ngô Đình Diệm seemed to be making some changes. There were moves to publicize high-profile corruption cases such as the one that dealt with the former chief of Biao district in Lâm Đồng province who had been accused of torturing detainees.[25] Ngô Đình Diệm also discussed at a February 6 press conference the reorganization of village administrations, the problems of decentralization, and a number of other governmental reforms.[26] The next week, it was announced that Lieutenant Trận Trận Hà, chief of Câu Ngan district in Vĩnh Bình province was suspended based upon complaints by district and village authorities.[27] This was followed by several more publicized removals of district chiefs for actions against the Republic.[28] Ngô Đình Diệm also impressed Durbrow with his campaigning for the April 1961 election, during which he worked to interact with the people at a variety of venues and events.

Durbrow was less optimistic about Lansdale's plans for a two-party system. Ironically, he argued that Lansdale's plan would encourage another attempt at a coup d'état or reaffirm to Ngô Đình Diệm that the United States was encouraging his opposition. This would allow Ngô Đình Diệm to move further away from American advice and support. Durbrow did not consider the fact that Lansdale's plan included Ngô Đình Diệm in the process rather than trying to work around the Saigon government as had been the practice in the previous months. Because of the unsophisticated nature of the opposition to Ngô Đình Diệm in the RVN, Durbrow recommended that the United States continue to put pressure on Ngô Đình Diệm to adopt as many liberal procedures and reforms as possible, which would "plant the seeds of democracy and eventually create a solid enough base on which to build still further democratic institutions."29 While the United States applied the pressure, Durbrow maintained that American representatives should make it known to the opposition that another coup d'état attempt was out of the question. Additionally, he argued that American diplomats should try to channel their energy and attention to push for constructive programs within the constitutional framework. What was missing in the Durbrow alternative to Lansdale was the role of Ngô Đình Diệm and the Saigon government. Durbrow envisioned the United States controlling the political opposition in Vietnam; Lansdale saw the United States as a facilitator to join the opposition with the existing government to work out their differences and focus the energy and attention of all the Vietnamese politicians toward their common problems.

As the Kennedy administration began to formulate its foreign policy toward Ngô Đình Diệm and Vietnam, based in part on the *Basic Counterinsurgency Plan for Viet Nam* and the Lansdale report, the personalities in Washington found themselves in the position of deciding which side of the coin to back. Robert Komer, who served as a staff member of the National Security Council, offered his personal and unofficial views in a February 1 memorandum to Deputy Special Assistant to the President for National Security Affairs Walter Rostow.30 Komer backed the Lansdale and CIA position that there was no alternative to Ngô Đình Diệm in 1961. Ngô Đình Diệm, he maintained, had demonstrated courage and leadership despite growing opposition, which was evident in the new media reporting and Durbrow's telegrams. Ngô Đình Diệm still held more loyalty of the people than any of his possible successors. As such, Komer argued that the events of November 11 had severely shaken Ngô Đình Diệm's confidence in the United States, and the fragile relationship needed to be refortified. He called for American sympathy and support from the highest levels as well as U.S. action on Ngô Đình Diệm's reasonable requests for money, equipment, and technical assistance. While all of this needed to be accomplished with the new administration, Komer also asserted that Ngô Đình Diệm must be made to realize that the United States could only provide the means to combat the communist insurgents; the people of Vietnam had to provide the will, initiative, and determination.

Komer argued that these steps needed to be taken to avoid a crisis in South Vietnam, but he also looked to the future and the U.S. role in supporting the Ngô Đình Diệm government: "Re-establishing close ties with Diem will get us little in the long run unless we keep working on him."31 Komer advocated long-range planning in addition to the stopgap measures designed to bring the United States–Ngô Đình Diệm relationship back to where it was before November 11. Komer represented the new thinking in Washington that tried to synthesize the Durbrow-Lansdale differences. This approach would pay immediate dividends so long as the Americans in charge of U.S. diplomacy in Vietnam continued to remain sympathetic to the plight of Ngô Đình Diệm. Once Washington leaned toward the old Durbrow position, which it would do in 1962, that balance would be lost, as would any possible reconciliation between the United States and Ngô Đình Diệm.

On February 3, Rusk sent a dispatch to Durbrow informing him of the approval of the *Basic Counterinsurgency Plan for Viet Nam*, specifically mentioning the 20,000-man increase and the extra training and equipment of 32,000 Civil Guard.32 The plan was to be funded by US$29 million from MAP for expanding the armed forces, US$12.7 million from MAP for the Civil Guard, and US$650,000 for psychological operations and communications equipment. In the dispatch, which was drafted by Wood and approved by Parsons, Rusk instructed Durbrow to present the plan to Ngô Đình Diệm and recommend that it be implemented "promptly and vigorously" to overcome the Việt Cộng advances and improve South Vietnam's defense against an overt invasion from the North. The Wood-drafted dispatch also had Rusk reaffirming the need for Ngô Đình Diệm to act toward the liberalization of his government to shore up local support. Rusk also instructed Durbrow to inform Ngô Đình Diệm that the counter-insurgency plan was only for the fiscal year 1961. Approval for an additional year would be dependent upon congressional approval, and that, so it was implied, would depend upon the political as well as the military situation.

The border was also on the mind of Kennedy, who questioned the chairman of the JCS General Lyman L. Lemnitzer as to whether existing forces in South Vietnam could not be redistributed to increase anti-guerrilla activities while the new troops were trained and equipped.[33] Kennedy continued to focus on the fact that there were only between 7,000 and 15,000 Việt Cộng in South Vietnam and that the RVN armed forces totaled 150,000, to be increased to 170,000. Kennedy was willing to increase the effort, but he wanted results.[34]

While Kennedy was looking for solutions to the military struggle in South Vietnam and determining how best the United States could aid Ngô Đình Diệm toward that goal, Ngô Đình Diệm responded to pieces of Lansdale's advice from his January visit. On February 6, Ngô Đình Diệm gave his first press conference to foreign correspondences in Saigon. In it, he did his best to connect with the media, offering candid answers and even joking with the reporters at the end of the session.[35] Ngô Đình Diệm was asked how he planned to reorganize different levels of his government to better serve the people and defend against Việt Cộng activities. In response, he openly discussed the plan to increase youth participation in village councils through additional elections and the process of decentralizing the councils. He introduced two new ministries, the Department of Civic Action and the Department of Rural Affairs, which brought the total number of ministers to twelve and the number of secretaries of state to sixteen. The four Secretaries without a special portfolio included a secretary to the president and three secretaries whose role it was to coordinate between departments: The secretary of security acted as a liaison between Defense and Interior, the secretary of economic development coordinated Economy, Finance, Public Works, and Rural Affairs, while the secretary of culture and social welfare worked with Education, Health, and Labor. These positions, as well as the creation of institutions like the Superior Council of Judiciary and the National Economic Council were designed to ease the pressure and responsibilities of the president as well as blunt the arguments of the Saigon critics.

Ngô Đình Diệm acknowledged that these reforms were only a start and reaffirmed that more could not be accomplished, such as complete village council elections, until greater security reigned. He argued that elections would only be successful if the citizenry had a degree of education and level of competence in the political process and lived in a stable environment that was free of security concerns. He acknowledged that his government had yet to meet these conditions. Even as Ngô Đình Diệm was expanding the Saigon government, he decreased the number of offices that reported directly to the Office of the President from twenty to six. The restructuring of the government was one of the few more significant changes called for by the United States and consistently pushed by Durbrow.

Durbrow was also complimentary of Ngô Đình Diệm's performance at the press conference, as the president provided clear and informed answers to the foreign and Vietnamese press.[36] Durbrow commented on Ngô Đình Diệm's relaxed manner and his joking with the reporters after the session. He was encouraged by the reforms mentioned by Ngô Đình Diệm and believed that if he granted more authority to his secretaries, the RVN would function much more efficiently. Durbrow noted that the announced reforms were more than had been expected based on his assessment at the end of January, and while there was not enough in the way of immediate concessions for democratic reform, Ngô Đình Diệm's call for decentralization, the creation of new institutions, and his forward-looking approach promised real potential for new initiatives in South Vietnam. Durbrow's impression of Ngô Đình Diệm had moved a long way since the turbulent days in November when he called for the ouster of the South Vietnamese leader. Whether that was a result of Ngô Đình Diệm's change after his meetings with Lansdale, Durbrow's continued insistence on change, or the fact that the ambassador's days were numbered is unclear. With the new Vietnamese year, it appeared that the RVN and the United States were finally working from the same perspective.

In Durbrow's next meeting with Ngô Đình Diệm in the presence of Nguyễn Đình Thuận, during a February 13 farewell visit by Command in Chief, U.S. Army, Pacific, General Isaac D. White, he and McGarr gave Ngô Đình Diệm an abridged copy of the *Basic Counterinsurgency Plan for Viet Nam*.[37] Ngô Đình Diệm's main concern was how the RVN would be able to finance the piaster cost for the additional 20,000 men when coupled with other major expenses such as the planned road from Tây Ninh along the Cambodian border to the Gulf of Thailand and the extra security forces needed to protect the construction crews building the Kontom-Tourane (Danang) road. While Ngô Đình Diệm and Nguyễn Đình Thuận pressed Durbrow and McGarr on what would happen if the South Vietnamese could not finance the increase, Durbrow indicated that the plan was flexible to a certain extent. This was a significant departure from Durbrow's original supposition that Ngô Đình Diệm had only requested the additional troops to increase the amount of money the United States would spend in Vietnam.

The April 1961 election was also discussed at the meeting when Ngô Đình Diệm outlined the insurgency plan to disrupt the event by preventing individuals from voting or forcing them to vote for weak candidates in order to lessen the power of the government. Ngô Đình Diệm cited captured documents that indicated the Việt Cộng's plan to cause riots, demonstrations, and bombing in the cities to deter or influence the vote. Through the course of this farewell visit, Durbrow listened patiently and was sympathetic to the piaster problem as it related to the armed forces increase and other RVN commitments. He was less encouraged by Ngô Đình Diệm and Nguyễn Đình Thuận's assurance that they would review and comment on the *Basic Counterinsurgency Plan for Viet Nam* before the tentative end-of-February deadline.[38]

While Ngô Đình Diệm and Durbrow were making progress in Saigon, even if the effects of November 11 were still evident, the discussions in Washington between State Department officials and America's allies continued to offer evidence on the transforming relationship. Under-Secretary of State Chester Bowles pushed the idea of reform on the South Vietnamese government with Trần Văn Chương while Wood worked on the British.[39] Bowles, who had been in this position since January 25, highlighted the importance of land redistribution for the Vietnamese people, specifically mentioning the communist efforts in doing this and the effect it had on the peasants. Bowles might not have been aware of the extent of the RVN's redistribution of land which had already been significant. He also had to be reminded by Trần Văn Chương of the failure of the communists in moving too fast, which resulted in disaster in the latter part of the 1950s.

Bowles acknowledged the difficulties, suggesting that he envisioned a program like

Thailand or Japan. The problem with this approach was that neither country had the threat of external invasion or the worries of a growing communist insurgency. There was also the added problem that Japan's redistribution was a result of its defeat by the United States and the active American occupation of the Japanese territories after the Second World War. While Bowles certainly was not making that connection, the post–November 11 atmosphere would have made it difficult for Trần Văn Chương or Ngô Đình Diệm not to consider the parallel.

Bowles also demonstrated a very Western approach to the Asian problem when he offered to Trần Văn Chương the position that the United States wanted to bring the people of Southeast Asia together to share in a common destiny. While Bowles acknowledged the local differences in Southeast Asia, he offered the analogy of the nineteenth-century British navy in its role of protector to the United States, which allowed the Americans to grow and prosper. Bowles' interpretation of American-British relations in the nineteenth century was unique, and even if one were to accept his dubious premise, he surely must have realized that the British, and French, were equated with colonialism and imperialism. Having the United Sates assume the role of protectorate using a nineteenth-century analogy of colonialism might have sent the wrong message to the Vietnamese ambassador. Trần Văn Chương did not give away any negative inclination on the analogy, choosing only to agree on the necessity of closer relations between the countries of Southeast Asia.

A week after the Bowles–Trần Văn Chương exchange, Wood briefed British Minister in the United States Viscount Samuel Hood and members of the British embassy on the situation in Vietnam. Wood offered an overview of Durbrow's effort at getting Ngô Đình Diệm to liberalize his government and discussed the *Basic Counterinsurgency Plan for Viet Nam* and Ngô Đình Diệm's February 6 press conference.⁴⁰ Overall, the Wood synopsis showed encouraging prospects for the immediate future of Ngô Đình Diệm's Vietnam. There was a sense that Ngô Đình Diệm might move toward greater liberalization, while his interaction with the foreign and Vietnamese press offered the hope that he was relaxing and moving outside the narrow confines he had entered after November 11. Lord Hood agreed that Ngô Đình Diệm's recent actions offered hope of a better future, though he suggested that the British position on Ngô Đình Diệm was a little more pessimistic.

By the end of February, Nguyễn Đình Thuận gave a response to the *Basic Counterinsurgency Plan for Viet Nam* as had been the arrangement, despite the fact that Durbrow believed the Vietnamese would not be so quick to respond.⁴¹ Nguyễn Đình Thuận maintained support for most of the military aspects of the plan with the exception of a few instances that called for a consolidation of power, while Nguyễn Đình Thuận, and presumably Ngô Đình Diệm, did not believe the Vietnamese had the personnel to provide the leadership or expertise. Nguyễn Đình Thuận reported the acceptance of the 20,000-man increase, which was not a surprise, though he cautioned against creating a "no man's land" along the Cambodian border, as McGarr had suggested, because of the number of people that would be displaced by the project. Nguyễn Đình Thuận did acknowledge the difficulty in controlling the waterways, which would remain a problem for the South Vietnamese and Americans for almost another decade.

The initial reaction of Ngô Đình Diệm and Nguyễn Đình Thuận when they received the *Basic Counterinsurgency Plan for Viet Nam* questioned how the RVN would pay for it. Nguyễn Đình Thuận's February 18 response showed that this concern had been addressed. There were also a number of political issues detailed in the *Basic Counterinsurgency Plan for*

Viet Nam that Nguyễn Đình Thuận addressed in his response though his reply was not complete. Some of the more significant issues included in Nguyễn Đình Thuận's response were the greater role of the National Assembly in questioning individual government departments about their operating expenses, appointing oppositionists to cabinet posts as Lansdale had suggested, encouraging a more liberal press code as had been introduced earlier, and easing restrictions on Vietnamese studying abroad. Nguyễn Đình Thuận also agreed to discuss the reformation, or abolishment, of the Cần Lao Party with Ngô Đình Diệm. This initial response would set the stage for further negotiations that would last through the end of Durbrow's tenure as the U.S. ambassador to the RVN. Much had been accomplished in the opening weeks of 1961, though there still remained many items that needed attention. Lansdale, Durbrow and McGarr would remain at the center of that attention as the new year continued.

On February 1, Lansdale wrote a piece, *Bình Hưng: A Counter Guerrilla Case Study*, about that village at the tip of the Cà Mau Peninsula that had been settled in March 1959 in an area dominated by the communist insurgents since 1945.[42] Lansdale visited Bình Hưng during his January trip to South Vietnam, during which he talked with the people of the village and interviewed members of the Self-Defense Corps protecting the area. Near the tip of the Cà Mau Peninsula, Bình Hưng was as far as one could go south in the RVN and was representative of all of the problems that the South Vietnamese faced in conducting their war against the Việt Cộng. It was positioned not too far from the Cambodian border where the Việt Cộng had infiltrated, was near the U Minh forest which was a safe haven for the insurgents, and was within the embarkation area for the Việt Minh forces that left the South to go north as a result of the 1954 Geneva Agreements, resulting in a concentration of insurgents who stayed behind to organize personnel and gathered a large cache of weapons should hostilities recommence.

Three hundred and seventy-five southern Chinese established Bình Hưng in 1959. This group, who had resisted Japanese occupation during the Second World War and later fought the Communist Chinese, moved to Kratje province in Cambodia. Led by Father Nguyễn Lộc Hóa, a former lieutenant colonel in the Chinese Nationalist Army, the group requested and was granted leave to establish Bình Hưng. Lansdale eloquently told the story of the plight of Bình Hưng and its constant struggle against the Việt Cộng. In part, the purpose of the story was to inform the policy makers in Washington that there were individuals in Vietnam who were risking their lives every day to resist the communist insurgents and struggled to survive in harsh conditions. These were the people that made up the bulk of support for Ngô Đình Diệm, though their story was seldom told. In passing the story to Parsons, Daniel Anderson commented on a cover sheet that Lansdale's work need not be read professionally, though he thought it was a good story or magazine piece.[43] Anderson suggested forwarding it to the scriptwriters of *The Ugly American*.[44]

The embassy personnel in Saigon never traveled to villages like Bình Hưng and rarely met with Vietnamese who genuinely struggled on a daily basis with the actions and activities of the Việt Cộng. The Vietnamese that the embassy personnel contacted and shared meals with lived in Saigon and were part of the educated elite. Lansdale's Bình Hưng was Vietnam, but organizations like the Free Democratic Party of Vietnam catered to the interests of the foreign diplomats. Published in English and French, the Free Democratic Party of Vietnam produced a *White Paper on Ngô Đình Diệm's Reign* which, as the editor Phạm Huy Cơ asserted, revealed the real Ngô Đình Diệm and purported to expose all of his crimes and corruption.⁴⁵ The sixteen-page pamphlet, based on newspaper articles and editorials, was a perfect example of the unabashed and selective criticisms put forth by Ngô Đình Diệm's opposition. Ngô Đình Diệm had his faults and would do little to improve his image in the post–Durbrow period, but it was an American failing to concentrate on Ngô Đình Diệm's critics who produced such items as the white paper and give less attention to the story of people like the villagers of Bình Hưng.

Another one of the reforms promised by Ngô Đình Diệm and encouraged by Durbrow and his supporters was judicial reform. The RVN had been contemplating the creation of a High Judiciary Court since 1958, but the government had failed to come to any consensus on the composition or function of the organization. The National Assembly had received three draft bills since 1958 and, in February 1961, merged them all into a workable draft bill that complied with articles 4, 70, and 73 of the RVN Constitution.⁴⁶ On February 23, the National Assembly deliberated on the draft bill, with discussion centering on the question of the composition of the High Council of the Judiciary, but were unable to reach any agreement. Various groups within the National Assembly, such as the Personalist Community and the Socialist Union, also met separately to discuss the draft bill in order to reach a compromise and progress toward the completion of the process.

By February 23, the National Assembly passed the first five articles of bill 36/II, which established the High Council of the Judiciary.⁴⁷ The National Assembly created the High Council of the Judiciary with a chairman, who would be the president of the RVN or his representative and one automatic member who would be the first chairman of the Cassation Court. Five other members would serve on the court, three of which would be elected by the judges of the Court of Cassation and the Court of Appeals and the other two elected by the judges of the Tribunals of First Instance, Courts of Peace with extended competence, and Tribunals of Peace. Members served three-year appointments with the opportunity for reelection. The creation of the court was a serious step forward for the RVN in creating the necessary bureaucratic machinery to continue improving the government and move forward in the transformation of South Vietnam from a former colonial possession to a viable anticommunist state and a model nation for the Free World in Asia and the Pacific.

The National Assembly, voting in secret on February 23, endorsed Vương Quang Nhường's appointment as the first chairman of the Constitutional Court.⁴⁸ Seventy-four of the 123 deputies in the National Assembly voted for Vương Quang Nhường, who was appointed by Ngô Đình Diệm in conformity with article 86 of the Constitution and article 2 of Law 7/60 which was passed on December 23, 1960. Vương Quang Nhường was highly praised by Lại Tử of the Personalist Community and Lê Trọng Quát of the Socialist Union for his work as a barrister. On February 24, the National Assembly passed the remaining fourteen articles of draft bill 36/II, which established the guidelines for electing members and operating the day-to-day functions of the court.⁴⁹ The final articles of the bill also stipulated that the new High Council of the Judiciary could issue punitive measures against magistrates for disciplinary problems, but it could not issue admonitions or indictments. The High Council of the Judiciary also earned the right to approve any appointment or transfer of judges made by the secretary of state for justice. The creation of this organization was another example of Ngô Đình Diệm and the Saigon government working toward the ideals of a Republic in Vietnam, though not all critics of the Saigon government were satisfied.

At the first plenary meeting of the second extraordinary session on March 2, the

National Assembly passed legislation creating the National Economic Council, an organization promised by Ngô Đình Diệm to Durbrow and the Americans as part of his overall reform plan.[50] In the session, the National Assembly finished debate on the final four articles of the new council, adopting articles 2, 6, and 7 and deleting article 16, which required the council to submit its opinion, when requested, on draft bills on economic questions within seven months. In the three articles passed by the National Assembly in this first reading, the National Economic Council was designed as an advisory council to the president and chairman of the National Assembly and was given the power to establish provisional commissions to examine specific economic questions or policy, all of which was funded by the National Budget. On February 18, the National Assembly passed article 3 of the draft bill to create the National Economic Council, which established the composition of the organization. The council would have fifty-five regular members and twenty-four alternates representing various branches of the economy.[51]

Continuing the path toward his Republic, Ngô Đình Diệm appointed four lawyers to serve as magistrates on the Constitutional Court, under Order 80-TTP on March 15.[52] They were Vu Tien Tuấn, president of the Court of Cassation; Đình Văn Huấn who was the attorney general in the Saigon Court of Appeals and head of the Judiciary Service in the Southern Area; Nguyễn Trúc Chi, president of the Court of Appeals in Hue; and Trần Tắc Lâm, chairman of the State Council. These men would join Vương Quang Nhường, who had been appointed chairman of the Constitutional Court by Ngô Đình Diệm, under Order 76-TTP, and had been endorsed by the National Assembly. Ngô Đình Diệm promulgated Laws 5/61 and 6/61 on March 17 establishing the National Economic Council and the High Court of the Judiciary, thus accomplishing, albeit over a longer period of time than anticipated, two critical reforms to the Saigon government that not only demonstrated his willingness to seek and follow through on American counsel but also to broaden the power of the government bureaucracy as was called for in the 1956 Constitution.[53] While the Saigon government moved forward, so did the United States as Durbrow's replacement was announced.

On February 20, the RVN endorsed the appointment of Frederick E. Nolting, Jr., as the new ambassador extraordinary and plenipotentiary of the United States.[54] Nolting, who was born in Richmond, Virginia, on August 24, 1911, had been with the U.S. Department of State since 1946 after serving as a lieutenant commander in the U.S. Navy during the Second World War. From 1950 to 1955, he served as the assistant to the deputy under-secretary of state and special assistant to the secretary of state for mutual security affairs. He was then appointed the director of the Office of Political Affairs of the U.S. delegation to the North Atlantic Treaty Organization with the rank of minister. In 1957, when Durbrow arrived in Vietnam, Nolting became the deputy U.S. representative to the North Atlantic Council in Paris with the rank of minister-counselor. Not too much was known about Nolting in the RVN, but his insertion into this new role was welcomed by many who stood opposite of Durbrow and his handling of Ngô Đình Diệm.

11

A New Plan for an Old Problem

Within the first two months of the Kennedy administration, Vietnam became one of the highest priorities in American foreign relations. As such, Kennedy wanted to engage U.S. forces more energetically in Vietnam rather than wait for the *Basic Counterinsurgency Plan for Viet Nam* to take effect in eighteen to twenty-four months.[1] It must be remembered that Kennedy ushered in a new vision of the United States in world affairs in his inaugural address with the challenge to "Let every nation know, whether it wishes us well or ill, that we shall pay any price, bear any burden, meet any hardship, support any friend, oppose any foe to assure the survival and the success of liberty."[2] To wait in Vietnam with the potential of seeing that region slip closer to the communist sphere was anathema to the Kennedy administration's goals and objectives in diplomacy.

On March 1, Durbrow received instructions from Rusk outlining potential American action before the *Basic Counterinsurgency Plan for Viet Nam* was implemented, or even approved, by the RVN in order to do something against the communist insurgents. These instructions, drafted by Wood and cleared with Anderson, called on Durbrow to begin implementing parts of the *Basic Counterinsurgency Plan for Viet Nam*, unless the ambassador objected, with or without the RVN's approval. Included in the instructions were the weeding out of less-qualified MAAG personnel and the insertion of better-qualified advisers who had counter-guerrilla training as well as the introduction of British and/or Malayans to work with the ARVN and the Civil Guard. Earlier conversations on the differences between Malaya's communist insurgency and the process by which colonial Britain engaged with its rebels appeared to be lost with the new administration.

Rusk also called for Durbrow to implement parts of the *Basic Counterinsurgency Plan for Viet Nam* that focused on eliminating the Việt Cộng from South Vietnam and reorganizing the ARVN to increase its ranger companies and decrease its regular infantry by prioritizing MAP assistance. Outside of the military, Rusk instructed Durbrow to use his best judgment in beginning economic programs of the *Basic Counterinsurgency Plan for Viet Nam* that focused on improving peasant loyalty to the Saigon government, to include such benefits as security, money, land, health, education, and better farming methods. Rusk continued to link the British experience in Malaya with that of Vietnam by suggesting that the treatment of Việt Cộng prisoners follow the British model in order to maximize intelligence and propaganda value.

A week later, Durbrow responded to the instructions in a nineteen-page reply in which he agreed with the Department of State plan to implement parts of the *Basic Counterinsurgency Plan for Viet Nam* with or without South Vietnamese approval.[3] Durbrow lamented the slow response of Ngô Đình Diệm and Nguyễn Đình Thuận in addressing the plan despite, in Durbrow's view, the rigorous manner in which the embassy had pushed the plan or the necessity of the *Basic Counterinsurgency Plan for Viet Nam*'s approval before MAAG could proceed. Durbrow suggested that Ngô Đình Diệm's delay was a result of his inability to relinquish personal power as the *Basic Counterinsurgency Plan for Viet Nam* called for or to share power with members outside of his family.

Durbrow's criticism may be correct, but it was made in an atmosphere of distrust and discontent on the heels of the November 11 abortive coup d'état. It is hard to imagine any president, so soon after surviving an attempted coup d'état, voluntarily giving up power. This is especially true when it was Ngô Đình Diệm's principal ally making the request. Durbrow concluded that he did not have the authority to demand that Ngô Đình Diệm and Nguyễn Đình Thuận approve the *Basic Counterinsurgency Plan for Viet Nam*—only the RVN could implement it—but he would continue to push the plan and recommended that Kennedy send Ngô Đình Diệm a personal message if Durbrow failed to convince Ngô Đình Diệm and Nguyễn Đình Thuận of the necessity of a quick implementation of the programs.

Durbrow's remarks about his limits in forcing the *Basic Counterinsurgency Plan for Viet Nam* on the South Vietnamese echoed an earlier message by McGarr to General Williston Palmer, the director of military assistance in the Office of the Assistant Secretary of Defense.[4] McGarr argued that the Department of State instructions would seriously hamper the progress made by the United States in South Vietnam, suggesting that implementation of the instructions would move away from the approved *Basic Counterinsurgency Plan for Viet Nam* rather than advance it. McGarr worried that the Rusk telegram was too much in the form of a directive where McGarr believed what was needed was time to allow the plan to take shape. At the heart of the McGarr argument was the underlying tension left over from November.

The last thing the United States needed to do was start making demands of the Saigon government to implement a plan that it was not ready to fully support, or begin the process of implementing parts of the plan itself, which would not only limit the positives of the entire effort but also parallel the old colonial model of acting in a host country without approval, due consideration, or respect for the laws, leadership, or sovereignty of that country. Engaging in the *Basic Counterinsurgency Plan for Viet Nam* before it was approved by the RVN could easily, and rightly, be judged by the Saigon government as an American effort to begin its own form of control, or imperialism, in the RVN. Even if that was as far from the American position as possible, perception was what mattered at that moment, and the prevailing atmosphere within Saigon was tense.

Durbrow met with Nguyễn Đình Thuận and Secretary of State for Foreign Affairs Vũ Văn Mẫu on March 11.[5] Among the subjects discussed was the status of the RVN's approval for the *Basic Counterinsurgency Plan for Viet Nam*. One of the recurring problems for the Vietnamese was financing the plan. Nguyễn Đình Thuận informed Durbrow that his government was working on a VN$1.5 billion loan but had run into problems with the banks, who did not want to fund just the military aspects of the plan and demanded that a part of the loan be used for economic development. While the Vietnamese had no problem with this, it did create the problem of finding other loans for the rest of the military aspects of the plan. Durbrow, Nguyễn Đình Thuận, and Vũ Văn Mẫu also discussed various aspects of the *Basic Counterinsurgency Plan for Viet Nam* that dealt with liberalization. Nguyễn Đình Thuận was worried about bringing opposition members into the cabinet if they did not agree with the government position, though Durbrow dismissed that concern and remarked that there were loyal oppositionists in the RVN who needed to be a part of the Saigon government.

Nguyễn Đình Thuận was also skeptical about giving the National Assembly the power of oversight over governmental agencies as was the practice in the United States. Nguyễn Đình Thuận, however, did get Ngô Đình Diệm's approval to allow the press to witness the National Assembly hearings with ministers in order to counter the criticism of the government and the stories emanating from Radio Catinat. Nguyễn Đình Thuận was particularly pleased with the improved relations between the government and the press, which Durbrow acknowledged. The Saigon government had worked hard at improving this aspect of its public-relations problem and had made real progress. There was less positive information to report on the situation with the Cần Lao Party and the American call to either reform or abolish it. Nguyễn Đình Thuận had spoken with Ngô Đình Diệm about the proposal, but there appeared to be no movement. Durbrow was encouraged by his meeting with Nguyễn Đình Thuận and Vũ Văn Mẫu, though he stopped short of endorsing the position of full implementation until the Vietnamese provided more details on the approved plan.

McGarr had also met with Ngô Đình Diệm on March 6 to discuss the *Basic Counterinsurgency Plan for Viet Nam* and left confident that the president was ready to approve it as it had been presented by Durbrow on February 13.[6] A week later, after the Durbrow–Ngô Đình Diệm exchange, McGarr addressed a letter to Nguyễn Đình Thuận expressing doubt for his earlier optimism. McGarr communicated his concern to Nguyễn Đình Thuận that the military aspects of the plan not be approved piecemeal before the overall plan was approved and implemented. McGarr focused on the 20,000-man increase as well as the additional MAP assistance that could only become available after the plan was finalized. McGarr outlined nine military aspects of the plan that were essential to the overall success of the struggle against the communist insurgency, including an entirely new military chain of command from the Joint General Staff of the RVN armed forces to the units in the field. The control of the military units by civilian agents, such as the provincial chiefs, was counterintuitive to the *Basic Counterinsurgency Plan for Viet Nam*. McGarr also highlighted the need for a more effective logistical system and the elimination of duplicate technical services. These points, and others, such as force composition, intelligence, border and coastal surveillance, psychological warfare, and improved communication, were essential to the success of the *Basic Counterinsurgency Plan for Viet Nam*. McGarr, like Durbrow, implored Ngô Đình Diệm and Nguyễn Đình Thuận to act quickly to implement the plan, which would allow for greater U.S. participation in the RVN.

Durbrow met with Ngô Đình Diệm on March 16 for seventy-five minutes to again urge him to accept the *Basic Counterinsurgency Plan for Viet Nam*.[7] Both he and McGarr had worked on Nguyễn Đình Thuận enough to get a tentative agreement on most of the military aspects of the plan. Durbrow initiated this conversation by telling Ngô Đình Diệm that he was going to see Rusk in Bangkok at the end of the month and would be asked about the *Basic Counterinsurgency Plan for Viet Nam*. Durbrow was to leave in ten days and used that deadline as the time frame for Ngô Đình Diệm to nominate military and civilian individuals to meet with and discuss the plan with American counterparts and reconcile any differences.

While Durbrow acknowledged the common ground already established by mutual agreement of parts of the plan, there were still several areas that needed to be addressed before the United States proceeded with the *Basic Counterinsurgency Plan for Viet Nam*. The first issue was the inclusion of oppositionists in the cabinet. This was a major concession for Ngô Đình Diệm and one that even Lansdale recognized as important for political stability in South Vietnam. While Ngô Đình Diệm understood the logic of the argument, it must have been a difficult concept to accept as some of the oppositionists had openly sided with the coup d'état plotters less than five months earlier. Even as these oppositionists had denounced the rebels and appeared to have reconciled their opposition with the need to support the Saigon government, Ngô Đình Diệm was justified in delaying their entry into power so soon after November 11.

Durbrow also brought up the question of the Cần Lao Party and rumors of secret activities that harmed the image of the Saigon government. Durbrow argued that the Cần Lao membership needed to become public, or, better yet, the party needed to be dissolved. Ngô Đình Diệm did not reply directly to these suggestions. To dissolve the organization would have been harmful to Ngô Đình Diệm, and even if the group created bad public relations, its organizational strength benefited the president. Durbrow finished the conversation by urging a better intelligence network and improved relations with Cambodia. The two also discussed press liberalization, village elections to add youth into leadership positions, and other proposed reforms that had been discussed. Durbrow was pleased by the exchange as well as Ngô Đình Diệm's gratitude for the *Basic Counterinsurgency Plan for Viet Nam*. Though Durbrow was cautiously optimistic and McGarr had begun ordering MAP equipment for the new 20,000 troops, he maintained that the United States needed to wait for full implementation until after lower-level military and civilian meetings concluded between the RVN and the United States.

Durbrow's mentioning of Cambodia forced the resurfacing of the long and turbulent relationship between it and the RVN. The two Southeast Asian neighbors had never been able to reconcile their quarrelsome past nor overcome the by-products of French colonialism. Cambodia remained an irritant for the RVN while Durbrow used the issue of improved relations as another way to force Ngô Đình Diệm to conform to his position. Unfortunately for the Americans and Vietnamese, the Cambodians were not willing to compromise on any of the significant issues related to regional security, while the RVN was less than sympathetic to the American calls for Southeast Asian partnerships if it meant assuming a secondary role to the Cambodians.

The South Vietnamese did not help to improve the relationship with Cambodia. *Sài Gòn Mới*, which had recently been created in December 1960, had been very unfavorable in its reporting of the Cambodian situation and even published, as had the *Times of Vietnam*, anti–Sihanouk cartoons. When Durbrow met with Nguyễn Đình Thuận and Secretary of State for Foreign Affairs Vũ Văn Mẫu on March 11, the issue of Cambodia surfaced. While Nguyễn Đình Thuận and Vũ Văn Mẫu were critical of the Cambodian press and its coverage of Vietnam, Durbrow countered that it was a response to what the Vietnamese press had been publishing.[8] Durbrow urged them to issue a press truce and mentioned that the Cambodian press had already attempted one earlier. Vũ Văn Mẫu agreed to issue a truce, to start on March 15, but did not seem encouraged with the potential results, as he had already tried to do the same in February without success. It was extremely important for the RVN to control its border with Cambodia if the fight against the communist insurgency was to improve. Sour relations between the two countries, stimulated by the press wars, would do nothing to improve the situation. Nguyễn Đình Thuận was not confident that an agreement could be reached between the two countries as long as there were outstanding issues that the Cambodians refused to resolve.

One of those issues was the C-47 transport aircraft used by the rebels who orchestrated the abortive coup d'état on November 11 and 12, 1960. Nguyễn Đình Thuận had requested its return only to receive the reply that there had been several instances where Cambodian barges or other transports had been seized by the Vietnamese; as such, the Cambodians informed Nguyễn Đình Thuận that he should not be concerned with the C-47 transport that carried the rebels to Phnom Penh which "happened to fall from the skies into RKG hands."[9] Durbrow was sympathetic to Nguyễn Đình Thuận's plight but urged him to make concessions in order to work out an arrangement with the Cambodians to resolve the border issue.

Another issue that plagued the relationship between the two countries was a March 4 incident in Tịnh Biên district, An Giang province, when Vietnamese security forces met a group of approximately 200 individuals, of which twenty to thirty were armed, and engaged in a firefight, but the South Vietnamese patrol did not pursue the group because it was outnumbered; however it did observe that approximately 150 Vietnamese had been taken as prisoners. As the force crossed into Cambodia, the South Vietnamese claimed that the Khmer frontier posts provided support fire as it left South Vietnam. While the Vietnamese admitted that some of the individuals might have voluntarily gone with the group to avoid military service, Minister of the Interior Lam Lê Trinh, who was also present for this discussion, expressed his frustration at the failure of the Cambodian government to acknowledge the incident or provide any further information on the Vietnamese citizens.

Lam Lê Trinh indicated to Durbrow that he might blame the Việt Cộng for the incident and argued that it was their intent to sabotage Vietnamese–Cambodian relations; Durbrow believed that Lam Lê Trinh actually thought this was true. Whatever the RVN reaction, Lam Lê Trinh informed Durbrow that the incident could not go unmentioned given the extent to which the Cambodians had publicized alleged Vietnamese executions and extortions as well as their statements regarding the March 4 event. Lam Lê Trinh was at a loss as to why the Cambodians were making the affair an international incident, including bringing it to the attention of secretary general of the United Nations, Dag Hammarskjold, though it was the American view that the articles in *Sài Gòn Mãi* were the primary cause. Lam Lê Trinh was reminded of the Sihanouk fourteen-nation proposal in January 1961, which coincided with the *Sài Gòn Mãi* articles that ridiculed the prince. Durbrow ended the conversation by reiterating the need to for the Vietnamese to come to some understanding with the Cambodians so that the two countries could, if not work together, at least co-exist and provide mutual support against the communist insurgency.

On March 8, the Vietnamese responded to claims made by the *Agence France Presse* that the 300 Vietnamese involved in the incident were simply Vietnamese of Cambodian origin who returned to Cambodia.[10] The *Agence France Presse* asserted that these Vietnamese had fled the RVN to seek the protection of the Cambodian government because Vietnamese officials had arrested them, taken their property, and, in some cases, executed their people without trial. These claims did nothing to ease the tension between the Vietnamese and Khmer governments and only helped to focus Ngô Đình Diệm's attention toward the real problem of Cambodia being used as a staging area for Việt Cộng raids into the RVN.

Tensions mounted in An Giang province on March 11 when approximately 400 bonzes and thousands of Vietnamese of Cambodian origin held a mass rally in Tri Tôn district.[11]

After holding religious ceremonies in remembrance of victims of the communist insurgency, the crowd listened to speakers who denounced the Việt Cộng activities in their province, which included murder, terror, and extortion. The demonstrations also raised VN$20,000 to repair pagodas destroyed by the Việt Cộng and assist families who had been victimized by the communist insurgents.

The border dispute continued to dominate the news relating to Vietnamese–Khmer relations when, on March 13, the Vietnamese mission to the International Control Commission published a letter it sent to the organization regarding the March 4 incident between the government patrol and the thirty armed men who were leading the approximately 200 Vietnamese across the Vĩnh Tế canal in Tịnh Biên district, An Giang province, into Cambodia.[12] The Vietnamese mission demanded that the ICC investigate this incident as the RVN officials claimed it was the Việt Cộng who were the armed men that fired on the government forces and had been operating for some time in the region in violation of international law and the 1954 Geneva Agreements.

When Durbrow met with Ngô Đình Diệm on March 16 to discuss the *Basic Counterinsurgency Plan for Viet Nam*, the issue of Cambodia resurfaced.[13] Durbrow reinforced to Ngô Đình Diệm what he had said to Nguyễn Đình Thuận; *Sài Gòn Mãi* was doing more harm than good in responding to the Cambodian claims of Vietnamese ill treatment of Vietnamese-Khmers within the RVN. Good relations with Cambodia and a secure border were important aspects of the *Basic Counterinsurgency Plan for Viet Nam*. McGarr had argued that the suppression of the Việt Cộng was improbable without cooperation from the Cambodians and stronger border control. Ngô Đình Diệm was not blind to this matter, but he also shared a Vietnamese loathing for the Khmer people. He informed Durbrow that he "sent word" to the *Sài Gòn Mãi* editors to refrain from attacking the Cambodians but received a reply that suggested the newspaper had to respond to Cambodian verbal attacks. As much as Ngô Đình Diệm acknowledged the necessity of the freedom of the press, he could have easily forced the editors to stop pushing the inflammatory articles to ease tension between the two countries if that was his end goal.

Ngô Đình Diệm also reiterated his often-voiced complaint about the difficulty of working with Sihanouk. Ngô Đình Diệm described Sihanouk as a self-anointed world statesman who worked with ex-colonial French officers and French-collaborationist Vietnamese to gain, and then maintain, power.

Ngô Đình Diệm also provided two examples of Sihanouk's insincerity in promoting better Vietnamese–Cambodian relations. The first involved an independent deputy in the French National Assembly, Antoine Pinay, who tried to explain to Sihanouk the nature of the communist insurgency in South Vietnam and its relationship to eventual instability in Cambodia should the Việt Cộng be successful in overthrowing the government in the Republic. Sihanouk, according to Ngô Đình Diệm, responded with a tirade against the Vietnamese and their treatment of the Khmer people in Vietnam. Another example saw the sacking of a Cambodian province chief who met with the Kiến Tường province chief to work out a joint effort to stop the Việt Cộng from operating freely between the two provinces. Ngô Đình Diệm complained of his, and Nguyễn Ngọc Thơ's, inability to even begin the conversation leading to negotiations for better relations with Cambodia because of Sihanouk's intransigence. Durbrow had no advice other than that it was a South Vietnamese issue and needed to be addressed to better fight the Việt Cộng. Durbrow's reinforcement of the importance of the issue was timely, but it was also irrelevant. Ngô Đình Diệm already understood the importance of border security and did not need to be reminded. What was his most significant problem was his inability to reconcile the need for better relations with the Cambodians with his personal dislike for the Khmer people and his animosity, assuredly earned, of Sihanouk.

The issue of Cambodia came up again during a March 27 meeting between Nguyễn Đình Thuần and Rusk in Bangkok while Rusk and Durbrow were attending the April 1961 SEATO Council meeting.[14] As part of a longer discussion about the *Basic Counterinsurgency Plan for Viet Nam* and the need to improve RVN international relations in the region, Rusk reaffirmed the American desire that this occur to better aid the economic and military aspects of the *Basic Counterinsurgency Plan for Viet Nam*. Nguyễn Đình Thuần agreed, letting the secretary of state know that the RVN had plans for Malaya prime minister Abdul Rahman Tunku and General Abdul Haris Nasution to visit the country shortly after the April 9 elections. Durbrow took the opportunity to bring Cambodia into the discussion, reminding Nguyễn Đình Thuần that improved relations with its western neighbor was a part of the *Basic Counterinsurgency Plan for Viet Nam*. Nguyễn Đình Thuần used Durbrow's remark as an opportunity to tell Rusk about the March 4 incident, which Phnom Penh had referred to as a "flight of hundreds of Vietnamese of Cambodian origin."[15] Nguyễn Đình Thuần lamented the Cambodian position, that the Việt Cộng had organized the event, and the fact that the Cambodian press used it as an excuse to intensify its anti–Vietnam campaign. Nguyễn Đình Thuần also commented on the March 24 Cambodian Assembly resolution that criticized the RVN, though he acknowledged Durbrow's assessment that the assembly's move had been motivated by communist elements in that country and was not representative of the people or the government.

Vietnamese-Cambodian relations were not all negative, even if the U.S. embassy was reluctant to report the positive stories emanating from the RVN. On April 5, Vietnamese of Cambodian descent in the village of Đại Tâm, Ba Xuyên province hosted Vietnamese and foreign correspondents who were in Vietnam to cover the April 9 election. The villagers emphasized the point that they had experienced no discrimination because of their ancestry as the North Vietnamese and some Cambodians had claimed.[16] The military representative who accompanied the media, Major Kim Khánh, used himself as an example. Kim Khánh was a Vietnamese citizen from a Khmer family and had risen to the rank of major based on his performance. He cautioned the reporters not to believe the accusations levied against the Saigon government without first exploring the evidence.

The Cambodia issue continued to plague Ngô Đình Diệm for the rest of his tenure in office and would remain a controversial issue during the presidencies of Kennedy, Johnson, and Nixon. The United States was never able to reconcile Cambodia neutrality and Sihanouk's un-neutral actions during the war, while Ngô Đình Diệm's position was not fully appreciated, nor were his calls to force the Cambodians to take a stand in Southeast Asia as had the RVN.

The subject of the *Basic Counterinsurgency Plan for Viet Nam* came up again on March 24 when the Country Team Staff Group met with Nguyễn Đình Thuần and ARVN chief of staff Nguyễn Khánh.[17] Mendenhall chaired the meeting, during which time Nguyễn Đình Thuần, who had seen the plan in detail, offered the status of Vietnamese thinking on the military and economic aspects outlined in the document. Nguyễn Đình Thuần informed the Americans that a draft decree from Ngô Đình Diệm and orders from the Internal Security Council had addressed a number of military issues including giving the field commanders operational control over the counter-insurgency operations and making the corps rather than the military region commander be responsible for conducting these operations under the field commander.

This MAAG recommendation was designed to improve the efficiency of resource use for the RVN armed forces in its counter-insurgency operations and to increase military cohesion in this aspect of the fight. Nguyễn Đình Thuận also informed the group that the Vietnamese were going to convert each military region commander into a logistic commander for his provinces under a military chain of command. McGarr had called for this improvement in communication and coordination of counter-insurgency efforts within a province. While Ngô Đình Diệm had agreed to this latter recommendation, Nguyễn Ngọc Thơ held it up because he questioned two items. First, he wanted to know which command the Sagion–Cholon–Gia Định Special Military District should fall under and, second, he opposed making the province chiefs responsible to a military chain of command when they had so many non-military responsibilities in their provinces.

Nguyễn Ngọc Thơ also wanted civilians in the position of province chiefs rather than military officers even though both Ngô Đình Diệm and Nguyễn Đình Thuận had repeatedly stated that there simply were not enough qualified individuals in the RVN to fill the positions. Nguyễn Đình Thuận also told the Country Team that Ngô Đình Diệm was prepared to issue a decree that formalized the regional and provincial internal security councils but refrained from district and village internal security councils because of the added bureaucracy and limited benefits.

The meeting also resolved the *Basic Counterinsurgency Plan for Viet Nam* issue of establishing a central intelligence agency with a director of the new organization in place by April 15. Mendenhall was skeptical of the timeline. The two sides did not reach an agreement on the American plan to create a 500-meter "no man's land" on the Cambodian border, with Nguyễn Đình Thuận citing the same objections of unnecessary displacement of Vietnamese and expense. The South Vietnamese did agree that ranger companies would have priority within the 20,000-man increase, though the Saigon government wanted one regiment replaced with an airborne and two marine battalions.

In relation to the political issues, Nguyễn Đình Thuận offered encouragement with his confirmation of greater press opportunities to witness National Assembly committee hearings on legislation and the questioning of government ministers and other high-ranking officials when they visited the National Assembly. Nguyễn Đình Thuận then promised a new press code for the next National Assembly session. In another effort to improve public perception of the Saigon government, Nguyễn Đình Thuận let the Country Team know about the plan to stop using community development labor in the Agrovilles unless the entire village benefited from the experience. This had been one of the primary criticisms of the program since its inception.[18] When asked whether the government would instruct its provincial chiefs on this policy and publicize the change, Nguyễn Đình Thuận agreed. At no time did Ngô Đình Diệm, Ngô Đình Nhu, or Nguyễn Đình Thuận shirk away from their responsibility toward the negative aspects of the Agroville Program once it was shown how mismanaged the program had become. The theory was sound but the implementation was not. Another issue, the introduction of oppositionists into the cabinet, was still a long way from being settled.[19]

The final issue discussed was the financing of the *Basic Counterinsurgency Plan for Viet Nam*, which was most likely one of the reasons the negotiations had been delayed for so long. Nguyễn Đình Thuận and his government did not like the idea of funding the entire

VN$1.5 billion of the plan, though the Saigon government was resigned to taking care of 1961 with a series of loans. There were two concerns with the financial process: one was the "Buy American" problem, which limited what the RVN could purchase and would require the South Vietnamese to use approximately 18 million piasters of its exchange reserve to meet these requirements. The other anxiety was inflation as a result of increasing the currency circulation by 45 percent over a two-year period.

Despite these concerns, the two sides were relaxed and, in Mendenhall's words, "congenial," while Mendenhall concluded that the Vietnamese were prepared to go a considerable way to meet most, if not all, of the *Basic Counterinsurgency Plan for Viet Nam* proposals. He also asserted that because of the impending election, finalization of the plan would not occur until after its results became known. The Nguyễn Đình Thuận–Country Team meeting was a precursor to the next exchange that would take place in Bangkok.

Nguyễn Đình Thuận had the opportunity to discuss the *Basic Counterinsurgency Plan for Viet Nam* again on March 27 with Rusk and Durbrow while the latter two were attending a SEATO Council meeting in Thailand.[20] Nguyễn Đình Thuận reviewed the history of recent Việt Cộng activities for Rusk, expanding upon how the communist insurgents had intensified their campaign against the Vietnamese people and explained why, as a result, Ngô Đình Diệm had not been able to initiate all of the democratic reforms he had proposed or for which the United States had hoped. Nguyễn Đình Thuận used the meeting to reinforce the RVN position that it was completely anti-communist and had always been a firm ally of the United States. He then focused on the financial aspects of the *Basic Counterinsurgency Plan for Viet Nam* and reiterated what he had discussed with Mendenhall three days earlier. At the very least, Rusk offered reassurances that the new administration was serious in its commitment to Vietnam.

He let Nguyễn Đình Thuận know that Kennedy had personally approved the *Basic Counterinsurgency Plan for Viet Nam* and was cognizant of the South Vietnamese financial situation. He even reinforced the movement away from the Durbrow approach of reform before assistance by echoing what Lansdale, Colby, and McGarr had advocated: "economic and military aid will do no good if efforts are not made simultaneously to explain to the people what the government is doing, the goals they hope to attain and the sacrifices needed."[21] This expression of commitment and understanding must have been welcomed, though the good intentions would only last as long as the personalities involved on both sides remained committed to the same process of achieving the desired goals.

The issue of finances arose again on April 8 when Trần Văn Chương met with the acting assistant secretary for Far Eastern affairs, John M. Steeves. While his principle reason for the interview was to discuss the recent SEATO meeting in Bangkok and get clarification on what Kennedy and British prime minister Harold McMillen had discussed during the April 4–8 visit by the British head of state to the United States, Trần Văn Chương asked for, and received, confirmation that the US$41 million offer of help through the *Basic Counterinsurgency Plan for Viet Nam* was tied to the counter-effort of VN$1.5 billion by the Vietnamese. He pleaded for aid, reaffirming the Vietnamese people's willingness to fight and his government's plans for introducing reforms but warning that the two would not be effective without American aid. Trần Văn Chương reaffirmed the basis of the RVN's approach; the Vietnamese people could do the job once properly trained and equipped by an ally whose interests called for a free Vietnam. The time for conditions attached to that aid was not when a crisis was mounting and on the heels of an attempt to overthrow the legitimate government by forces that were suspected of having American encouragement. Implied, though perhaps not understood by Steeves, was the fact that Durbrow had dangled a carrot while he held a stick and had set back relations between the two countries after November 1960. Trần Văn Chương did not want to see these same mistakes repeated with the new administration.

Meanwhile, the focus in Washington was to get things moving. This was reinforced on the military side through a visit to Vietnam by the commanding general of the 18th Airborne Corps, General Thomas Trapnell, and on the civilian side by Walt Rostow. Rostow's plan of action called for the United States to approach Ngô Đình Diệm after the April 9 election to finish the process of approving the *Basic Counterinsurgency Plan for Viet Nam* and win the war. He recommended bringing McGarr to Washington to meet with Fritz Nolting, the ambassador-designate and receive "fresh instructions" so that the two could return to Vietnam as a team. Rostow also called for another Ngô Đình Diệm trip to the United States or a Lyndon Johnson visit to Vietnam to reinforce the new phase of U.S.-Vietnamese relations and impress upon Ngô Đình Diệm "that he must face up to the political and morale elements of the job, as well as its military components."[22] Finally, in addition to creating a position similar to a Vietnam czar to oversee all of the policies, Rostow urged the increase of unexploited assets from the United States which could be brought to bear against the Việt Cộng. Quoting Knute Rockne, "we are not saving them for the Junior prom," Rostow wanted action rather than discussions, task forces, and counter-insurgency plans.[23]

As the deputy assistant for national security affairs, Rostow spent some time on the Vietnam issue and the implementation of the *Basic Counterinsurgency Plan for Viet Nam*. One area where he believed the United States could assist in confronting the Việt Cộng was in the use of helicopters. When Trapnell visited Saigon, McGarr had informed him that the fourteen H-19 and eleven H-34 helicopters employed in the RVN were as many as the South Vietnamese could handle. Rostow believed that the helicopter was not being exploited enough in counter-insurgency operations.[24] He, in promoting Kennedy's vision, wanted action and the full efforts of the United States and its Vietnamese ally committed to winning the war. It was this mentality that would eventually mean the end for Ngô Đình Diệm as he moved further away from American advice in conducting his own counter-insurgency campaign.

On April 3, Foreign Secretary Vũ Văn Mẫu and Durbrow signed a Treaty of Amity and Economic Relations, which was the culmination of three years of negotiations between the two countries. The treaty focused on defining the conditions by which citizens of each country could operate businesses in the other as well as set the parameters for active trade and ventures of private American investors to help advance the RVN's industries. Vũ Văn Mẫu, upon signing the document, maintained that the treaty marked "a new step in the history of Vietnamese–American relations which would lead to new prosperity." Durbrow responded by expressing his "great admiration for the outstanding achievements and progress made by the government and people of Viet Nam, whose spirit and determination against heavy odds have evoked the admiration and respect of the free world."[25] While Durbrow may have been entirely sincere in his remarks, he had expressed something less than great admiration for Ngô Đình Diệm in the past six months. The treaty, however, did prove to be one of the positive marks on his records, but it fell short of reconciling the intrigue and duplicity that emanated from the American embassy in Saigon during Durbrow's tenure.

As the ink on the treaty dried, the National Assembly convened for its first ordinary session in 1961, less than one week before the election. Trương Vĩnh Lê praised the economic and social development in the RVN and offered tribute to the armed forces engaged in the struggle against the Việt Cộng. He maintained that in the Republic, "our revolution must be carried out in the spirit of Personalism, collective advancement and community development if we want to eradicate Communism and avoid all political adventures dangerous to the very existence of the nation."[26] Trương Vĩnh Lê commented on the elections and the importance of the democratic experiment: "Each ballot that the citizen will place in the ballot box on April 9 will be not only a stone in the construction of Viet Nam but also an efficient arm for the defence of the nation." The election would showcase the RVN to the world, through which other emerging post-colonial nations would take note and hopefully use as a model or as inspiration in their own democratic experiments.

On April 7, it was publicly announced in Vietnam that Durbrow would leave the RVN around May 1 to take up the post of deputy chief of missions in Paris and be replaced by Frederick E. Nolting, Jr., who had been the U.S. representative to the NATO Council in Paris.[27] While the changing of the guard had been known for some time, the timing of the public announcement, two days before the election, was significant in that many in Saigon knew of the tension and conflict between Ngô Đình Diệm and Durbrow. Durbrow's departure was a symbolic victory for Ngô Đình Diệm in his fight against the public perception that he took his marching orders from Washington. Given that Durbrow, Mendenhall, and Cunningham had privately sided against Ngô Đình Diệm's continued rule, the removal of the primary American opponent demonstrated, at least in Vietnamese terms, the power of the president of the RVN.

12

Vietnamese Democracy in Action

The looming April 1961 election would not only be a test of the Saigon government to showcase the democratic evolution of the RVN, but it also could be used as a potential catalyst for the political and military opposition to initiate another coup d'état attempt if the elections proved to be a sham. The Constitution of the RVN called for the election of a president and vice president to take place on a Sunday three months before the expiration of the presidential five-year term of duty. To prepare for an April 1961 election, the National Assembly created an inter-parliamentary committee that included members of the interior, justice, and legislation committees to work on a bill for the election.[1]

The new election law, No. 1/61, was promulgated on January 6, though elements of it had been discussed in the press.[2] Before its release, Saigon lawyer Trương Đình Dzu met with Cunningham at a social gathering in Saigon and informed him that the *Vietnam Press* had failed to report sections of the new election law that made it less likely that the opposition would ever agree to the results.[3] The parts that the *Vietnam Press* did print were what, he argued, the United States could accept. What was not included in the newspaper account was the fact that a committee of the National Assembly, half named by Ngô Đình Diệm and half appointed by the Assembly, would determine the extent of all campaigning activities and literature. This committee had to approve, and would regulate, all campaigning, to include radio time, campaign posters, and other means of publicizing the candidates. Because Ngô Đình Diệm had a hand in selecting this committee, Trương Đình Dzu maintained that he would essentially control it. As a result, he concluded that the new election laws were a joke. He asserted, after being questioned by Cunningham, that because of the "almost warlike conditions" in the RVN, Ngô Đình Diệm was not being honest with the Vietnamese people. This type of assessment was readily accepted by the U.S. embassy as it geared toward, and reported, the political campaign.

Law 1/61 contained forty-three articles divided into seven chapters that covered rules and regulations governing the voters, candidates, campaign process, voting procedures, election validity and proclamation of the returns, and punitive measures for individuals who tried to obstruct the election process.[4] The new election law also determined the election date, which was set for the Sunday three weeks before the expiration of the mandate for the outgoing president and vice president. On January 13, the Saigon government confirmed that April 9 would be the date for the election in conformity with the election law.[5] Four days later, the secretariat of the National Assembly announced that applications to run in the election for president or vice president had to be submitted before February 7, which conformed to article 34 of the Constitution and articles 2, 3, and 12 of the election law, though two days later the secretariat announced that applications filed after February 7 would still be considered. The National Assembly set up a special election service for those interested in running for office and announced that all candidates who had fulfilled the requirements would have their names posted at the National Assembly, all city halls, and administrative seats in the provinces, districts, and villages.[6]

As the election began to unfold, Ngô Đình Diệm started to make more appearances in the countryside. While he was not actively campaigning, he did make himself visible to the people. One such example was an inspection tour of Tuyên Đức and Pleiku between January 16 and 17. On January 19, Ngô Đình Diệm inspected Phước Long province.[7] These types of appearances, within the role as president, did give Ngô Đình Diệm an advantage over his political rivals as he was able to unofficially campaign before other candidates had similar opportunities. As a result, he was criticized for running an unfair campaign. However, Ngô Đình Diệm had earlier been criticized for not going into the countryside. Despite what he did and regardless of the motives, Ngô Đình Diệm's actions were viewed in a negative way.

With the election law promulgated and the filing procedures set, various organizations began to offer educational workshops on the election and its process. On January 21, the Civil Servants' League decided to conduct courses on Law 1/61 in order to better inform the voters and candidates of how the election would be conducted.[8] Civil Servants who wanted to run in the presidential election needed to attach a certificate of leave without pay, as was provided for in article 14 of Law 1/61 as well as gather 100 signatures of voters who endorsed the candidate.[9] On January 23, Bùi Văn Lương, secretary of state for the interior, initiated a three-day seminar on the presidential election at the city hall in Saigon. The seminar, sponsored by the Interior Ministry, the Office for Civic Action, and the General Office of Information, covered Law 1/61 questions related to the role of the Constitutional Court in the process, and the organization of the election campaign.[10] Additional training courses were conducted in the provinces of Ba Xuyên, Vĩnh Bình, Long An, Kông Khánh, Biên Hòa, Phước Tuy, Quảng Nam, Darlac, and Kontom.[11]

Participants in these sessions learned of the election law and the process for campaigning and voting on April 9 and were instructed to take this knowledge back to their neighborhoods in order to reach as large an audience as possible. Three additional special training courses were conducted in Lộc Ninh and Bình Dương districts for approximately 716 people.[12] Like the courses and sessions before, these trainees would serve as the principle cadres to teach the general population about the election process. In other efforts to disseminate information about the election, the National Motion Picture Production Centre of the Information Office produced a black-and-white, twenty-two-minute, 16 mm documentary that outlined how the election would proceed and explained the process by which a voter could lodge a complaint if his name did not appear on the voters' list.[13] The film also explained how to vote. The Information Office distributed eighty copies of the film to provincial Information Services with orders to show the film to as many people as possible. Workshops continued to be offered throughout the RVN to educate as many people as possible about the election law and their responsibilities as members of the participatory Republic for which they were striving.[14] More than 10,000 people watched the final product on March 13 and 14 in Bình Thuận province in what would be the first of many viewings.[15] While the Saigon government worked diligently on training its people in the election process, the candidates began to emerge. Not surprisingly, Ngô Đình Diệm was one of the first as he began to gather support from organizations around the country.[16] Ngô Đình Diệm had a well-organized political machine to garner support for his candidacy, and he used the print media, especially the *Vietnam Press*, to publicize his national appeal; but Ngô Đình Diệm also had earned many of the accolades he received.

With the publication of the election law and the deadline for announcing one's candidacy, February 7, drawing closer, there was a significant grassroots effort to publicize and encourage the reelection bid of Ngô Đình Diệm and Nguyễn Ngọc Thơ. At a January 25 meeting of Buddhists and Cao Đài in Vĩnh Lợi, Ba Xuyên province, the group issued one of the first appeals to Ngô Đình Diệm to run again, arguing that he was "the man who founded the Republic at a moment when the situation was particularly difficult, has brought prosperity to the country despite the communist threat. He is the only man qualified to be our leader."[17] This sentiment was reinforced by the Lawyers' Fraternity at the Court of Appeals in Hue on January 28 and by a member of the former imperial family, Nguyễn Phước, in front of 12,000 members of that group. On January 28 and 29, thousands marched in support of Ngô Đình Diệm, passing resolutions asking for him to run for another term. Various demonstrations in Kiến Hòa, Thừa Thiên, and Bình Thuận provinces, which numbered approximately 50,000, maintained that Ngô Đình Diệm was the best hope to fight against the communist insurgency and led the people in achieving the RVN's national revolution. In Vĩnh Long, representatives of fifty-eight different groups that included physicians, educators, and religious leaders passed a similar resolution while the Association for Buddhist Studies and the organization Aid to Deserving Families in Bình Long sent like petitions.[18] Even if Ngô Đình Diệm was not actively campaigning, those who supported him had begun the process of organizing the people for the April 9 election. Nearly 40,000 Vietnamese attended a pro–Ngô Đình Diệm rally on January 30 at the sports ground in Nha Trang, Khánh Hòa province, while Ngô Đình Diệm enjoyed the support of the Central Committee of the Viet Nam Labour Union, who passed a resolution in support of the president.[19]

Ngô Đình Diệm also received support for his reelection bid, even though it was not official, in the form of telegrams from the Association of Oriental Medicine Practitioners, Thừa Thiên province schoolchildren, the Hue chapter of the Vietnam Jaycees, and the Red Cross Society, Central Area branch. Youth groups in Thừa Thiên gathered to approximately 20,000 strong at the Phu Văn Lâu palace in Hue for a mass rally on January 29 while Buddhists in Ba Xuyên and Bình Long province endorsed the president. By February 3, Ngô Đình Diệm had received additional endorsements from youth, civil, and religious groups from ten provinces in the south.

While Ngô Đình Diệm received endorsements and accolades from villages throughout the RVN's provinces, his government also ensured that the election process would be as efficient as possible. This included special workshops for Vietnamese who had either never participated in an election or required additional information about the election process under Law 1/61. Between February 3 and 7, study sessions and workshops about the election process and law were held for local administrative officers and executives of civil groups who, once mastering the process, could then explain it to the residents in their areas.[20] Sessions were held in the provinces of An Giang, Kiên Giang, Định Tường, Vĩnh Long, and Long An. There was also a special workshop in Danang.

By February 6, one day before the filing deadline, Ngô Đình Diệm had received an additional 112 resolutions passed by various civic, religious, and youth groups from all over the RVN.[21] Individual signatures on the cables, resolutions, and other proclamations that were publicized numbered in the tens of thousands. The prevailing assumption of the Saigon government opposition was that the Vietnamese villager was indifferent to politics or uniformly opposed to Ngô Đình Diệm's rule. Ngô Đình Diệm did have significant support or, at the very least, positive name recognition in the countryside. Even if he had caused some grief through his earlier plans of national mobilization and had failed to eliminate the communist insurgency threat in the countryside, his name and face were still synonymous with the RVN government and the hope for a better Vietnamese future. It would be difficult for any other candidate to become that well known, despite his efforts before the April 9 election. This was not a result of any underhandedness by Ngô Đình Diệm or attempts at election fraud but rather the reality of the political landscape of Vietnam in 1961 and a result of the simple fact that Ngô Đình Diệm had been leading the country since the inception of the Republic. There was no other representative in the RVN who could boast of a public record or offer evidence of a stronger commitment to his people than Ngô Đình Diệm.

Despite all of the accolades, Ngô Đình Diệm was still not considered an official candidate until after the February 7 deadline for filing had passed. Article 13 of Law 1/61 stated that the candidate list would not be available until seven days after the filing deadline for the applications for the election.[22] This did not stop the speculation emanating from the press who had already determined the candidate list. The delay was a result of the need for the National Assembly to validate the applications before they could be posted and the slates given the opportunity to begin campaigning.

Ngô Đình Diệm picked up significant endorsements from members of Labour on February 7.[23] The 30,000-strong Trade Union Federation of Saigon–Cholon–Gia Định demanded that Ngô Đình Diệm run for reelection, while the Refugee Workers Federation, the Vietnamese Railway Workers Federation, and the Vietnamese Confederation of Workers Unions sent Ngô Đình Diệm resolutions of support and called on him to run in the election. Even if these organizations were associated with Ngô Đình Nhu, they still represented a strong move forward in the election for the incumbent.

These messages of support were among the forty-eight received from eight provinces that day. The messages were similar in tone as displayed by the petition sent by the Vietnamese citizens of Chinese descent in Phước Thành province: "Considering that only the President is capable of combating successfully against the feudalists, colonialists and Communists, enemies of the Vietnamese people: We ask him to run again for another term as to continue leading the people toward social betterment and prosperity."[24] The effects of this overwhelming outpouring of support helped to keep Ngô Đình Diệm's name in the news in a very positive way. Even if many Vietnamese living in the countryside did not read the *Vietnam Press*, the mass rallies and demonstrations of support for the president could not have failed to attract attention. Ngô Đình Diệm was the only potential candidate who had the organization to garner petitions and maintain exposure as the campaign season began. It is worth noting that no mention of the mass rallies made their way into American embassy reporting during the month. The only references to the election that made their way back to Washington were reports of possible fraud and intimidation.

The extent of Ngô Đình Diệm's command over the Vietnamese media was clearly demonstrated by the pre-reporting of the Vietnamese people's support for his reelection bid and the first-page advertisement in the February 7 evening edition of the *Vietnam Press* that announced Ngô Đình Diệm and vice presidential candidate Nguyễn Ngọc Thơ would join together to form a slate for the election.[25] In publicizing his campaign, Ngô Đình Diệm referred to the wishes of the people as a significant part of his decision to seek reelection.

Ngô Đình Diệm also mentioned the unfinished work that the RVN needed to accomplish to fulfill its goal of becoming free, independent, and prosperous.²⁶ Ngô Đình Diệm's letter announcing his candidacy received top billing in the February 8 *Vietnam Press* morning edition followed by a brief article announcing that two other slates would take part in the election.

The other two slates were filled with Nguyễn Đình Quát as the presidential candidate and Nguyễn Thành Phương as the vice presidential candidate in Slate II. Nguyễn Đình Quát, who was born in 1917, was from Hà Tĩnh while Nguyễn Thành Phương, who served as the Vietnamese minister of state until May 1955 and was commander of the Cao Đài forces, was born in 1915 in Cần Thơ and had strong nationalist, anti–French credentials. Slate III had Hồ Nhật Tân as the presidential candidate and Nguyễn Thế Truyền as his running mate. Hồ Nhật Tân, born in 1886 at Long Xuyên, was a practitioner of oriental medicine while Nguyễn Thế Truyền was an engineer by profession, born in 1898 in Nam Định.²⁷ A fourth slate was expected with Nguyễn Ngọc Bích and Nguyễn Văn Thỏa, both living in Paris, but the candidates did not fill out and submit the application by the February 7 deadline. The Vietnamese Socialist Party had announced earlier that it did not intend to submit its own candidate for the election, offering instead its support for Ngô Đình Diệm and Nguyễn Ngọc Thơ. In their January 26 statement, the Socialists called for the next president to be "virtuous, courageous, resolute and able people to lead the country on a basis of respect for the human person and social justice."²⁸

With the official campaign slates announced, Ngô Đình Diệm and Nguyễn Ngọc Thơ wasted no time in starting the process. On February 8, approximately 1,250 Saigon children received Tết gifts at a spring tree party at the Independence Palace.²⁹ Nguyễn Ngọc Thơ, who presided over the event, told the children to stay in school, obey their parents, work hard, and be good to their brothers and sisters. Baby kissing had not made its way to Vietnam yet, but everything else suggested that the campaign was in full swing. While Nguyễn Ngọc Thơ entertained the children, Ngô Đình Diệm inspected the new agricultural development centers in Tuyên Đức province, searched for sites on horseback for new servicemen's rest centers and camps for youth groups along the Đa Nhim River, and visited the Vĩnh Thượng porcelain factory and the construction site for the Dalat military academy.³⁰

Durbrow was impressed with Ngô Đình Diệm's campaigning and made remarks on a number of his events, such as his unannounced visit to a soccer match between the Saigon All-Star team and the Swiss Young Boys at Cộng hòa stadium on February 3 and a number of local markets, villages, schools, and orphanages during a visit to the western provinces on February 21.³¹ Just as many people called for Ngô Đình Diệm's reelection bid, news of the official announcement also garnered support from around South Vietnam. In Côn Sơn province, more than 1,000 people rallied for a demonstration in support of the president's decision, marching through the main street and gathering in front of the provincial administrative office to submit a petition for Ngô Đình Diệm to the provincial chief. This type of scene was repeated throughout Vietnam as more cables, petitions, and resolutions poured into Saigon in support of Slate I.³²

Amid the fanfare and ceremony marking the beginning of the campaign season, Trương Vĩnh Lễ held a press conference to announce that applications for the three slates had been validated. Trương Vĩnh Lễ also explained why the Nguyễn Ngọc Bích–Nguyễn Văn Thỏa ticket would not be added, citing articles 11 and 12 of Law 1/61.³³ The application arrived late, neither included a birth certificate, and the potential candidates failed to provide the list of 100 signatures supporting the slate required by the election law. Nguyễn Ngọc Bích and Nguyễn Văn Thỏa also attempted to file to run on one ticket and also tried to file on separate tickets, which violated the law. There was no real opposition to the Nguyễn Ngọc Bích–Nguyễn Văn Thỏa ticket being excluded from the election. The election law was clear on the process, and the two overseas Vietnamese had failed to follow the instructions.

The Presidential Election Campaign Committee met for the first time on February 13 to begin overseeing the election process and ensuring that all three slates follow the guidelines as outlined in article 22 of Law 1/61. The committee was chaired by Cao Văn Trường and included a delegate and alternate delegate for each of the three slates as required by article 16. The committee spent the day establishing the timeline for campaigning, including the deadlines for submitting the designs for emblems, posters, and handbills for the committee to approve. In this respect, the Presidential Election Campaign Committee assured that all three slates followed the same rules and competed on equal ground. While it is easy to criticize the equality of the process because of Ngô Đình Diệm's position and name recognition, the election law and its guidelines were designed to ensure that all of the candidates were given the same opportunity to campaign and get their message out.

Ngô Đình Diệm continued to make public appearances connected to his reelection bid even though none of the candidates were suppose to be officially campaigning. On February 14, he made an unannounced visit to the markets at Cholon and An Đôn. He talked with the merchants about their concerns and problems, viewed the merchandise, and interacted with the shoppers.[34] While this was clearly an election-related event, this type of interaction with the people was not rare. One of the complaints of the Americans in Vietnam was that Ngô Đình Diệm was aloof and out of touch with the people. This would become especially true as the Kennedy administration continued its tenure in office. This American perception was reinforced by the American officials in Saigon who failed to report this type of activity by the president of the RVN and, instead, focused on intrigue, discontent, and potential scandal.

Ngô Đình Diệm also had an advantage in the election of demonstrating how significantly improved the economic situation was in the RVN. He could point to a number of accomplishments achieved during his tenure as president. In land reform, his government had redistributed 312,976 hectares to 123,170 tenants by January 31.[35] An additional 113,025 hectares had been expropriated for distribution to tenants but had not been used because the fields were either fallow or were being illegally exploited by tenants who had refused to pay rent to the landowners. In a February 24 press conference, Nguyễn Xuân Khương, director of the Office of the Secretary of State for Land Reform, announced that VN$1,036,011,000 had been granted to landowners of 320,601 hectares, with approximately VN$127,971,000 paid in cash. He also provided information about an additional 6,362 hectares that were sold by the landowners directly to 2,857 tenants, bringing the total number of Vietnamese who benefited from the land redistribution policy to 126,027. Much of the land, 228,858 hectares, had been in the possession of French landowners, and a significant portion of it was used for such programs as the Agroville Plan. Still, the extent of the land redistribution and its large number of recipients made it difficult for critics of Ngô Đình Diệm to convince these people that he was indifferent to their plight. This was especially true when these critics represented the Saigon intelligentsia who were as removed from the countryside as they claimed Ngô Đình Diệm to be.

Another benchmark of the RVN's economic prosperity occurred on February 25 when

Ngô Đình Diệm at the Hưng Long Pagoda in Cholon, circa 1950s (United States Information Agency-Saigon, Photograph 61–11500, National Archives and Records Administration, College Park, Maryland).

the National Bank of Vietnam published its balance sheet for 1960 (see chart 2). Added to the tally of Ngô Đình Diệm's accomplishments while president of the RVN was an announcement by the Office of Land Development on March 12 that 21,733 hectares had been reclaimed from wasteland using an impressive array and quantity of bulldozers and tractors since 1957. The number of hectares plowed and furrowed was much higher.[36] The RVN had come a long way since 1954, and even if Ngô Đình Diệm was not intimately involved in every positive economic contribution, he had done much to ensure that individuals who were the experts had the means to improve and diversify the RVN economy.

Chart 2: National Bank of Vietnam Balance Sheet, 1960

Assets	Amount in VN$
Precious Metals and Foreign Exchange	7,577,058,597.69
Consolidated Government Bonds	10,681,187,174.46
Special Loans to the Treasury 1958 and 1959 Monetary Transactions	749,640,326.77
Temporary Loans to the Government	200,000,000.00
Loans to Banks	150,000,000.00
Immobilized Funds	136,514,481.20
Various Assets	341,621,869.21
Total	**19,836,022,449.33**

Liabilities	Amount in VN$
Currency in Circulation	12,158,171,644.88
Deposits	4,382,272,136.85
Sundry Creditors	2,180,816,048.89
Reserves and Stocks	780,759,400.03
Various Liabilities	334,003,218.68
Total	**19,836,022,449.33**

Source: "National Bank 1960 Balance Sheet Issued," *Vietnam Press* (Morning), February 26, 1961, H.14.

On February 20, the three slates announced their emblems for the presidential campaign.[37] Slate I (Ngô Đình Diệm–Nguyễn Ngọc Thơ) decided on a portrait of Ngô Đình Diệm, while Slate II (Nguyễn Đình Quát–Nguyễn Thành Phương) picked a buffalo and Slate III (Hồ Nhật Tân–Nguyễn Thế Truyền) chose the lotus flower. While the buffalo and lotus flower were symbols unique to Vietnam and images readily identified by the people, the portrait of Ngô Đình Diệm had the added value of distributing his image to a greater number of people. It was a politically astute choice from a seasoned candidate. The emblems were acknowledged by the Central Presidential Election Campaign Committee when it met for the second time on February 21. The committee also began to work out the campaign procedures and deliberate on when the candidates could officially start campaigning. The committee also examined the fees pertaining to the presidential election conforming to the provision of article 20 of Law 1/61.[38] In the public statements from the committee, Cao Văn Trường stressed the importance of the committee in creating guidelines that would achieve the "democratic spirit and national solidarity" the elections were suppose to bring to the people of Vietnam.[39] The role of the Central Presidential Election Campaign Committee was significant in the election process for the RVN. It was this committee that set the tone of the election and assured that all three slates would have an equal opportunity to compete when the campaign season began.

This intent was reasonable, but both Ngô Đình Diệm and Nguyễn Ngọc Thơ continued to use the office of the presidency and vice presidency to publicize themselves through personal appearances that were, technically, not campaigning but still achieved the goal of reinforcing their current positions within the government and emphasized, by default, the lack of position of responsibility of the opposing two slates. Ngô Đình Diệm visited five airports on February 21, highlighting the efficiency of his administration in modernizing the RVN and also showcasing the government's concern for reaching those people in the countryside who were practically isolated from the urban centers. During the same period, Nguyễn Ngọc Thơ opened the twelfth meeting of the Mekong Investigation Coordination Committee with a speech that emphasized the role that the Saigon government had played in developing industry along the Mekong River.[40]

On February 23, the Central Presidential Election Campaign Committee met again to discuss the printing of posters and handbills for the election and deliberated on how best to allow the candidates to interact with the people during the campaign season.[41] The committee announced on February 26 that the campaign season would begin on March 15 and that each candidate would be allowed four press conferences.[42] The committee also announced that the campaign would cost over VN$3 million, including VN$600,000 for the publication of 3.6 million handbills and 180,000 posters, while the rest of the money would be used for transportation and the hiring of vehicles.[43]

The national budget allocated VN$5,354,000 for the polling booth operations throughout the RVN and contributions to the candidates that equaled VN$.25 for each voter. The candidates had to pay any additional charges. All of this was in compliance with article 21 of Law 1/61 which also stipulated that if any of the candidates withdrew before the election or failed to poll at least 5 percent of the votes cast, the slate would have to reimburse the government 20 percent of the costs for handbills and posters produced for their use. This ensured that the candidates were serious and legitimate. It is interesting to note that Ngô Đình Diệm's representative on the Central Presidential Election Campaign Committee was often outvoted on election procedures, but he still followed the election rule. For instance, Ngô Đình Diệm's camp did not want radio used in the campaign, but the other two candidates' representatives outvoted his representative on the committee.[44]

On March 8, Cao Văn Trường held the first press conference for the Central Presidential Election Campaign Committee.[45] As chairman of the committee, he focused on the role the press and other media outlets would play in the election and called on those information organizations to make sure that each of the three slates received equal coverage. While Cao Văn Trường did not mention the United States, it would have been an obvious connection for those at the press conference, as the United States had just completed the Nixon-Kennedy contest. Cao Văn Trường also stressed the two central themes for the election: the democratic process and the preservation of national unity. For the Vietnamese and especially Ngô Đình Diệm, the April 9 election was an opportunity to showcase to the world and the Americans the extent to which the RVN had progressed.

Cao Văn Trường also laid out the procedures for the election. There would be twenty-five days of campaigning, March 15 through April 8, during which time each slate would receive 1.2 million handbills and 60,000 wall posters. The candidates or their designees would also be able to organize 210 talks with the electorate throughout the country, hold four press conferences and national broadcasts, write five articles for the press, and have access to the public address systems fitted onto trucks in order to campaign in the provinces. Cao Văn Trường also announced the new budget for the election, which came to a total of VN$5 million: Central Election Committee (VN$800,000); regional subcommittees (VN$3.1 million); handbills, posters, and transportation (VN$900,000); and miscellaneous expenses (VN$200,000). He concluded with a warning about inappropriate campaigning, personal attacks on the candidates, and the abuse of resources and power. These admonitions signified the real significance of the event. The RVN would showcase to the world the real possibilities of the democratic process as a counter to communist ideology that threatened the emerging nations who had shared a colonial past. If the elections proceeded without incident, it would serve as a model for other nations, and it would also reaffirm the role that Ngô Đình Diệm had played in helping to create the young Republic.

On March 7, the Saigon government announced the beginning of voter card distribution, which would start on March 12. The cards were necessary to ensure that all voters cast their ballots only once and that each vote cast came from a valid voter.[46] In order to get a voter card from the local administration or police station, each individual had to show their identity card. This also helped to limit the number of communist insurgents attempting to disrupt the election by voting for the weaker candidate.

Ngô Đình Diệm's role in the election and his handing over of the responsibilities of organizing the process to the Central Presidential Election Campaign Committee received praise from some Vietnamese in addition to the criticism reported by some Vietnamese to members of the U.S. embassy in Saigon. In a radio interview on March 10, Vũ Quốc Thúc,

Ngô Đình Diệm casts his ballot in the 1956 National Assembly elections (United States Information Agency, Photograph 56-5608, National Archives and Records Administration, College Park, Maryland).

dean of the Saigon University Law Faculty, praised the election process, asserting that Ngô Đình Diệm's prestige would be strengthened within Vietnam and throughout the international community after April 9 because of his adherence to the RVN's Constitution as it related to the election.[47] Vũ Quốc Thúc, who was clearly a supporter of Ngô Đình Diệm, argued that the Republic could finally come together after the election and prosper as a democracy under such organizations as the National Economic Council and the High Court of the Judiciary, both of which had been recently established by the National Assembly.

Where critics of Ngô Đình Diệm claimed that these organizations were a result of election politics and would not continue to function independently of the president after the election, Vũ Quốc Thúc disagreed, citing a speech he had made in 1957 during a seminar in Greece and elaborated on the role of the chief of staff, who needed to be "a leader who has faith in the democratic regime and entertain an immense prestige so that the people may be confidant in him and carry out his instructions in the march toward democracy."[48] Ngô Đình Diệm was the one individual who could confront the communists and lead the RVN forward down the path of democracy, according to Vũ Quốc Thúc. His words, heard throughout South Vietnam, reminded the people of Ngô Đình Diệm's record and the importance of the election. It is significant that this message and public utterance of support for Ngô Đình

Diệm coupled with the outpouring of support for the president within the provinces did not receive attention in the outgoing telegrams from the U.S. embassy in Saigon.

Another issue that Ngô Đình Diệm had to deal with was the constant criticism during and after the election that his slate added ballots during the election that resulted in his landslide victory. A first posting of names based on voting card information indicated that there were 6,948,466 voters eligible to case a ballot on April 9, with approximately 10 percent, or 692,699, registered in Saigon.[49] That 90 percent of the eligible voters were outside of the capital district was significant to Ngô Đình Diệm's reelection bid as it was widely assumed that he had a large majority of the non-urban vote while his two opponents had their best chance at making a political statement with the voters in Saigon. With so many voters outside Saigon, there seemed little likelihood that Ngô Đình Diệm would not be successful in his reelection attempt.

By mid-March, the Saigon government's focus split between the *Basic Counterinsurgency Plan for Viet Nam* and the impending April 9 election. Ngô Đình Diệm did not devote a lot of time to campaigning because the two opposing slates had not made too much of an impact, though that would change in the coming weeks. A March 15 radio broadcast was typical of the message Ngô Đình Diệm offered.[50] He equated a vote for him as a vote for the RVN, imploring the Vietnamese to consider their future as they cast their ballot rather than worrying about Ngô Đình Diệm's future. He harkened on the difficulties faced by the South Vietnamese in the six previous years but focused more on the opportunities for the future. Ngô Đình Diệm had been accused of being a mandarin who was out of touch with his people and their needs, though the radio broadcast suggested the opposite. The tone and language employed was reminiscent of Franklin Delano Roosevelt's fireside chats as Ngô Đình Diệm not only communicated to the Vietnamese the importance of a participatory democracy but also encouraged the people to mobilize to improve security, the economy, and society.

Reminding the Vietnamese of their heroic tradition, Ngô Đình Diệm sought to inspire the people into action: "Dear compatriots, you can believe what is sincerely told you today by a man who during all his life has had only one aspiration that is to serve the people and whose only will has been to promote a policy subject to the only ideal worthy of consideration, that of the Common Good and an active and realistic democracy."[51] Ngô Đình Diệm appealed to the people just as he had done to the Saigon intelligentsia and the emerging youth leadership. His call was no different than John F. Kennedy's call to action in his inaugural address, though Kennedy's country was in an entirely different situation: The RVN was at war with an enemy to the North and an insurgency from within while attempting to maintain a relationship with the American embassy that oftentimes had conflicting views about how the country should be run and who should lead.[52]

A short time after the Ngô Đình Diệm speech, Saigon businessman and confidant of Francis Cunningham, Lê Trung Nghĩa, met with the embassy counselor to discuss the nature of the campaigning for the April election.[53] Lê Trung Nghĩa made it a point to see Cunningham who was preparing to return to the United States and was not expected back until June, after the election. Lê Trung Nghĩa reported that Ngô Đình Diệm had not been taking the two other slates seriously until a March 20 press conference during which the leaders of each slate, Hồ Nhật Tân and Nguyễn Đình Quát, received a strong public reaction to their programs and message.[54] While both were still considered lesser slates to his group, there were rumors that Nguyễn Đình Quát's Slate II might withdraw in favor of Hồ Nhật Tân's Slate III. The combined popularity of the groups gave Ngô Đình Diệm pause for consideration and had forced him to begin campaigning in earnest beyond what he had done on March 15.

Lê Trung Nghĩa predicted that, as the situation stood, Ngô Đình Diệm would lose the election in Saigon and Biên Hòa because these two areas would be scrutinized by the public and press for fairness, but that Ngô Đình Diệm's men would rig the election in the countryside in spite of Việt Cộng efforts to pressure the people into voting against the president. Lê Trung Nghĩa seemed confident that the election would have to be rigged in order for Ngô Đình Diệm to win and that Ngô Đình Diệm's increased campaigning was only to improve his vote count in Saigon. Despite Lê Trung Nghĩa's prediction of election fraud, he still maintained that Ngô Đình Diệm needed to win the election, as he was the only Vietnamese leader who could run the country and fight the insurgency. The inexperience of Slate II and Slate III would provide a clear path for a communist victory. Lê Trung Nghĩa called on Cunningham to inform the U.S. government that it needed to direct Ngô Đình Diệm toward democracy after the election, and when faced with a Cunningham response that placed the onus of responsibility on the Vietnamese people to do this, he asserted that "the friendly help of the United States would continued to be needed."[55]

Lê Trung Nghĩa was also worried that the election would provide a catalyst for the Việt Cộng to gain popular support if Ngô Đình Diệm won. They would claim the election was a fraud and use it as justification for the removal of the president. It would be difficult, according to Lê Trung Nghĩa, to reconcile democracy in the RVN with a fixed election. Lê Trung Nghĩa, whose brother was General Lê Văn Tất—one of the leaders of the Cao Đài—might have been correct in his analysis, though he, like Cunningham, Mendenhall, and Durbrow, under-estimated the support that Ngô Đình Diệm had in the countryside. It also demonstrated, again, the tendency of those in Saigon to negate the political savvy of the Vietnamese peasants in choosing a leader who could best serve their needs and desires. Cunningham concluded from the conversation that Lê Trung Nghĩa might have exaggerated the popularity of Slate II and Slate III but indicated that the recent Saigon press campaign to dismiss the opposition candidates did suggest that Ngô Đình Diệm was taking the election a little more seriously than he had previously.

Ngô Đình Diệm opened the election campaign season on March 15 with an address to the nation on the National Radio Broadcasting System.[56] He had earned the right to go first, as the incumbent and only president the RVN had ever known. The schedule for radio broadcasts gave each candidate equal time at similar hours of the day.

Chart 3: 1961 National Election Radio Broadcast Schedule

March 15	Slate I	7:30 p.m.–7:45 p.m.
March 17	Slate II	12:15 p.m.–12:30 p.m.
March 20	Slate III	7:15 a.m.–7:30 a.m.
March 22	Slate II	7:30 p.m.–7:45 p.m.
March 24	Slate III	12:45 p.m.–1:00 p.m.
March 27	Slate I	7:15 a.m.–7:30 a.m.
March 29	Slate III	7:30 p.m.–7:45 p.m.
March 31	Slate I	12:15 p.m.–12:30 p.m.
April 3	Slate II	7:15 a.m.–7:30 a.m.
April 5	Slate III	7:30 p.m.–7:45 p.m.
April 6	Slate II	7:30 p.m.–7:45 p.m.
April 7	Slate I	7:30 p.m.–7:45 p.m.

Source: "Presidential Candidates to Go on the Air," *Vietnam Press* (Morning), March 16, 1961, H.10–H.11.

The same equity was demonstrated in public meetings that were allowed by the Central Presidential Election Campaign Committee.

**Chart 4: 1961 National Election
Public Meeting Schedule in Saigon**

April 1	Slate I	City Hall: 6:00 p.m.–8:00 p.m.
April 2	Slate II	City Hall: 8:00 a.m.–10:00 a.m.
April 3	Slate III	Điện Hồng Hall: 6:00 p.m.–8:00 p.m.
April 4	Slate I	Palace Cinema, Đồng Khánh Boulevard: 6:00 p.m.–8:00 p.m.
April 5	Slate II	Kinh Đô Cinema, Lê Văn Duyệt Street: 6:00 p.m.–8:00 p.m.
April 6	Slate III	Văn Hóa Cinema, Trần Quang Khải Street: 6:00 p.m.–8:00 p.m.

Open Air Meetings

March 23	Slate I	In Front of City Hall: 6:00 p.m.–8:00 p.m.
March 24	Slate II	In Front of Nguyễn Tri Phương Market: 6:00 p.m.–8:00 p.m.
March 25	Slate III	Hoàng Diệu Car Station: 6:00 p.m.–8:00 p.m.
March 26	Slate I	In Front of Nguyễn Tri Phương Market: 6:00 p.m.–8:00 p.m.
March 27	Slate II	Hoàng Diệu Car Station: 6:00 p.m.–8:00 p.m.
March 28	Slate III	In Front of City Hall: 6:00 p.m.–8:00 p.m.
March 29	Slate I	Hoàng Diệu Car Station: 6:00 p.m.–8:00 p.m.
March 30	Slate II	In Front of Hòa Huế Cinema, Nguyễn Hoàng Boulevard: 6:00 p.m.–8:00 p.m.
March 31	Slate III	In Front of Nguyễn Tri Phương Market: 6:00 p.m.–8:00 p.m.

Source: "Calendar of Candidates' Meetings with the Public," *Vietnam Press* (Morning), March 20, 1961, H.4–H.5.

In Ngô Đình Diệm's first radio broadcast, he spoke of the importance of the election for the future of the Vietnamese people and the Republic, but he also reminded his listeners of the vast progress that had been accomplished since 1955.[57] In reviewing the record, Ngô Đình Diệm accomplished one of the primary goals toward his reelection; he showed the people the significance of the progress accomplished since the end of French colonialism during a time when the Vietnamese had started with practically nothing but had accomplished a great deal in the economy, agriculture, politics, social advancement, diplomacy, and government.

Ngô Đình Diệm did not mention the United States by name during his address, but he acknowledged the economic and technical assistance of foreign nations. He also reminded his listeners that the April elections did not have to occur, but he had insisted on them because of the necessity of keeping the democratic spirit alive in the RVN. The 1956 Vietnamese Constitution stipulated that the president could prolong his term in office in times of emergency such as the one Vietnam was currently experiencing with the Việt Cộng. He asserted that other foreign leaders had done this and had suspended their constitutions in the process to maintain a hold on power.

Ngô Đình Diệm, however, appealed to the people by arguing that it was not his future at stake but that of the Republic: "You can believe what is sincerely told [to] you today by a man who during all his life has had only one aspiration that is to serve the people and whose only will has been to promote a policy subject to the only ideal worthy of consideration, that of the Common Good and an active and realistic democracy."[58] While his words and sentiment came as a result of the start of the campaign season, they do represent what was at the core of his political philosophy and presidential objectives. He wanted to create a viable, non-communist government in Southeast Asia that would assume a leadership position in Asia and the Pacific as the bulwark of democracy against the unrelenting attempts of subversion under the direction of the communists.

With the April 1961 presidential elections begun, the RVN had entered a new, significant phase in its short history. The election would show the world that the Republic was a model of democracy and a viable alternative to communism. Ngô Đình Diệm continued to have his detractors, but his government did work to ensure that the spirit of the electoral process was followed. The three slates had been established, and each provided the resources and guidance to conduct their election bid. There was little doubt that Ngô Đình Diệm and Nguyễn Ngọc Thơ held an advantage over the other candidates. Whether this resulted in an unfair election was open to interpretation. For those who were critical of Ngô Đình Diệm and his rule, there was little chance that he would receive a fair assessment when they communicated with members of the U.S. embassy.

13

April 1961 Election and the Departure of Durbrow

As Ngô Đình Diệm prepared for, and delivered, the first radio address of the election campaign, the sub-committees of Central Presidential Election Campaign Committee throughout the country prepared for the process. In the Saigon-Cholon area, the most significant and contested in the election, the sub-committee for the presidential election announced that it had a fund of VN$178,540 for the campaign, VN$40,000 of which had come from the Central Presidential Election Campaign Committee while the national budget funded the remaining VN$138,540.[1] The sub-committee announced that each candidate would have 55,000 handbills and posters, of which there were two versions, that would be distributed, or affixed to walls, by campaign officials. Each slate would also receive 50,000 additional handbills to distribute from their offices. The sub-committee authorized the distribution of these items by the candidate or their delegates from only their homes or offices starting on March 20. No candidate was allowed to distribute handbills in the streets.

The sub-committee also ordered that the three candidates' posters be grouped together when displayed, with the order of the posters following the number of the slate from left to right, with the position of Ngô Đình Diệm to the left, Nguyễn Đình Quát in the center, and Hồ Nhật Tân on the right. There was to be no deviation from this order.[2] In organizing the campaign in this manner, each slate was given equal access to resources and forced to follow the same rules in conducting their political campaigns. In theory, all three slates would operate on a level playing field even though the reality of the situation determined that the Ngô Đình Diệm–Nguyễn Ngọc Thơ slate had a distinct advantage because they were the incumbents and enjoyed name recognition, whether good or bad, and opportunities to make public appearances in connection with their office unavailable to the other candidates.

On March 16, Slate II's presidential candidate, Nguyễn Đình Quát, held his first press conference of the four allotted to him during the campaign season.[3] He promised to bring prosperity back to the RVN within six months and revalue the Vietnamese piaster to equal the U.S. dollar. The rate at the time of the conference was 73.50 piasters to the dollar. He also promised, after this rate was equalized, to revalue the British pound sterling to the piaster to equality. One pound sterling equaled 205.70 piasters. He outlined a program for the country based on the model of Ludwig Erhardt's Federal Republic of Germany, which called for a national union government with good relations with the West and alliances in Southeast Asia. Nguyễn Đình Quát called for a revision of the 1956 Constitution and more national focus on solving unemployment and introducing new principles in the fields of economics, politics, cultural affairs, and the military.

Nguyễn Đình Quát's three-hour press conference was short of substantive measures to accomplish these goals, though one could not expect detailed plans so quickly. The *Vietnam Press* did report that Nguyễn Đình Quát complained of the election process, which he argued favored Slate I, though Cao Văn Trường, who was also at the press conference, interrupted him to deny the charges and maintained that all three candidates had representation on the Central Presidential Election Campaign Committee and none had objected to the election guidelines and procedures. In fact, the sub-committee within the Saigon-Cholon area had met between March 15 and 20 to discuss all of the details of the election campaigning, and representatives from all three slates signed a joint statement that their deliberations and decisions had taken place in an atmosphere of "mutual understanding and concessions and a perfect democratic spirit."[4] All of the delegates were united in the assessment that the only force that would attempt to disrupt the April 9 elections was the communists. The delegates, Nguyễn Thanh Lớp (Slate I), Nguyễn Thanh Sơn and Nguyễn Ngọc Lễ (Slate II), and Phạm Văn Ngô (Slate III), agreed that their rules and regulations were freely arrived at without any outside pressure. Other sub-committees met with the same time frame with similar sentiment and results.[5]

Nguyễn Đình Quát experienced, in this first press conference, the difficult path he would need to take to challenge Ngô Đình Diệm and Nguyễn Ngọc Thơ in the election. Even if the Central Presidential Election Campaign Committee worked to make the process equitable, both he and Hồ Nhật Tân would have to face news media personnel who supported Ngô Đình Diệm and framed their questions accordingly. One example of this came in the form of a question that asked if Nguyễn Đình Quát was running for president "in order to halt legal procedures concerning the liquidation of his properties."[6] Nguyễn Đình Quát's running mate, Nguyễn Thành Phương, was also asked about his role in the 1955 politico-religious intrigue. Both questions produced vehement responses that must have shown the candidates of Slate II in less of the chief-of-state role than they would have liked. Ngô Đình Diệm would not receive these types of questions in his press conferences.

Nguyễn Đình Quát was able to further outline his platform during his March 17 radio broadcast.[7] He offered a fourteen-point plan under a united government of all political parties and called for a revision of the Constitution that clearly separated the legislative, judicial, and executive branches. Nguyễn Đình Quát's plan had some reasonable suggestions and offered a valuable direction for the RVN, but some of his points required much more than what the Saigon government could achieve given the nature of the communist insurgency, such as his call for the unification of the land by peaceful means. In a world void of political and military strife, Nguyễn Đình Quát's fourteen points would have had mass appeal. However, the RVN was far from the point at which it could devote all of its time and energy to such pursuits. The difference between reality and words would not be lost on the Vietnamese people.

In Nguyễn Đình Quát's second radio broadcast, he focused on the votes of the military, police, civil servants, workers, and farmers. These individuals, most of who came from an urban background or were directly tied to the city, represented Slate II's best chance for victory.[8] Nguyễn Đình Quát repeated earlier promises outlined in his fourteen points and continued to maintain that he alone was capable of improving the lives of the Vietnamese people.

As the election process intensified, a second and final counting of voters in the Saigon-

Cholon area on March 20 increased the total number of eligible voters to 732,248, which was an increase of 39,549 from the first count. This increase was significant as it countered accusations that Ngô Đình Diệm supporters were actively trying to limit the number of voters in Saigon to decrease the turnout for Nguyễn Đình Quát and Hồ Nhật Tân, or the claim that the Cần Lao Party was fraudulently fixing the number of voters to get rid of those who did not support Slate I. As a result of the increased numbers, the sub-committee announced that Saigon would have seventy-nine different polling locations and 528 polling stations to accommodate the voters.[9]

Chart 5: Eligible Voters in Saigon-Cholon Area, March 20, 1961

1st District	2nd District	3rd District	4th District
50,987	82,896	148,452	67,387
5th District	6th District	7th District	8th District
244,509	77,148	14,669	46,230

	Voters
Saigon and Cholon	732,248
Eastern Eleven Provinces	1,137,016
Western Twelve Provinces	2,786,588
Delta, Central Nine Provinces plus Hue and Danang	2,205,111
High Plateux of Six Provinces and Dalat	370,174
Total	**7,231,137**

Source: "City Has 732,248," *Vietnam Press* (Morning), March 20, 1961, H.6; and "7,231,137 to Go to Poll," *Vietnam Press* (Evening), April 3, 1961, H.9.

As the Saigon-Cholon numbers were released, Slate III held its first broadcast, completing the first round of radio speeches by the candidates. Presidential candidate Hồ Nhật Tân spent his fifteen minutes by criticizing the Ngô Đình Diệm government that, after six years, had failed to bring the RVN peace, security, and prosperity. He asserted that Ngô Đình Diệm's policies had placed the Vietnamese people between the "communist hammer and the anvil of the legal authorities," who called for the levying of "heavy taxes and the useless and harmful obligation of standing in the blazing sun in welcoming parties."[10] There was no doubt that Hồ Nhật Tân referred to the rallies and mass demonstrations held in support of Ngô Đình Diệm in the countryside, which was something that neither he nor Nguyễn Đình Quát experienced. Critics of the election argued that that Slate II and Slate III did not experience these rallies because Slate I delegates sabotaged their efforts by threats and cajoling. The election commission did not report any such instances.

On March 21, Hồ Nhật Tân and Nguyễn Thế Truyền held a press conference during which they announced a five-point program to the voters.[11] Slate III promised to work toward the establishment of a true democracy with economic and political opportunity for all, greater educational choices, a pro–Free World diplomacy, and the continued fight against the communist insurgents. The candidates had a much more focused message in this interaction with the press than they had in their radio broadcast. The slate began to develop a platform that was more than just critical of Ngô Đình Diệm. The five-point program turned into an eight-point plan on March 24 when Hồ Nhật Tân presented his new platform during his regularly scheduled radio broadcast.[12] Hồ Nhật Tân focused on the youth and student vote in this round of the campaign and called for them to vote for the old man of the election—Hồ Nhật Tân was seventy-five—because he was determined to serve the people and the Republic.

On March 23, Ngô Đình Diệm held the first press conference for Slate I, during which time he outlined his vision for Vietnam's economic and social future.[13] Ngô Đình Diệm alluded to the communist insurgency throughout the press conference. In doing so, he reminded his people, and the Americans, of the difficulties of practicing democracy during a time of war, especially when the RVN was still in its infant stage of democracy: "The moral rehabilitation and material reconstruction of a country burdened at the outset by these triple handicaps [underdevelopment, division, and communist threat] confront the whole nation with the necessity to accept a discipline all the more strict because it desires to liberate itself all the more rapidly."[14] Ngô Đình Diệm's version of discipline and sacrifice, while used to achieve similar objectives as outlined by Durbrow and the Americans, conflicted with American efforts to obtain those goals. Where Ngô Đình Diệm saw the rigid discipline as a necessary step to overcome Vietnam's three handicaps, Durbrow understood the RVN's actions to be a sign of stubborn pride and as unrealistic in translating thought into action. Some within the Kennedy administration would find the rigidity refreshing at first but would slowly turn against Ngô Đình Diệm, who they believed had lost touch with his people, but more importantly had turned away from American advice.

On the same day, Phần Ba Thực, delegate for Ngô Đình Diệm and Nguyễn Ngọc Thơ, began the public meetings in Saigon for the election campaign.[15] The two-hour affair marked the first of five such opportunities for each of the candidates. Phần Ba Thực repeated the familiar theme of Ngô Đình Diệm's record since 1955 and the progress he had made for the Republic in the past six years. There was a strong effort to get out the vote for the election. In addition to the mock polling station designed to teach the people how to vote and the radio broadcasts, press conferences, and rallies, members of the National Revolutionary Movement Civil Servants League worked with the Republican Youth to campaign for a mass turnout for the election.[16] Not only would this help to validate the eventual winner of the election—both organizations supported Ngô Đình Diệm—but it would also demonstrate to the DRV and members of the international community watching that the RVN was capable of participatory democracy and that its people were enthusiastic about this form of government. Because of the very real fear of Việt Cộng activity on Election Day, both the National Revolutionary Movement Civil Servants League and Republican Youth made it their mission to ensure that the elections proceeded without incident and that the voters arrived at the polls educated and aware of the significance of the event in which they were a participant.

While the three slates were strictly limited in the type and quantity of personal appearances, Ngô Đình Diệm and Nguyễn Ngọc Thơ had an unfair advantage as the incumbents. On March 24, Ngô Đình Diệm attended the inaugural of a new coal-washing station and railroad trunk line for the transportation of the coal at Nông Sơn.[17] The event afforded him the opportunity to speak with a number of potential voters who certainly welcomed the new industry and employment in their region. Ngô Đình Diệm addressed several audiences during the day, repeating some of the central messages of his campaign.[18] While it was his prerogative as president to attend this function and he would have been criticized for not being present, this type of media exposure and contact with the voting public was cause for complaint by the other slates. Ngô Đình Diệm, however, was in a difficult position, as he would have been criticized for either fulfilling his presidential duty and skirting the election procedures or neglecting his duties as chief of state to adhere to the rules and regulations of the campaign.

Delegates for all three slates held campaign meetings in the provinces of Phong Dinh, An Xuyên, Bình Long, Phước Thành, Long Khánh, Quảng Trị, Pleiku, and Côn Sơn between March 25 and 26 under the watchful eyes of the local election campaign committees. Each slate's delegates had to follow the same procedures and regulations, and there were no reports of incidents. In many respects, these delegate appearances and the personal appearances by the candidates ensured that each slate was given an opportunity to spread their message and project their vision for the future of the Republic.

As orderly as the Saigon-Cholon sub-committee of the Central Presidential Election Campaign Committee wished the campaign to proceed, there were moments of tension and chaos. On March 26, "over-enthusiastic voters" fought for the use of the loudspeakers at the Slate I open-air meeting in front of the Nguyễn Tri Phương market, breaking the loudspeaker system and forcing the city election campaign committee chairman, Trần Văn Sơn, to suspend the meeting.[19] The same type of incident occurred during the Slate III meeting at the Hoàng Diệu bus station in Khánh Hội, after Hồ Nhật Tân broke down in tears during his speech on the conditions of the Vietnamese people. Like the Slate I meeting, Hồ Nhật Tân's talk ended early as the crowd became too active and unruly. As a result of these two events, the city election campaign committee requested security officers present at future meetings and called upon the three slates to ensure that their delegates and supporters did not engage in disturbances that disrupted the campaigning. The March 27 meeting for Slate II was the first to fall under these new rules and proceeded smoothly.[20]

As the election drew nearer, accusations of potential election fraud surfaced. These accusations helped to reinforce the negative opinion of Ngô Đình Diệm held by those who were inclined to see him depart the office while, at the same time, making it difficult for pro–Ngô Đình Diệm representatives to assuage fears that the election would be fixed. One such charge was issued by Directorate General of Customs Hoàng Huy, who reported to John J. Helble in the American embassy that during the week of March 27 all RVN employees had received instructions on how to publicize the election.[21] According to the instructions, each government employee had to go to ten families to explain the election process so that a more informed voter could participate in the democratic experience and experiment. Hoàng Huy informed Helble that there was a secret instruction attached to the form handed out that ordered the government employees to push Slate I (Ngô Đình Diệm–Nguyễn Ngọc Thơ) and then find out how the family intended to vote. The employees then turned over the list with the family's name, address, and voting preference to the Saigon government.

Suggested in the report of the memorandum of conversation was the accusation that the government would use the list as retribution for those who failed to vote for Ngô Đình Diệm. Helble had heard rumors of these special instructions and because of his friendship with, and the reliability of, Hoàng Huy believed the report to be true. Hoàng Huy, as the head of a major government organization, did not provide a copy of the special instructions nor was one leaked to the American embassy from the many thousands of Saigon government employees, not all of whom were sympathetic to Ngô Đình Diệm and Nguyễn Ngọc Thơ. For Helble and those of a similar mind, rumor was enough to discredit Ngô Đình Diệm and the election process; physical evidence was not necessary.

As the election campaign proceeded, the candidates continued to delineate their messages to the people. Hồ Nhật Tân met with the voters of Saigon in front of city hall on

March 29 during which he maintained that "a proper implementation of the Constitution and the exercise of democratic liberties will automatically lead to a truly united nation; and thus we will easily overcome the Communists."[22] In front of a large audience, Hồ Nhật Tân outlined his plan to restore prosperity to the people. He was asked, however, about his and Nguyễn Thế Truyền's position during the Japanese occupation to the end of the Bảo Đại regime with a suggestion, from the *Vietnam Press*, that neither of them was a revolutionary as they had made themselves out to be, nor were they, by implication, as nationalistic.

Nguyễn Đình Quát had received similar treatment in his public appearance the day before at the Hoàng Diệu bus station when he was challenged to explain how he would lower taxes and raise salaries for civil servants and the military as he had outlined in his platform. Later in the campaign he was questioned about his self-financing projects that he advocated for his economic development program and was pressed to relate the plan to economic theory.[23] The *Vietnam Press* commented on his confused answer that left many frustrated. The *Vietnam Press* also reported of an exchange with a questioner who asked Nguyễn Đình Quát to translate the sentence, "A frog which wants to be as big as an ox," into French, English, and Chinese to prove his claims that he had authored a series of dictionaries in these languages. This type of interaction did nothing to help the election process and demonstrated one of many things: the candidates for Slates II and III were not taken seriously; the *Vietnam Press* reports of Slate II and III meetings were askew; or Ngô Đình Diệm's supporters dominated the other slate meetings and refocused the attention away from qualifications and toward personal attacks. Regardless, Slates II and III had a much more difficult time developing their vision for the Republic and its people than Ngô Đình Diệm had.

In some respects, the questions posed to Slate II and III candidates reflected a shift in election tactics that occurred at the end of March as Election Day drew nearer. On March 29, delegate to Slate I, Huỳnh Ngọc Diệp, confronted the criticisms of his candidate by Nguyễn Đình Quát and Hồ Nhật Tân and their delegates who disparaged Ngô Đình Diệm's economic, financial, and social policies as well as his nepotism and dictatorial methods.[24] Huỳnh Ngọc Diệp admitted that there had been mistakes during Ngô Đình Diệm's presidency, though he did not provide specifics. He maintained that any administration was bound to have difficulties. Any shortcomings, he asserted, were more than offset by the positive results during the nearly six years of Ngô Đình Diệm's rule. This was a theme repeated by Nguyễn Ngọc Thơ a few days later during a campaign meeting in Saigon.[25] Huỳnh Ngọc Diệp then went on to criticize Slates II and III for misrepresenting themselves and their political activities during the Second World War and the First Indochinese Conflict, concluding that each candidate had made exaggerated promises without offering any substantive plan to accomplish their goals. As with most campaigns in democratic countries with a much longer tradition of free elections, the Vietnamese people demonstrated their ability to redirect, and sometimes misdirect, the focus of the campaign away from the real issues of the day and toward the personal issues. Through this display of politics, the South Vietnamese showed that they were much more practiced and sophisticated in the democratic process than the Americans had given them credit for.

On March 30, Ngô Đình Diệm and Nguyễn Ngọc Thơ held their first press conference for the election at the Presidential Palace.[26] Ngô Đình Diệm was asked to explain his future plans for the Republic, as his election focus had only examined achievements to that point, and he spent most of the time outlining his vision for educational opportunities at all age groups and skill levels. He also discussed his health program, labor reforms including the

Ngô Đình Diệm addresses the nation, circa 1950s (United States Information Agency–Saigon, Photograph 55-218, National Archives and Records Administration, College Park, Maryland).

new National Economic Council, social welfare, and his economic development plan. Of the six questions asked, the most difficult or critical was the one that asked him to elaborate on the Saigon government's shortcomings in implementing its program, which was something he had freely acknowledged in his earlier election radio broadcast. Ngô Đình Diệm's press conference allowed him to further elaborate on the successes during his tenure as president and comment on his vision for the future. Unlike the other candidates' press conferences, Ngô Đình Diệm did not have to delve into personal issues or defend himself against attacks on past actions or policy. This was not to suggest that Ngô Đình Diệm received a free ride in the campaigning but rather that he was able, unlike the other two slates, to focus on an established record and provide legitimacy for future plans and projects for the Republic and its people.

At the third campaign meeting for Slate III held at the Nguyễn Tri Phương residential area in Cholon, Định Khắc Quyết, the delegate for Hồ Nhật Tân, provided some biographical information about the presidential candidate.[27] Vice presidential candidate Nguyễn Thế Truyền, who was at the meeting, argued that a change in government was necessary because Ngô Đình Diệm had failed to maintain security for the people. In what had become a popular refrain for Slate III, Nguyễn Thế Truyền asserted that the Saigon government was incapable of dealing with the Việt Cộng activity that had terrorized the people and declared that Ngô Đình Diệm's response to these threats was to adopt old French colonial methods to rule the country. Nguyễn Thế Truyền wanted to highlight what Slate III believed was a real difference between their ticket and Slate I. Both Hồ Nhật Tân and Nguyễn Thế Truyền believed that they belonged to the old revolutionary movement that had fought against the French and centralized authority while Ngô Đình Diệm had moved too much toward centralized control. Nguyễn Thế Truyền had been active in smuggling Vietnamese nationalists out of the country during the French colonial rule, and both he and Hồ Nhật Tân maintained that only their revolutionary zeal, along with a military solution, could rid the Republic of the communist insurgents, which would ultimately lead to the liberation of the North.

As Election Day drew closer, the tension within Saigon increased. The chairman of the city election campaign committee, Trần Văn Sơn, clashed with Nguyễn Đình Quát over remarks made by the candidate of Slate II at a public appearance in front of city hall.[28] In his April 2 talk, Nguyễn Đình Quát criticized the National Assembly, which was to convene for the first ordinary session of 1961 the next day. Trần Văn Sơn, who was a delegate in the National Assembly, walked out of the April 2 campaign meeting after Nguyễn Đình Quát called the National Assembly a group of puppets to the Saigon government and leveled sharp criticism at Ngô Đình Diệm. Trần Văn Sơn seized the microphone to end the meeting before walking out and then, at his own press conference on April 3, demanded an apology from Nguyễn Đình Quát before the city election campaign committee would resume its organizational duties for future Slate II events.[29]

While Nguyễn Đình Quát had his problems with Trần Văn Sơn, Slate III was occupied with an increasingly aggressive audience who responded negatively to its claims that Ngô Đình Diệm was responsible for all of the problems in the Republic.[30] At the campaign meeting in Thống Nhứt theater, Slate III delegate Nghiêm Xuân Thiện, who was the editor of the Saigon daily *Thời luân*, was very critical of Ngô Đình Diệm, but he predicted a Slate I victory because neither his candidates or those of Slate II had the same resources at their disposal.[31] Nghiêm Xuân Thiện implied that Ngô Đình Diệm was not playing by the same election rules and was taking advantage of his political office to further his reelection bid. While he was technically correct, this was much less true in Saigon where the people wanted to hear why they should vote for a candidate rather than why they needed to vote against the others. Nghiêm Xuân Thiện continued for nearly thirty minutes when the audience began to leave noisily, shouting for Slate III to withdraw. Trần Văn Sơn, who was present at the meeting, called for order but failed to restrain the crowd, resulting in the Saigon police intervening. The city election campaign committee agreed, as a group, to suspend the meeting before it got further out of hand. Two days later, Hồ Nhật Tân and Nghiêm Xuân Thiện experienced a similar backlash at a Slate III press conference when the opening question focused on Nguyễn Thế Truyền's failed promises and alleged drinking problems when he was elected to the Hanoi town council before the partition.[32]

Even as tension in Saigon increased as Election Day approached, there were no similar outbursts in the provinces.³³ The lack of violence or disruption in the campaign meetings and rallies in all but the Saigon area altered the assumption that Ngô Đình Diệm and Ngô Đình Nhu had ordered their people to disrupt the Slate II and Slate III campaigns. A further piece of evidence against these charges was that violence in Saigon had originated at a Slate I meeting. The disruptions and increased tension were more a result of the politically charged atmosphere in the city than any coordinated effort by one slate to derail the other two slates.

Ngô Đình Diệm received a major endorsement on April 3 from the Association of Communists' Victims, an organization that had received government support as well as private support from the Vietnamese Women's Solidarity Movement, organized by Madame Nhu.³⁴ The association's endorsement was significant, especially when considering the fact that it had been run by one of his opponents, Nguyễn Đình Quát, before he announced his candidacy for the presidency. It was also important for Ngô Đình Diệm because of what the association stood for in the RVN: "We thus are defenders of an ideology which conforms to our operation," remarked the association's secretary general, Lưu Hưng, referring to the desire to avenge communist attacks of terror and intimidation against the Vietnamese people, "and we wish to be on the vanguard of a regime which meets our vocation."³⁵ Lưu Hưng rejected Slate II and Slate III as big children and whimpering old men unsuited to face the challenges of the day. With the support of the association, it was difficult for Nguyễn Đình Quát or Hồ Nhật Tân to make the charge that Ngô Đình Diệm was not doing enough to provide security for the people or quell the communist insurgency to the people's satisfaction. Madame Nhu had also been in the public eye much since the beginning of the election to rally support for Ngô Đình Diệm and his vision for the Republic.³⁶

On April 7, just two days before the election, Ngô Đình Diệm met with reporters in one of his last official appearances before the election.³⁷ In the press conference, Ngô Đình Diệm was asked to respond to some of the criticisms leveled against him by Slate II and Slate III during the campaign. That Ngô Đình Diệm was asked to address these issues was another sign of the validity of the campaigns of Nguyễn Đình Quát and Hồ Nhật Tân and further evidence that Ngô Đình Diệm, even if he was treated differently, still had to answer the difficult questions. One criticism of Ngô Đình Diệm's rule was unemployment. Ngô Đình Diệm responded to this issue by arguing that under-employment was a better term for what was happening in the Republic as seasonal farmers were often unemployed for eight or nine months but still had an occupation and livelihood. Ngô Đình Diệm admitted that more could be done for these individuals other than the government efforts, such as doubling the number of crops and diversifying the agricultural output to include animal husbandry. While Ngô Đình Diệm acknowledged under-employment, he denied that unemployment was as serious an issue as the Saigon slates made it out to be, especially when one considered that the RVN had been the recipient of 810,000 refugees from the North as a result of the petitioning of the country from the 1954 Geneva Agreements.

Ngô Đình Diệm was also asked about nepotism in his government, which was a charge leveled by his critics as well as the presidential candidates. His response was worth repeating, not only in the context of the April election but as a counter-argument to the accusations asserted by his opponents who orchestrated his assassination in November 1963. He maintained that it was not uncommon to have family members in prominent position within a government; Ngô Đình Diệm cited India and the relationship between Pandit Nehru, his wife, and his daughter Indira Gandhi. He did not mention John F. Kennedy, who had two brothers in prominent political positions in the United States within a family that continued to dominate New England politics for the remainder of the century. Ngô Đình Diệm then went through his family list of those who had been involved in the nepotism controversy. Ngô Đình Luyện was a highly qualified engineer who became an ambassador for Vietnam well before Ngô Đình Diệm entered high office; in fact, he was the longest-tenured Vietnamese diplomat. Ngô Đình Nhu had formal education training at the École Nationale des Chartes and was a well-known trade unionist leader before Ngô Đình Diệm returned to Vietnam. It was difficult to question his credentials or ability to get things done when compared to the available talent in the Republic. Ngô Đình Thục received his religion rank of archbishop not from Ngô Đình Diệm but from the Holy See in Rome, while Madame Nhu had been charged with countless crimes of a financial nature without evidence being made available. For Ngô Đình Diệm, family was very important, and the charges of nepotism were a real source of frustration for him, especially when he relied on family members to fulfill many of the roles needed for the new nation. Ngô Đình Diệm also had a proven track record of giving increasing responsibility to non-family members who proved themselves worthy. That the question was raised, and addressed by Ngô Đình Diệm, on the eve of the election lent itself to the credibility of the election process.

Nguyễn Đình Quát held his last press conference on April 6, repeating his claims that the city election campaign committee had shown undue favoritism toward Slate I even though he and Hồ Nhật Tân had representation in that group. These charges were really nothing more than an attempt to justify what was expected to be a landslide victory for Ngô Đình Diệm. From Nguyễn Đình Quát's perspective, the rigging of the election was a better reason for what would become a significant defeat than the fact that his campaign message— restoring "democracy and prosperity to the country 'in such a way that the population in North Viet Nam will want to live under the same regime'"—rang hollow to the voters.[38]

In his last press conference before the election, Ngô Đình Diệm appealed to the media to join him in calling for moderation and respect for the Constitution: "Let us now unite against the attempts of sabotage by the Communists so that we can be sure of the best conditions for all to vote in a free election."[39] Ngô Đình Diệm spent most of his time focused on the threat of the communist insurgents and how the RVN had to respond in order to be successful in ensuring peace and prosperity for the people. The majority of the questions focused on foreign policy, from the value of SEATO aid to Ngô Đình Diệm's position on the fourteen-nation conference on Laos scheduled to discuss the neutralization option.

Ngô Đình Diệm was asked about the impact of the November 11 abortive coup d'état on morale, which he dismissed, stating that the event was isolated and had not affected the Vietnamese military or civilian population. There was, of course, no mention of the effect of the incident on Vietnamese–American relations, though that same day the Department of State issued a statement of full support for the RVN, asserting that the United States did "not intend to let the Vietnamese down in the dangerous situation they are now facing" and Senator Mike Mansfield (D–Montana) had earlier called for additional aid for the RVN to counter Việt Cộng activities.[40]

While Ngô Đình Diệm set the mood for the election as one in which the people needed to come together to ensure a successful Election Day, the National Assembly still found it difficult to reconcile with Slate II.[41] The National Assembly sent a protest note to Nguyễn Đình Quát for his remarks of April 2, announcing that it would reserve the right to sue any person or group that attacked the National Assembly without due cause. The protest note argued that the letter and spirit of the January 5 election law 1/61 concerning the organization of the presidential election had been followed faithfully and that any reports to the contrary would be dealt with accordingly. Clearly, this did not conform with the tone of Ngô Đình Diệm's remarks, but it was indicative of the type of campaign Slate II had run. Nguyễn Thế Truyền oversaw Slate III's final public appearance at the Moderne Cinema; he focused on reunification with the North by elections under the supervision of the United Nations. In 1961, this type of plan might have won popular sentiment, but it was not practical for those with any political savvy. It also assured the very real possibility that the 810,000 Vietnamese who had fled the North in Operation Exodus and Operation Passage to Freedom would feel less inclined to vote for Slate III over Slate I.[42]

Polling booths opened at 7:00 a.m. in Saigon to the sound of a siren, signaling the beginning of the first real national election under the RVN's Constitution. Voters began to line up at the polls, in part because of the heavy voter turnout but also as a result of some logistical problems such as all voters entering polling stations through one door. The voting process, aided by Saigon police and members of the Republican Youth, was smooth, save for one woman collapsing in line and being rushed to the hospital and two individual arrested for trying to persuade voters in line to cast their ballots for Slate III.[43] At 9:25 a.m. Ngô Đình Diệm left the Presidential Palace to cast his vote, which he was able to do in ten minutes, and walked through Tao Đàn Park on his return.[44] There were no reports of Việt Cộng interference in the capital in the morning hours, though at 11:00 p.m. on election eve a hand grenade exploded near the Xóm Côi School in the Eighth District where polling booths had been set up.[45]

By 3:00 p.m. 518,183 of the 732,248 registered voters in Saigon had cast their ballots. The process was well covered by the Vietnamese and foreign press, who witnessed numerous inspiring demonstrations of individuals exercising their democratic rights.[46] This included patients leaving the Saigon hospital to vote, a ninety-eight-year-old woman being helped by two young relatives to the polling booth, disabled war victims arriving by wheelchairs to cast their ballots, and voters from the fourth district's Nguyễn Văn Kiến Islet crowding onto the three boats furnished by the city election campaign committee to make their way off the island to the polling stations. Reports from the provinces confirmed that there was a heavy voter turnout, and for the most part individuals did not experience any obstacles getting to the polling stations.[47]

Local Saigon dailies devoted much of their print to the election on April 9, with each one reminding the voters of the paper's choice and the individual's responsibility to participate in the democratic process. *Sài Gòn Mới* called Election Day "A Historic Day" while *Tiếng dân* reminded voters that "each one is free to vote for the candidates of his choice." *Sài Gòn Thời Báo* appealed to patriotism: "Let the voters not lose sight of the Communist danger when going to the polls: Let them be proud to have been living under the Republic Regime and enjoying freedom in selecting the man who meets their wishes to be the nation's leader."[48] This theme was repeated in most of the front pages of the dailies as the papers heeded the call of Ngô Đình Diệm to mark the historical significance of April 9 and rally around the Constitution. While the Saigon papers were willing to follow Ngô Đình Diệm's lead, the Việt Cộng had other ideas.

There were exceptions to the calm on Election Day. In Kiên Giang province, a grenade exploded in front of the Rạch Giá market with no casualties, while the chief of Hà Tiên district fought off a Việt Cộng ambush without injury to his party. There were reports of suspected Việt Cộng taking away voting cards in the countryside, but special circumstances were made for those individuals who still wanted to vote. There was also a major Việt Cộng plot to disrupt the elections in Saigon that was foiled on the night of April 8. Approximately 2,000 Vietnamese, mostly women and from the countryside, were arrested and detained in an abandoned rice-husking plant along the Chinese canal at Bình Đông in the seventh district.[49] According to Colonel Lâm Văn Phát, director general of the Civil Guard, the Việt Cộng mobilized the peasants, who were mostly from Bình Đông and Kiến Hòa provinces, and infiltrated them in twos and threes into the city on April 8. Their plan was to hold a massive demonstration on Election Day, distribute communist leaflets, and disrupt the vote with homemade and foreign-manufactured grenades.

Of the more than 2,000 captured, Colonel Lâm Văn Phát revealed that 200 were Việt Cộng cadre, while the unwilling remainder had been tricked into participating in the demonstrations or had been threatened with reprisals against their lives and property if they refused to comply. The Việt Cộng also attempted to prevent the collection of ballot boxes in the countryside.[50] The Việt Cộng damaged roads to delay or stop ballot boxes from reaching their designated counting place. This was especially true in the provinces of Phước Long, Phú Yên, Khánh Hòa, and Quảng Ngãi. Despite the Việt Cộng attempts of sabotage, the boxes all arrived, albeit very late in some cases, and the returns from these provinces were eventually added to the total number of votes validated by the commission set up via the National Assembly.

On April 11, Secretary of State for the Interior Bùi Văn Lương held a press conference to go over the totality of the Việt Cộng efforts to disrupt the election.[51] His report was much more extensive than had been previously reported in the press, though the end result was the same: the Việt Cộng had failed to stop or alter the election. Bùi Văn Lương reported Việt Cộng attacks on isolated military outposts, assassination and kidnapping of village council members, destruction of bridges, cut-off of roads, damaging of electoral cards and identification papers, ransacking of polling booths, and direct threats by the Việt Cộng to individual voters.[52] Bùi Văn Lương also reported that the Việt Cộng had plans to seize power through a general uprising, though no other evidence collaborated this assertion. While he may have overstated the final Việt Cộng strategy, the tactics of subversion, violence, and terror were real but also flawed, as the power of the ballot won over the politics of fear.[53] Ngô Đình Diệm also held a press conference on April 11 to confirm his election victory.[54]

The Saigon election campaign committee acknowledged that the Việt Cộng might have played a role in only 560,876 of the 732,232 registered voters casting ballots but also conceded that other factors played a role.[55] Saigon residents had moved out of the city without notifying the election authorities, moved between districts and failed to have their names in their former district struck from the record, were away from Saigon because of work, died between registering to vote and Election Day, or were prevented from casting a ballot because of work or illness. The committee did not list apathy or the fact that Ngô Đình Diệm had a clear majority, though those two factors probably accounted for a majority of the no-shows.[56]

In an attempt to preempt claims of impropriety during the campaign and Election Day, candidate representatives in Saigon issued a joint statement that the election was conducted in an "atmosphere of complete liberty and true democracy."[57] The representatives commended the officials at the polling stations and volunteer groups who helped to ensure that the Election Day went smoothly. All three slate representatives affirmed that none of them had cause to lodge any type of complaint. The sub-committee of Quảng Nam issued a similar statement.⁵⁸

Even before the election results were officially counted and verified by the National Assembly special committee, Ngô Đình Diệm began receiving congratulations from other international leaders and media outlets. The Department of State called Ngô Đình Diệm's win a great victory over the communist insurgency, which failed to dampen the democratic spirit with sabotage and violence while the heavy turnout showed the "extent and efficiency of the control the Saigon government has over the country."⁵⁹ Similar messages were received from regional allies such as Laotian prime minister Prince Boun Oum Na Champassak and Philippine president Carlos P. Garcia. Other country leaders whose nations shared a colonial past, such as Republic of Gabon president Leo M'Ba, Republic of Senegal president Leopold Sedar Senghor, and Congo information director Louis Loubassou, sent messages of congratulations. There were also countless congratulatory letters, telegrams, and proclamations from Vietnamese citizens, councils, and organizations from both within and outside the RVN.

On April 15, the National Assembly reconvened to certify the final vote count in conformity with article 33 of Law 1/61 (see chart 6). Voter turnout in these three areas was particularly high, with 75 percent voting in Saigon, 99 percent in Dalat, and 98 percent in Tuyên Đức. In addition to the high voter turnout, the fears of a Việt Cộng disruption of the election process proved to be unnecessary. Saigon, as reported by Mendenhall, was quiet throughout Election Day and the night, though later reports would show some Việt Cộng activity and a more significant attempt foiled.⁶⁰

Chart 6: 1961 National Election—Final Vote Count, April 15, 1961

Location	Slate I	Slate II	Slate III	Non-Valid Votes
Saigon Perfecture	354,732	51,078	146,518	8,956
Eastern Provinces				
Biên Hòa	105,140	10,570	13,923	732
Bình Dương	95,987	23,123	25,895	1,334
Bình Long	25,340	3,519	6,532	435
Bình Tuy	25,100	16	41	25
Gia Định	304,934	27,533	53,421	4,994
Long Khánh	47,472	1,283	1,549	198
Phước Long	26,732	587	656	66
Phước Thành	27,858	3,126	3,078	161
Phước Tuy	54,931	5,714	7,472	468
Tây Ninh	120,770	12,989	7,901	993
Côn Sơn	776	0	0	0
Western Provinces				
An Giang	363,963	9,026	21,347	440
An Xuyên	76,781	1,563	1,364	264
Ba Xuyên	309,221	16,084	13,014	69
Định Tường	291,109	7,823	8,300	1,899
Kiên Giang	195,336	4,151	4,385	63
Kiến Hòa	173,490	20,634	27,475	233
Kiến Phong	112,245	3,345	2,608	194
Kiến Tường	29,935	91	100	17

Location	Slate I	Slate II	Slate III	Non-Valid Votes
Long An	221,954	5,290	7,256	351
Phong Dinh	194,282	10,595	13,583	930
Vĩnh Bình	200,257	17,011	16,666	808
Vĩnh Long	238,470	6,023	8,611	337
Delta, Central Area				
Da Nang	42,484	1,174	5,213	464
Hue	41,869	654	1,766	288
Bình Định	386,640	2,586	17,436	792
Bình Thuận	119,569	1,062	999	704
Khánh Hòa	123,619	1,557	11,433	897
Ninh Thuận	67,373	334	266	70
Phú Yên	156,420	2,385	8,562	331
Quảng Nam	457,992	5,811	4,206	532
Quảng Ngãi	292,297	8,612	11,089	571
Quảng Trị	137,978	138	112	14
Thừa Thiên	219,499	304	563	11
High Plateaux, Central Area				
Dalat	27,995	536	456	135
Darlac	86,429	1,458	2,191	428
Kontum	59,848	104	244	48
Lâm Đồng	30,746	244	356	98
Plieku	101,396	4	3	11
Quảng Đức	17,299	51	88	21
Tuyên Đức	31,669	480	447	88
Total	**5,997,937**	**268,668**	**457,125**	**29,470**

Source: "National Assembly Confirms Victory of Slate I," *Vietnam Press* (Morning), April 19, 1961, H.1–H.3.

Durbrow sent Ngô Đình Diệm and Nguyễn Ngọc Thơ a congratulatory message on April 12, which followed the standard diplomatic formula but lacked the emotional conviction such a letter would have had from a friend.[61] Durbrow recalled Ngô Đình Diệm's "calm courage and tenacity of purpose" that he had shown during the Durbrow years in Saigon, confiding to Ngô Đình Diệm that he believed the president would continue this path and lead Vietnam to "greater and greater heights." Given the tension in Saigon at the time, after the attempted coup d'état and the failure to advance the *Basic Counterinsurgency Plan for Viet Nam*, one could also interpret these sentiments of calm courage and tenacity of purpose as calculating and stubborn, while Vietnam's ascent to greater and greater heights would occur under the leadership of Ngô Đình Diệm but with the guidance of the United States.

After reminding Ngô Đình Diệm that he would be leaving Vietnam soon, Durbrow remarked on his time in the country. The best he could say was that it was both pleasant and fruitful. There was no genuine friendship expressed in the letter, which is not to say that an ambassador must be friends with the leadership of the country in which he represents the United States. Nonetheless, the stiff and formal pronouncement of congratulations, while diplomatically professional and appropriate, suggested that the animosity and distaste that had developed between these two individuals had not improved, despite Lansdale's advice, and had fallen well short of healed.

The special committee created under article 34 of Law 1/61 to validate the final returns convened on April 19.[62] This committee was charged with reviewing all of the provincial and municipal reports related to the election and the National Assembly minutes from the time the vote was certified. It was also charged with investigating any candidate's claim of fraud. The committee had, under article 36, five days to validate the election. On April 24, the committee issued a communiqué officially certifying the validity of the election, maintaining that it took place in conformity with Law 1/61.[63]

Durbrow might have offered a rather stale, diplomatic congratulations to Ngô Đình Diệm, but he did recommend that Kennedy send Ngô Đình Diệm a message, though he suggested that Kennedy wait until the president's inauguration on April 30.[64] Durbrow could then deliver Kennedy's message at a formal ceremony, which would make it more meaningful. The message, if delivered on April 30, would also come one day after the opening of the Saigon–Biên Hòa highway, which was the largest U.S. economic aid project in the RVN to date, and three days before Durbrow was set to depart Vietnam.

With the election complete and Durbrow's replacement announced, the ambassador began to make the rounds of farewell visits. The secretary of state for foreign affairs, Vũ Văn Mẫu, held a dinner in his honor at the Hotel Caravelle on April 19, with Vice President Nguyễn Ngọc Thơ in attendance.[65] Durbrow next visited the Saigon Lion's Club for a farewell dinner, during which he offered some observations on the status of the Republic after the elections. He argued that Vietnam had successfully completed two phases toward a stable Republic; it had survived the period of division and relocation of refugees and had achieved significant economic development. He suggested that Vietnam had entered a third stage: the defeat of the Việt Cộng and the broadening of the democratic base that would allow for greater prosperity and security.[66] While Durbrow made the diplomatic rounds, Secretary of State Dean Rusk swore in Frederick E. Nolting, Jr., as the new ambassador, with Trần Văn Chương witnessing the ceremony. Nolting had planned to arrive in Saigon during the second week of May with his wife and four daughters.[67]

Meanwhile, in Washington, the executive secretary of the Department of State, Lucius D. Battle, recommended approving Durbrow's request and authorizing him to inform Ngô Đình Diệm that a congratulatory message would be forthcoming on inaugural day and also to let Ngô Đình Diệm know how pleased Kennedy was that the RVN president had received such a strong mandate even though the Việt Cộng had threatened to disrupt the election process. Kennedy's congratulatory letter was drafted between April 14 and 24. The letter in itself was not remarkable, as it offered the reasonable congratulations to Ngô Đình Diệm on his victory and commented on his efforts during his six years in office.

The final paragraph, however, might have caused Ngô Đình Diệm to pause and reconsider whether anything had changed in the United States–Vietnamese relationship with the new administration: "It is fitting that Ambassador Durbrow should be present on this occasion to deliver my message to you, for he has worked tirelessly and with understanding for the common good of our countries. I look forward to his return, when I shall have opportunity to hear from him first hand of his service in your country."[68] Ngô Đình Diệm might not have shared Kennedy's conviction of the appropriateness of Durbrow at his inauguration. Certainly Lansdale had tried to have the new ambassador in place before the election to achieve a fresh start. While Durbrow would leave a few days later, Ngô Đình Diệm could not have been encouraged to learn that Kennedy was waiting for a firsthand account, as there was no other single individual who had done more to harm the relationship between Ngô Đình Diệm and the Americans than Elbridge Durbrow.

When Durbrow resumed his farewell tour, he next visited Trương Vĩnh Lê before he, with Ngô Đình Diệm, presided over the opening of the Bien Hoa–Saigon highway.[69] At

13. April 1961 Election and the Departure of Durbrow

Ngô Đình Nhu with Ambassador Frederick Nolting (Republic of Vietnam Director of Information Photograph Room, Folder 5, Box 39. Frederick [Fritz] Earnest Nolting, Jr. Papers, Accession #12804, Albert and Shirley Small Special Collections Library, University of Virginia).

Ngô Đình Diệm with new Ambassador Frederick Nolting (Republic of Vietnam Director of Information Photograph Room, Folder 3, Box 39. Frederick [Fritz] Earnest Nolting, Jr., Papers, Accession #12804, Albert and Shirley Small Special Collections Library, University of Virginia).

that event, one of the last that would see Durbrow and Ngô Đình Diệm together in public, the ambassador declared that the road was "an outstanding example of Vietnamese and American cooperation in bringing to a successful conclusion a most difficult and challenging engineering problem."[70] The highway had also been a source of fodder for the North Vietnamese propaganda machine, who argued that it was nothing more than a big airbase rather than the civil communications line as defined by the Saigon government.[71] Durbrow complimented the Saigon government and its president on the achievement, in what would also be one of the last utterances of support for Ngô Đình Diệm. Ngô Đình Diệm responded with kind words for the Americans who had worked on the four-year program, which had enhanced "the feeling of solidarity in the face of the threats from the Communist world."[72] Durbrow was not singled out in Ngô Đình Diệm's remarks; the ill feeling of the previous months coupled with the overwhelming mandate of the April 9 election continued to make their presence known in the Ngô Đình Diệm–Durbrow relationship. Durbrow was then honored in a farewell reception at McGarr's house the evening before the inauguration at an event sponsored by USOM, USIS, and MAAG.[73]

The final Durbrow–Ngô Đình Diệm public appearance occurred during the inauguration festivities, which was an all-day event on April 29.[74] Durbrow did not make any public pronouncements, though he delivered Kennedy's note of congratulations. On April 30, Durbrow and Ngô Đình Diệm would hold their final private meeting when, as dean of the diplomatic and Consular Corp, Durbrow offered the official congratulations for a second term to Ngô Đình Diệm from the Saigon diplomats. Durbrow, a professional to the end even if one who had actively conspired to thwart the Ngô Đình Diệm presidency and even suggested the possible removal of the RVN leader if he did not initiate American suggestions for reform, completed the diplomatic formalities expected of him within his capacity as the dean of the corps. Durbrow then departed Vietnam on Wednesday, May 3, nearly 1,500 days after presenting his credentials to become the ambassador.

Conclusion

Even as the April 1961 election was under way, other events around the world helped to shape American foreign policy in Southeast Asia. The failure at the Bay of Pigs on April 17, 1961, strengthened Kennedy's conviction that he needed to get tough with the communists around the world.[1] Vietnam would become the area of focus, and the United States would recommit itself to the defense of the RVN and Ngô Đình Diệm. However, the events of 1960 had forever changed how the RVN's president viewed the Americans. Ironically, Kennedy offered the best hope for the Vietnamese because he was willing to provide them with the resources they needed to fight the insurgency. His moves, however, occurred at a time when Ngô Đình Diệm's trust of his principal ally was at an all-time low. While it is true that Durbrow was out, which provided Ngô Đình Diệm with some incentives to begin matching American actions, the new ambassador was an unproven actor. Frederick Nolting would show himself to be a supporter of Ngô Đình Diệm during his tenure in office, but he lacked the political clout to combat the State Department and compete with individuals who had served in Durbrow's embassy but now held significant positions in the State Department, such as Joseph Mendenhall.

Likewise, new Kennedy administration advisers sought to take control of American diplomacy and provide a fresh, more active policy to ensure that communism was checked around the world. In Laos, Kennedy trusted his ambassador at large, W. Averell Harriman, to begin the process of neutralizing that country.[2] On January 19, 1961, the day before his inauguration, Eisenhower met with Kennedy to discuss foreign policy concerns. Within the region of Southeast Asia, Eisenhower focused on Laos rather than the RVN. The Laotian communist insurgency had intensified in the late 1950s while the events of 1960 confirmed the country's instability. Kennedy turned to Harriman to resolve this problem even as he moved to escalate in Vietnam.[3] Harriman's solution was neutrality, which he helped to set in motion with the International Conference on the Settlement of the Laotian Question, as it was formally titled. This newest Geneva Conference began on May 16, 1961, and lasted until July 23, 1962. While Harriman pushed for neutrality, Ngô Đình Diệm reacted forcibly against such a move, which he believed, rightfully so, would allow the North Vietnamese access to, and transit through, Laos as they escalated their war in the RVN. *The Declaration on the Neutrality of Laos*, issued on July 8, 1962, allowed for the Laotians to maintain a coalition government that was supposedly neutral. Within Laos, three political parties conflicted with one another as they individually pushed for support of the United States, the communist Pathet Lao, and neutrality, respectively. *The International Agreement on the Neutrality of Laos*, signed on July 23, 1962, affirmed that the fourteen nations at the conference would respect Laotian neutrality by ending direct or indirect interference in Laotian internal affairs and by keeping Laos out of military alliances.

The American move in Laos was an indication to Ngô Đình Diệm that the once-complementary policy shared by the United States and the RVN was at an end. As Ngô Đình Diệm pushed against the American plan to make Laos neutral, the ghosts of Durbrow's past seeped into the Kennedy administration's foreign policy direction for the RVN. For Ngô Đình Diệm, Harriman's attitudes reflected a continuation of Durbrow's aloofness even though Nolting sided with the RVN president. Ngô Đình Diệm had learned in 1960 that the United States, despite its increased aid which was essential to the war effort, was no longer a steadfast ally that would support him without limit or qualification. In this respect, 1960 marked the beginning of the end of the Ngô Đình Diệm–United States relationship.

Other events, which followed in 1962 and 1963, confirmed Ngô Đình Diệm's suspicion that the United States no longer had his best interests in mind. The clash over the Strategic Hamlet Program, the American reaction to the Buddhist uprisings in 1963, and the replacement of Nolting by Henry Cabot Lodge signaled a moving away from Ngô Đình Diệm even as the United States increased its aid and personnel in the fight against communism in the RVN. While Ngô Đình Diệm's actions and reactions to these events fell short of satisfactory, he was more than just motivated by personal greed or a need for power. Ngô Đình Diệm responded to the Americans during the critical times in 1962 and 1963 based upon his experiences in 1960. That story, however, is a much longer one to tell. Still, it cannot be fully understood unless the Year of the Rat, 1960, is placed into the proper context of the early years of the RVN and the presidency of Ngô Đình Diệm.

Ngô Đình Diệm had failed in 1960, but so had Durbrow and the Americans. For those who supported the Durbrow position, the constant pressure against Ngô Đình Diệm coupled with the unquestioned support of his Vietnamese rivals forced an already stubborn man into an inflexible position. Likewise, within the American community, the continued bickering and clashes between the military and diplomats resulted in an expenditure of personal resources that would have been better served supporting the RVN. While individuals like Lansdale, Williams, and McGarr worked to support Ngô Đình Diệm, their pressure against Durbrow, the embassy, and the State Department had the unfortunate effect of forcing these individuals and organizations into a confirmed anti–Ngô Đình Diệm position. What Ngô Đình Diệm needed from the United States was unity and support. He received division, questionable advice, limited support, and, at times, outright hostility. Ngô Đình Diệm did not respond as Durbrow and his allies had expected, but this did not mean that the two sides were no longer seeking the same objectives. Their means differed while their ability to justify their actions failed to satisfy the other side. Neither Ngô Đình Diệm and his allies nor Durbrow and his cohort were able to reconcile these differences, and as a result, the path down the long road of the United States' greatest failure in the twentieth century continued and was accelerated.

Appendix

The Republic of Vietnam's Economy

At the end of 1959, rubber exports totaled 73,433 tons, which was an increase of 4,696 tons from 1958. The total number of hectares under production also increased from 76,300 hectares to 100,440 hectares in 1959, while the amount of profit in exporting rubber also increased from VN$1,932 (US$55.2) million in 1958 to VN$2,627 (US$75.05) million in 1959.[1] Rubber remained the leading profit-making export for Vietnam, followed by rice, tea, cinnamon, and beer.[2] Further, at the end of 1959–1960, Vietnamese rice crops had yielded more than 5,300,000 tons of rice, which was an increase from the 3,995,333 tons produced during the 1958–1959 crop. More than half of the thirty-seven rice-producing provinces achieved bi-annual harvests, and the per-hectare output was estimated at 2,220 tons for the first and 1,150 tons for the second harvest. Rice exports in 1958 had been 171,100 tons and jumped to 368,500 tons in 1959. This meant that the amount of exportable rice more than doubled its 1957 levels, reaching the 400,000-ton level.[3] As reported by Agriculture Secretary Lê Văn Đông, rice production and exports had increased significantly since the 1954–1955 period, rising from 2,566,000 tons to 5,312,000 tons during the 1959–1960 production period.[4]

Vietnam imported 143,852 tons of agricultural goods in 1959 worth VN$891,437,000 (US$25,469,628) which included VN$217,000,000 (US$6,200,000) in flour, VN$139,000,000 (US$3,971,428) in cotton and thread, and VN$139,000,000 (US$3,971,428) in sugar. During the same period, Vietnam imported 18,189 tons of farm products valued at approximately VN$882,300,000 (US$25,208,571), including VN$345,000,000 (US$9,857,142) in milk and VN$4,586,000 (US$1,310,285) in forestry products.[5] Fruit orchards in Vietnam covered 42,905 hectares in 1959 and produced 290,903 tons of fruit, which compared favorably to the 1958 levels of 37,276 hectares and 250,051 tons.

The Ministry of Agriculture also reported that sweet potato and manioc cultivation had increased in the same period from 136,650 tons to 203,245 tons and 161,767 tons to 180,878 tons respectively. While peanuts, corn, and vegetables declined because there was less cultivable land, Phước Tuy province had produced 1,200 tons of peanuts by October 1960, of which 1,000 tons were purchased by exporters in Saigon.[6] By the end of 1959, there were 8,964 hectares of tea plantations in South Vietnam, which was a slight increase from the 8,468 hectares under production in 1958, though there were only 6,590 hectares under production in 1955. The 1959 plantations produced 4,183 tons of tea as opposed to the 3,410 tons yielded in 1958, and more than double the 1955 production.

South Vietnam imported over 17,000 tons of concentrated milk per year with a value of VN$344,000,000 (US$9,828,571). By the end of the year, the Bến Cát Pilot Dairy Farm, which was a joint operation between Australia and the National Directorate of Animal Husbandry under Colombo Plan aid, announced that it would be able to supply fresh milk to Saigon.[7] The farm produced between 700 and 1,000 liters of milk per day. The poultry industry also improved, producing 9,191,702 chicks in 1958 compared to 9,627,447 chicks in 1959.[8] There was also an increase in ducks from 6,394,522 in 1958 to 7,328,600 in 1959. While none of the meat from these animals was exported, approximately 1,000,000 duck eggs were sent to foreign markets out of the 288,623,650 eggs produced in 1959. This egg count was up from 249,336,200 in 1958. While these indicators were only a few for the Vietnamese economy, they did suggest that the country was moving in a positive direction.

Chapter Notes

Preface

1. Bùi Diễm, with David Chanoff, *In the Jaws of History*, 95. Joseph Buttinger, *Vietnam: A Dragon Embattled*, 962–964. Buttinger does not conclude that all signers were arrested, though he does defend the reputation of the men as prominent.
2. Seth Jacobs, *Cold War Mandarin*, 115.
3. Chester Cooper, *Lost Crusade*, 159.
4. George Kahin, *Intervention*, 123.
5. Malcolm Browne, *The New Face of War*, 307. Other Historians, such as Anthony Trawick Bouscaren, devote only a few sentences to the abortive coup d'état. Anthony Trawick Bouscaren, *Last of the Mandarins: Diem of Vietnam*, 69.
6. David Anderson, *Trapped by Success*; and Ronald Spector, *Advice and Support*.
7. John Ernst, *Forging a Fateful Alliance*; and Arthur J. Dommen, *The Indochinese Experience of the French and the Americans*.

Chapter 1

1. Ronald B. Frankum, Jr., *Operation Passage to Freedom*.
2. The term "politico-religious group" is used here rather than the more commonly used "religious sects" to better reflect the political orientation of the three organizations. See Jessica M. Chapman, *Cauldron of Resistance*.
3. In May 1955, Michigan State University established a technical assistance program for Vietnam. One of its early leaders, political science professor Welsey Fishel, was on good terms with Ngô Đình Diệm, while each shared common political and social views. The Michigan State University Group provided advice and assistance to the young Republic, including consultation during the creation of the Constitution. During the seven years that Michigan State University was involved in Vietnam, it offered expertise in a number of projects designed to improve Vietnam. Tension between the group and Ngô Đình Diệm developed after group members published a series of articles and reports critical of Ngô Đình Diệm. A few of these occurred during the lunar year 1960, though the relationship had begun to sour earlier. Ngô Đình Diệm rejected the criticism and eventually ended the relationship in June 1962.
4. The national election was not without controversy or signs of the fragile nature of the Republic of Vietnam's experimentations with democracy. There were charges of intimidation by the Saigon government, National Revolutionary Movement members, and those loyal to Ngô Đình Nhu who focused on candidates opposed to Ngô Đình Diệm or were outside the National Revolutionary Movement's approved candidate list. See Nguyễn Tuyết Mai, "Electioneering: Vietnamese Style," *Asian Survey* 2, no. 9 (1962): 11–18; P.J. Honey, "The Problem of Democracy in Vietnam," *The World Today* 16, no. 2 (1960): 71–79; Robert G. Scigliano, "The Electoral Process in South Vietnam: Politics in an Underdeveloped State," *Midwest Journal of Political Science* 4, no. 2 (1960): 138–161; and Robert G. Scigliano, "Political Parties in South Vietnam under the Republic," *Pacific Affairs*, 33, no. 4 (1960): 327–346.
5. The Country Team in Vietnam consisted of representatives of the Military Assistance and Advisory Group, United States Operations Mission, United States Information Service, Office of the Special Assistant to the Ambassador in Vietnam, and U.S. embassy in Saigon.
6. Elbridge Durbrow to the Department of State, Dispatch 163, December 7, 1959, *Foreign Relations of the United States* [hereafter referred to as *FRUS*], *1958–1960, Volume I: Vietnam*, 260.
7. Durbrow to the Department of State, Dispatch 163, December 7, 1959, *FRUS, 1958–1960, Volume I: Vietnam*, 261.
8. On December 6, government security agents, Civil Guard, and ARVN units in Cái Nước district, An Xuyên province, attacked a group of communist insurgents, killing five, as they approached the hamlet of Rach Lang by boat. A similar incident occurred on December 11 in Đức Lập village, Long An province, that resulted in the deaths of three Việt Cộng and the seizure of many weapons and documents. Long An province was the focal point for a number of intense clashes between government forces and the Việt Cộng because of its strategic location and value. It was the site of additional attacks on December 11 in Bàu Sen hamlet, Đức Lập village, and December 14 between the Civil Guard and thirty Việt Cộng that focused around the hamlet of Thành Đông and would continue to play a major role in the insurgents' battle for the hearts and minds of the Vietnamese people. Not only was the fighting intensifying, but the targets were also becoming more prominent. On December 13, Việt Cộng cadre assassinated Nguyễn Thành Tòn, chief of An Khương village in Vĩnh

Long province. He would be one of many that would die as a result of *Trụ Gian* (targeted assassinations). See *Cách mạng Quốc gia*, December 6, 1959, and December 11, 1959, Foreign Broadcast Information Service [hereafter referred to as FBIS], December 16, 1959, G2; *Ngôn Luận*, December 14, 1959, FBIS, December 16, 1959, G2; and *Chuông Mai*, December 13, 1959, FBIS, December 16, 1959, G2.

9. Lansdale joined the Office of Strategic Services in 1943 and, as a lieutenant in the U.S. Army, worked in military intelligence. In 1950, he was transferred to the Joint United States Military Assistance Group, Philippines, where he earned a reputation as someone who could get the job done. On June 1, 1954, Lansdale joined the Saigon Military Mission where he advised the State of Vietnam in counter-insurgency strategy and became the confidant of Ngô Đình Diệm. In the early years of the Republic of Vietnam, Lansdale continued to support Ngô Đình Diệm even when other high-ranking Americans did not. When the French-supported Bình Xuyên, Cao Đài, and Hòa Hảo attempted to overthrow Ngô Đình Diệm in March 1955, Lansdale worked to secure his safety and ensure that Ngô Đình Diệm would win and consolidate his power.

10. Durbrow to the Department of State, Dispatch 163, December 7, 1959, *FRUS, 1958–1960, Volume I: Vietnam*, 255–271.

11. Colby would replace Natsios as the Central Intelligence Agency station chief in Saigon in June 1960. See Ahern, *House of Ngo*, 135.

12. Fall, *The Two Viet-Nams*, 237–238.

13. Durbrow to the Department of State, Dispatch 163, December 7, 1959, *FRUS, 1958–1960, Volume I: Vietnam*, 255.

14. Robert G. Scigliano, "The Electoral Process in South Vietnam," 138–161.

15. In the case of the Department of Information, the budget decrease was approximately VN$1,500,000 less than the already proposed VN$24,742,000 decrease from the previous year, while the Department of Finance saw a reduction of VN$14,518,000. The Department of Information's budget was VN$169,039,000 in 1959, and the proposed 1960 budget was VN$144,297,000. *Vietnam Press*, December 18, 1959, FBIS, December 22, 1959, G3.

16. Durbrow to Gore, January 6, 1960, Central Decimal Files [hereafter referred to as CDF], 751K.00/1–660, RG 59: Records of the Department of State [hereafter referred to as RG 59], National Archives and Records Administration, College Park, MD [hereafter referred to as NARA].

17. Durbrow to the Department of State, Telegram 2165, January 17, 1960, CDF 751K.00/1–1860, RG 59, NARA. See also Durbrow correspondence related to Gore's follow-up letter, CDF 751K.00/2–1760, RG 59, NARA. See also Robert G. Scigliano, "The Electoral Process in South Vietnam," 138–161; and P.J. Honey, "The Problem of Democracy in Vietnam," 71–79.

18. *Buổi sang*, December 21, 1959, FBIS, December 22, 1959, G4.

19. "Deputies Urge End to Police Brutality," *Chuông Mai*, December 22, 1959, FBIS, December 24, 1959, G1–G2.

20. *Chuông Mai*, December 22, 1959, FBIS, December 24, 1959, G1. Phan Khắc Sửu would also be one of the leading members of the April 1960 Caravelle Manifesto Group that openly opposed Ngô Đình Diệm and his rule.

21. Mendenhall to the Department of State, Dispatch 233, February 4, 1960, CDF 751G.00/2–460, Box 1745, RG 59, NARA.

22. Durbrow to the Department of State, Dispatch 163, December 7, 1959, *FRUS, 1958–1960, Volume I: Vietnam*, 258.

23. Durbrow to the Department of State, Dispatch 163, December 7, 1959, *FRUS, 1958–1960, Volume I: Vietnam*, 263. Personalism, as adopted by Ngô Đình Diệm, derived from the French Personalist philosophy as enumerated by Emmanuel Mounier during the interwar period. See Chapman, *Cauldron of Resistance*, 121–124.

24. Durbrow to the Department of State, Dispatch 163, December 7, 1959, *FRUS, 1958–1960, Volume I: Vietnam*, 264.

25. Durbrow to the Department of State, Dispatch 163, December 7, 1959, *FRUS, 1958–1960, Volume I: Vietnam*, 264.

26. On December 15, the Saigon Supreme Court issued a decision to sentence ARVN lieutenant Trần Quốc Thái to five years' imprisonment for embezzling public funds. On December 21, Colonel Trần Quốc Dũng and Lieutenant Lê Văn Đức were sentenced to three and four years in prison for embezzling public funds while the chief of Long Dinh village, Mỹ Tho province, Ngô Văn Tinh, was arrested for extortion. These cases never made their way into the American reports even when Durbrow and his embassy devoted space in the dispatches to including information from the Saigon intelligentsia who complained about the failure to address corruption. They usually focused on the Ngô family and the Cần Lao Party. *Ngôn Luận*, December 14, 1959, FBIS, December 16, 1959, G2; and *Cách mạng Quốc gia*, December 21, 1959, December 23, 1959, G2.

27. "Press Interview with President Diem," December 8, 1959, Dispatch 186, enclosure 1, CDF 751G.11/2–1159, Box 3347, RG 59, NARA.

28. "Press Interview with President Diem," December 8, 1959, Dispatch 186, enclosure 1, CDF 751G.11/2–1159, Box 3347, RG 59, NARA.

29. The Civil Guard was officially established by Ngô Đình Diệm in April 1955 and was organized as a paramilitary organization to assist the ARVN. It had units in nearly every district of each province and was responsible for internal security. The Self-Defense Corps was similar, though it operated only at the district level. Both the Civil Guard and the Self-Defense Corps were generally poorly trained and equipped. Their purpose was to patrol the countryside and keep the insurgents off balance. The Republican Youth was also a paramilitary organization designed to recruit the youth toward supporting the Republic of Vietnam and Ngô Đình Diệm.

30. "News Conference and Briefing Given by Mr. Dung Secretary of State for National Defense at DOD," December 8, 1959, Dispatch 186, enclosure 2, CDF 751G.11/2–1159, Box 3347, RG 59, NARA.

31. "Spare the Rich, Hit the Poor, Buy American," *Times of Vietnam*, December 5, 1969, FBIS, Decem-

ber 7, 1959, G1–G2. The *Times of Vietnam* was the first English-language newspaper in the Republic of Vietnam. After 1957, it was run by Gene Gregory, a supporter of Ngô Đình Nhu, and published stories that supported his position and policy in the Republic of Vietnam. See Nguyễn Thái, "South Vietnam," in *The Asian Newspapers' Reluctant Revolution*, 249.

32. FBIS, December 7, 1959, G2.
33. FBIS, December 7, 1959, G7.
34. Durbrow to the Department of State, Telegram 1921, December 11, 1959, CDF 751G.5/12–1159, Box 3351, RG 59, NARA.
35. *Vietnam Press*, December 24, 1959, FBIS, December 28, 1959, G1.

Chapter 2

1. *Vietnam Press*, January 27, 1960, FBIS, January 29, 1960, G1–G2. See also Mendenhall to the Department of State, Dispatch 235, February 4, 1960, CDF 751G.00/2-460, Box 1745, RG 59, NARA. The significance of the French effect on the Vietnamese was a constant theme of Ngô Đình Diệm and Ngô Đình Nhu. Ngô Đình Nhu provided an eloquent explanation of the nature of the under-developed country in a February 9 meeting with Wolf Ladejinsky and Leo Cherne while Ngô Đình Diệm outlined the negative role of the French and their influence on the RVN's development in a February 20 meeting with Lieutenant General Isaac White, commander in chief, Pacific. See Memoranda of Conversation, February 9, 1960, and February 26, 1960. Both are located in Folder 1, Box 14, Papers of Samuel T. Williams, Hoover Institute, Stanford University, Palo Alto, Calif. See also Durbrow to the Department of State, Dispatch 261, "Anti-Guerrilla Training for Civil Guard and ARVN," February 27, 1960, CDF 751K.5/2-2760, RG 59, NARA.
2. *Vietnam Press*, January 27, 1960, FBIS, January 29, 1960, G2.
3. See appendix A.
4. Colby, *Lost Victory*, 69.
5. Brucker arrived on January 6 and departed on January 8. He was briefed and held discussions with Durbrow and Williams in addition to meeting with Ngô Đình Diệm. See Durbrow to the Department of State, Telegram 2107, January 9, 2011, CDF 751K.00(W)/1-960, RG 59, NARA.
6. Memorandum of Conversation, January 7, 1960, Folder 1, Box 14, Papers of Samuel T. Williams, Hoover Institute, Stanford University, Palo Alto, Calif.
7. Williams' handwritten notes on the Memorandum of Conversation, January 7, 1960, Folder 1, Box 14, Papers of Samuel T. Williams, Hoover Institute, Stanford University, Palo Alto, Calif. See also Williams' Memorandum for Record, March 1971, which refutes many of Durbrow's claims about the meeting, in Folder 1, Box 14, Papers of Samuel T. Williams, Hoover Institute, Stanford University, Palo Alto, Calif. Durbrow offers no account of the heated visit in his WeekA to the Department of State, Durbrow to the Department of State, Telegram 2107, January 9, 2011, CDF 751K.00(W)/1-960, RG 59, NARA.

8. On January 25, 1960, Chalmers B. Wood, the officer in charge of Vietnam affairs in the Department of State, and former subordinate to Durbrow in the U.S. embassy in Saigon, wrote a memorandum for the record in which he defended Durbrow's actions and argued that "one of the greatest problems which Ambassador Durbrow has overcome has been Diem's proclivity for playing one American official against another." "Secretary Brucker and the Geneva Agreements," January 25, 1960, CDF 751K.00/1–2560, RG 59, NARA.
9. In June 1956, TERM personnel began to arrive in Vietnam with two major objectives. Its public mission was supervising the recovery and removal of Mutual Defense Assistance Program equipment the United States had provided to the French during the First Indochina War. Privately, its mission was also to improve the newly created ARVN logistical capabilities. The TERM increased the number of U.S. personnel in Vietnam from 342 to 692. TERM personnel were assigned to ARVN military units and focused on logistics, medical, quartermaster, transportation, ordnance, engineering, and signal units. The International Control Commission never agreed to the TERM and, in December 1958, it passed a resolution that called for the mission to leave by June 30, 1959. In May 1960, the TERM was absorbed into the MAAG, making the temporary mission permanent, while the U.S. ceiling for advisers rose to 685. See Ronald Frankum, *Historical Dictionary of the War in Vietnam*, 443–444.
10. The second conversation was recorded as an addendum to the first Memorandum of Conversation of January 7, 1960, Folder 1, Box 14, Papers of Samuel T. Williams, Hoover Institute, Stanford University, Palo Alto, Calif. Williams' memory of the events is recorded in Williams' Memorandum for Record, March 1971, Folder 1, Box 14, Papers of Samuel T. Williams, Hoover Institute, Stanford University, Palo Alto, Calif.
11. In February, Durbrow would push to have the RVN request the MAAG ceiling raised to 685 rather than having the request come from the United States. See Durbrow to the Department of State, Telegram 2430, February 16, 1960, CDF 751K.5-MSP/2–1660, RG 59, NARA; Durbrow to the Department of State, Telegram 2443, February 18, 1960, CDF 751K.5-MSP/2–1860, RG 59, NARA. Williams' analysis is found in Williams to the secretary of state, Telegram MAGCC-OP 259, February 24, 1960, CDF 751K.5-MSP/2–2460, RG 59, NARA.
12. Memorandum of Conversation, January 7, 1960, Folder 1, Box 14, Papers of Samuel T. Williams, Hoover Institute, Stanford University, Palo Alto, Calif.
13. Durbrow's January 8, 1960, letter; Parsons' February 1, 1960, reply; and Williams' February 10, 1960, observation of the exchange are located in Folder 1, Box 14, Papers of Samuel T. Williams, Hoover Institute, Stanford University, Palo Alto, Calif. See also Williams' memory of the events in Williams' Memorandum for Record, March 1971, Folder 1, Box 14, Papers of Samuel T. Williams, Hoover Institute, Stanford University, Palo Alto, Calif.
14. The USOM is not to be confused with the United States Overseas Missions, also abbreviated as USOM, which was the precursor to the United States Agency for International Development.
15. There is no additional evidence to confirm

Williams' assertion that only Durbrow was asked to stay away from the meeting. However, it is reasonable to accept Williams' claim given his 1971 Memorandum for the Record which outlined the course of events as compared to Durbrow's reporting of it to Washington. Williams' Memorandum for Record, March 1971, Folder 1, Box 14, Papers of Samuel T. Williams, Hoover Institute, Stanford University, Palo Alto, Calif.

16. Memorandum of Conversation, January 7, 1960, Folder 1, Box 14, Papers of Samuel T. Williams, Hoover Institute, Stanford University, Palo Alto, Calif.

17. Durbrow to the Department of State, Telegram 2431, February 16, 1960, CDF 751K.5-MSP/2-1660, RG 59, NARA.

18. Memorandum of Conversation, February 1, 1960, Folder 1, Box 14, Papers of Samuel T. Williams, Hoover Institute, Stanford University, Palo Alto, Calif.; and Durbrow to the Department of State, Telegram 2337, February 6, 1960, CDF 751K.00(W)/2-660, RG 59, NARA. See also the press conference by Secretary of State for Information Trần Chánh Tranh and Secretary of State for the Presidency Nguyễn Đình Thuận as reported by *Tuan Tung Jih Pao*, February 2, 1960, FBIS, February 3, 1960, G1–G2. A.J. Langguth argued that three companies, or approximately 300 men, attacked approximately 1,700 troops. See Langguth, *Our Vietnam*, 101. See also Spector, *Advice and Support*, 338–339. Spector correctly identifies the four companies and details Williams' conversation with Ngô Đình Diệm as a result of the failure of the 32nd Regiment.

19. *Vietnam Press*, January 31, 1960, and February 1, 1960, FBIS, February 2, 1960, G1. See also *Times of Vietnam*, February 3, 1960, FBIS, February 4, 1960, G1; and *May Jih Luan Zan*, February 4, 1960, FBIS, February 4, 1960, G3.

20. This assessment is based on a conversation between Lieutenant Colonel Joseph A. Flesch OASD/ISA Far East Region and Chalmers B. Wood, officer in charge of Vietnam affairs in the Department of State, February 4, 1960, Folder 108 "VN 1960—National Defense Affairs (General)," Box 2, Entry 5155, Bureau of East Asian Affairs, Vietnam Desk, Vietnam Subject Files, 1955–1962, RG 59, NARA.

21. Memorandum of Conversation, February 1, 1960, Folder 1, Box 14, Papers of Samuel T. Williams, Hoover Institute, Stanford University, Palo Alto, Calif.

22. The weapons were locked in a shed in order to control the distribution of the weapons and ensure that they were not sold by individual soldiers.

23. The Agroville Program, established by the Ngô Đình Diệm government in 1959, was a pacification program created as a response to the increased communist insurgent activities of Trụ Giãn. In a July 1959 radio broadcast commemorating the fifth anniversary of his rise to power, Ngô Đình Diệm announced the creation of the program, which was described as a plan to concentrate the people into protected villages. Agrovilles would have all the amenities that villages lacked. Peasants would have access to electricity, schools, medical facilities, and doctors as well as other infrastructure that would markedly increase their quality of life. While not mentioned in the broadcast, another important goal of the Agroville Program was the creation of centers for the people to protect them against the increased communist insurgent threat. The insurgents had preyed upon the people by taxing them, recruiting from their ranks, and receiving intelligence on the disposition of the ARVN troops operating in their area. By denying the insurgency access to the people and providing the peasants with the benefits of modernization, Ngô Đình Diệm hoped to deny the insurgency its most potent resource. See Joseph J. Zasloff, "Rural Resettlement in South Viet Nam: The Agroville Program," *Pacific Affairs* 35, no. 4 (Winter 1962–1963): 327–340; Catton, *Diem's Final Failure*, 66–71; Colby, *Lost Victory*, 69–71; Miller, *Misalliance*, 177–184; and Spector, *Advice and Support*, 332–334.

24. In Long An province, twenty-six people were killed, either shot or executed in a brutal way. This led to a certain paralysis in the Vietnamese countryside. The Việt Cộng assassinated the chief of Phú Thạnh hamlet in Phú Hòa Đông village, Bình Dương province; murdered the hamlet chief in Thới Vĩnh village, Bình Đại district, Kiến Hòa province; and killed the village police chief in Hữu Định village, Trúc Giang district. The significance of these attacks was enhanced by an uprising in Kiến Hòa province, known by the insurgents as Bến Tre province, in January. *Tự do*, February 2, 1960, FBIS, February 2, 1960, G2. See also Race, *War Comes to Long An*, 113–115; Duiker, *Sacred War*, 124–126; and Langguth, *Our Vietnam*, 105–107. See also Nguyen Thi Dinh, *No Other Road to Take*, 17–18.

25. Mendenhall to the Department of State, Telegram 230, February 2, 1960, CDF 751G.00/1-2060, RG 59, NARA.

26. *Cách mạng Quốc gia*, February 5, 1960, FBIS, February 8, 1960, G2. *Cách mạng Quốc gia* was published by the Movement for National Revolution and was decidedly pro–Ngô Đình Diệm. See Nguyễn Thái, "South Vietnam," in *The Asian Newspapers' Reluctant Revolution*, 243.

27. *Tự do* and *Ngôn Luận* on February 8, 1960, FBIS, February 9, 1960, G1; and *Ngôn Luận*, February 12, 1960, FBIS, February 12, 1960, G1. See also *Cách mạng Quốc gia*, February 9, 1960, FBIS, February 9, 1960, G3; *Ngôn Luận*, *Cách mạng Quốc gia*, and *Tiếng Chuông* on February 10, 1960, FBIS, February 10, 1960, G1; *Cách mạng Quốc gia*, February 11, 1960, FBIS, February 11, 1960, G1; and, *Tự do*, February 15, 1960, FBIS, February 17, 1960, G1–G3.

28. Durbrow to the Department of State, Telegram 2014, December 24, 1959, *FRUS, 1958–1960, Volume I: Vietnam*, 276–278.

29. Durbrow to the Department of State, Telegram 2014, December 24, 1959, *FRUS, 1958–1960, Volume I: Vietnam*, 278.

30. Memorandum of Conversation, April 6, 1960, Folder 1, Box 14, Papers of Samuel T. Williams, Hoover Institute, Stanford University, Palo Alto, Calif.

31. Durbrow to the Department of State, Dispatch 251, "Current Security Problems Facing the GVN," February 16, 1960, CDF 751K.5/2-1660, RG 59, NARA. A Memorandum of Conversation between Ngô Đình Diệm and Durbrow is attached. Ngô Đình Diệm's trip to Malaya was his second state trip of the year (the first was to Taiwan). In preparing for the trip, Durbrow pushed for Ngô Đình Diệm to visit the Jungle Warfare School in order to see how the British were fighting their own insurgents. Time did not permit the visit, though

British counter-insurgency experts would play a significant role in aiding the Vietnamese as a result of this visit. Durbrow to the Department of State, Telegram 2372, February 11, 1960, CDF 751K.11/2–1160, RG 59, NARA; Durbrow to the Department of State, Telegram 2411, February 13, 1960, CDF 751K.11/2–1360, RG 59, NARA; and U.S. Ambassador in Malaysia Homer M. Byington to the Department of State, Telegram 428, February 15, 1960, CDF 751K.11/2–1560, RG 59, NARA.

32. Durbrow reported his arguments on the budget in Durbrow to the Department of State, Telegram 2519, February 27, 1960, CDF 751K.5-MSP/2–2760, RG 59, NARA.

33. One complaint that many Americans pursued was their inability to have a balanced conversation with Ngô Đình Diệm. While the American perception was that Ngô Đình Diệm needed to dominate the conversation because they believed he was not interested in their perspective or advice, Ngô Đình Diệm often provided new visitors or others with background information as an attempt to get them to understand the Vietnamese perspective. This eventually caused Durbrow an inordinate amount of frustration as Ngô Đình Diệm never really believed that the ambassador understood him, the Vietnamese, or the Republic of Vietnam.

34. Memorandum of Conversation, February 1, 1960, Folder 1, Box 14, Papers of Samuel T. Williams, Hoover Institute, Stanford University, Palo Alto, Calif. In a February 20, 1960, conversation between Williams and Ngô Đình Diệm, he confirmed to the general that he needed 10,000 men as well as a number of small boats so that he could better access the Plaine de Joncs. The Plaine de Joncs was located to the west and southwest of Saigon and included the city of Mỹ Tho. Memorandum of Conversation, February 20, 1960, Folder 1, Box 14, Papers of Samuel T. Williams, Hoover Institute, Stanford University, Palo Alto, Calif.

35. Durbrow to the Department of State, Dispatch 251, "Current Security Problems Facing the GVN," February 12, 1960, CDF 751K.5/2–1660, RG 59, NARA.

Chapter 3

1. See Nashel, *Edward Lansdale's Cold War*.
2. See Anderson, *Trapped by Success*, 177. Ngô Đình Nhu had made this argument as early as 1957 during his visit to the United States.
3. Lansdale to Douglas, February 12, 1960, CDF 751K.5/3–460, RG 59, NARA.
4. Lansdale to Douglas, February 12, 1960, CDF 751K.5/3–460, RG 59, NARA.
5. Memorandum from Lansdale to the assistant secretary of defense for international security affairs, John N. Irwin II, February 19, 1960, *FRUS, 1958–1960, Volume I: Vietnam*, 288–289.
6. Memorandum from Lansdale to Irwin, February 19, 1960, *FRUS, 1958–1960, Volume I: Vietnam*, 289.
7. One example of this action was the attempt to create a postal exchange between North and South Vietnam. The DRV, on January 26, sent a letter to the ICC proposing that it intercede in the negotiations because the South Vietnamese, despite making "a great noise," had not communicated their desires directly to Hanoi. The implication was that the North Vietnamese were ready and willing to open an exchange, save for Saigon's reluctance to accomplish what it had originally proposed. The North used the ICC procedures against the South to further advance this implication, which in turn caused the Saigon government to protest that the ICC favored the North Vietnamese. This type of issue also diverted ICC attention away from the real violations occurring on both sides of the DMZ. See Mendenhall to the Department of State, Dispatch 241, February 10, 1960, CDF 751K.00/2–1060, RG 59, NARA. Additional material related to protests to the ICC and decisions by the ICC that affected its staff are located in the CDF for the dates between February 26 and February 29, 1960. See also *Lê Sống* editorial, February 9, 1960, FBIS, February 9, 1960, G3.

8. There were several examples of this in the early days of February such as the relationship between the Southeast Asia Treaty Organization and the RVN, or as Hanoi VNA referred to it, "the ever-closer military collusion between the South Vietnam authorities and the aggressive Southeast Asian military bloc headed by the United States." A few days later, the North Vietnamese issued protests over the visit of the Republic of Korea's navy to Saigon. Hanoi, VNA, January 31, 1960, FBIS, February 1, 1960, E3; see also Hanoi VNA, February 2, 1960, FBIS, February 3, 1960, E3; and Hanoi, VNA, February 8, 1960, FBIS, February 9, 1960, E4.

9. *Vietnam Press*, February 4, 1960, FBIS, February 8, 1960, G1.

10. The Personalism adopted by Ngô Đình Diệm and Ngô Đình Nhu was developed between the First World War and Second World War in France and espoused by Emmanuel Mounier. This form of Personalism sought a middle ground between the exploitative nature of capitalism and the subjugated ideology of communism. See Miller, *Misalliance*, 43–46; and Chapman, *Cauldron of Resistance*, 121–124.

11. *Sun Wun Jih Pao*, February 9, 1960, FBIS, February 9, 1960, G4.

12. *Voice of Vietnam*, February 9, 1960, FBIS, February 12, 1960, E4–E5.

13. *Ngôn Luận*, February 24, 1960, FBIS, February 24, 1960, G1.

14. FBIS, March 4, 1960, G2.

15. *Chung Juo Jih Pao* editorial, May 7, 1960, FBIS, May 11, 1960, G3.

16. Memorandum of Conversation, "Internal Security Situation and Corruption," March 2, 1960, CDF 751K.00/3–260, RG 59, NARA. See also Colby, *Lost Victory*, 70.

17. Memorandum of Conversation, "Internal Security Situation and Corruption," March 2, 1960, CDF 751K.00/3–260, RG 59, NARA.

18. Joseph J. Zasloff, "Rural Resettlement in South Viet Nam: The Agroville Program," *Pacific Affairs* 35, no. 4 (Winter 1962–1963): 327–340.

19. Memorandum of Conversation, "Internal Security Situation and Corruption," March 2, 1960, CDF 751K.00/3–260, RG 59, NARA.

20. Memorandum of Conversation, "Internal Secu-

rity Situation and Corruption," March 2, 1960, CDF 751K.00/3-260, RG 59, NARA.

21. Memorandum of Conversation between Williams and Ngô Đình Diệm, January 12, 1960, Folder 1, Box 14, Papers of Samuel T. Williams, Hoover Institute, Stanford University, Palo Alto, Calif.

22. Memorandum of Conversation, "Internal Security Situation and Corruption," March 2, 1960, CDF 751K.00/3-260, RG 59, NARA. See also Memorandum of Conversation, the Pentagon, March 18, 1960, *FRUS, 1958–1960, Volume I: Vietnam*, 340. There was a similar complaint reported by Theodore Heavner, vice consul in Hue, from Phạm Ngọc Vinh who had been a former member of the Cần Lao; "Comments on the Can Lao Party and Ngo Dinh Can by an 'Inactive' Party Member," CDF 751K.00/2-860, RG 59, NARA.

23. Memorandum of Conversation, "Internal Security Situation and Corruption," March 2, 1960, CDF 751K.00/3-260, RG 59, NARA.

24. Memorandum of Conversation, "Internal Security Situation and Corruption," March 2, 1960, CDF 751K.00/3-260, RG 59, NARA.

25. Memorandum of Conversation, "Internal Security Situation and Corruption," March 2, 1960, CDF 751K.00/3-260, RG 59, NARA. Norodom Sihanouk, the son of King Norodom Suramarit and Queen Sisowath Kossamak, became king in September 1941 after the death of his maternal father, Chea Sim, on April 23, 1941. Sihanouk was anti-colonial and advocated an end to French rule in Indochina. On March 2, 1955, Sihanouk abdicated the throne to his father, Norodom Suramarit, and took the position of prime minister. He became head of state when his father died in 1960. His rule in Cambodia was characterized by an anti–Vietnamese, anti–Ngô Đình Diệm position that helped to maintain a tense relationship between Cambodia and the Republic of Vietnam.

26. FBIS, March 11, 1960, G1–G2.

27. "Saigon-Cholon Press Review," March 24, 1960, FBIS, G1.

28. FBIS, April 5, 1960, G4.

29. Memorandum of Conversation, "The Can Lao Party and Ngo Dinh Can," February 8, 1960, CDF 751K.00/2-860, RG 59, NARA.

30. Dispatch from Durbrow to the Department of State, March 7, 1960, *FRUS, 1958–1960, Volume I: Vietnam*, 300. Much of Durbrow's comments come from a special report from the Country Team titled "Special Report on Internal Security Situation in Viet-Nam" that was included as an enclosure to the dispatch and reprinted in *FRUS, 1958–1960, Volume I: Vietnam*, 303–320. See also Kahin, *Intervention*, 122.

31. "Security Anxiety in S. Viet Nam: Two Newspapers Suspended," *London Times*, March 8, 1960. See also Robert Ballantyne, second secretary of the American embassy in London to the Department of State, "Comment in London Press re Security Situation in South Vietnam," Dispatch 2895, March 14, 1960, CDF 751K.00/3-1460, RG 59, NARA; and Durbrow to the Department of State, Telegram 2639, March 12, 1960, CDF 751K.00(W)/3-1260, RG 59, NARA. *Tự do* was established by a group of journalists who fled the Democratic Republic of Vietnam during the 300 days following the 1954 Geneva Agreements. It was funded, in part, by the government and American investors. See Nguyễn Thái, "South Vietnam," in *The Asian Newspapers' Reluctant Revolution*, 243.

32. "'Tu Do' and 'Buoi Sang' are Suspended," *Vietnam Press*, March 8, 1960, FBIS, G1. *Tự do* was authorized to resume publishing in early April if they dismissed the two employees responsible for the stories. The publishers of the paper refused. See Durbrow to the Department of State, Telegram 2850, April 2, 1960, CDF 751K.00(W)/4-260, RG 59, NARA.

33. FBIS, March 26, 1960, G3; and "Former Communists Denounce Vietcong," March 28, 1960, FBIS, G4.

34. Hồ Chí Minh helped to establish the Đảng Lao động Việt Nam (Lao Động Party) in 1951 to replace the Indochinese Communist Party. Its mission was to bring together the Vietnamese people in opposition to the French and then the Republic of Vietnam (RVN) and United States.

35. Dispatch from Durbrow to the Department of State, March 7, 1960, *FRUS, 1958–1960, Volume I: Vietnam*, 301. The first Agroville at Vị Thanh–Hỏa Lựu in Phong Dinh province was inaugurated during the week of March 12. See Cunningham to the Department of State, Telegram 2692, March 19, 1960, CDF 751K.3-1960, RG 59, NARA.

36. Dispatch from Durbrow to the Department of State, March 7, 1960, *FRUS, 1958–1960, Volume I: Vietnam*, 302.

37. Memorandum of Conversation between Williams and Ngô Đình Diệm, March 15, 1960, Folder 1, Box 14, Papers of Samuel T. Williams, Hoover Institute, Stanford University, Palo Alto, Calif. Durbrow's report of the conversation is located in Cunningham to the Department of State, Telegram 2691, March 19, 1960, CDF 751K.5/3-1960, RG 59, NARA.

38. Memorandum of Conversation between Williams and Ngô Đình Diệm, March 19, 1960, Folder 1, Box 14, Papers of Samuel T. Williams, Hoover Institute, Stanford University, Palo Alto, Calif.

39. Telegram from Williams to Lansdale, March 10, 1960, *FRUS, 1958–1960, Volume I: Vietnam*, 320–324.

40. Nguyễn Đình Thuận informed Williams on February 20 of Ngô Đình Diệm's intention to create the 10,000-man commando force though Ngô Đình Diệm had proposed a smaller number of commandos when he first mentioned the concept. Briefing paper prepared in the Department of Defense, undated, *FRUS, 1958–1960, Volume I: Vietnam*, 357. See also Telegram 2567, Durbrow to the Department of State, March 3, 1960, CDF 751K.00/3-360, RG 59, NARA. See Spector, *Advice and Support*, 349–355.

41. Telegram 2567, Durbrow to the Department of State, March 3, 1960, CDF 751K.00/3-360, RG 59, NARA.

42. Memorandum of Conversation between Williams and Ngô Đình Diệm, March 7, 1960, Folder 1, Box 14, Papers of Samuel T. Williams, Hoover Institute, Stanford University, Palo Alto, Calif.

43. Memorandum of Conversation between Williams and Ngô Đình Diệm, March 15 and 19, 1960. Both documents located in Folder 1, Box 14, Papers of Samuel T. Williams, Hoover Institute, Stanford University, Palo Alto, Calif. A predominate analysis of this policy suggests that Ngô Đình Diệm was more concerned about roads and Agrovilles, as he maintained that the com-

munist insurgency was more a military and administrative problem. See Spector, *Advice and Support*, 335–336.

44. Memorandum of Conversation between Williams and Ngô Đình Diệm, March 19, 1960, Folder 1, Box 14, Papers of Samuel T. Williams, Hoover Institute, Stanford University, Palo Alto, Calif.

45. Several examples of the give-and-take between Ngô Đình Diệm and Williams are evident in their conversations. A few examples include the Memorandum of Conversations on January 12, February 1, and March 15 and 19, 1960, Folder 1, Box 14, Papers of Samuel T. Williams, Hoover Institute, Stanford University, Palo Alto, Calif.

46. Colonel Nguyễn Khánh replaced Colonel Nguyễn Văn Y as commander of the 5th Military Region in late January 1960. See "Conversations with President DIEM during PLEIKU Area—DALAT Visit, 0715–2010 hours 22 January 1960," Folder 1, Box 14, Papers of Samuel T. Williams, Hoover Institute, Stanford University, Palo Alto, Calif.

47. Memorandum from Lansdale to the deputy secretary of defense, C. Douglas Dillon, March 17, 1960, *FRUS, 1958–1960, Volume I: Vietnam*, 336–338. See also Memorandum of Conversation, the Pentagon, March 18, 1960, *FRUS, 1958–1960, Volume I: Vietnam*, 339–340.

48. Telegram from Williams to Lansdale, March 10, 1960, *FRUS, 1958–1960, Volume I: Vietnam*, 324. For additional comments by Williams on Nguyễn Khánh, see Williams to Myers, March 20, 1960, *FRUS, 1958–1960, Volume I: Vietnam*, 342.

49. Memorandum of Conversation, April 6, 1960, Folder 1, Box 14, Papers of Samuel T. Williams, Hoover Institute, Stanford University, Palo Alto, Calif.

50. Williams to Myers, March 20, 1960, *FRUS, 1958–1960, Volume I: Vietnam*, 343. See also Spector, *Advice and Support*, 349–355.

51. Williams continued to influence Ngô Đình Diệm throughout the month. Williams to Lansdale, March 25, 1960, *FRUS, 1958–1960, Volume I: Vietnam*, 348–349.

52. Memorandum of Conversation, April 6, 1960, Folder 1, Box 14, Papers of Samuel T. Williams, Hoover Institute, Stanford University, Palo Alto, Calif.

53. Durbrow to the Department of State, Telegram 2622, March 10, 1960, CDF 751K.00/3–160, RG 59, NARA.

54. Durbrow to the Department of State, Telegram 2622, March 10, 1960, CDF 751K.00/3–1060, RG 59, NARA.

55. Felt to Irwin, Telegram 142355Z, March 14, 1960, *FRUS, 1958–1960, Volume I: Vietnam*, 328–329.

56. Participants at the conference included Admiral E.J. O'Donnell, USN, East Region, ISA; Colonel Edward G. Lansdale, OSO/OSD; Ben Wood, Department of State; Lieutenant Colonel J.M. Flesch, USA, Far East Region, ISA; Lieutenant Colonel J.A. Murphy, USA OCS, D/A Civil Affairs; and Jerry French, OSO/OSD. Memorandum of Conversation, "Conference on Internal Security in Vietnam and Related Problem of Civil Administration," March 18, 1960, *FRUS, 1958–1960, Volume I: Vietnam*, 339.

57. Memorandum of Conversation, the Pentagon, March 18, 1960, *FRUS, 1958–1960, Volume I: Vietnam*, 339–341.

58. Memorandum on Counter-Guerrilla Training in Vietnam, Lansdale to Williams, April 14, 1960, *FRUS, 1958–1960, Volume I: Vietnam*, 386–387.

59. Durbrow to the Department of State, Dispatch 306, March 26, 1960, CDF 751K.00/3–2660, RG 59, NARA. A Memorandum of Conversation of the March 21 meeting is attached to the document. See also Memorandum of Conversation, the Pentagon, March 18, 1960, as noted in footnote 2, *FRUS, 1958–1960, Volume I: Vietnam*, 342.

60. Durbrow had already offered his position on the issue of money in his Telegram 2753, March 24, 1960, CDF 751K.5-MPS/3–2460, RG 59, NARA, in which he had sought to resolve the matter before Nguyễn Đình Thuận's arrival in Washington to end his attempts to circumvent the process, that is, go through Durbrow for all of the Vietnamese needs. A Memorandum of Conversation titled "General Discussion of U.S. Aid to Viet-Nam, Internal Security Situation in Viet-Nam, and Vietnamese Relations with Cambodia," April 4, 1960, is located in CDF 751K.5-MSP/4–460, RG 59, NARA.

61. Memorandum of Conversation, "General Discussion of U.S. Aid to Viet-Nam, Internal Security Situation in Viet-Nam and Vietnamese Relations with Cambodia," April 4, 1960, CDF 751K.5-MSP/4–460, RG 59, NARA. It is ironic that this conversation occurred immediately after an April 1 article appeared in *Réalités Cambodgiennes* severely criticizing Ngô Đình Diệm, Ngô Đình Cẩn, and the Republic of Vietnam. See "Khmer Paper on S. Vietnam Situation," *Réalités Cambodgiennes*, FBIS, April 7, 1961, G2.

62. Memorandum of Conversation, "General Discussion of U.S. Aid to Viet-Nam, Internal Security Situation in Viet-Nam and Vietnamese Relations with Cambodia," April 4, 1960, CDF 751K.5-MSP/4–460, RG 59, NARA.

63. Nguyễn Đình Thuận visited Parsons on April 9 alone and at his request to let him know that the RVN was planning to release 3 billion French francs for payment to Cambodia and to confirm that an RVN mission to Cambodia was firm. Parsons to the U.S. embassy in Saigon, April 11, 1960, CDF 751G.00/4–1160, RG 59, NARA.

64. Memorandum of Conversation, Department of State, April 8, 1960, *FRUS, 1958–1960, Volume I: Vietnam*, 383–384. See also the Memorandum of Conversation between Nguyễn Đình Thuận, Senator Gale W. McGee, and Chalmers Wood, "Situation in Viet-Nam," April 8, 1960, CDF 751K.5-MSP/4–860, RG 59, NARA.

65. An additional concern with the Cần Lao Party was that they had been feeding Ngô Đình Diệm information about the internal security of the Republic of Vietnam that did not match the reality of the situation. These informants, so the argument went, told Ngô Đình Diệm what they believed he wanted to hear. This created a disconnect between American advisers who reported to Williams and others who then discussed the situation with Ngô Đình Diệm. See Spector, *Advice and Support*, 344–347.

66. When Nguyễn Đình Thuận met with Durbrow on April 21, the subject of the military budget did not materialize. Durbrow reported that Nguyễn Đình Thuận was pleased with his visit, though the Vietnamese had told individuals more sympathetic to the

Vietnamese plight that the visits did not go as planned and the Vietnamese were frustrated by the inability to communicate their needs to Parsons. See Durbrow to the Department of State, Dispatch 391, "Conversation between Ambassador Durbrow and Secretary of State for the Presidency Nguyen Dinh Thuan," May 17, 1960, CDF 751K.13/501760, RG 59, NARA.

67. Durbrow to the Department of State, Telegram 2885, April 8, 1960, CDF 751K.5/4-860, RG 59, NARA.

68. This number was lower than the figure cited by Ngô Đình Diệm in his conversation with Durbrow in March.

69. Durbrow to the State Department, Telegram 2884, April 7, 1960, CDF 751K.00/4-760, RG 59, NARA. See Anderson, *Trapped by Success*, 183.

70. Durbrow to the State Department, Telegram 2884, April 7, 1960, CDF 751K.00/4-760, RG 59, NARA.

71. Durbrow to the State Department, Telegram 2884, April 7, 1960, CDF 751K.00/4-760, RG 59, NARA. See also Durbrow to the Department of State, "Morale of Vietnamese Armed Forces," Dispatch 348, April 15, 1960, CDF 751K.00/4-1560, RG 59, NARA. The Memorandum of Conversation between Ladejinsky and Ngô Đình Diệm is attached to this document.

72. Later in the day on April 8, Durbrow reported to the Department of State that the Vietnamese had informed MAAG that the $165 million budget would only cover a force level of 135,000 instead of the projected 144,217. It needed an additional $3,781,512 to meet its financial obligations or an additional $6 million if the force level reached 148,000. Durbrow to the Department of State, Telegram 2893, April 8, 1960, CDF 751K.5/4-860, RG 59, NARA.

73. Wood to Usher, April 15, 1960, *FRUS, 1958-1960, Volume I: Vietnam*, 390-392; and Durbrow to Usher, April 18, 1960, *FRUS, 1958-1960, Volume I: Vietnam*, 392-294. Durbrow sent another telegram to Washington on April 16 in which he continued to complain about Ngô Đình Diệm going outside the chain of command when dealing with the ARVN, suggesting that it had caused a disruption in morale and within the military organization. See Durbrow to the Department of State, Telegram 2962, April 16, 1960, CDF 751K.00/4-1660, RG 59, NARA.

74. "Assembly Set Up Liberation Commission," *Vietnam Press*, April 9, 1960, FBIS, April 11, 1960, G1; and "Assembly Needs Commission on Security," *Ngôn Luận*, April 13, FBIS, April 14, G1-G2.

75. Durbrow argued that the National Assembly was being used as a psychological and propaganda vehicle to counter Việt Cộng terrorism. Durbrow to the Department of State, Telegram 2908, April 9, 1960, CDF 751K.00(W)/4-960, RG 59, NARA. 10/59 was the culmination of a series of acts passed in 1959 that made it easier for the Saigon government to arrest or detain individuals who were suspected of communist activity. While the program did trouble the communist insurgency, it did so at a cost of goodwill from the many innocent individuals who were caught up in the drive to eliminate the communists.

76. The islands were named by the Cambodians as Koh Thmey (Middle Island), Koh Ses (Water Island), Koh Antay (Peak Island), Koh Takeav (Bay Island), and Koh Po (North Pirates Archipelago). See U.S. Ambassador to Cambodia William Trimble to the Department of State, Telegram 1333, April 15, 1960, CDF 751K.022/4-1560, RG 59, NARA.

77. Trimble to the Department of State, Telegram 1386, April 27, 1960, CDF 751.

78. Durbrow to Parsons, April 19, 1960, CDF 751K.5-MSP/4-1960, RG 59, NARA.

79. Durbrow to Williams, April 19, 1960, CDF 751K.5-MSP/4-1960, RG 59, NARA.

80. Memorandum of Conversation, April 13, 1960, Folder 1, Box 14, Papers of Samuel T. Williams, Hoover Institute, Stanford University, Palo Alto, Calif. It was not clear from the correspondence whether the Williams-Durbrow telephone conversation of April 13 occurred before or after Williams interview with Ngô Đình Diệm, though it seems likely that it did occur before the two met. Williams also had to defend himself in relation to the RVN naval demonstration against the Cambodians. Durbrow expected an immediate report on the incident even though Williams left for the CINCPAC conference early the next day. Williams to Durbrow listed as CINCPAC to the secretary of state, Telegram 172145Z April (Navy Message), April 17, 1960, CDF 751K.022/4-1760, RG 59, NARA.

81. Between April 11 and April 14, thousands of Vietnamese in Phước Tuy province had meetings and rallies condemning the Việt Cộng looting of the Bên Sân leprosarium and the killing of two workers at the Binh Ba rubber plantation. This was one of several demonstrations against the communists and in support of the Saigon government that went unreported by the U.S. embassy. See *Sài Gòn Mới*, April 18, 1960, FBIS, April 19, 1960, G1; and *Cách mạng Quốc gia*, April 18, 1960, FBIS, April 19, 1960, G2.

Chapter 4

1. Mendenhall to the Department of State, "Internal Security during May 1960," Report No. 23, Dispatch 37, July 25, 1960, CDF 751K.00/7-2560, RG 59, NARA.

2. One of the signees, Phan Huy Quát, had been involved in the maneuvering to remove Ngô Đình Diệm from power in the spring of 1955 and was championed by then-MAAG commander, J. Lawton Collins. See Jacobs, *Cold War Mandarin*, 115; Kahin, *Intervention*, 122-123; and Anderson, *Trapped by Success*, 183-184. Historians have made claims that these were eighteen distinguished politicians, though their influence in 1960 was, in some cases, questionable. See Karnow, *Vietnam: A History*, 235.

3. Mendenhall to the Department of State, "Reports of Opposition Activities," Dispatch 358, April 22, 1960, enclosure 4, CDF 751K.00/4-2260, RG 59, NARA. A second version went out in the May 1960 Dispatch 400. For a similar version, see Fall, *The Two Vietnams*, 435-436.

4. Fall, *The Two Vietnams*, 436.
5. Fall, *The Two Vietnams*, 437.
6. Fall, *The Two Vietnams*, 438.
7. In July 1959, Albert Colegrove wrote a series of

articles for the *Scripps-Howard* newspaper chair that severely criticized Ngô Đình Diệm and the U.S. effort in the Republic of Vietnam. The six articles Colegrove contributed maintained that there was corruption in the giving of American aid to the Vietnamese. This prompted hearings within the State Foreign Relations Committee's Sub-committee on State Department Organization chaired by Senator Mike Mansfield (D-Montana). See Mann, *A Grand Delusion*, 216–218. Additional hearings occurred in the House under the chairmanship of Clement Zablocki (D-Wisconsin). See Anderson, *Trapped by Success*, 180–182.

8. Mendenhall to the Department of State, "Reports of Opposition Activities," Dispatch 358, April 22, 1960, enclosure 4, CDF 751K.00/4-2260, RG 59, NARA.

9. Mendenhall to the Department of State, "Reports of Opposition Activities," Dispatch 358, April 22, 1960, enclosure 4, CDF 751K.00/4-2260, RG 59, NARA.

10. Mendenhall to the Department of State, "Reports of Opposition Activities," Dispatch 358, April 22, 1960, enclosure 4, CDF 751K.00/4-2260, RG 59, NARA.

11. Durbrow to the Department of State, Telegram 2981, April 19, 1960, *FRUS, 1958–1960, Volume I: Vietnam*, 404–406.

12. Durbrow to the Department of State, Telegram 2981, April 19, 1960, *FRUS, 1958–1960, Volume I: Vietnam*, 404–406.

13. Between March 7 and March 13, 1960, Mendenhall and Thomas Barnes from the embassy and James Howe and Igor Javrotsky from USOM toured the region, visiting Bản Mê Thuột, Nha Trang, Qui Nhơn, An Khê, and Pleiku. Mendenhall to the Department of State, "Trip to Six Provinces in Central Viet-Nam," April 1, 1960, CDF 751K.00/4-160, RG 59, NARA.

14. U.S. Ambassador John H. Whitney to the Department of State, Telegram 4797, April 1, CDF 751K.00/4-160, RG 59, NARA. See also U.S. Representative to the United Nations Henry Cabot Lodge to the Department of State, Telegram 1050, April 12, 1960, CDF 751K.00/4-1260, RG 59, NARA; William Trimble to the Department of State, Telegram G-74, April 14, 1960, CDF 751K.00/4-1460, RG 59, NARA.

15. Durbrow to the Department of State, Telegram 2954, April 15, 1960, CDF 751K.00/4-1560, RG 59, NARA. *Réalités Cambodgiennes* continued to publish provocative articles in its "confidential" column that linked the Republic of Vietnam with the Free Khmer Movement and reported on the critical internal security situation in the Mekong Delta.

16. Cunningham to the Department of State, Dispatch 364, "Rumored Corruption in the Government of South Viet-Nam," April 23, 1960, CDF 751K.00/4-2360, RG 59, NARA. See also Durbrow to the Department of State, Dispatch 371, "Can Lao Party Financial Activities as a Source of Unpopularity of the Diem Regime," April 28, 1960, CDF 751K.00/4-281960, RG 59, NARA.

17. Durbrow to the Department of State, Dispatch 371, "Can Lao Party Financial Activities as a Source of Unpopularity of the Diem Regime," April 28, 1960, CDF 751K.00/4-281960, RG 59, NARA.

18. Durbrow to the Department of State, Dispatch 370, "Internal Political and Security Situation in Vietnam," April 28, 1960, CDF 751K.00/4-2860, RG 59, NARA. Gonder continued to operate in Vietnam until his departure on May 22 as one who had intimate knowledge of the political scene and multiple contacts, though he really did not. In part, his departure might have been hastened by the fact that he owed back taxes to the Republic of Vietnam in the sum of approximately VN$200,000. Even Durbrow and Mendenhall were pleased when they learned that Gonder would depart Saigon because of his connection with the Colegrove articles and his intrigue with the Caravelle Group. See Durbrow to the Department of State, Telegram 3243, May 19, 1960, CDF 751K.00/5-1960, RG 59, NARA; Mendenhall to the Department of State, "Activities of 'Opposition Group,'" Dispatch 410, May 20, 1960, CDF 751K.00/5-2060, RG 59, NARA; Durbrow to the Department of State, Airgram G-205, May 26, 1960, CDF 751K.00/5-2660, RG 59, NARA; and Memorandum of Conversation between Ngô Đình Diệm and Williams, May 19, 1960. Folder 1, Box 14, Papers of Samuel T. Williams, Hoover Institute, Stanford University, Palo Alto, Calif.

19. Operation Exodus was the code name for the South Vietnamese effort to aid in the movement of Vietnamese who wished to leave the Democratic Republic of Vietnam and resettle in the State of Vietnam. This was made possible as a result of the 1954 Geneva Agreements, which established the guidelines for the movement of Vietnamese.

20. Durbrow to the Department of State, Telegram 3185, May 12, 1960, CDF 751K.00/5-1260, RG 59, NARA.

21. Mendenhall to the Department of State, Dispatch 423, June 7, 1960, CDF 751K.00/6-760, RG 59, NARA.

22. Memorandum of Conversation between Ngô Đình Diệm and Williams, May 19, 1960, Memorandum of Conversation, May 11, 1960, Folder 1, Box 14, Papers of Samuel T. Williams, Hoover Institute, Stanford University, Palo Alto, Calif.

23. In July, it was reported that a number of intellectuals had been arrested in early June for their attempts to try to disrupt Saigon politics in May. Included in the group, known as the Mobilization among Intellectuals, were three doctors, six journalists and teachers, and a number of students. See "Police Arrest Dissident Intellectuals," *Times of Vietnam*, July 4, 1960, FBIS, July 5, 1960, G1; and FBIS, July 6, G3.

24. Durbrow to the Department of State, Telegram 3185, May 12, 1960, CDF 751K.00/5-1260, RG 59, NARA.

25. *Sài Gòn Mới* editorial, May 7, 1960, FBIS, May 11, 1960, G2. *Sài Gòn Mới* was a commercial newspaper that did not receive funding from the Saigon government. It was one of the best-selling Saigon dailies. See Nguyễn Thái, "South Vietnam," in *The Asian Newspapers' Reluctant Revolution*, 243.

26. *Cách mạng Quốc gia* editorial, May 13, 1960; and *Sài Gòn Mới* editorial, May 13, 1960, both located in FBIS, May 17, 1960, G6. See also *Cách mạng Quốc gia* editorial, May 17, 1960, FBIS, May 19, 1960, G1.

27. Durbrow to the Department of State, "'Explanation' by Members of Opposition Group," Dispatch 6, July 5, 1960, CDG 751K.00/7-560.

28. Both sides of the argument used the Saigon rumor mill to their advantage. As William Colby, CIA station chief in Saigon starting in June 1960, would argue, "The absence of free discussion and communication in Vietnamese political circles also played a role. In the absence of authoritative correctives, rumor and speculation replaced solid information as the basis for political discourse." Colby, *Lost Victory*, 71.

29. Memorandum prepared for the president, "Situation in Viet-Nam," April 21, 1960, *FRUS, 1958–1960, Volume I: Vietnam*, 407–408.

30. After the conclusion of the 1954 Geneva Conference that marked the end of France's influence in Indochina, the CIA sponsored the Saigon Military Mission under the leadership of Edward Lansdale to conduct psychological warfare in the Democratic Republic of Vietnam in order to damage the northern Vietnamese reputation and encourage the flight of Vietnamese from the North to the South. The Saigon Military Mission had actually entered Vietnam before the fall of the French fortress at Điện Biên Phủ with the mission of assisting the Vietnamese in conducting unconventional warfare. Its numbers were too small to make a difference before the French fortress fell and the 1954 Geneva Conference concluded. The Saigon Military Mission also helped Ngô Đình Diệm consolidate his power in Vietnam, which eventually led to the establishment of the Republic of Vietnam in October 1955.

31. Memorandum of Conversation, "President Diem Requests Lansdale," between Nguyễn Duy Liên; Deputy Director of the Office of Southeast Asian Affairs Richard Usher; and the officer in charge of Cambodian Affairs, Laurin Askew, April 19, 1960, CDF 751K.58/4–1960, RG 59, NARA. The Lansdale visit served as a catalyst for further Department of State and Department of Defense tensions. See Anderson, *Trapped by Success*, 185.

32. Durbrow to the Department of State, Telegram 3013, April 22, 1960, *FRUS, 1958–1960, Volume I: Vietnam*, 409.

33. Durbrow to the Department of State, Telegram 3013, April 22, 1960, *FRUS, 1958–1960, Volume I: Vietnam*, 409.

34. Lansdale to Bonesteel, "'Third Country' Doctrine, Internal Security," April 25, 1960, *FRUS, 1958–1960, Volume I: Vietnam*, 410–411.

35. Lansdale to Bonesteel, "'Third Country' Doctrine, Internal Security," April 25, 1960, *FRUS, 1958–1960, Volume I: Vietnam*, 410.

36. Lansdale letter to Williams, April 30, 1960, *FRUS, 1958–1960, Volume I: Vietnam*, 425–426.

37. Lansdale letter to Williams, April 30, 1960, *FRUS, 1958–1960, Volume I: Vietnam*, 425–426.

38. Williams to Lansdale, May 9, 1960, *FRUS, 1958–1960, Volume I: Vietnam*, 443.

39. Memorandum of Conversation between Williams and Ngô Đình Diệm, May 9, 1960, Folder 1, Box 14, Papers of Samuel T. Williams, Hoover Institute, Stanford University, Palo Alto, Calif. See also Anderson, *Trapped by Success*, 186.

40. Williams to Lansdale, May 9, 1960, *FRUS, 1958–1960, Volume I: Vietnam*, 443.

41. Williams to Lansdale, May 9, 1960, *FRUS, 1958–1960, Volume I: Vietnam*, 444–445. See also Williams to Mansfield, May 20, 1960, *FRUS, 1958–1960, Volume I: Vietnam*, 467–471.

42. "Resume of the Visit of Admiral Stump with President Ngo Dinh Diem at Dalat, 26–26 April 1960," April 30, 1960, Folder 1, Box 14, Papers of Samuel T. Williams, Hoover Institute, Stanford University, Palo Alto, Calif.

43. Durbrow to the Department of State, Telegram 3095, May 3, 1960, *FRUS, 1958–1960, Volume I: Vietnam*, 433–437. See Anderson, *Trapped by Success*, 187. Sam Sary had been a cabinet member in Norodom Sihanouk's government in the 1950s but turned against the government. He founded a newspaper and political organization that criticized the Phnom Penh government and was generally a nuisance to Sihanouk.

44. Durbrow to the Department of State, May 3, 1960, *FRUS, 1958–1960, Volume I: Vietnam*, 434.

45. Durbrow to the Department of State, May 3, 1960, *FRUS, 1958–1960, Volume I: Vietnam*, 435.

46. Draft telegram from the acting secretary of state to the embassy in Vietnam, May 3, 1960, *FRUS, 1958–1960, Volume I: Vietnam*, 437.

47. Parsons to Durbrow, Telegram 2038, May 3, 1960, CDF 751K.00/5–360, RG 59, NARA.

48. Parsons to Durbrow, Telegram 2038, May 3, 1960, CDF 751K.00/5–360, RG 59, NARA.

49. Hugh Cummings, the director of intelligence and research, Department of State, to the acting secretary of state, May 3, 1960, CDF 751K.00/5–360, RG 59, NARA.

50. Jacobs, *Cold War Madarin*, 116; and Colby, *Lost Victory*, 73.

51. *Tin Mới* editorial, May 6, 1960, FBIS, May 10, 1960, G1. See also *Dân chúng* editorial, April 27, 1960, FBIS, April 27, 1960, G3; *Dân chúng* editorial, April 28, 1960, FBIS, April 29, 1960, G1; and *Ah Chau Jih Pao* and *May Jih Luan Zan* editorials, FBIS, May 3, 1960.

52. *Tiếng Chuông*, May 13, 1960, FBIS, May 20, 1960, G1–G8. The articles in *Tiếng Chuông* appeared in all of the Vietnamese-language newspapers in Saigon.

53. Memorandum of Conversation, "Question of Withholding Emergency Military Equipment from Viet-Nam," May 5, 1960, CDF 751K.00/5–51960, RG 59, NARA.

54. Durbrow to the Department of State, Telegram 3133, May 6, 1960, CDF 751K.00/5–660, RG 59, NARA. See also Durbrow to the Department of State, "Political and Security Situation in Viet-Nam," Dispatch 403, May 16, 1960, CDF 751K.005–1660, RG 59, NARA. See also Durbrow to the Department of State, Telegram 3272, May 23, 1960, CDF 751K.00/5–2360, RG 59, NARA.

55. Durbrow to the Department of State, Telegram 3152, May 9, 1960, CDF 751K.00/5–960, RG 59, NARA.

56. Durbrow to the Department of State, Dispatch 392, May 10, 1960, CDF 751K.00/5–1060, RG 59, NARA. A Memorandum of Conversation between Trần Cửu Thiên and Durbrow is attached to this document.

57. Durbrow to the Department of State, "GVN Agroville Program," Dispatch 426, June 6, 1960, CDF 751K.00/6–660, RG 59, NARA.

58. Department of State to Durbrow, Telegram 2037, May 9, 1960, *FRUS, 1958–1960, Volume I: Vietnam*, 448–449. See also Anderson, *Trapped by Success*, 188.

59. Durbrow to the Department of State, Telegram 3196, May 13, 1960, *FRUS, 1958–1960, Volume I: Vietnam*, 453–457.
60. Memorandum of Conversation, May 11, 1960, Folder 1, Box 14, Papers of Samuel T. Williams, Hoover Institute, Stanford University, Palo Alto, Calif.
61. Memorandum of Conversation, May 11, 1960, Folder 1, Box 14, Papers of Samuel T. Williams, Hoover Institute, Stanford University, Palo Alto, Calif.
62. Williams to Lansdale, May 17, 1960, *FRUS, 1958–1960, Volume I: Vietnam*, 464.
63. Department of State to the American embassy in Saigon, Telegram 2277, June 21, CDF 751K.00/6-2160, RG 59, NARA.
64. Durbrow to the Department of State, Telegram 3196, May 13, 1960, *FRUS, 1958–1960, Volume I: Vietnam*, 453–457.
65. William Henderson and Wesley R. Fishel, "The Foreign Policy of Ngo Dinh Diem," *Vietnam Perspectives* 2, no. 1 (August 1966): 3–30.
66. Memorandum of Conversation, "Possible TDY to Viet-Nam for Brigadier General Lansdale," May 13, 1960, *FRUS, 1958–1960, Volume I: Vietnam*, 457–458.
67. Memorandum of Conversation, "Possible TDY to Viet-Nam for Brigadier General Lansdale," May 13, 1960, *FRUS, 1958–1960, Volume I: Vietnam*, 457–458.
68. Memorandum of Conversation, "Possible TDY to Viet-Nam for Brigadier General Lansdale," May 13, 1960, *FRUS, 1958–1960, Volume I: Vietnam*, 457–458.
69. Durbrow to the Department of State, Telegram 3218, May 17, 1960, *FRUS, 1958–1960, Volume I: Vietnam*, 462.
70. Williams refers to the fact that his friendship and correspondence with Lansdale was not known by members of the embassy staff. Williams to Lansdale, May 17, 1960, *FRUS, 1958–1960, Volume I: Vietnam*, 463–464.
71. Williams to Lansdale, May 17, 1960, *FRUS, 1958–1960, Volume I: Vietnam*, 463–464.
72. Williams to Lansdale, May 17, 1960, *FRUS, 1958–1960, Volume I: Vietnam*, 464.
73. Williams to Lansdale, May 17, 1960, *FRUS, 1958–1960, Volume I: Vietnam*, 464.
74. Durbrow to the Department of State, Telegram 3220, May 17, 1960, CDF 751K.00/5-1760, RG 59, NARA.
75. It should be noted that during this time of American infighting and jockeying for position, Ngô Đình Diệm was busy running his country and doing his best to inspire his people. A good example of this is his June 20 address to a group of Republican Youth who were attending a general convention in Thừa Thiên province. See "Diem Counsels Youth to Be Self-Reliant," *Buổi sang*, June 20, 1960, FBIS, June 23, 1960, G1–G2.
76. Memorandum of a telephone conversation between Parsons and Knight, "Proposed Assignment of Brigadier General Lansdale as Adviser to President Diem," May 19, 1960, *FRUS, 1958–1960, Volume I: Vietnam*, 465.
77. Memorandum of a telephone conversation between Parsons and Knight, "Proposed Assignment of Brigadier General Lansdale as Adviser to President Diem," May 19, 1960, *FRUS, 1958–1960, Volume I: Vietnam*, 466.
78. Williams to Mansfield, May 20, 1960, *FRUS, 1958–1960, Volume I: Vietnam*, 467–471; and Williams to Durbrow, "Training of the RVNAF (U)," June 1, 1960, *FRUS, 1958–1960, Volume I: Vietnam*, 471–483.
79. Parsons to Durbrow, June 9, 1960, *FRUS, 1958–1960, Volume I: Vietnam*, 492–493.
80. Lansdale to Williams, June 21, 1960, *FRUS, 1958–1960, Volume I: Vietnam*, 501–502.
81. Lansdale to Williams, June 21, 1960, *FRUS, 1958–1960, Volume I: Vietnam*, 501.
82. Williams to Lansdale, June 28, 1960, as noted in footnote 8, *FRUS, 1958–1960, Volume I: Vietnam*, 502.
83. Memorandum of Conversation, June 24, 1960, *FRUS, 1958–1960, Volume I: Vietnam*, 502–508.
84. Ngô Đình Diệm had recently inaugurated National Route 21, linking Ninh Hòa to Bản Mê Thuột on May 31, which was significant because it connected the highlands to the coastal areas of Central Vietnam. The road improved economic opportunities as well as internal security. See "Opening of Route 21 a Signal Event," *Lê Sống* editorial, May 31, 1960, FBIS, June 3, G2–G3.
85. Memorandum of Conversation, June 24, 1960, *FRUS, 1958–1960, Volume I: Vietnam*, 508.
86. Williams handwritten note on Memorandum of Conversation, June 24, 1960, as noted in footnote 6, *FRUS, 1958–1960, Volume I: Vietnam*, 508.

Chapter 5

1. Durbrow to the Department of State, Telegram 3342, June 1, 1960, CDF 751K.00/6-160, RG 59, NARA.
2. Durbrow to the Department of State, Telegram 3342, June 1, 1960, CDF 751K.00/6-160, RG 59, NARA.
3. Mendenhall to the Department of State, "Internal Security in Vietnam during May 1960, Report No. 23," Dispatch 37, July 25, 1960, CDF 751K.00/7-2560, RG 59, NARA.
4. Durbrow continued to work against the commando scheme, suggesting that they were "volunteers," that is to say, forced into service against their wishes and not recognized within the 150,000-man force level. By June, he argued that the "time has come to put teeth into our approaches to GVN on level security forces." See Durbrow to the Department of State, Telegram 3412, June 10, 1960, CDF 751K.5/6-1060, RG 59, NARA. Durbrow was sowing the seeds for his next démarche against Ngô Đình Diệm. Williams received confirmation from the Vietnamese that the commando force level was included in the 150,000 ceiling, and its addition was not to exceed this cap. Durbrow to the Department of State, Telegram 3512, June 22, 1960, CDF 751K.5/6-2260, RG 59, NARA.
5. Mendenhall to the Department of State, "Conversation with Minister Lê Văn Đông on Internal Political Situation," Dispatch 440, June 10, 1960, CDF 751K.00/6-1060 HBS, RG 59, NARA.
6. Memorandum of Conversation, "Situation in Viet-Nam," June 2, 1960, CDF 751K.00/6-260, RG 59, NARA.
7. Memorandum of Conversation, "Situation in Viet-Nam," June 2, 1960, CDF 751K.00/6-260, RG 59,

NARA. See also Department of State to the American embassy in Saigon, Telegram 2186, June 2, 1960, CDF 751K.00/6-160, RG 59, NARA.

8. Memorandum of Conversation between Williams and Ngô Đình Diệm, June 2, 1960, Folder 1, Box 14, Papers of Samuel T. Williams, Hoover Institute, Stanford University, Palo Alto, Calif.

9. "Diem Says Press Free to Criticize," *Times of Vietnam*, May 17, 1960, FBIS, May 18, 1960, G1–G2. See also *Ngôn Luận*, *Cách mạng Quốc gia*, and *Dân chúng* editorials of May 16, 1960, FBIS, May 18, 1960, G5.

10. *Dân chúng* editorial, May 21, 1960, FBIS, May 24, 1960, G1. See also *Dân chúng* editorial, May 23, 1960, FBIS, May 25, 1960, G1.

11. *Sài Gòn Mới*, June 7, 1960, FBIS, June 8, 1960, G3.

12. *Dân chúng* editorial, June 6, 1960, FBIS, June 7, 1960, G2–G3.

13. *Tin Mới* editorial, June 28, 1960, FBIS, June 29, 1960, G1.

14. *Dân chúng* editorial, July 29, 1960, FBIS, August 1, 1960, G1.

15. As the month progressed, the success in road building and the ARVN victories in the Mekong Delta were often mentioned by Ngô Đình Diệm to anyone who would listen. Durbrow did faithfully report these conversations, though he often inserted commentary or another bit of information to distract from the success. For an example, see Durbrow to the Department of State, "Opening of Route 21 on May 28, 1960," Dispatch 436, June 7, 1960, CDF 751K.00/6-760, RG 59, NARA.

16. Durbrow to the Department of State, June 4, 1960, Airgram G-212, CDF 751K.00/6-460, RG 59, NARA. See also Memorandum of Conversation between Williams and Ngô Đình Diệm, June 2, 1960, Folder 1, Box 14, Papers of Samuel T. Williams, Hoover Institute, Stanford University, Palo Alto, Calif.

17. This type of reporting from the U.S. embassy to the Department of State was frequently authored by Joseph Mendenhall and Francis Cunningham, though Durbrow approved and authored his fair share during the time period. An example of such reporting can be found in Mendenhall to the Department of State, "Conversation with Tran Van Dinh, Vietnamese Consul General, Rangoon, on Internal Political Situation in Viet-Nam," Dispatch 429, June 6, 1960, CDF 751K.00/6-660, RG 59, NARA. See also domestic news report, FBIS, May 31, 1960, G2.

18. *Tiếng Chuông* editorial, May 28, 1960, FBIS, June 1, 1960, G1.

19. "It Rests with Us to Carry Out Our Sound Slogan," *Ngôn Luận* editorial, June 1, 1960, FBIS, June 7, G1–G2. In Turkey, police attacked a seventy-two-year-old university rector, which caused students to revolt, while the Republic of Korea incident was thought to have originated and intensified by the death of a voter at the hands of the police.

20. See Mendenhall to the Department of State, "Conversation with Indian Official re Political Situation in Viet-Nam," Dispatch 450, June 17, 1960, CDF 751K.00/6-1760, RG 59, NARA.

21. Durbrow to the Department of State, Telegram 3430, June 11, 1960, CDF 751K.00/6-1160, RG 59, NARA.

22. Memorandum of Conversation between Williams and Ngô Đình Diệm, June 15, 1960, Folder 1, Box 14, Papers of Samuel T. Williams, Hoover Institute, Stanford University, Palo Alto, Calif. See also U.S. embassy in Saigon to the secretary of state, Airgram G-230, June 30, 1960, CDF 751K.5-MSP/6-3060, RG 59, NARA.

23. Heavner to the Department of State, "Remarks by Nguyen Van Buu on Corruption and Communism in the Government of Vietnam," Dispatch 23, June 28, 1960, CDF 751K.00/6-2860, RG 59, NARA.

24. Durbrow to the Department of State, Airgram G-01, July 1, 1960, CDF 751K.00/7-160, RG 59, NARA.

25. Durbrow to the Department of State, "Uneasiness among GVN Top Officials," Airgram G-5, July 9, 1960, CDF 751K.00/7-960, RG 59, NARA. See also Durbrow to the Department of State, Telegram 81, July 9, 1960, CDF 751K.5-MSP/7-960, RG 59, NARA.

26. FBIS, July 7, 1960, G2.

27. "Diem Reaffirms Revolution's Goals," *Times of Vietnam*, July 7, 1960, FBIS, July 8, 1960, G1–G2. Following the Double-Seven speech, Ngô Đình Diệm took several trips into the countryside, attending inauguration ceremonies of new Agrovilles. During these trips, he deviated from his schedule to interact with the people. This was noted by Durbrow. Durbrow to the Department of State, July 22, 1960, CDF 751K.00(W)/7-2260 HBS, RG 59, NARA.

28. Durbrow to the Department of State, "Conversation with Ngo Dinh Luyen about the Internal Situation in Viet-Nam, American Aid, and Relations with Cambodia," Dispatch 22, July 14, 1960, CDF 751K.00/7-1960, RG 59, NARA; and Durbrow to the Department of State, "Peasant Views on Tan Luoc Agroville, Vinh Long Province," Dispatch 24, July 14, 1960, CDF 751K.00/7-1460, RG 59, NARA. See also Mendenhall to the Department of State, "Conversation with Dang Doc Khoi re Political Situation in Viet-Nam, U.S.-GVN Relations and RKG-GVN Relations," Dispatch 42, July 29, 1960, CDF 751K.00/7-2960, RG 59, NARA. A Memorandum of Conversation between Mendenhall and Đặng Độc Khối, Vietnamese chargé d'affaires in Bangkok, is attached to this dispatch. A June 16 Memorandum of Conversation between Đặng Độc Khối and the U.S. chargé d'affaires ad interim to Cambodia, Leonard Unger, is attached to Unger to the Department of State, Dispatch 715, "Conversation between Charge d'Affaires ad interim and Vietnamese Charge concerning International Situation South Viet-Nam and Vietnamese actions against Cambodia," June 20, 1960, CDF 751G.00/6-2060, RG 59, NARA.

29. Zasloff continued to argue this point even though the second Agroville in Kiên Giang Province, which was completed in April 1960, was done with paid labor. Durbrow to the Department of State, Telegram 3369, June 4, 1960, CDF 751K.00(W)/6-460 HBS, RG 59, NARA. See also Mann, *A Grand Delusion*, 218–219.

30. Durbrow to the Department of State, "Conversation with Ngo Dinh Luyen about the Internal Situation in Viet-Nam, American Aid, and Relations with Cambodia," Dispatch 22, July 14, 1960, CDF 751K.00/7-1960, RG 59, NARA.

31. Ironically, before the speech, Durbrow recommended to Washington that he send a special letter to

Ngô Đình Diệm after the speech because of reports that had been received which indicated that the United States was looking for another leader for the Republic of Vietnam. See Durbrow to the Department of State, Telegram 47, July 6, 1960, CDF 751K.11/7-660, RG 59, NARA.

32. Memorandum of Conversation between Williams and Ngô Đình Diệm, July 25, 1960, Folder 1, Box 14, Papers of Samuel T. Williams, Hoover Institute, Stanford University, Palo Alto, Calif.

33. General Tôn Thất Đính commanded the II Corps and was a leading member in the Cần Lao Party.

34. Durbrow to the Department of State, July 1, 1960, CDF 751K.5/7-160, RG 59, NARA.

35. Mendenhall to the Department of State, "The Women's Social Solidarity Movement," Dispatch 58, August 16, 1960, CDF 751K.00/8-1660, RG 59, NARA.

36. FBIS, March 10, 1960, G3.

37. "New Province Functionaries Draw Advice," *Vietnam Press*, March 12, FBIS, G3-G4.

38. Editorial Note, *FRUS, 1958-1960, Volume XVI: East Asia-Pacific Region; Cambodia; Laos*, 782. For details of the coup d'état, see also Dommen, *The Indochinese Experience of the French and the Americans*, 388-399; and Duiker, *Sacred War*, 127.

39. Radio Vientiane as quoted by Peking NCNA, August 11, 1960, FBIS, August 15, 1960, I1.

40. *Ah Chau Jih Pao* editorial, August 11, 1960, FBIS, August 12, 1960, G3.

41. *Dân chúng* editorial, August 15, 1960, FBIS, August 15, 1960, G1.

42. Laotian Home Service, August 29, 1960, FBIS, August 29, 1960, I2.

43. *Tin Mới* and *Dân chúng* editorials, August 29, 1960, FBIS, August 30, 1960, G3.

44. Memorandum of Conversation, "Situation in Viet-Nam," August 1, 1960, CDF 751K.00/8-160, RG 59, NARA. See also Memorandum of Conversation, "U.S.-Vietnamese Relations," August 3, 1960, CDF 751K.5-MSP/8-360, RG 59, NARA.

45. Durbrow to the Department of State, Airgram G-66, August 18, 1960, CDF 751K.00/8-1860, RG 59, NARA.

46. "Assembly Hears Community Village Report," *Vietnam Press*, April 4, 1960, FBIS, April 6, 1960, G1.

47. Durbrow to the Department of State, "'Freedom and Progress Bloc' Petitions Diem re Agroville and GVN Responds," Airgram G-50, August 11, 1960, CDF 751K.00/8-1160, RG 59, NARA. See also Mendenhall to the Department of State, "Freedom and Progress Bloc Petition re Agrovilles and GVN Response," Dispatch 63, August 17, 1960, CDF 751K.00/8-1760, RG 59, NARA; and Mendenhall to the Department of State, "Phan Quang Dan Petition to President Diem for Institution Habeas Corpus," Dispatch 62, August 17, 1960, CDF 751K.00/8-1760, RG 59, NARA. When Trương Vĩnh Lê and his delegation met with Eisenhower on August 25, he restated many of the positives he had used earlier in the month. See Memorandum of Conversation, "Vietnamese–U.S. Relations," August 25, 1960, CDF 751K.00/8-2560, RG 59, NARA.

48. Durbrow to the Department of State, "Phan Quan Dan Petitions re Habeas Corpus," Airgram G-52, August 12, 1960, CDF 751K.00/8-1260, RG 59, NARA.

49. Durbrow to the Department of State, Telegram 432, August 22, 1960, CDF 751K.00/8-2260, RG 59, NARA. See also Durbrow to the Department of State, Telegram 455, August 24, 1960, CDF 751K.00/8-2460, RG 59, NARA.

50. "Police Bar Anti-Government Demonstrations," London, Reuters, August 22, 1960, FBIS, August 23, 1960, G1; and "Communist Adopt 'Nationalist' Disguise," *Chuông Mai*, August 23, 1960, FBIS, August 26, 1960, G5-G6.

51. Kahin, *Intervention*, 123.

52. Durbrow to the Department of State, Airgram G-79, August 25, 1960, CDF 751K.00/8-2560, RG 59, NARA.

53. Durbrow to the Department of State, Airgram G-83, August 26, 1960, CDF 751K.00/8-2660, RG 59, NARA.

54. Durbrow to the Department of State, Airgram G-92, August 26, 1960, CDF 751K.00/8-2660, RG 59, NARA. See also Durbrow to the Department of State, Telegram 492, August 30, 1960, CDF 751K.00/8-3060, RG 59, NARA; and Durbrow to the Department of State, Telegram 495, August 30, 1960, CDF 751K.00/8-3060, RG 59, NARA. On September 7, Ambassador Trần Văn Chương called the Department of State and requested a minimum of fifty instructors as well as having the Civil Guard be trained by MAAG. Robert Cleveland, officer in charge of Southeast Asian economic affairs to the American embassy, Saigon, September 13, 1960, CDF 751K.5-MSP/9-1360, RG 59, NARA. Even though Durbrow opposed placing the Civil Guard under the Vietnamese Department of Defense, he consented because of the emergency in the internal security of the RVN. Durbrow to the Department of State, Telegram 605, September 14, 1960, CDF 751K.5-MSP/9-1460, RG 59, NARA.

55. Durbrow to the Department of State, Telegram 435, August 22, 1960, CDF 751K.5-MSP/8-2260, RG 59, NARA.

56. Mendenhall to the Department of State, air pouch 104, September 10, 1960, CDF 751K.00/9-1060, RG 59, NARA. An August 17 Memorandum of Conversation, "Political Situation in South Viet-Nam," is attached to the document.

57. Memorandum of Conversation, "Situation in Viet-Nam," September 1, 1960, CDF 751K.00/9-160, RG 59, NARA.

58. Memorandum of Conversation, "Internal Situation in Viet-Nam," September 1, 1960, enclosure 1 of Dispatch 105, CDF 751K.00/9-160, RG 59, NARA.

59. Houghton to the Department of State, Telegram 912, September 2, 1960, CDF 751K.00/9-260, RG 59, NARA.

60. Houghton to the Department of State, Telegram 964, September 7, 1960, CDF 751K.00/9-760, RG 59, NARA.

61. Durbrow to the Department of State, Airgram G-93, September 3, 1960, CDF 751K.00/9-360, RG 59, NARA.

62. Durbrow to the Department of State, Telegram 538 (in two sections), September 5, 1960, CDF 751K.00/9-560, RG 59, NARA.

63. Durbrow to the Department of State, Telegram 727, October 1, 1960, CDF 751K.00/10-160, RG 59, NARA. See also Department of State to the American

embassy, Saigon, Telegram 624, October 1, 1960, CDF 751K.00/10-160, RG 59, NARA; and Durbrow to the Department of State, Telegram 735, October 3, 1960, CDF 751K.00/10-360, RG 59, NARA.

64. Durbrow to the Department of State, Telegram 624, September 16, 1960, CDF 751K.00/9-1660, RG 59, NARA. See also Colby, *Lost Victory*, 73–74; and Anderson, *Trapped by Success*, 189.

65. Langguth, *Our Vietnam*, 104–105.

66. Durbrow to the Department of State, Telegram 638, September 17, 1960, CDF 751K.00/9-1760, RG 59, NARA. See also Dillon to Durbrow, September 17, 1960, CDF 751K.00/9-1760, RG 59, NARA. See Kahin, *Intervention*, 123; and Colby, *Lost Victory*, 74–75.

67. Lansdale to O'Donnell, "State Message, Saigon 624," September 20, 1960, *FRUS, 1958–1960, Volume I: Vietnam*, 579–585.

68. Lansdale to O'Donnell, "State Message, Saigon 624," September 20, 1960, *FRUS, 1958–1960, Volume I: Vietnam*, 580.

69. Houghton to the Department of State, Airgram G-409, September 21, 1960, CDF 751K.00/9-2160, RG 59, NARA.

70. Durbrow to the Department of State, Telegram 645, September 19, 1960, CDF 751G.00/9-1960 HBS, RG 59, NARA.

71. Cunningham to the Department of State, Dispatch 119, "President DIEM Asks American Businessman if His Firm Has Been Approached in Behalf of President's Family, and Hints at Postponing Presidential Election," September 21, 1960, CDF 751K.5/9-2160, RG 59, NARA. The American Trading Company was connected, through Frank Gondor, with the Caravelle Group earlier in April.

Chapter 6

1. Special National Intelligence Estimate 63.1-60, August 23, 1960, *FRUS, 1958–1960, Volume I: Vietnam*, 536–541.

2. Special National Intelligence Estimate 63.1-60, August 23, 1960, *FRUS, 1958–1960, Volume I: Vietnam*, 536.

3. Lansdale to Kent, "Approaching Crisis in South Vietnam?," August 10, 1960, *FRUS, 1958–1960, Volume I: Vietnam*, 526–528. Kent had sent his memorandum to the director of central intelligence on July 28.

4. Lansdale to Kent, "Approaching Crisis in South Vietnam?," August 10, 1960, *FRUS, 1958–1960, Volume I: Vietnam*, 526.

5. Lansdale to McGarr, "Vietnam," August 11, 1960, *FRUS, 1958–1960, Volume I: Vietnam*, 528–536. Lansdale included a copy of Kent's memorandum that had been the source of his concern earlier.

6. Parsons to Livingston T. Merchant, September 8, 1960; and Durbrow to the Department of State, Airgram G-130, September 26, 1960. Both documents found in Entry 5155, Bureau of East Asian Affairs, Vietnam Desk, Vietnam Subject Files, 1955–1962, Box 2, Folder 102 VN 1960—Internal Security, RG59, NARA. See also Durbrow to the Department of State, Telegram 539, September 5, 1960, CDF 751K.5-MSP/9-560, RG 59, NARA. The cost of MAAG taking over the training from USOM for the remainder of fiscal year 1961 was $8.13 million, while the fiscal year 1962 cost was estimated at $24 million. Durbrow to the Department of State, Telegram 745, October 5, 1960, CDF 751K.5-MSP/10-560, RG 59, NARA.

7. "Paper Prepared by the Military Assistance Advisory Group in Vietnam," *FRUS, 1958–1960, Volume I: Vietnam*, 550–556; and Durbrow to Parsons, September 6, 1960, RG59 Entry 5155, Bureau of East Asian Affairs, Vietnam Desk, Vietnam Subject Files, 1955–1962, Box 2, Folder 108 VN 1960—National Defense Affairs (General), RG 59, NARA. The document in *FRUS* was not the original one as mentioned by Durbrow to Parsons on September 6. Rather, it was the revised copy that reflected the recommendations and revisions agreed upon during the September 4 Country Team meeting.

8. Durbrow's exact words were, "This is a rather sad commentary on the slowness of the MAAG training during the relatively quiet period 1956–59," Durbrow to Parsons, September 6, 1960, RG59 Entry 5155, Bureau of East Asian Affairs, Vietnam Desk, Vietnam Subject Files, 1955–1962, Box 2, Folder 108 VN 1960—National Defense Affairs (General), RG 59, NARA. See also Durbrow to the Department of State, Dispatch 145, "Conversation between President Diem and General W.B. Palmer, September 29, 1960," October 5, 1960, CDF 751K.5-MSP/10-560 HBS, RG 59, NARA. A Memorandum of Conversation between Ngô Đình Diệm, Palmer, and Durbrow is attached. Another Memorandum of Conversation between the three is located in Durbrow to the Department of State, Dispatch 146, "Memorandum of Conversation with President Diem on September 30," October 6, 1960, CDF 751K.5-MSP/10-660, RG 59, NARA. This conversation also included McGarr.

9. Durbrow did compliment McGarr for his "completely cooperative and realistic attitude" on the issue of training the Civil Guard. Durbrow to Parsons, September 6, 1960, Entry 5155, Bureau of East Asian Affairs, Vietnam Desk, Vietnam Subject Files, 1955–1962, Box 2, Folder 108 VN 1960—National Defense Affairs (General), RG 59, NARA.

10. There were several points in the MAAG paper with which Durbrow concurred, though that agreement was often with qualifications. See Durbrow to the Department of State, Telegram 539, September 5, 1960, CDF 751K.5-MSP/9-560, RG 59, NARA.

11. Durbrow to Parsons, September 6, 1960, RG59 Entry 5155, Bureau of East Asian Affairs, Vietnam Desk, Vietnam Subject Files, 1955–1962, Box 2, Folder 108 VN 1960—National Defense Affairs (General), RG 59, NARA.

12. Lansdale worked hard to convince Americans on the right way to deal with the Vietnamese and used a variety of strategies to see though his perspective. See Lansdale to Desmond Fitzgerald, CIA Far East Division, "Madame Nhu," September 9, 1960, *FRUS, 1958–1960, Volume I: Vietnam*, 568–569.

13. Ngô Đình Diệm's State of the Union Message, October 3, 1960, Box 5, Folder "350 Internal Political Affairs: Vietnam, 1959–1961," Entry 3340B—Vietnam, Saigon Embassy, General Records, 1956–1963, RG 84:

Department of State Records, Foreign Service Posts [hereafter referred to as RG 84], NARA. A full copy of the text is located at "President Open National Assembly's October Regular Session; Reviews National Achievements," *Vietnam Press* (Evening), October 3, 1960, H.1–H.22. See also Arthur Gardiner, counselor of the U.S. embassy in Saigon for economic affairs to the Department of State, "The State of the Union and President Diem's Address to the National Assembly, October 3, 1960: Economic Aspects," Dispatch 169, October 22, 1960, CDF 751K.00/10-2260 HBS, RG 59, NARA. Another copy of the speech is attached to the dispatch as enclosure 1.

14. Ngô Đình Diệm's State of the Union Message, October 3, 1960, Box 5, Folder "350 Internal Political Affairs: Vietnam, 1959–1961," Entry 3340B—Vietnam, Saigon Embassy, General Records, 1956–1963, RG 84, NARA.

15. This Saigon government plan was offset by Việt Cộng efforts to redistribute southern lands to the peasants. As Jeffrey Race argued in his study of Long An province, "Land redistribution was an integral part of the Party takeover in the rural areas." It offered an effective weapon against the Saigon government by providing the redistribution on Việt Cộng terms as well as negating the positive effects of Ngô Đình Diệm's plan by refusing to acknowledge the government policy and punishing those who took advantage of it. See Race, *War Comes to Long An*, 126–127.

16. Ngô Đình Diệm's State of the Union Message, October 3, 1960, Box 5, Folder "350 Internal Political Affairs: Vietnam, 1959–1961," Entry 3340B—Vietnam, Saigon Embassy, General Records, 1956–1963, RG 84, NARA.

17. See appendix A.

18. *Tự do* editorial, October 2, 1960, FBIS, October 4, 1960, G3.

19. *Dân chúng* editorial, October 2, 1960, FBIS, October 4, 1960, G3.

20. Durbrow to the Department of State, Airgram G-146, October 6, 1960, CDF 751K.00/10-660, RG 59, NARA.

21. See Durbrow to the Department of State, Telegram 751, October 6, 1960, CDF 751K.00/10-660, RG 59, NARA.

22. "The Suspension of U.S. Military Aid to Laos," *Times of Vietnam*, October 13, 1960, FBIS, October 19, 1960, G1.

23. Durbrow to the Department of State, Telegram 751, October 6, 1960, CDF 751K.00/10-660, RG 59, NARA.

24. Acting Secretary of State John Steeves to the embassy in Vietnam, Telegram 581, October 7, 1960, *FRUS, 1958–1960, Volume I: Vietnam*, 593. See also Anderson, *Trapped by Success*, 189.

25. To reinforce this point, Mendenhall sent a dispatch to the Department of State on October 6 in which he attached an open letter from Dr. Phan Quang Đán, whom he characterized as a prominent oppositionist, which criticized the implementation of the Agroville Program but praised the concept. Mendenhall to the Department of State, Dispatch 170, October 24, 1960, CDF 751K.00/10-2460, RG 59, NARA. A copy of the Memorandum of Conversation is attached.

26. Durbrow to the Department of State, Telegram 802, October 15, 1960, CDF 751K.00/10-160, RG 59, NARA. See also Durbrow to the Department of State, Telegram 805, October 15, 1960, CDF 751K.5-MSP/10-1560, RG 59, NARA; and Mendenhall to the Department of State, Dispatch 159, "Civil Guard: Memorandum Given to President Diem," October 15, 1960, CDF 751K.5-MSP/10-1560, RG 59, NARA. McGarr presented the plan to reorganize Civil Guard training on October 28, 1960. See Mendenhall to the Department of State, Dispatch 182, "MAAG Plan for Reorganization, Training, Equipping and Employment of Civil Guard," November 4, 1960, CDF 751K.5-MSP/11-460 HBS, RG 59, NARA. The plan is located in enclosure 1. See also Anderson, *Trapped by Success*, 189; and Spector, *Advice and Support*, 366–367.

27. Memorandum from the secretary of state to the president, October 20, 1960, CDF 751K.00/10-2060, RG 59, NARA.

28. Mendenhall to the Department of State, "Approach to President Diem on Suggested Political Action," Dispatch 157, October 15, 1960, CDF 751K.00/10-160, RG 59, NARA. "English Text of Memorandum Handed to President Diem," referred to in Telegram 802 that was handed to Ngô Đình Diệm in French by Durbrow during their October 14 meeting, and "English Text of Notes on Ngô Đình Nhu and Dr. Tran Kim Tuyen," Enclosure 2, Dispatch from the Ambassador in Vietnam to the Department of State, October 15, 1960, are attached to this dispatch.

29. Durbrow to the Department of State, Telegram 866, October 20, 1960, CDF 751K.00/10-2060, RG 59, NARA. See also Anderson, *Trapped by Success*, 190.

30. The Ngô Đình Diệm–Parsons discussion was followed up by a request from Ambassador Trần Văn Chương to John Steeves, who was acting assistant secretary of state for Far Eastern affairs in Parsons' absence. The November 1 conversation centered around the 20,000-man increase and additional military funding. Memorandum of Conversation, "Viet-Nam: Request for Increased Military Assistance," between Ambassador Trần Văn Chương, Counselor Nguyễn Duy Liên, Steeves, and Wood is located in CDF 751K.5-MSP/11/160, RG 59, NARA. In *America's Longest War*, Herring argued that Durbrow "tactfully urged the president to broaden his government by appointing a new cabinet, relax controls on the press and civil liberties, and pacify the rural population by restoring village elections and making credit easily available." While Durbrow did make these urgings, though perhaps that is not strong enough a word, there is some evidence to suggest that Durbrow was less than tactful in his approach. Durbrow had been angling for a "frank" talk for a while and was keen on making his point to Ngô Đình Diệm. See Herring, *America's Longest War*, 84.

31. Durbrow to the Department of State, Telegram 866, October 20, 1960, CDF 751K.00/10-2060, RG 59, NARA.

32. Durbrow to Irwin, October 31, 1960, *FRUS, 1958–1960, Volume I: Vietnam*, 622.

33. Durbrow to the Department of State, Telegram 861, October 20, 1960, CDF 751K.00/10-2060, RG 59, NARA.

34. Department of State to the American embassy, Saigon, October 20, 1960, CDF 751K.00/10-2060, RG 59, NARA. See also Memorandum of Conversation,

"Situation in Viet-Nam," between first secretary of the French embassy in Washington, Marcel Berthelemy, and Chalmers Wood, October 20, 1960, CDF 751K.00/10-2060, RG 59, NARA. Durbrow seemed to continually advocate keeping the French at a distance but also had frequent conversations with Lalouette that discussed matters that he had suggested not be discussed. See Durbrow to the Department of State, Telegram 868, October 21, 1960, CDF 751K.00/10-2160, RG 59, NARA.

35. Airgram G-196 from the ambassador in Vietnam to the Department of State, November 3, 1960, CDF 751K.11/11-360 HBS, RG 59, NARA.

36. "Cabinet Reshuffled; Information Minister Becomes Directorate General," *Vietnam Press* (Evening), October 18, 1960, H.1; and "Mr. Tran Van Dinh Appointed Information Director General," *Vietnam Press* (Evening), October 19, 1960, H.3. The men replaced would be appointed to diplomatic posts abroad. See *Cách mạng Quốc gia* editorial, October 22, 1960, FBIS, October 25, 1960, G1. Durbrow's reaction is located in Durbrow to the Department of State, Telegram 852, October 19, 1960, CDF 751K.13/10-1960, RG 59, NARA; and Durbrow to the Department of State, Telegram 867, October 21, 1960, CDF 751K.13/10-2160, RG 59, NARA.

37. "Argentine Minister Plenipotentiary Presents Credentials," *Vietnam Press* (Evening), October 20, 1960, H.1.

38. Floyd Whittington, counselor of the U.S. embassy in Thailand for economic affairs to the Department of State, October 20, 1960, CDF 751K.00/10-20/60 RG 59, NARA. A copy of the Memorandum of Conversation, "Security Situation in Vietnam," between Dixon and Đặng Độc Khôi is attached. For some U.S.-reported Vietnam media reaction, see Mendenhall to the Department of State, "Editorial Reaction to GVN Cabinet Changes," Dispatch 181, November 4, 1960, CDF 751K.00/11-460, RG 59, NARA.

39. Durbrow to the Department of State, Telegram 873, October 21, 1960, CDF 751K.00/10-2160, RG 59, NARA.

40. "Socialist Union to Submit Draft on Press Freedom," *Vietnam Press* (Morning), October 25, 1960, H.6.

41. Durbrow to the Department of State, Telegram 904, October 27, 1960, CDF 751K.00/10-2760, RG 59, NARA; and Durbrow to the Department of State, "Memorandum of Conversation with President Diem, October 22, 1960, concerning Internal Security," Dispatch 175, October 29, 1960, CDF 751K.00/10-2960, RG 59, NARA. A copy of the Memorandum of Conversation, which also included McGarr, is attached.

42. "'Neutrality Is a Luxury We Cannot Afford,' Ambassador Says," *Vietnam Press* (Morning), October 24, 1960, H.2.

43. "Presidential Message Delivered on National Day, October 26, 1960," *Vietnam Press* (Morning), October 26, 1960, H.1–H.3.

44. "Presidential Message Delivered on National Day, October 26, 1960," *Vietnam Press* (Morning), October 26, 1960, H.1. An abstract is also located in FBIS, October 27, 1960, G1.

45. "Order of the Day of the President of the Republic of Viet Nam to the Armed Forces on the Occasion of the National Day (October 26, 1960)," *Vietnam Press* (Morning), October 26, 1960, H.4; and "President Ngo Dinh Diem Takes Salute of the Armed Forces," *Vietnam Press* (Evening), October 26, 1960, H.1–H.3.

46. "U.S. President Greets Republic Day," *Vietnam Press* (Morning), October 26, 1960, H.8–H.9; "Military Parades and Sports Contexts Highlight Republic Day in Provinces," *Vietnam Press* (Evening), October 27, 1960, H.1; and "Vietnamese Republic Day in Phnom Penh and Vientiane," *Vietnam Press* (Evening), October 27, 1960, H.2.

47. Barnes to the Department of State, "Three Who Dislike the Diem Regime," Dispatch 9, November 3, 1960, CDF 751K.00/11-360, RG 59, NARA.

48. Counselor for political affairs of the embassy in France, Randolph Kidder, to the Department of State, Airgram G-683, November 6, 1960, CDF 751K.00/11-660, RG 59, NARA.

49. Mendenhall to the Department of State, Airgram G-196, November 3, 1960, CDF 751K.11/11-360, RG 59, NARA.

50. "US17.5 Million Loan to Improve Water Supply System in City," *Vietnam Press* (Morning), November 3, 1960, H.5.

51. Lê Trọng Quát had announced the bill at an October 24 press conference along with other measures he hoped to pass, including an increase in the price of rice and a purge of inefficient civil servants. See Mendenhall to the Department of State, "Socialist Bloc in National Assembly Announces Policy Goals," Dispatch 184, November 8, 1960, CDF 751K.00/11-860, RG 59, NARA.

52. "Government Asked to Take 'Emergency Measures' to Check Red Subversion," *Vietnam Press* (Single), November 6, 1960, H.1. See also "Explanation of Resolution," *Sài Gòn Mới*, November 7, 1960, FBIS, November 8, G1.

53. "People Demonstrate Anti-Red Feelings," *Vietnam Press* (Morning), November 8, 1960, H.13.

54. Durbrow to the Department of State, Dispatch 221, "Trip to Kontum, Pleiku, and Qui Nhon on November 5, 1960," December 3, 1960, CDF 751K.00/12-360, RG 59, NARA.

55. "National Assembly Approves Budget's Revenue," *Vietnam Press* (Evening), November 10, 1960, H.5–H.7.

Chapter 7

1. Air attaché in Vietnam (Toland) to the chief of staff, United States Air Force (White), Telegram C-115, November 11, 1960, *FRUS, 1958–1960, Volume I: Vietnam*, 638. See also Joseph A. Mendenhall's letter to his parents reprinted as an editorial note in *FRUS, 1958–1960, Volume I: Vietnam*, 660. A telegram from Durbrow to the director of naval intelligence has the coup d'état beginning around 3:00 a.m. Folder 350 "Internal Political Affairs: Vietnam—November Coup d'etat," Box 5, Entry 3340B—Vietnam, Saigon Embassy, General Records, 1956–1963, RG 84, NARA. A Telegram sent thirty minutes later by Durbrow to the Department of State timed the start of the attack at 3:30 a.m. Durbrow to Department of State, Telegram 993, Folder 350 "Internal Political Affairs: Vietnam—November Coup d'etat," Box 5, Entry 3340B—Vietnam, Saigon Embassy,

General Records, 1956–1963, RG 84, NARA. A copy of the Telegram is also located in CDF 751K.54/11-1060, RG 59, NARA. See also ALUSNA, Saigon to the Department of State, Telegram 102114Z, November 10, 1960, CDF 751K.00/11-1060, RG 59, NARA; and Durbrow to the Department of State, MAGCH 1422, November 10, 1960, CDF 751K.00/11-1060, RG 59, NARA. See also Spector, *Advice and Support*, 369–370.

2. A detailed analysis of the military units involved in the coup d'état attempt is located in McGarr to Department of the Army CX-166, November 17, 1960, Folder 83 "VN 1960—Attempted Coup d'Etat," Box, 1 Entry 5155, General Records of the Department of State, Bureau of East Asian Affairs, Vietnam Desk, Vietnam Subject Files, 1955–1962, RG 59, NARA.

3. "Abortive Coup as Told by Rebel Officer," *Vietnam Press* (Evening), November 25, 1960, H.4.

4. Joseph A. Mendenhall's letter to his parents reprinted as an editorial note in *FRUS, 1958–1960, Volume I: Vietnam*, 660–661. See also Durbrow to Department of State, Telegram 994, November 11, 1960, Folder 350 "Internal Political Affairs: Vietnam—November Coup d'etat," Box 5, Entry 3340B—Vietnam, Saigon Embassy, General Records, 1956–1963, RG 84, NARA.

5. Saigon to the secretary of state, Telegram Critic 3, November 10, 1960, CDF 751K.00/11-1060, RG 59, NARA; and Durbrow to the Department of State, Telegram 996, November 11, 1960, CDF 751K.00/11-1160, RG 59, NARA. Stanley Karnow argued that Ngô Đình Diệm, his brother Nhu, and Madame Nhu took refuge in the cellar of the palace. Other historians have repeated this claim, calling it a wine cellar, though no evidence suggests that this is true. See Karnow, *Vietnam: A History*, 236; Anderson, *Trapped by Success*, 192; and Spector, *Advice and Support*, 370. All three repeat the story without documentation.

6. William Colby observed this pitched battle from his home and reported it to Durbrow via telephone. Durbrow to Department of State, Telegram 993, Folder 350 "Internal Political Affairs: Vietnam—November Coup d'etat," Box 5, Entry 3340B—Vietnam, Saigon Embassy, General Records, 1956–1963, RG 84, NARA.

7. "Chronology of November 11–12 Events," *Vietnam Press* (Evening), November 21, 1960, H.6–H.8.

8. Durbrow to Department of State, Telegram 998, November 11, 1960, CDF 751K.00/11-1160, RG 59, NARA. See also Saigon to secretary of state, Telegram 4, November 10, 1960, CDF 751K.00/11-1060 HBS, RG 59, NARA.

9. Durbrow to Department of State, Telegram 998, November 11, 1960, CDF 751K.00/11-1160, RG 59, NARA. See also Saigon to secretary of state, Telegram 4, November 10, 1960, CDF 751K.00/11-1060 HBS, RG 59, NARA.

10. Durbrow to Department of State, Telegram 1035, November 12, 1960, CDF 751K.00/11-1260, RG 59, NARA. See also Durbrow to the Department of State, Telegram 1000, November 11, 1960, CDF 751K.00/11-1160, RG 59, NARA.

11. "Saigon Radio Mirrors Course of Coup," FBIS, November 14, 1960, G1–G6. The *Voice of the Republic of Vietnam* broadcast began at approximately 8:45 a.m. and continued until approximately 10:15 a.m.

12. Critic CIA Saigon Number 1645, Folder 350 "Internal Political Affairs: Vietnam—November Coup d'etat," Box 5, Entry 3340B—Vietnam, Saigon Embassy, General Records, 1956–1963, RG 84, NARA. Durbrow reported another conversation between an unnamed embassy officer and Secretary General of the Ministry of Foreign Affairs Phạm Đăng Lâm in which he reported the confused situation but also confirmed the pessimistic outlook shared by Durbrow. See Saigon to the Department of State, Telegram 1003, November 10, 1960, CDF 751K.00/11-1060, RG 59, NARA.

13. OUSARMA, Saigon to the secretary of state, CX-154, November 11, 1960, CDF 751K.00/11-1160, RG 59, NARA. In this same telegram, it was reported that the guards at the Palace gates had surrendered. Forty minutes later, another telegram from the same source reported that the civil police were throwing away their weapons but staying at their posts as heavy weapons fired upon the Palace, with small-arms fire responding. OUSARMA, Saigon to the secretary of state, CX-156, November 11, 1960, CDF 751K.00/11-1160, RG 59, NARA. Colby confirmed the loss of one of the guardhouses at 9:00 a.m. See Saigon to the secretary of state, CIA Message Critic 8, November 11, 1960, CDF 751K.00/11-1160, RG 59, NARA.

14. Durbrow to Department of State, Telegram 1015, November 11, 1960, CDF 751K.00/11-1160, RG 59, NARA.

15. Critic CIA Saigon Number 1645, Folder 350 "Internal Political Affairs: Vietnam—November Coup d'etat," Box 5, Entry 3340B—Vietnam, Saigon Embassy, General Records, 1956–1963, RG 84, NARA. Colby offers two accounts of the November 11–12 events, in *Lost Victory*, 76–79, and *Honorable Men*, 163–165.

16. "Chronology of November 11–12 Events," *Vietnam Press* (Evening), November 21, 1960, H.6–H.8. See also Saigon to the secretary of state, CIA Message 5, November 10, 1960, CDF 751K.00/11-1060, RG 59, NARA.

17. Saigon to the secretary of state, CIA Message 5, November 10, 1960, CDF 751K.00/11-1060, RG 59, NARA.

18. Several reports confirmed that the Việt Cộng did not take advantage of the situation. "Situation Reported Calm in Provinces during November 11 Coup," *Vietnam Press* (Evening), November 16, 1960, H.4. See also Durbrow to the Department of State, Telegram 1084, November 15, 1960, CDF 751K.00/11-1460, RG 59, NARA.

19. Durbrow to the Department of State, Telegram 994, November 10, 1960, CDF 751K.00/11-1060, RG 59, NARA.

20. Cunningham Memorandum of Conversation, November 13, 1960, Folder 71 "VN 1960—Political Affairs (General)," Box 1, Entry 5155, General Records of the Department of State, Bureau of East Asian Affairs, Vietnam Desk, Vietnam Subject Files, 1955–1962, RG 59, NARA; and Durbrow to Department of State, Telegram 1082, November 15, 1960, CDF 751K.00/11-1560, RG 59, NARA.

21. "Chronology of November 11–12 Events," *Vietnam Press* (Evening), November 21, 1960, H.6–H.8; and McGarr to Department of the Army CX-166, November 17, 1960, Folder 83 "VN 1960—Attempted Coup d'Etat," Box 1, Entry 5155, General Records of the Department of State, Bureau of East Asian Affairs, Vietnam Desk, Vietnam Subject Files, 1955–1962, RG 59, NARA.

22. Air attaché in Vietnam (Toland) to the chief of staff, United States Air Force (White), Telegram C-115, November 11, 1960, *FRUS, 1958–1960, Volume I: Vietnam*, 638–639.

23. CIA Telegram 6 to the Department of State reported Colby's view from his position as of 8:30 a.m. when the fighting was in a lull and the palace was confronted by four armored cars that had been apparently captured from the defenders. The telegram concluded that the end of the fighting was in sight. Saigon to the secretary of state, CIA Message 6, November 10, 1960, CDF 751K.00/11-1060, RG 59, NARA.

24. Critic CIA Saigon Number 1645, Folder 350 "Internal Political Affairs: Vietnam—November Coup d'etat," Box 5, Entry 3340B—Vietnam, Saigon Embassy, General Records, 1956–1963, RG 84, NARA.

25. Durbrow to the Department of State, Telegram 1009, November 11, 1960, CDF 751K.00/11-1160, RG 59, NARA.

26. Meloy to Department of State, November 12, 1960, Folder 350 "Internal Political Affairs: Vietnam—November Coup d'etat," Box 5, Entry 3340B—Vietnam, Saigon Embassy, General Records, 1956–1963, RG 84, NARA.

27. Details of the events around 10:30 a.m. are located in OUSARMA, Saigon to the Department of State, CX-155, November 10, 1960, CDF 751K.00/11-1060, RG 59, NARA. See also USARMA Saigon to CINCPAC, CX-155 and CX-156, November 11, 1960, Folder 84 "VN 1960—Attempted Coup d'Etat," Box 1, Entry 5155, General Records of the Department of State, Bureau of East Asian Affairs, Vietnam Desk, Vietnam Subject Files, 1955–1962, RG 59, NARA; and Durbrow to Department of State, Telegram 1006, November 11, 1960, Folder 350 "Internal Political Affairs: Vietnam—November Coup d'etat," Box 5, Entry 3340B—Vietnam, Saigon Embassy, General Records, 1956–1963, RG 84, NARA. The telegram is also located in CDF 751K.00/11-1160, RG 59, NARA. See also McGarr to the Department of State, MAAG-CH 1426, November 10, 1960, CDF 751K.00/00-1060, RG 59, NARA.

28. "Saigon Radio Mirrors Course of Coup," FBIS, November 14, 1960, G1–G6. Durbrow to the Department of State, Telegram 1007, November 11, 1960, CDF 751K.00/11-1160, RG 59, NARA. Soon afterward, Durbrow sent a telegram in which it was revealed that Generals Lê Văn Ty and Thái Quang Hoàng were prisoners to Colonel Nguyễn Chánh Thi. Durbrow to the Department of State, Telegram 1012, 1960, CDF 751K.00/11-1160, RG 59, NARA. See Kahin, *Intervention*, 123–125.

29. USARMA, Saigon to the secretary of state, CX-157, November 11, 1960, CDF 751K.00/11-1160, RG 59, NARA. This telegram reported three F-8F rather than four planes that were involved in the leaflet-dropping operation.

30. Durbrow to Department of State, Telegram 1035, November 12, 1960, CDF 751K.00/11-1260, RG 59, NARA. See also Saigon to the secretary of state, CIA Message 9, November 11, 1960, CDF 751K.00/11-1160, RG 59, NARA; and Saigon to secretary of state, CIA Message 10, November 11, 1960, CDF 751K.00/11-1160, RG 59, NARA. In *Cold War Madarin*, Seth Jacobs argued that Nguyễn Chánh Thi and Vương Văn Đông were two of the finest officers in the country and were motivated by their frustration at the lack of progress in prosecuting the war. He also suggests that the two did not seek to remove Ngô Đình Diệm. This seems curious given the nature of the opening attacks directed against Ngô Đình Diệm's living quarters and the process by which they motivated their troops to attack. See Jacobs, *Cold War Mandarin*, 117.

31. "Names of Officers of 'Revolutionary Committee' Revealed," *Vietnam Press* (Evening), November 17, 1960, H.5; and "Real Nature of Abortive Coup Revealed at News Conference," *Vietnam Press* (Morning), November 18, 1960, H.5–H.8.

32. Durbrow to Department of State, Telegram 1015, November 11, 1960, CDF 751K.00/11-1160, RG 59, NARA. See also Durbrow to the Department of State, Telegram 1012, November 11, 1960, CDF 751K.00/11-1160, RG 59, NARA.

33. Bùi Diễm, with David Chanoff, *In the Jaws of History*, 95. Bùi Diễm argued that the abortive coup d'état was similar to the Caravelle Manifesto in that both were a call for reform.

34. An element of Vietnam War historiography has maintained that the U.S. military was more involved, though this assertion is not validated by the data available. See Lederer, *Our Own Worst Enemy*, 22–23.

35. Joseph A. Mendenhall's letter to his parents reprinted as an editorial note in *FRUS, 1958–1960, Volume I: Vietnam*, 662–663.

36. Excerpt of Mendenhall Oral History with members of the Office of the Historian, December 27, 1983, *FRUS, 1958–1960, Volume I: Vietnam*, 662. During the same oral history interview, Mendenhall maintained that Durbrow was "shocked" and "stunned" by the coup d'état, though his actions during and after suggest that this was not the case.

37. Excerpt of a Colby Oral History with the Department of State Historian, January 6, 1984, *FRUS, 1958–1960, Volume I: Vietnam*, 663. See Kahin, *Intervention*, 125–126; and Catton, *Diem's Final Failure*, 79. Colby offers his analysis in *Lost Victory*, 78–79. See also Anderson, *Trapped by Success*, 192–193; Spector, *Advice and Support*, 370–371; and Ahern, *House of Ngo*, 141–142.

38. "Chronology of November 11–12 Events," *Vietnam Press* (Evening), November 21, 1960, H.6–H.8; McGarr to CINCPAC, MAGER 1444, November 12, 1960, Folder 83 "VN 1960—Attempted Coup d'Etat," Box 1, Entry 5155, General Records of the Department of State, Bureau of East Asian Affairs, Vietnam Desk, Vietnam Subject Files, 1955–1962, RG 59, NARA; and McGarr to Department of the Army CX-166, November 17, 1960, Folder 83 "VN 1960—Attempted Coup d'Etat," Box 1, Entry 5155, General Records of the Department of State, Bureau of East Asian Affairs, Vietnam Desk, Vietnam Subject Files, 1955–1962, RG 59, NARA.

39. The efficiency of the ARVN troops coming into Saigon from the countryside was increased by members of the Republican Youth who met the troops at the outskirts of the city and guided them through the confusing, and sometimes blocked, roads to their objective. "Cong Hoa Youth Given Recognition," *Vietnam Press*, November 17, 1960, H.14.

40. Durbrow to Department of State, Telegram 1019, November 11, CDF 751K.00/11-1160, RG 59, NARA.

41. Parsons to Durbrow, Telegram 774, November 11, 1960, CDF 751K.00/11–1160, RG 59, NARA.

42. Durbrow to Department of State, Telegram 1019, November 11, CDF 751K.00/11–1160, RG 59, NARA; and Durbrow to Department of State, Telegram 1035, November 12, 1960, CDF 751K.00/11–1260, RG 59, NARA.

43. Durbrow to Department of State, Telegram 1019, November 11, CDF 751K.00/11–1160, RG 59, NARA.

44. Durbrow to Department of State, Telegram 1022, November 11, CDF 751K.00/11–1160, RG 59, NARA.

45. Durbrow to Department of State, Telegram 1025, November 11, 1960, CDF 751K.00/11–1160, RG 59, NARA.

46. McGarr to Department of the Army CX-166, November 17, 1960, Folder 83 "VN 1960—Attempted Coup d'Etat," Box 1, Entry 5155, General Records of the Department of State, Bureau of East Asian Affairs, Vietnam Desk, Vietnam Subject Files, 1955–1962, RG 59, NARA; "Viet Cong Fails in Attack on Government Troops at Phuoc Long," *Vietnam Press* (Morning), November 17, 1960, H.3; and "Chronology of November 11–12 Events," *Vietnam Press* (Evening), November 21, 1960, H.6–H.8.

47. "Chronology of November 11–12 Events," *Vietnam Press* (Evening), November 21, 1960, H.6–H.8.

48. McGarr to Felt, MAGTN-PO 1432, November 12, 1960, CDF 751K.00/11–1160, RG 59, NARA; and Durbrow to Department of State, Telegram 1082, November 15, 1960, CDF 751K.00/11–1560, RG 59, NARA.

49. Durbrow to the Department of State, Telegram 1029, November 11, 1960, CDF 751K.00/11–1160, RG 59, NARA.

50. McGarr to Felt, MAGTN-PO 1432, November 12, 1960, CDF 751K.00/11–1160, RG 59, NARA.

51. Telephone conversation from CIA, November 11, 1960, Folder 84 "VN 1960—Attempted Coup d'Etat," Box 1, Entry 5155, General Records of the Department of State, Bureau of East Asian Affairs, Vietnam Desk, Vietnam Subject Files, 1955–1962, RG 59, NARA.

52. McGarr to CINCPAC, MAGCH-CS 13061, November 11, 1960, Folder 83 "VN 1960—Attempted Coup d'Etat," Box 1, Entry 5155, General Records of the Department of State, Bureau of East Asian Affairs, Vietnam Desk, Vietnam Subject Files, 1955–1962, RG 59, NARA. See also Durbrow to the Department of State, Telegram 1031, November 11, 1960, CDF 751K.00/11–1160, RG 59, NARA.

53. McGarr to CINCPAC, MAGCH-CS 13061, November 11, 1960, Folder 83 "VN 1960—Attempted Coup d'Etat," Box 1, Entry 5155, General Records of the Department of State, Bureau of East Asian Affairs, Vietnam Desk, Vietnam Subject Files, 1955–1962, RG 59, NARA. See also McGarr to the Department of State, MAGTN-PO 1433, November 11, 1960, CDF 751K.00/11–1160, RG 59, NARA.

54. Durbrow to the Department of State, Telegram 1034, November 12, 1960, CDF 751K.00/11–1260, RG 59, NARA.

55. Durbrow to Department of State, Telegram 1029, November 11, 1960, Folder 83 "VN 1960—Attempted Coup d'Etat," Box 1, Entry 5155, General Records of the Department of State, Bureau of East Asian Affairs, Vietnam Desk, Vietnam Subject Files, 1955–1962, RG 59, NARA; and Mendenhall to Department of State, Telegram 1034, November 12, 1960, Folder 350 "Internal Political Affairs: Vietnam—November Coup d'etat," Box 5, Entry 3340B—Vietnam, Saigon Embassy, General Records, 1956–1963, RG 84, NARA.

56. McGarr to Department of the Army CX-166, November 17, 1960, Folder 83 "VN 1960—Attempted Coup d'Etat," Box 1, Entry 5155, General Records of the Department of State, Bureau of East Asian Affairs, Vietnam Desk, Vietnam Subject Files, 1955–1962, RG 59, NARA.

57. Joseph A. Mendenhall's letter to his parents reprinted as an editorial note in *FRUS, 1958–1960, Volume I: Vietnam*, 662–663. Durbrow reported the conversation occurring at 2:10 a.m. and made no reference to Võ Văn Hải being a captive of the rebel leaders. In fact, Durbrow reported that Võ Văn Hải was speaking for the rebels and would not negotiate with him. Durbrow to the Department of State, Telegram 1060, November 12, 1960, CDF 751K.00/11–1260, RG 59, NARA.

58. Memorandum of Conversation between Francis Cunningham and Nguyễn Thái, director general of the *Vietnam Press*, November 18, 1960, Folder 71 "VN 1960—Political Affairs (General)," Box 1, Entry 5155, General Records of the Department of State, Bureau of East Asian Affairs, Vietnam Desk, Vietnam Subject Files, 1955–1962, RG 59, NARA.

59. Durbrow Oral History interviews with the Department of State historian held April 2 and May 4, 1984, as referred to in the editorial note, *FRUS, 1958–1960, Volume I: Vietnam*, 662–663.

60. "Chronology of November 11–12 Events," *Vietnam Press* (Evening), November 21, 1960, H.6–H.8. See also OUSARMA, Saigon to the secretary of state, Telegram CX-158, November 11, 1960, CDF 751K.00/11–1160, RG 59, NARA.

61. McGarr to Felt, MAGTN-PO 1434, November 12, 1960, CDF 751K.00/11–1260, RG 59, NARA; and Durbrow to Department of State, Telegram 1045, November 11, 1960, Folder 350 "Internal Political Affairs: Vietnam—November Coup d'etat," Box 5, Entry 3340B—Vietnam, Saigon Embassy, General Records, 1956–1963, RG 84, NARA. Durbrow offers a summary of the day's events in Telegram 1065, November 12, 1960, CDF 751K.00/11–1260, RG 59, NARA.

62. Durbrow to the Department of State, Telegram 1042, November 12, 1960, CDF 751K.00/11–1260, RG 59, NARA.

63. OUSARMA to the secretary of state, CX-161, November 12, 1960, CDF 751K.00/11–1260, RG 59, NARA; and McGarr to Department of the Army CX-166, November 17, 1960, Folder 83 "VN 1960—Attempted Coup d'Etat," Box 1, Entry 5155, General Records of the Department of State, Bureau of East Asian Affairs, Vietnam Desk, Vietnam Subject Files, 1955–1962, RG 59, NARA. See also McGarr to the Department of State, Telegram MAGTN/PO 1429, November 11, 1960, CDF 751K.00/11–1160, RG 59, NARA; and McGarr to the Department of State, Telegram MAGCH-CH 1430, November 11, 1960, CDF 751K.00/11–1160, RG 59, NARA.

64. Joseph A. Mendenhall letter to his parents reprinted as an editorial note in *FRUS, 1958–1960, Volume I: Vietnam*, 661; and November 14, 1960, Durbrow off-the-record press conference, Folder 350 "Internal Political Affairs: Vietnam—November Coup d'etat," Box 5, Entry 3340B—Vietnam, Saigon Embassy, General Records, 1956–1963, RG 84, NARA.
65. "Saigon Radio Mirrors Course of Coup," FBIS, November 14, 1960, G1–G6. See Jacobs, *Cold War Mandarin*, 118.
66. Joseph A. Mendenhall letter to his parents reprinted as an editorial note in *FRUS, 1958–1960, Volume I: Vietnam*, 661. See also "Saigon Radio Mirrors Course of Coup," FBIS, November 14, 1960, G1–G6.
67. The demonstrators were asked to carry signs reading "Down with feudalism and dictatorship! Support the army! Support the Revolutionary Council: The entire nation unites against the communists!" See "Saigon Radio Mirrors Course of Coup," FBIS, November 14, 1960, G1–G6.
68. Telegram MAGCH-CS 1435 to the secretary of state, November 12, 1960, CDF 751K.00/11–1260, RG 59, NARA.
69. CX-160 to the secretary of state, November 12, 1960, CDF 751K.00/11–1260, RG 59, NARA.
70. Durbrow to Department of State, Telegram 1049, November 12, 1960, CDF 751K.00/11–1260, RG 59, NARA; and McGarr to CINCPAC, MAGCH-CS 1438, November 12, 1960, Folder 83 "VN 1960—Attempted Coup d'Etat," Box 1, Entry 5155, General Records of the Department of State, Bureau of East Asian Affairs, Vietnam Desk, Vietnam Subject Files, 1955–1962, RG 59, NARA.
71. "Saigon Radio Mirrors Course of Coup," FBIS, November 14, 1960, G1–G6.
72. Durbrow to Department of State, Telegram 1049, November 12, 1960, CDF 751K.00/11–1260, RG 59, NARA.
73. On December 28, Durbrow sent Parsons a letter in response to a December 3 letter from Parsons in which the latter informed Durbrow of army chief of staff general Lyman Lemnitzer's strong urging to push Ngô Đình Diệm to be moderate with the rebels. Durbrow, as was seen with other events during the year, backpedaled and defended his position which he argued was not as severe as his critics asserted. In this case, however, General Williams was not around to set the record straight.
74. Parsons to Durbrow, Telegram 782, November 12, 1960, CDF 751K.00/11–1260, RG 59, NARA.
75. Durbrow to the Department of State, Telegram 1043, November 12, 1960, CDF 751K.00/11–1260, RG 59, NARA; and CX-160 to the secretary of state, November 12, 1960, CDF 751K.00/11–1260, RG 59, NARA.
76. Mendenhall to Department of State, Telegram 1043, November 12, 1960, Folder 350 "Internal Political Affairs: Vietnam—November Coup d'etat," Box 5, Entry 3340B—Vietnam, Saigon Embassy, General Records, 1956–1963, RG 84, NARA.
77. Durbrow to the Department of State, Telegram 1050, November 12, 1960, Folder 350 "Internal Political Affairs: Vietnam—November Coup d'etat," Box 5, Entry 3340B—Vietnam, Saigon Embassy, General Records, 1956–1963, RG 84, NARA; and MAGCH-CS 1436 to the secretary of state, November 12, 1960, CDF 751K.00/11–1260, RG 59, NARA.
78. Durbrow to the Department of State, Telegram 1050, November 12, 1960, CDF 751K.00/11–1260, RG 59, NARA; and Durbrow to the Department of State, Telegram 1051, November 12, 1960, CDF 751K.00/11–1260, RG 59, NARA. See also "Saigon Radio Mirrors Course of Coup," FBIS, November 14, 1960, G1–G6.
79. "Chronology of November 11–12 Events," *Vietnam Press* (Evening), November 21, 1960, H.6–H.8; and Radio Broadcasts, November 12, 1960, Folder 350 "Internal Political Affairs: Vietnam—November Coup d'etat," Box 5, Entry 3340B—Vietnam, Saigon Embassy, General Records, 1956–1963, RG 84, NARA.
80. McGarr to CINCPAC, MAGCH-CS 1439, November 12, 1960, Folder 83 "VN 1960—Attempted Coup d'Etat," Box 1, Entry 5155, General Records of the Department of State, Bureau of East Asian Affairs, Vietnam Desk, Vietnam Subject Files, 1955–1962, RG 59, NARA.
81. One such leaflet was from the newly formed People's Revolutionary Committee against Rebellion that called upon the civilians and military in Saigon to rally to the government's cause. Durbrow to the Department of State, Telegram 1054, November 12, 1960, CDF 751K.00/11–1260, RG 59, NARA; and Durbrow to the Department of State, Telegram 1056, November 12, 1960, CDF 751K.00/11–1260, RG 59, NARA.
82. "Air Traffic Resumes at Tan Son Nhut," *Vietnam Press* (Morning), November 15, 1960, H.16. See also USARMA, Saigon to the secretary of state, CX-162, November 12, 1960, CDF 751K.00/11–1260, RG 59, NARA.
83. Durbrow was focused on the issue of the bloodbath. When it did not occur, he telephoned Ngô Đình Diệm late in the night of November 12 to tell him how pleased he was that it did not occur. Durbrow remarked that Ngô Đình Diệm seemed pleased that he called, though Durbrow did press the conversation to rehash his views against Ngô Đình Nhu. There is no indication of Ngô Đình Diệm's response to this so soon after his life was in peril. See Durbrow to the Department of State, Telegram 1066, November 12, 1960, CDF 751K.00/11–1260, RG 59, NARA; and Parsons to Durbrow, Telegram 788, November 12, 1960, CDF 751K.00/11–1260, RG 59, NARA. Durbrow then telephoned Nguyễn Đình Thuận with the same message. See Durbrow to the Department of State, Telegram 1067, November 12, 1960, CDF 751K.00/11–1260, RG 59, NARA.
84. Albert Jenkins, regional planning adviser in the Far East to Cleveland, November 14, 1960, CDF 751K.00/11–1460, RG 59, NARA.
85. A list of the plane's occupants is located in William Trimble to the Department of State, Telegram 540, November 16, 1960, CDF 751K.00/11–1660, RG 59, NARA.
86. McGarr to CINCPAC, MAGTN-PO 1445, November 12, 1960, Folder 83 "VN 1960—Attempted Coup d'Etat," Box 1, Entry 5155, General Records of the Department of State, Bureau of East Asian Affairs, Vietnam Desk, Vietnam Subject Files, 1955–1962, RG 59, NARA. Priority cable 175 from Phnom Penh to the Department of State confirmed that the aircraft had requested an emergency landing in Phnom Penh, Folder

350 "Internal Political Affairs: Vietnam—November Coup d'etat," Box 5, Entry 3340B—Vietnam, Saigon Embassy, General Records, 1956–1963, RG 84, NARA. See also "Coup Leaders Arrested in Phnom Penh," *Vietnam Press* (Morning), November 14, H.7; and "Negotiations Under Way with Cambodia for Extradition of Treacherous Officers," *Vietnam Press* (Morning), November 18, 1960, H.2.

87. "Major Ngo Xuan Soan Killed by Rebels for Opposition to Coup," *Vietnam Press* (Evening), November 17, 1960, H.2. See also Trimble to the Department of State, Telegram 530, November 13, 1960, CDF 751K.00/11–1360, RG 59, NARA; and Trimble to the Department of State, Telegram 531, November 14, 1960, CDF 751K.00/11–1460, RG 59, NARA. General Thái Quang Hoàng was eventually released on November 15, 1960. See Trimble to the Department of State, Telegram 535, November 15, 1960, CDF 751K.00/11–1560, RG 59, NARA; and Trimble to the Department of State, Telegram 537, November 16, 1960, CDF 751K.00/11–1660, RG 59, NARA.

88. Durbrow to the Department of State, Telegram 1075, November 14, 1960, CDF 751K.00/11–1460, RG 59, NARA. Only these four were arrested, though historians of the Vietnam War had made claims or implied that all were arrested because of their activities associated with the Caravelle Manifesto. See Herring, *America's Longest War*, 84.

89. MAAG (Richard P. Scott) to CINCPAC, MAGCH-SO 13066, November 12, 1960, Folder 350 "Internal Political Affairs: Vietnam—November Coup d'etat," Box 5, Entry 3340B—Vietnam, Saigon Embassy, General Records, 1956–1963, RG 84, NARA; MAGCH-CS 1441 to the secretary of state, November 12, 1960, CDF 751K.00/11–1260, RG 59, NARA; Durbrow to the Department of State, Telegram 1063, November 12, 1960, CDF 751K.00/11–1260, RG 59, NARA; and Durbrow to Department of State, Telegram 1088, November 16, 1960, CDF 751K.00/11–1660 CS, RG 59, NARA.

90. See also "Saigon Radio Mirrors Course of Coup," FBIS, November 14, 1960, G1–G6.

91. Durbrow to the Department of State, Telegram 1064, November 12, 1960, CDF 751K.00/11–1260, RG 59, NARA. See also "Saigon Radio Mirrors Course of Coup," FBIS, November 14, 1960, G1–G6.

92. "Assembly Voices Confidence in President; Asks Punishment for Coup Leaders," *Vietnam Press* (Single), November 13, 1960, H.1–H.2; and "Appeal of the President of the Republic to the Nation," *Vietnam Press* (Single), November 13, 1960, H.1.

93. McGarr to Lansdale, November 13, 1960, *FRUS, 1958–1960, Volume I: Vietnam*, 659–660; and McGarr to CINCPAC, MAGTN-PO 1445, November 12, 1960, Folder 83 "VN 1960—Attempted Coup d'Etat," Box 1, Entry 5155, General Records of the Department of State, Bureau of East Asian Affairs, Vietnam Desk, Vietnam Subject Files, 1955–1962, RG 59, NARA.

94. Durbrow to Department of State, Telegram 1082, November 15, 1960, CDF 751K.00/11–1560, RG 59, NARA.

95. See also the November 16 *Voice of the Republic of Vietnam* broadcast, "Paratroopers Blameless in Coup Attempt," FBIS, November 17, 1960, G1–G2; and "Rebels Were Instigated by Colonialists," *Times of Vietnam*, November 15, 1960, FBIS, November 17, 1960, G2. The suggestion that the attempt by the paratroopers to drive Ngô Đình Diệm from office was an indication of how poorly he fared is a common one in Vietnam War historiography, as they are considered to have been his most loyal force. While this is technically true, the missing part of the story is that the paratroopers remained loyal to Ngô Đình Diệm and were guided into their attack because of that loyalty. That is, they were told that they were going to rescue Ngô Đình Diệm from an attempted coup d'état rather than initiating one. Once word of this duplicity reached the troops, there was a general inclination to switch sides to those who were fighting for Ngô Đình Diệm and the Republic of Vietnam. See Jacobs, *Cold War Mandarin*, 119; and Herring, *America's Longest War*, 83.

96. Durbrow to Department of State, Telegram 1082, November 15, 1960, CDF 751K.00/11–1560, RG 59, NARA.

Chapter 8

1. McGarr to CINCPAC, MAGTN-PO 1451, November 13, 1960, and MAGCH-CS 13075, November 13, 1960, both documents located in Folder 83 "VN 1960—Attempted Coup d'Etat," Box 1, Entry 5155, General Records of the Department of State, Bureau of East Asian Affairs, Vietnam Desk, Vietnam Subject Files, 1955–1962, RG 59, NARA. See also Durbrow to the Department of State, Telegram 1076, November 14, 1960, CDF 751K.00/11–1460, RG 59, NARA.

2. "People Fete Failure of Coup d'Etat," *Vietnam Press* (Single), November 14, H.1.

3. Memorandum from Lansdale to Douglas, November 15, 1960, *FRUS, 1958–1960, Volume I: Vietnam*, 667–668. Douglas passed along Lansdale's thoughts to Secretary of Defense Thomas Gates.

4. French to Lansdale, Telegram SGN 239, November 17, 1960, *FRUS, 1958–1960, Volume I: Vietnam*, 669–670.

5. French to Lansdale, Telegram SGN 239, November 17, 1960, *FRUS, 1958–1960, Volume I: Vietnam*, 670.

6. "Counter-Coup D'Etat Committee Chairman Meets the Press," *Vietnam Press* (Morning), November 15, 1960, H.5.

7. At around 3:10 p.m. on November 12, the People's Counter-Coup d'État Committee broadcast a communiqué calling on the people of Saigon to turn in supporters of the abortive coup d'état. See "Saigon Radio Mirrors Course of Coup," FBIS, November 14, 1960, G1–G6. Other members of the central executive committee included vice chairmen Colonel Nguyễn Văn Y and Ngô Trọng Hiếu, secretary general Lieutenant Colonel Nguyễn Văn Châu, and several others, including Brigadier Generals Lê Văn Nghiệm and Tôn Thất Đính. See "Antirebel Committee Issues Communique," *Sài Gòn Mới*, November 15, 1960, FBIS November 16, 1960, G1–G2. See also Durbrow to the Department of State, Airgram G-219, November 21, 1960, CDF 751K.00(W)/11–2160, RG 59, NARA.

8. Durbrow to the Department of State, Telegram

1054, November 12, 1960, Folder 350 "Internal Political Affairs: Vietnam—November Coup d'etat," Box 5, Entry 3340B—Vietnam, Saigon Embassy, General Records, 1956–1963, RG 84, NARA.

9. "Flags Out to Fete Crushing of Rebels," *Vietnam Press* (Single), November 13, H.10.

10. "People's Committee against Rebels and Communists Set Up," *Vietnam Press* (Evening), November 14, 1960, H.4.

11. "People's Counter Coup D'Etat Committee's Officers Named," *Vietnam Press*, November 15, 1960, H.2–H.3. See also Durbrow to the Department of State, Telegram 1090, November 16, 1960, CDF 751K.00/11-1660, RG 59, NARA; and Durbrow to the Department of State, Telegram 1091, November 16, 1960, CDF 751K.00/11-1660, RG 59, NARA.

12. Durbrow to Department of State, Telegram 1096, CDF 751K.00/11-1760, RG 59, NARA. On November 16, another leaflet was distributed by the committee that stated clearly that the United States, Britain, and France were not involved in the abortive coup d'état. For whatever reason, Durbrow was slow to report this new leaflet. On November 23, in a meeting with the Indian commissioner to the ICC, Gopala Menon, Ngô Đình Diệm identified the French as the colonial element that influenced and encouraged the rebel leaders. See Durbrow to the Department of State, Telegram 1120, November 23, 1960, CDF 751K.11/11-2360, RG 59, NARA.

13. The committee was renamed the People's Committee against Rebels and Communists. See also Memorandum of Conversation between Joseph Mendenhall and Trần Văn Lắm, November 16, 1960, Folder 90 "VN 1960—Government (General)," Box 1, Entry 5155, General Records of the Department of State, Bureau of East Asian Affairs, Vietnam Desk, Subject Files, 1955–1962, RG 59, NARA. Mendenhall to the Department of State, Dispatch 210, "People's Committee against Rebels and Communists," November 28, 1960, CDF 751K.001/11-2660, RG 59, NARA, contains a detailed study of the group.

14. Durbrow to Department of State, Telegram 1096, CDF 751K.00/11-1760, RG 59, NARA.

15. "Drastic Measures against Rebels Demanded," *Vietnam Press*, November 15, 1960, H.4.

16. "Two Saigon Dailies under Seals," *Vietnam Press*, November 15, 1960, H.3. See also "Offices of Several Newspapers Sealed," *Tự do*, November 13, 1960, FBIS, November 15, 1960, G2. A November 15 broadcast on *Voice of the Republic of Vietnam* by members of the Committee for the Struggle against the Rebels and Communists also singled out these papers and *Đại chúng* as ones that distorted the truth and "heightened the role of the traitorous acts of the rebels." "Four Saigon Newspapers Are Suspended," *Voice of the Republic of Vietnam*, November 15, FBIS, November 16, 1960, G3.

17. Trần Văn Thọ became the director general of information on November 13. See Mendenhall to the Department of State, Dispatch 216, "Dr. Tran Van Tho Appointed Director General of Information," November 30, 1960, CDF 751K.521/11-3060, RG 59, NARA.

18. Nguyễn Đình Thuận Press Conference at the Điện Hồng Palace, November 17, 1960, Folder 98 "VN 1960—Internal Security," Box 1, Entry 5155, General Records of the Department of State, Bureau of East Asian Affairs, Vietnam Desk, Subject Files, 1955–1962, RG 59, NARA. "Newspapers Continue to Hail Government Victory over Rebels," *Vietnam Press* (Morning), November 14, C.1. See also "Tran Van Tho Analyzes Attempted Coup," *Vietnam Press*, November 18, 1960, FBIS, November 21, 1960, G1–G2, which is based upon a November 17 press conference.

19. Press conference transcript, November 14, 1960, 6–8, Folder 350 "Internal Political Affairs: Vietnam—November Coup d'etat," Box 5, Entry 3340B—Vietnam, Saigon Embassy, General Records, 1956–1963, RG 84, NARA. See also Durbrow to Department of State, Telegram 1015, November 11, 1960, CDF 751K.00/11-1160, RG 59, NARA; Durbrow to Department of State, Telegram 1019, November 11, CDF 751K.00/11-1160, RG 59, NARA; and Durbrow to Department of State, Telegram 1025, November 11, CDF 751K.00/11-1160, RG 59, NARA.

20. Colby and Forbath, *Honorable Men: My Life in the CIA*, 164–165.

21. Ahern, *House of Ngo*, 142–143.

22. Durbrow to Department of State, Telegram 1088, November 16, 1960, CDF 751K.00/11-1660, RG 59, NARA; and Durbrow to Department of State, Telegram 1081, November 14, 1960, CDF 751K.00/11-1460, RG 59, NARA. A thirty-four-page transcript of the November 14, 1960, exchange is available at Folder 350 "Internal Political Affairs: Vietnam—November Coup d'etat," Box 5, Entry 3340B—Vietnam, Saigon Embassy, General Records, 1956–1963, RG 84, NARA. Present at the press conference, in addition to Durbrow and McGarr, were the reporters Stanley Karnow, Frank Robertson, François Sully, Bud Briggs, Woody Edwards, G. Leavitt, Jim Robinson, Pepper Martin, James Wilde, and Jacques Nevard.

23. Durbrow to Department of State, Telegram 1088, November 16, 1960, CDF 751K.00/11-1660, RG 59, NARA. See also Durbrow to Department of State, Telegram 1081, November 14, 1960, CDF 751K.00/11-1460, RG 59, NARA.

24. Press conference transcript, November 14, 1960, Folder 350 "Internal Political Affairs: Vietnam—November Coup d'etat," Box 5, Entry 3340B—Vietnam, Saigon Embassy, General Records, 1956–1963, RG 84, NARA. See also Durbrow to the Department of State, Telegram 1081, November 14, 1960, CDF 751K.00/11-1460, RG 59, NARA; and Durbrow to the Department of State, Telegram 1088, November 16, CDF 751K.00/11-1660, RG 59, NARA.

25. Press conference transcript, November 14, 1960, Folder 350 "Internal Political Affairs: Vietnam—November Coup d'etat," Box 5, Entry 3340B—Vietnam, Saigon Embassy, General Records, 1956–1963, RG 84, NARA.

26. Press conference transcript, November 14, 1960, Folder 350 "Internal Political Affairs: Vietnam—November Coup d'etat," Box 5, Entry 3340B—Vietnam, Saigon Embassy, General Records, 1956–1963, RG 84, NARA.

27. Mention of both examples is scattered through the press conference transcript, November 14, 1960, Folder 350 "Internal Political Affairs: Vietnam—November Coup d'etat," Box 5, Entry 3340B—Vietnam, Saigon Embassy, General Records, 1956–1963, RG 84, NARA.

28. Memorandum of Conversation, Sawin and Cunningham, November 14, 1960, Folder 71, "VN 1960—Political Affairs (General), Box 1, Entry 5155, General Records of the Department of State, Bureau of East Asian Affairs, Vietnam Desk, Vietnam Subject Files, 1955–1962, RG 59, NARA.

29. Memorandum of Conversation between Mendenhall and Trần Văn Lắm, November 16, 1960, Folder 90 "VN 1960—Government (General), Box 1, Entry 5155, General Records of the Department of State, Bureau of East Asian Affairs, Vietnam Desk, Subject Files, 1955–1962, RG 59, NARA.

30. Memorandum of Conversation between Cunningham and Trần Đình An, November 16, 1960, Folder 71 "VN 1960—Political Affairs (General)," Box 1, Entry 5155, General Records of the Department of State, Bureau of East Asian Affairs, Vietnam Desk, Subject Files, 1955–1962, RG 59, NARA.

31. Letter from Durbrow to Allen, November 29, 1960, Folder 350 "Internal Political Affairs: Vietnam—November Coup d'etat," Box 5, Entry 3340B—Vietnam, Saigon Embassy, General Records, 1956–1963, RG 84, NARA. See also Luther Allen, "Crisis in Saigon: The Sunday Morning Visitor Returns," *Massachusetts Review* 3, no. 1 (Autumn 1961): 170–187.

32. Letter from Durbrow to Allen, November 29, 1960, Folder 350 "Internal Political Affairs: Vietnam—November Coup d'etat," Box 5, Entry 3340B—Vietnam, Saigon Embassy, General Records, 1956–1963, RG 84, NARA. The Việt Cộng did not take advantage of the abortive coup d'état, in part because the troops were alert and ready for any attempt to do so. See "Provinces Calm during Coup Attempt," *Vietnam Press*, November 16, 1960, FBIS, November 18, 1960, G3.

33. "268 People Wounded in Uprising," *Vietnam Press* (Morning), November 16, 1960, H.5.

34. Examples of which are seen in Memorandum of Conversation between the Reverend John S. Sawin and Francis Cunningham, counselor, Saigon embassy, November 14, 1960, and Memorandum of Conversation between Vietnamese National Assemblymen Trần Văn Lắm and Joseph A. Mendenhall, counselor, Saigon embassy, November 16, 1960. These and other records are found in Folder 71 "VN 1960—Political Affairs (General)," Box 1, Entry 5155, General Records of the Department of State, Bureau of East Asian Affairs, Vietnam Desk, Subject Files, 1955–1962, RG 59, NARA.

35. Memorandum of Conversation between University of Saigon professor of linguistics Nguyễn Đình Hoà; Joseph A. Mendenhall, political counselor; and Thomas F. Conlon, POL, November 30, 1960, Folder 83 "VN 1960—Attempted Coup d'Etat," Box 1, Entry 5155, General Records of the Department of State, Bureau of East Asian Affairs, Vietnam Desk, Vietnam Subject Files, 1955–1962, RG 59, NARA.

36. Durbrow to the Department of State, Telegram 1089, November 16, 1960, CDF 751K.00/11–1660, RG 59, NARA.

37. Durbrow to the Department of State, Telegram 1091, November 16, 1960, CDF 751K.00/11–1660, RG 59, NARA.

38. It did not help that McGarr and Nguyễn Đình Thuận met on November 16 to discuss the abortive coup d'état and the state of the Vietnamese military. There was no indication of what was to come in the press conference. See Mendenhall to the Department of State, Dispatch 208, "Conversation between Chief MAAG and Assistant Secretary of State for National Defense," November 26, 1960, CDF 751K.5/11–2660, RG 59, NARA. A Memorandum of Conversation between McGarr and Nguyễn Đình Thuận is attached as enclosure 1. A memorandum handed to Nguyễn Đình Thuận by Williams on October 28 is attached as enclosure 2.

39. Ironically, no public mention was made of the French press even though it would produce a series of critical reports about Ngô Đình Diệm and the reasons for the coup d'état. It was not until the next week that the RVN went after the French press accounts. See Memorandum of Conversation between Ambassador Trần Văn Chương and Chalmers Wood, article about Viet-Nam in *Le Monde Diplomatique*, Marcel Barthelemy, November 22, 1960, CDF 751K.00/11–2260, RG 59, NARA; and Memorandum of Conversation between first secretary of the French embassy in the U.S. and Chalmers Wood, "Article about Viet-Nam in *Le Monde Diplomatique*," November 22, 1960, CDF 751K.00/11–2260, RG 59, NARA.

40. Nguyễn Đình Thuận press conference at the Điện Hồng Palace, November 17, 1960, 3–12, Folder 98 "VN 1960—Internal Security," Box 1, Entry 5155, General Records of the Department of State, Bureau of East Asian Affairs, Vietnam Desk, Subject Files, 1955–1962, RG 59, NARA. See also "No Foreign Government Involved in Nov. 11 Coup, Presidency Secretary Says," *Vietnam Press* (Morning), November 18, 1960, H.1; and Durbrow to the Department of State, Telegram 1104, November 18, 1960, CDF 751K.00/11–1860, RG 59, NARA.

41. The text of the leaflet is reported in Durbrow to the Department of State, Telegram 1093, November 17, 1960, CDF 751K.00/11–1760, RG 59, NARA; and Durbrow to the Department of State, Telegram 1096, November 17, 1960, CDF 751K.00/11–1760, RG 59, NARA.

42. Nguyễn Đình Thuận press conference at the Điện Hồng Palace, 3, November 17, 1960, Folder 98 "VN 1960—Internal Security," Box 1, Entry 5155, General Records of the Department of State, Bureau of East Asian Affairs, Vietnam Desk, Subject Files, 1955–1962, RG 59, NARA.

43. Nguyễn Đình Thuận press conference at the Điện Hồng Palace, 9, November 17, 1960, Folder 98 "VN 1960—Internal Security," Box 1, Entry 5155, General Records of the Department of State, Bureau of East Asian Affairs, Vietnam Desk, Subject Files, 1955–1962, RG 59, NARA.

44. Memorandum of Conversation, McGarr and Ngô Đình Diệm, November 17, 1960, transmitted to Durbrow, *FRUS, 1958–1960, Volume I: Vietnam*, 677–678.

45. Memorandum of Conversation, McGarr and Ngô Đình Diệm, November 17, 1960, transmitted to Durbrow, *FRUS, 1958–1960, Volume I: Vietnam*, 677–678.

46. Memorandum of Conversation, McGarr and Ngô Đình Diệm, November 17, 1960, transmitted to Durbrow as noted in footnote 2, *FRUS, 1958–1960, Volume I: Vietnam*, 677. Mendenhall would continue to report conversations of corruption by the Ngo family

that he had with Vietnamese, see Folder 92 "VN 1960—Presidency," Box 2, Entry 5155, General Records of the Department of State, Bureau of East Asian Affairs, Vietnam Desk, Subject Files, 1955–1962, RG 59, NARA.

47. Memorandum of Conversation, McGarr and Ngô Đình Diệm, November 17, 1960, transmitted to Durbrow as noted in footnote 3, *FRUS, 1958–1960, Volume I: Vietnam*, 678.

48. Durbrow to the Department of State, Telegram 1099, November 18, 1960, CDF 751K.00/11–1860, RG 59, NARA.

49. Durbrow to the Department of State, Telegram 1105, November 18, 1960, CDF 751K.00/11–1860, RG 59, NARA.

50. Durbrow to the Department of State, Telegram 1107, November 19, 1960, CDF 751K.00/11–1860, RG 59, NARA. Foreign Press accounts of the abortive coup d'état that discussed the reasons it had occurred were highly critical of Ngô Đình Diệm.

51. Memorandum of Conversation, "Vietnamese Pamphlet Alleging Americans Involved in Coup Attempt," November 18, 1960, CDF 751K.00/11–1860, RG 59, NARA.

52. Memorandum of Conversation, "Vietnamese Pamphlet Alleging Americans Involved in Coup Attempt," November 18, 1960, CDF 751K.00/11–1860, RG 59, NARA.

53. State Department to Durbrow, Telegram 1103, November 18, 1960, CDF 751K.00/11–1860, RG 59, NARA.

54. Durbrow to the Department of State, Telegram 1105, November 18, 1960, CDF 751K.00/11–1860, RG 59, NARA.

55. The committee eventually lost influence as a result of the leaflets that had accused the United States, France, and Britain of being involved in the abortive coup d'état. By November 21, Durbrow no longer considered the group a real threat to American interests. See Durbrow to the Department of State, Telegram 1114, November 21, 1960, CDF 751K.00/11–2160, RG 59, NARA; and Durbrow to the Department of State, Telegram 1115, November 21, 1960, CDF 751K.00/11–2160, RG 59, NARA.

56. Durbrow to the Department of State, Telegram 1105, November 18, 1960, *FRUS, 1958–1960, Volume I: Vietnam*, 685.

57. The Department of State instructions are located in Telegram 806 to Saigon as noted in footnote 10, *FRUS, 1958–1960, Volume I: Vietnam*, 685.

58. Durbrow to the Department of State, Telegram 1119, November 23, 1960, CDF 751K.00/11–2360, RG 59, NARA.

59. Memorandum on the substance of discussion at a Department of State–JCS meeting in the Pentagon, Washington, November 18, 1960, *FRUS, 1958–1960, Volume I: Vietnam*, 681–682.

60. Memorandum on the substance of discussion at a Department of State–JCS meeting in the Pentagon, Washington, November 18, 1960, *FRUS, 1958–1960, Volume I: Vietnam*, 682.

61. Durbrow believed his repeated calls to avoid a bloodbath were justified given the People's Counter-Coup d'État Committee's broadcast of November 15 and his fear that Ngô Đình Diệm would need to retaliate. See "Call for Surrender of Traitors," *Voice of the Republic of Vietnam*, November 15, 1960, FBIS, November 16, 1960, G2.

62. Durbrow to the Department of State, Telegram 1130, November 27, 1960, CDF 751K.5811/11–2760 HBS, RG 59, NARA.

63. Durbrow to the Department of State, Telegram 1130, November 27, 1960, CDF 751K.5811/11–2760 HBS, RG 59, NARA.

64. Lansdale to Parsons, November 29, 1960, *FRUS, 1958–1960, Volume I: Vietnam*, 692–693. For French's version of the episode, see the Memorandum from Jerome T. French of the Office of Special Operations, Department of Defense, to the Secretary of Defense's assistant for special operations, General Graves B. Erskine, December 6, 1960, *FRUS, 1958–1960, Volume I: Vietnam*, 713–717.

65. French to Erskine, December 6, 1960, *FRUS, 1958–1960, Volume I: Vietnam*, 713–717.

66. In a conversation with Jerome French at the 2008 Texas Tech University Vietnam Symposium, the author asked him about the affair. He maintained that he did not dismiss his escort because, in fact, he did not have one. He did have a driver, but he did not think it was necessary to have him at a lunch with his Vietnamese friends. French also was surprised to learn of the uproar that he had created when he visited Saigon, as his visit with his Vietnamese friends was personal rather than official. That Durbrow, given the nature of his need for control, saw it differently should not be surprising.

67. French to Erskine, December 6, 1960, *FRUS, 1958–1960, Volume I: Vietnam*, 716.

68. "Cuu States Aims of People's Committee," *Times of Vietnam*, November 25, 1960, FBIS, November 28, 1960, G1.

69. Durbrow to the Department of State, Telegram 1129, November 26, 1960, *FRUS, 1958–1960, Volume I: Vietnam*, 688–691.

70. "Defence Department to Train Civil Guard," *Vietnam Press* (Morning), November 23, 1960, H.3.

Chapter 9

1. While the committee announced on November 25 that it would extend its activities into the provinces, the chairman of the group, Trương Công Cửu, announced on November 29 that they would receive no more contributions from the public starting on December 1. Mendenhall to the Department of State, Dispatch 220, "December 1, 1960, WEEKA 49, for State, Army, Navy, and Air Departments from SANA," December 2, 1960, CDF 751K.00(W)/12–260, RG 59, NARA.

2. Ngô Đình Diệm's annoyance is expressed in various conversations with American leaders. See Memorandum for File, interview with the president of the Republic of Vietnam, G.P. Case and S.M. Strasburger, December 30, 1960, Folder 91 "VN 1960—Chief of Executive Ngo Dinh Diem," Box 1, Entry 5155, General Records of the Department of State, Bureau of East Asian Affairs, Vietnam Desk, Subject Files, 1955–1962, RG 59, NARA. Statements by international leaders include Australian minister for external affairs Sir Robert G. Menzies' remarks to the Australian House of

Representatives, December 6, 1960, Folder 30 "VN 1960 GVN Australian Relations," Box 1, Entry 5155, General Records of the Department of State, Bureau of East Asian Affairs, Vietnam Desk, Subject Files, 1955–1962, RG 59, NARA; and "Australian Premier Urges More Western Understanding and Support for Viet Nam," *Vietnam Press* (Evening), December 8, 1960, H.1.

3. Outline plan prepared by the Military Assistance Advisory Group, Vietnam, October 27, 1960, *FRUS, 1958–1960, Volume I: Vietnam*, 613–620.

4. Durbrow to Parsons, November 8, 1960, *FRUS, 1958–1960, Volume I: Vietnam*, 626–631.

5. McGarr to Felt, November 21, 1960, with MAAG comments on recommended 20,000 increase in RVNAF force level, Folder 16 "VN 1960—Embassy Saigon, Official-Informal Miscellaneous Letters," Box 1, Entry 5155, General Records of the Department of State, Bureau of East Asian Affairs, Vietnam Desk, Subject Files, 1955–1962, RG 59, NARA.

6. McGarr to Felt, November 21, 1960, Box 1, Entry 5155, General Records of the Department of State, Bureau of East Asian Affairs, Vietnam Desk, Subject Files, 1955–1962, RG 59, NARA.

7. McGarr to Felt, November 21, 1960, Box 1, Entry 5155, General Records of the Department of State, Bureau of East Asian Affairs, Vietnam Desk, Subject Files, 1955–1962, RG 59, NARA.

8. Durbrow to Parsons, November 30, 1960, Folder 16 "VN 1960—Embassy Saigon, Official-Informal Miscellaneous Letters," Box 1, Entry 5155, General Records of the Department of State, Bureau of East Asian Affairs, Vietnam Desk, Subject Files, 1955–1962, RG 59, NARA.

9. Durbrow to the Department of State, Telegram 1156, December 7, 1960, CDF 751K.00/12–760, RG 59, NARA. The actual decree is located in Airgram G-245, December 8, 1960, CDF 751K.00/12–860, RG 59, NARA.

10. Durbrow to the Department of State, Airgram G-240, December 3, 1960, CDF 751K.5-MSP/12–360, RG 59, NARA.

11. Durbrow to Parsons, November 30, 1960, *FRUS, 1958–1960, Volume I: Vietnam*, 694–703.

12. Special staff note prepared by the Department of Defense as noted in footnote 2, *FRUS, 1958–1960, Volume I: Vietnam*, 705.

13. "AD-6 Aircraft Replaces F8F Fighter," *Vietnam Press* (Morning), November 24, 1960, H.5. See also Ronald Frankum, *Like Rolling Thunder*, 185.

14. "U.S. Submarine Chaser Transferred to Viet Nam Navy," *Vietnam Press* (Evening), November 25, 1960, H.1–H.3. The VNS *Vân Đồn* arrived in Saigon on March 24 to much fanfare and ceremony; "VNS Van Don Arrives," *Vietnam Press* (Evening), March 24, 1961, H.4–H.5; and "VNS Van Don Official Commissioned in Vietnamese Navy," *Vietnam Press* (Morning), March 25, 1961, H.4.

15. Durbrow to the Department of State, Telegram 1143, December 1, 1960, CDF 751K.00/12–160, RG 59, NARA.

16. Durbrow to the Department of State, Telegram 1204, December 22, 1960, CDF 751K.00/12–2260, RG 59, NARA. See also Mendenhall to the Department of State, Dispatch 249, "Suspension of Conscription," December 16, 1960, CDF 751K.5511/12–1660 HBS, RG 59, NARA.

17. Mendenhall to the Department of State, Dispatch 227, "December 3 Press Conference of New Director General of Information," December 9, 1960, CDF 751K.00/12–960, RG 59, NARA.

18. *Cách mạng Quốc gia* editorial, December 1, 1960, FBIS, December 1, 1960, G1. Another article in *Cách mạng Quốc gia* on December 11 echoed the earlier call and compared inefficient or corrupt officials as dangerous as the communists trying to subvert the authorities in the RVN. "Overbearing Officials Endanger Regime," *Cách mạng Quốc gia*, December 11, 1960, FBIS, December 14, 1960, G1.

19. "General Director of Information Makes Contact with the Press," *Vietnam Press* (Evening), December 3, 1960, H.4.

20. "Public Relations Service Created at Information Center," *Vietnam Press* (Morning), December 10, 1960, H.1.

21. "Three New Dailies Here," *Vietnam Press* (Morning), December 21, 1960, H.4.

22. "Propriety Key to Freedom of the Press," *Times of Vietnam*, December 7, 1960, FBIS, December 9, 1960. *Sài Gòn Mới* was a political newspaper that was pro–Ngô Đình Diệm. See Nguyễn Thái, "South Vietnam," in *The Asian Newspapers' Reluctant Revolution*, 243.

23. Durbrow to the Department of State, Telegram 1150, December 4, 1960, CDF 751K.00/12–460, RG 59, NARA. See also Karnow, *Vietnam: A History*, 235; and Anderson, *Trapped by Success*, 195.

24. Durbrow to the Department of State, Dispatch 209, "November 26, 1960, WEEKA 48, for State, Army, Navy, Air Departments from SANA," November 26, 1960, CDF 751K.00(W)/11–2660, RG 59, NARA.

25. Mendenhall to the Department of State, Dispatch 244, "Whereabouts of Dr. Phan Quang Dan, and Phan Huy Quat," December 15, 1960, CDF 751K.00/12–1560, RG 59, NARA. A Memorandum of Conversation between Mendenhall and Andre Lane, president of Brownell, Lane International, Ltd., is attached. Buttinger, *Vietnam: A Dragon Embattled*, 964.

26. A December 15 English broadcast from Phnom Penh maintained that he had been arrested and offered the rumor that he had been convicted in a secret trial. "Doctor Dan Reported Arrested, Tried," FBIS, December 16, 1960, G2.

27. Vietnamese continued to press for information about Dr. Phan Quang Đán as the year ended. See the December 27, 1960, letter from Huynh Sanh Thong to Secretary of State Christian Herter, CDF 751K.00/12–2760, RG 59, NARA.

28. Durbrow to the Department of State, Telegram 1151, December 4, 1960, CDF 751K.00/12–460, RG 59, NARA.

29. Dixon to the Department of State, Dispatch 343, "Conversation with Dang-Doc-Khoi concerning the Past Coup Government of President Diem of Vietnam," November 8, 1960, CDF 751K.00/12–860, RG 59, NARA. A Memorandum of Conversation is attached to the telegram. A few days later, another airgram from the U.S. embassy in Bangkok reported that Wolf Ladejinsky completely dismissed the position of Đặng Độc Khôi, arguing that his positive attitude was only a front to the real problems in Saigon. See U.S. ambassador to

Thailand, U. Alexis Johnson, to the Department of State, Airgram G-208, December 13, 1960, CDF 751K.00/12-1360, RG 59, NARA.

30. "S. Vietnam Has No True Opposition Party," *Voice of the Republic of Vietnam*, November 30, 1960, FBIS, December 2, 1960, G1-G2. While there is no Mendenhall reaction to the broadcast, it seems fair to argue that he would have dismissed it as government propaganda, with the denial of a legitimate opposition party by the Saigon government serving as proof that it actually did exist.

31. See Durbrow to the Department of State, Dispatch 230, "Misgivings of Air Force Commander on Prospects for Effective Reform in the GVN," December 10, 1960, CDF 751K.00/12-1060, RG 59, NARA. A Memorandum of Conversation is attached to the dispatch.

32. Mendenhall to the Department of State, Dispatch 240, "Views of GVN Official on Political Situation Following Attempted Coup d'Etat," December 15, 1960, CDF 751K.00/12-1560, RG 59, NARA. A Memorandum of Conversation between Andrew Fink from the American embassy in Saigon and Colonel Hoàng Thùy Nam, chief of the RVN mission charged with relations with the ICC, is attached.

33. Mendenhall to the Department of State, Dispatch 259, "Conversation with Nguyen Dinh Quat," December 22, 1960, CDF 751K.00/12-2260, RG 59, NARA. A Memorandum of Conversation between Mendenhall and Nguyễn Đình Quát is attached. Mendenhall to the Department of State, Dispatch 261, "Political Views of Nguyen Phuong Thiep, Member of the National Assembly," December 23, 1960, CDF 751K.00/12-2360, RG 59, NARA. Three memoranda of conversation between Mendenhall and Nguyễn Phương Thiệp dated December 5, December 12, and December 20 are attached.

34. Durbrow to the Department of State, Dispatch 269, "Conversation with Chinese Ambassador Concerning Situation in Viet-Nam," December 28, 1960, CDF 751K.00/12-2860, RG 59, NARA. A Memorandum of Conversation between Durbrow and Yuen Tse Kien is attached.

35. Herter to Durbrow, Telegram 862, December 9, 1960, *FRUS, 1958-1960, Volume I: Vietnam*, 720-721.

36. Daniel V. Anderson to Parsons, "Memorandum on Talk with Mr. Merchant on Vietnamese Force Level," December 6, 1960, Folder 108 "VN 1960—National Defense Affairs (General)," Box 2, Entry 5155, General Records of the Department of State, Bureau of East Asian Affairs, Vietnam Desk, Subject Files, 1955-1962, RG 59, NARA.

37. Daniel V. Anderson to Parsons, "Memorandum on Talk with Mr. Merchant on Vietnamese Force Level," December 6, 1960, Folder 108 "VN 1960—National Defense Affairs (General)," Box 2, Entry 5155, General Records of the Department of State, Bureau of East Asian Affairs, Vietnam Desk, Subject Files, 1955-1962, RG 59, NARA.

38. Durbrow characterized the Self-Defense Force as a part-time, semi-uniformed, poorly armed village defense force, that was nominally under the control of the province chiefs. On December 17, he notified Washington that the Self-Defense Force had increased from approximately 40,000 in August to 48,900 in October.

Durbrow to the Department of State, Airgram G-257, December 17, 1960, CDF 751K.5-MSP/12-1760, RG 59, NARA.

39. Wood to Anderson, "Diem's Resentment," December 2, 1960, Folder 91 "VN 1960—Chief of Executive Ngo Dinh Diem," Box 2, Entry 5155, General Records of the Department of State, Bureau of East Asian Affairs, Vietnam Desk, Vietnam Subject Files, 1955-1962, RG 59, NARA.

40. Durbrow to the Department of State, Telegram 1175, December 15, 1960, CDF 751K.00/12-1560, RG 59, NARA. See also Durbrow to the Department of State, Telegram 1176, December 15, 1960, CDF 751K.00/12-1560, RG 59, NARA.

41. "Pope Creates Ecclesiastical Hierarchy throughout Viet Nam," *Vietnam Press* (Morning), December 8, 1960, H.1-H.3a; and "Almost Two Million Vietnamese Catholics," *Vietnam Press* (Evening), December 15, 1960, H.1-H.2. The *Osservatore Romano*, in reporting the Holy See dispatch, noted that the number of Catholics in Vietnam had increased from 812,000 in 1900 to 1,807,784 in 1960, with 393,819 in the new Hue archbishopric, 620,965 in the Saigon archbishopric, and 793,000 in the Hanoi archbishopric. The number of Catholic priests was 480, 650, and 321, respectively.

42. "Catholics Welcome Ecclesiastical Hierarchy in Viet Nam," *Vietnam Press* (Evening), December 10, 1960, H.1-H.3.

43. "Services Marking Establishment of Ecclesiastical Hierarchy in Viet Nam," *Vietnam Press* (Morning), December 19, 1960, H.1-H.4.

44. Mendenhall to the Department of State, Dispatch 250, "U.S. Reporter's Praise of Civil and Military Morale in Southern Viet-Nam," December 17, 1960, CDF 751K.00/12-1760, RG 59, NARA. A letter from public affairs officer John M. Anspacher to Durbrow is enclosed with the dispatch.

45. Anderson to Parsons, "General Lansdale's Call at 3 p.m. Today," December 19, 1960, Folder 20 "GVN 1961—General Lansdale," Box 3, Entry 5155, General Records of the Department of State, Bureau of East Asian Affairs, Vietnam Desk, Subject Files, 1955-1962, RG 59, NARA.

46. Felt to the Office of the Secretary of Defense, Telegram 102203Z, December 10, 1960, *FRUS, 1958-1960, Volume I: Vietnam*, 729.

47. Felt to the Office of the Secretary of Defense, Telegram 102203Z, December 10, 1960, as noted in footnote 2, *FRUS, 1958-1960, Volume I: Vietnam*, 729. It refers to Telegram Def 987048 to CINCPAC sent on December 9, 1960, that outlined Felt's instructions for Lansdale.

48. Lansdale Memorandum "Trip to Asia" to Douglas, December 14, 1960, *FRUS, 1958-1960, Volume I: Vietnam*, 730. See also footnote 3 in the same document that refers to message Def 987217 to CINCPAC dated December 14, 1960, that contains Douglas' reply to Felt.

49. Acting Secretary of State Steeves to Durbrow, Telegram 898, December 16, 1960, CDF 751K.00/12-1560, RG 59, NARA.

50. Acting Secretary of State Steeves to Durbrow, December 20, 1960, *FRUS, 1958-1960, Volume I: Vietnam*, 737-738.

51. Steeves to Durbrow, December 20, 1960, *FRUS, 1958-1960, Volume I: Vietnam*, 738.

52. Durbrow to the Department of State, Telegram 1216, December 24, 1960, CDF 751K.00/12-2360, RG 59, NARA; and Durbrow to the Department of State, Dispatch 264, "Memorandum Handed to President Diem on Liberalization," December 27, 1960, CDF 751K.00/12-2760, RG 59, NARA. The memorandum is attached.

53. Durbrow to the Department of State, Dispatch 264, "Memorandum Handed to President Diem on Liberalization," December 27, 1960, CDF 751K.00/12-2760, RG 59, NARA. The Saigon government continued to have problems with the French press and focused much of its ire, when not directed at the United States, on it. Mendenhall to the Department of State, Dispatch 294, "GVN-Inspired Magazine Article Attacks Western Press Coverage of *Coup d'Etat*," January 12, 1961, CDF 751K.00/1-1261, RG 59, NARA. Attached to this dispatch are copies from the *Vietnam Press*.

54. *Tiếng Chuông* editorial, December 22, 1960, FBIS, December 22, 1960, G3. While it might be an overstatement to suggest that the reporters did what they did for commercial purposes, it is fair to assume that the Vietnamese press was disgruntled with how the French and Americans were reporting. *Lê Sống* offered a similar position on December 26. *Le Song* editorial, December 26, 1960, FBIS, December 28, 1960, G3.

55. Acting Secretary of State Steeves letter to Durbrow, December 20, 1960, *FRUS, 1958-1960, Volume I: Vietnam*, 737-738.

56. "Republic of Viet Nam Protests against Violations of Geneva Agreements by Viet Cong," *Vietnam Press* (Evening), December 19, 1960, H.3-H.4.

57. Durbrow to the Department of State, Telegram 1217, December 24, 1960, CDF 751K.00/12-2460, RG 59, NARA.

58. Durbrow to the Department of State, Telegram 1217, December 24, 1960, CDF 751K.00/12-2460, RG 59, NARA.

59. Parsons to Durbrow, Telegram 961, December 29, 1960, CDF 751K.00/12-2960, RG 59, NARA.

60. Central Intelligence Agency Information Report, December 9, 1960, *FRUS, 1958-1960, Volume I: Vietnam*, 721-728.

61. Central Intelligence Agency Information Report, December 9, 1960, as noted in footnote 4, *FRUS, 1958-1960, Volume I: Vietnam*, 723. This document carried Mendenhall's handwritten note in the margin.

62. Memorandum of Conversation between Pauline Thọ, Nguyễn Văn Thọ, and Joseph Mendenhall, "Phan Khac Suu and Activities of National Assembly," December 2, 3, and 6, 1960, Folder 94 "VN 1960—Legislative Branch—National Assembly," Box 2, Entry 5155, General Records of the Department of State, Bureau of East Asian Affairs, Vietnam Desk, Subject Files, 1955-1962, RG 59, NARA.

63. It was estimated that there were 9,820 hard-core Việt Cộng in the RVN as of December 6. This was a significant increase from the 7,000 estimated for September. Durbrow to the Department of State, Airgram G-275, January 7, 1961, CDF 751K.5-MSP/1-761, RG 59, NARA.

64. Durbrow to the Department of State, Telegram 1231, December 29, 1960, *FRUS, 1958-1960, Volume I: Vietnam*, 749-750; and "Republic of Viet Nam Protests against Violations of Geneva Agreements by Viet Cong," *Vietnam Press* (Evening), December 19, 1960, H.3-H.4.

65. Gerald DeGroot, *A Noble Cause: America and the Vietnam War*, 69-70.

66. Duiker, *Sacred War*, 128-134. See also Cooper, *Lost Crusade*, 158; and Race, *War Comes to Long An*, 121-122.

67. The NLF was recognized in a Hanoi broadcast on January 26, 1961. See Colby, *Lost Victory*, 81.

68. "National Assembly Votes VN$105 Million Foreign Department Budget," *Vietnam Press* (Morning), December 17, 1960, H.4; "National Assembly Begins Debate on 1961 National Budget," *Vietnam Press* (Evening), December 13, 1960, H.1-H.2; "Assembly Approves VN$397-Million Health Budget," *Vietnam Press* (Single), December 18, 1960, H.1; and "National Assembly Votes VN$ 2,162 Million Budget for Interior Department," *Vietnam Press* (Morning), December 20, 1960, H.1-H.2.

69. "Assembly Votes VN$109 Million Justice Budget," *Vietnam Press* (Evening), December 20, 1960, H.1; "Assembly Discusses Education Budget," *Vietnam Press* (Evening), December 23, 1960, H.2; "Assembly Votes VN$912, 487,000 Education Budget, *Vietnam Press* (Morning), December 24, 1960, H.5; "Assembly Votes Presidency and Connected Services Budgets," *Vietnam Press* (Morning), December 27, 1960, H.2; "Assembly Votes VN$140 Million Information Budget," *Vietnam Press* (Evening), December 27, 1960, H.1; Assembly Votes on VN$175 Million Budget for Agriculture," *Vietnam Press* (Evening), December 28, 1960, H.3; and "VN$386 Million Budget Voted for Finance Department," *Vietnam Press* (Evening), December 29, 1960, H.6. Within the total budget, the Foreign Affairs Department received VN$105,843,000 and the Health Department received VN$396,708,000, which was more than originally planned, in order to increase the drug supplies and rural health development program. The Department of the Interior received VN$2,162,146,000 to further develop its administrative measures, including the creation of new village councils and improving intelligence operations at the village level. The Education Department received VN$912,487,000, which exceeded its total from the previous year by VN$116,487,000. The National Assembly also voted on a budget of VN$302,799,000 for the Office of the President of the Republic, with an additional VN$609,134,000 for services connected to the office, while it allocated VN$140,032,000 for the Information General Office, VN$175,046,000 for the Agriculture Department, and VN$386,511,000 for the Department of Finance. The Public Works Department received VN$1,256,823,000 while the Justice Department received VN$108,881,000 from the budget to increase the number of magistrates and replace the Courts of Peace with tribunals with extended powers.

70. "National Assembly Debates on Constitutional Court," *Vietnam Press* (Morning), December 21, 1960, H.1-H.2.

71. "Heated Debates Over Immunity of Constitutional Court Members," *Vietnam Press* (Evening), December 21, 1960, H.2-H.3.

72. "Constitutional Court Voted," *Vietnam Press* (Morning), December 22, 1960, H.2-H.3.

73. Mendenhall to the Department of State, Dis-

patch 329, "Establishment of the Constitutional Court," January 31, 1961, CDF 751K.34/1-3161, RG 59, NARA. A copy of the thirty-article decree is attached to the dispatch. See also "Constitutional Court Promulgated," *Vietnam Press* (Morning), December 27, 1960, H.1.

74. "Committee to Consider Draft on Presidential Election Procedures," *Vietnam Press* (Evening), December 23, 1960, H.3.

75. "Assembly Votes on Draft for Presidential Election Procedure," *Vietnam Press* (Morning), December 31, 1960, H.1–H.3.

76. "National Assembly Ends Second Ordinary Session," *Vietnam Press* (Evening), December 31, 1960, H.1.

77. "Charnel House of Viet Cong Victims Uncovered," *Vietnam Press* (Evening), December 31, 1960, H.2–H.3.

Chapter 10

1. Durbrow to the Department of State, January 3, 1961, Folder 361.1 "Executive. Royal Family Vietnam: Ngo Dinh Diem, 1951–1961," Box 6, Entry 3340B, RG 84, NARA.

2. "Religious Ceremonies Mark President's 60th Birthday," *Vietnam Press* (Morning), January 3, 1961, H.1; "Cong Hoa Youth Pledges Loyalty to President and Republican Regime," *Vietnam Press* (Morning), January 4, 1961, H.1–H.4; and "President Receives Birthday Well Wishers," *Vietnam Press* (Morning), January 4, 1961, H.5.

3. Presentation of Paul Revere bowl to President Ngô Đình Diệm, Folder 361.1 "Executive. Royal Family Vietnam: Ngo Dinh Diem, 1951–1961," Box 6, Entry 3340B, RG 84, NARA; and "President Receives Gift from Boston," *Vietnam Press* (Evening), January 4, 1961, H.1–H.2. Whether Durbrow really believed it essential to win over Ngô Đình Diệm is unclear. When the Thailand ambassador extraordinary and plenipotentiary, Pramote Chongeharoen, announced that he would be ending his tenure in Saigon to take up a new diplomatic post, Durbrow became the senior foreign diplomat in the Republic of Vietnam and was named the dean of the diplomatic corps. There is no indication that Durbrow used this position to improve his relationship with Ngô Đình Diệm; he seemed to be more focused on leaving. See "Thai Ambassador Advocates Closer Ties between His Country and Viet Nam," *Vietnam Press* (Evening), February 24, 1961, H.3–H.3; and "US Ambassador Is Dean of Diplomatic Corps," *Vietnam Press* (Morning), February 25, 1961, H.2.

4. *Basic Counterinsurgency Plan for Viet Nam* prepared by the Country Team Staff Committee, January 4, 1961, *FRUS, 1961–1963, Volume I: Vietnam,* 1961, 1–12. A copy of Appendix IV to Annex C is located in CDF 751K.5-MSP/1-661, RG 59, NARA. Tab A to this appendix is located in CDF 751K.5/MSP/1-961, RG 59, NARA. Tab C to this appendix is located in CDF 751K.5/MSP/1-2561, RG 59, NARA. Tab A to Appendix IV of Annex B is located in CDF 751K.5-MSP/2-1361, RG 59, NARA.

5. Lansdale to Gates, January 17, 1961, Folder 20 "GVN 1961—General Lansdale," Box 3, Entry 5155, General Records of the Department of State, Bureau of East Asian Affairs, Vietnam Desk, Vietnam Subject Files, 1955–1962, RG 59, NARA.

6. Lansdale had several conversations with Ngô Đình Diệm as well as local Americans and old Vietnamese friends in Saigon and in the provinces that served as the basis for his report. See Lansdale to Gates, January 17, 1961, Folder 20 "GVN 1961—General Lansdale," Box 3, Entry 5155, General Records of the Department of State, Bureau of East Asian Affairs, Vietnam Desk, Vietnam Subject Files, 1955–1962, RG 59, NARA. See Anderson, *Trapped by Success,* 175, 195–196.

7. Lansdale to Gates, January 17, 1961, Folder 20 "GVN 1961—General Lansdale," Box 3, Entry 5155, General Records of the Department of State, Bureau of East Asian Affairs, Vietnam Desk, Vietnam Subject Files, 1955–1962, RG 59, NARA.

8. Fred I. Greenstein and Richard H. Immerman, "What Did Eisenhower Tell Kennedy about Indochina? The Politics of Misperception," *Journal of American History* 79 (1992): 568–587. See also Cooper, *Lost Crusade,* 170–172.

9. Lansdale to Gates, January 17, 1961, Folder 20 "GVN 1961—General Lansdale," Box 3, Entry 5155, General Records of the Department of State, Bureau of East Asian Affairs, Vietnam Desk, Vietnam Subject Files, 1955–1962, RG 59, NARA. See also Jones, *Death of a Generation,* 20–22.

10. Lansdale to Gates, January 17, 1961, Folder 20 "GVN 1961—General Lansdale," Box 3, Entry 5155, General Records of the Department of State, Bureau of East Asian Affairs, Vietnam Desk, Vietnam Subject Files, 1955–1962, RG 59, NARA. See also Cooper, *Lost Crusade,* 169.

11. Lansdale to Gates, January 17, 1961, Folder 20 "GVN 1961—General Lansdale," Box 3, Entry 5155, General Records of the Department of State, Bureau of East Asian Affairs, Vietnam Desk, Vietnam Subject Files, 1955–1962, RG 59, NARA.

12. Lansdale to Gates, January 17, 1961, Folder 20 "GVN 1961—General Lansdale," Box 3, Entry 5155, General Records of the Department of State, Bureau of East Asian Affairs, Vietnam Desk, Vietnam Subject Files, 1955–1962, RG 59, NARA.

13. Lansdale to Gates, January 17, 1961, Folder 20 "GVN 1961—General Lansdale," Box 3, Entry 5155, General Records of the Department of State, Bureau of East Asian Affairs, Vietnam Desk, Vietnam Subject Files, 1955–1962, RG 59, NARA.

14. Memorandum of Conversation between Cunningham and Lê Trung Nghĩa, "Political Situation in Viet-Nam," January 21, 1961, Folder 14 "GVN 1961—Political Situation—General," Box 2, Entry 5155, General Records of the Department of State, Bureau of East Asian Affairs, Vietnam Desk, Vietnam Subject Files, 1955–1962, RG 59, NARA.

15. Summary Record of a Meeting, the White House, January 28, 1961, *FRUS, 1961–1963, Volume I: Vietnam,* 1961, 13–15. See also Kahin, *Intervention,* 129–131; and Karnow, *Vietnam: A History,* 248–249.

16. See Morgan, *The Vietnam Lobby: The American Friends of Vietnam, 1955–1975,* 8 and 41; and James T. Fisher, "The Second Catholic President: Ngo Dinh

Diem, John F. Kennedy, and the Vietnam Lobby, 1954–1963," *U.S. Catholic Historian* 15, no. 3, Catholics in a Non-Catholic World, part 2 (Summer 1997): 130–132.

17. Memorandum from the president's deputy special assistant for national security affairs, Walt W. Rostow, to the president's special assistant for national security affairs, William P. Bundy, January 30, 1961, Folder "General, 1/61–3/61," Box 193, National Security Country Files, Vietnam Files, John F. Kennedy Presidential Library, Boston, Massachusetts [hereafter referred to as NSF: Vietnam, JFK].

18. Notes on a Meeting between Rusk and Parsons, January 28, 1961, *FRUS, 1961–1963, Volume I: Vietnam*, 19–20. See also Jones, *Death of a Generation*, 23–38.

19. Ladejinsky did meet with Ngô Đình Diệm on January 24 for a farewell call and did inform the president that the RVN, when compared to Indonesia where Ladejinsky had just visited, was doing much better but still needed to seek reforms. Durbrow to the Department of State, Dispatch 330, "Conversation with Mr. Wolf Ladejinsky," January 31, 1961, CDF 751K.00/1-3161, RG 59, NARA. See also Memorandum of Conversation, "Viet-Nam" between Trần Văn Chương, Nguyễn Duy Liên, Daniel Anderson, and Chalmers Wood regarding Trần Văn Chương's visit with Ladejinsky, CDF 751K.00/2-1461, RG 59, NARA. See also Memorandum of Conversation between Ladejinsky and Wood, February 20, 1961, CDF 751K.00/2-2061, RG 59, NARA.

20. Memorandum for Rusk and McNamara, January 30, 1961, Folder "General, 1/61–3/61," Box 193, NSF: Vietnam, JFK.

21. Durbrow to the Department of State, Telegram 1366, February 13, 1961, CDF 751K.5-MSP/2-1361, RG 59, NARA. See also Cooper, *Lost Crusade*, 169–170.

22. Lansdale to Ngô Đình Diệm, January 30, 1961, *FRUS, 1961–1963, Volume I: Vietnam*, 20–24.

23. Lansdale to CINCPAC, Telegram 172157Z as noted in footnote 2, *FRUS, 1961–1963, Volume I: Vietnam*, 1961, 25.

24. Durbrow to the Department of State, Telegram 1329, January 31, 1961, CDF 751K.00/1-3161, RG 59, NARA.

25. Durbrow to the Department of State, Airgram G-326, February 7, 1961, CDF 751K.00/2-761 HBS, RG 59, NARA.

26. Durbrow to the Department of State, Telegram 1349, February 7, 1961, CDF 751K.00/2-761; Durbrow to the Department of State, Telegram 1351, February 8, 1961, CDF 751K.00/2-861 HBS, RG 59, NARA; and Durbrow to the Department of State, Dispatch 350, "February 10, 1961 WEEKA No. 6 for State, Army, Navy, and Air Departments for SANA," February 13, 1961, CDF 751K.00(W)/2-1361, RG 59, NARA.

27. Durbrow to the Department of State, Airgram G-342, February 14, 1961, CDF 751K.00/2-1461 HBS, RG 59, NARA.

28. Mendenhall to the Department of State, Airgram G-364, March 2, 1961, CDF 751K.00/3-261 HBS, RG 59, NARA; and Durbrow to the Department of State, Airgram G-376, March 11, 1961, CDF 751K.00/3-161 HBS, RG 59, NARA. Other examples are listed in Mendenhall to the Department of State, Airgram G-406, March 30, 1961, CDF 751K.00/3-3061, RG 59, NARA.

29. Durbrow to the Department of State, Telegram 1329, January 31, 1961, CDF 751K.00/1-3161, RG 59, NARA.

30. Komer to Rostow, "Forestalling a Crisis in South Vietnam," February 1, 1961, Folder "General, 1/61–3/61," Box 193, NSF: Vietnam, JFK. See also Mann, *A Grand Delusion*, 228.

31. Komer to Rostow, "Forestalling a Crisis in South Vietnam," February 1, 1961, Folder "General, 1/61–3/61," Box 193, NSF: Vietnam, JFK.

32. Department of State to Durbrow, Telegram 276, February 3, 1961, Folder "General, 1/61–3/61," Box 193, NSF: Vietnam, JFK. See also Mann, *A Grand Delusion*, 227–228.

33. National Security Action Memorandum Number 12, February 6, 1961, Folder 12 "Re: Distribution of forces in Vietnam (2/6/61)," Box 328, National Security Files: National Security Action Memoranda (NSAM) [NSF: NSAM], JFK.

34. Catton, *Diem's Final Failure*, 75.

35. Durbrow to the Department of State, Telegram 1349, February 7, 1961, Folder 350 "Internal Political Affairs: Vietnam, 1959–1961," Box 5, Entry 3340B, RG 84, NARA; Parsons to Rusk, "Viet-Nam—President Ngo Dinh Diem's Reforms (For Use on Hill Today)," February 15, 1961, Box 2, Entry 5155, General Records of the Department of State, Bureau of East Asian Affairs, Vietnam Desk, Vietnam Subject Files, 1955–1962, RG 59, NARA; and Durbrow to the Department of State, Telegram 1351, February 8, 1961, CDF 751K.00/2-861, RG 59, NARA. See also "Changes in Ministerial Department Envisaged," *Vietnam Press* (Morning), February 7, 1961, H.8–H.9.

36. Durbrow to the Department of State, Telegram 1351, February 8, 1961, CDF 751K.00/2-861, RG 59, NARA.

37. Durbrow to the Department of State, Telegram 1367, February 13, 1961, CDF 751K.5-MSP/2-1361; and Mendenhall to the Department of State, Dispatch 351, "Counterinsurgency Plan for South Viet-Nam," February 14, 1961, CDF 751K.5-MSP/2-1461, RG 59, NARA. A copy of the plan given to Ngô Đình Diệm is attached to this dispatch.

38. Catton, *Diem's Final Failure*, 77.

39. Memorandum of Conversation between Bowles and Trần Văn Chương, February 13, 1961, CDF 751K.00/2-1361; and Memorandum of Conversation, "Viet-Nam—Discussion with the British," February 21, CDF 751K.00/2-2161, RG 59, NARA.

40. Memorandum of Conversation, "Viet-Nam—Discussion with the British," February 21, 1961, CDF 751K.00/2-2161, RG 59, NARA.

41. Durbrow to the Department of State, Telegram 1414, February 28, 1961, CDF 751K.5-MSP/2-2861 HBS, RG 59, NARA. On February 22, Durbrow complained that he had not heard from the Vietnamese and called Nguyễn Đình Thuận to discuss the matter. See Durbrow to the Department of State, Telegram 1391, February 22, 1961, CDF 751K.5-MSP/2-2261 HBS, RG 59, NARA.

42. Brigadier General Edward G. Lansdale, "Binh-Hung: A Counter-Guerrilla Case Study," February 1, 1961, Folder 20 "GVN 1961—General Lansdale," Box

3, Entry 5155, General Records of the Department of State, Bureau of East Asian Affairs, Vietnam Desk, Vietnam Subject Files, 1955–1962, RG 59, NARA.

43. Anderson to Parsons, February 15, 1961, Folder 20 "GVN 1961—General Lansdale," Box 3, Entry 5155, General Records of the Department of State, Bureau of East Asian Affairs, Vietnam Desk, Vietnam Subject Files, 1955–1962, RG 59, NARA.

44. This is in reference to the 1958 book by Eugene Burdick and William Lederer which was eventually adapted to film by director George Englund. The film starred Marlon Brando as the U.S. ambassador to the fictional Southeast Asian nation of Sarkhan.

45. Though produced in the fall of 1961, this type of work serves as a good example of how the embassy reported anti–Ngo Dinh Diem material. Free Democratic Party of Vietnam, *White Paper on Ngo Dinh Diem's Reign*, October 1961, Folder "CO 312 Vietnam, General, 1/20/61–11/30/61," Box 75, White House Central Subject Files [WHCSF], JFK.

46. "Assembly Divided on Composition of High Judiciary Council," *Vietnam Press* (Morning), February 23, 1961, H.2.

47. "Assembly's Two Groups Discuss Draft Bill Separately," *Vietnam Press* (Morning), February 23, 1961, H.3; and "Assembly Passes First Five Articles of Judiciary Bill," *Vietnam Press* (Morning), February 24, 1961, H.2–H.3.

48. "Barrister Vuong Quang Nhuong First Chairman of Constitutional Court," *Vietnam Press* (Morning), February 25, 1961, H.3; and "Barrister Vuong Quang Nhuong Confirmed Constitutional Court Chairman," *Vietnam Press* (Evening), March 6, 1961, H.1.

49. "Assembly Passes Judiciary High Council Law," *Vietnam Press* (Morning), February 25, 1961, H.1–H.2.

50. "Assembly Passes National Economic Council Bill," *Vietnam Press* (Morning), March 3, 1961, H.2–H.3.

51. "Assembly Votes on Composition of National Economic Council," *Vietnam Press* (Single), February 19, 1961, H.1–H.3.

52. "Constitutional Court Magistrates Named," *Vietnam Press* (Evening), March 15, 1961, H.1; and "President Receives the Pledge of the Constitutional Court," *Vietnam Press* (Evening), March 20, 1961, H.1–H.2.

53. "National Economic Council and Judiciary High Court Laws Promulgated," *Vietnam Press* (Evening), March 17, 1961, H.1–H.3.

54. "New U.S. Ambassador Named," *Vietnam Press* (Morning), February 20, 1961, H.1.

Chapter 11

1. Department of State to Durbrow, Telegram 1115, March 1, 1961, *FRUS, 1961–1963, Volume I: Vietnam*, 1961, 40–42. For details on other Kennedy actions during his first year in office, see Stephen Pelz, "John F. Kennedy's 1961 Vietnam War Decisions," *Journal of Strategic Studies* (Great Britain) 4, no. 4 (1981): 356–385. In National Security Action Memorandum No. 28, McGeorge Bundy informed Secretary of Defense Robert McNamara and CIA Director Allen Dulles that, per Kennedy's instructions "to launch guerrilla operations in Viet-Minh territory at the earliest possible time," the two were to provide options on expanding operations in the Republic of Vietnam. National Security Action Memorandum No. 28, March 9, 1961, Folder 28 "Guerilla Operations in Viet-Minh Territory (3/9/61)," Box 329, NSF: Vietnam, JFK.

2. The Inaugural Address of John F. Kennedy, Thirty-Fifth President of the United States at the Capitol, Washington, DC, January 20, 1961, *Public Papers of the Presidents: John F. Kennedy, 1961*, 1–3.

3. See footnote 4, Department of State to Durbrow, Telegram 1115, March 1, 1961, *FRUS, 1961–1963, Volume I: Vietnam*, 1961, 42.

4. McGarr to Palmer, March 3, 1961, *FRUS, 1961–1963, Volume I: Vietnam*, 1961, 43–44.

5. Durbrow to the Department of State, Telegram 1414, March 11, 1961, Folder "General, 1/61–3/61," Box 193, NSF: Vietnam, JFK.

6. McGarr to Thuan, March 13, 1961, *FRUS, 1961–1963, Volume I: Vietnam*, 1961, 44–46.

7. Durbrow to the Department of State, Telegram 1466, March 16, 1961, CDF 751K.5-MSP/3–1661, RG 59, NARA.

8. Durbrow to the Department of State, Telegram 1447, March 11, 1961, Folder "General, 1/61–3/61," Box 193, NSF: Vietnam, JFK.

9. Durbrow to the Department of State, Telegram 1447, March 11, 1961, Folder "General, 1/61–3/61," Box 193, NSF: Vietnam, JFK.

10. "Report on Exodus to Cambodia is Groundless Authorities Say," *Vietnam Press* (Evening), March 8, 1961, H.4.

11. "People of Khmer Origin Demonstrate Anti-Red Feelings," *Vietnam Press* (Evening), March 15, 1961, H.8; and "Cambodian-Born Vietnamese Denounce External Subversion," *Vietnam Press* (Evening), March 21, 1961, H.1.

12. "Viet Cong Raid on Villagers at Cambodian Border, ICC Reported," *Vietnam Press* (Evening), March 13, 1961, H.2.

13. Durbrow to the Department of State, Telegram 1466, March 16, 1961, *FRUS, 1961–1963, Volume I: Vietnam*, 48–50.

14. Memorandum of Conversation, March 29, 1961, *FRUS, 1961–1963, Volume I: Vietnam*, Vietnam, 1961, 56–57.

15. Memorandum of Conversation, March 29, 1961, *FRUS, 1961–1963, Volume I: Vietnam*, 1961, 57.

16. "Newsmen Call on Cambodian-Born Vietnamese," *Vietnam Press* (Morning), April 6, 1961, H.13.

17. Mendenhall to the Department of State, Telegram 1523, March 27, 1961, Folder "General, 1/61–3/61," Box 193, NSF: Vietnam, JFK.

18. Joseph J. Zasloff, "Rural Resettlement in South Viet Nam: The Agroville Program," *Pacific Affairs* 35, no. 4 (Winter 1962–1963): 327–340.

19. On April 16, Ngô Đình Diệm inaugurated a newly renovated and improved canal at the Ba Thê Agroville in An Giang province. The significance of this event lay in the fact that the majority of the inhabitants in this Agroville were Khmer, who had been linked to abuses by the Saigon government by its opponents.

Mendenhall to the Department of State, Dispatch 479, "President Ngo Dinh Diem Inaugurates Canal in Khmer Minority Territory," April 22, 1961, CDF 751K.00/4-2261 HBS, RG 59, NARA.

20. Memorandum of Conversation, "Situation in Vietnam," March 27, 1961, *FRUS, 1961–1963, Volume I: Vietnam*, 1961, 52–57.

21. Memorandum of Conversation, "Situation in Vietnam," March 27, 1961, *FRUS, 1961–1963, Volume I: Vietnam*, 1961, 56.

22. Rostow to Kennedy, March 29, 1961, Folder "General, 1/61–3/61," Box 193, NSF: Vietnam, JFK.

23. Rostow to Kennedy, March 29, 1961, Folder "General, 1/61–3/61," Box 193, NSF: Vietnam, JFK.

24. Rostow to Kennedy, April 3, 1961, *FRUS, 1961–1963, Volume I: Vietnam*, 1961, 61–62.

25. The announcement of the treaty and statements of Vũ Văn Mẫu and Durbrow are found in "Viet Nam–U.S. Amity and Economic Relations Treaty Signed," *Vietnam Press* (Evening), April 3, 1961, H.1–H.3.

26. "National Assembly Convenes First 1961 Ordinary Session," *Vietnam Press* (Evening), April 3, 1961, H.4–H.6.

27. As a final straw, Durbrow complained to Washington that as he made his announcement, McGarr informed him that he had been called to Washington for consultation. Durbrow was angry because 650 people had been invited to a farewell reception at McGarr's residence, and the host was not going to be in town. Durbrow found this embarrassing and perhaps, as a final irony, worried more about how the Vietnamese would perceive this slight than the fact that McGarr was needed in Washington to help prepare the fiscal year 1962 aid program. See Durbrow to the Department of State, Telegram 1626, April 21, 1961, CDF 751K.5-MSP/4-2161, RG 59, NARA.

Chapter 12

1. "Inter-Departmental Committee Works on Presidential Election Bill," *Vietnam Press* (Evening), October 13, 1960, H.1.

2. Mendenhall to the Department of State, Dispatch 319, "Presidential Elections Law," January 27, 1961, CDF 751K.00/1-2761, RG 59, NARA. A copy of the forty-three-article election law is attached to the dispatch. See also Durbrow to the Department of State, Airgram G-270, January 7, 1961, CDF 751K.00/1-761, RG 59, NARA; and Durbrow to the Department of State, Airgram G-285, January 17, 1961, CDF 751K.00/1-1761, RG 59, NARA. A copy of the March 25, 1961, special issue of the *Vietnam Press* is also available as an attachment to Mendenhall to the Department of State, Dispatch 439, "Reference Material for the 1961 Presidential Election in South Viet-Nam," April 3, 1961, CDF 751K.00/4-361, RG 59, NARA.

3. Memorandum of Conversation between Cunningham and Trương Đình Dzu, January 3, 1961, Folder 14 "C-GVN 1961 Elections," Box 2, Entry 5155, General Records of the Department of State, Bureau of East Asian Affairs, Vietnam Desk, Vietnam Subject Files, 1955–1962, RG 59, NARA.

4. "Presidential Election Law Promulgated," *Vietnam Press* (Evening), January 6, 1961, H.1. Some of the important provisions included article 8, which stated that all candidates had to have Vietnamese citizenship by birth or have adopted it before the Constitution came into effect, be at least forty years old, and have enjoyed all civic rights. Those who did not enjoy all civic rights had the opportunity to appeal to the Court of Appeals for a certificate under the provisions of article 9. "Major Provisions in Presidential Election Law," *Vietnam Press* (Evening), January 21, 1961, H.2–H.3.

5. "Presidential Election to be Held on April 9," *Vietnam Press* (Evening), January 13, 1961, H.2.

6. "Attention Presidential Candidates," *Vietnam Press* (Evening), January 17, 1961, H.3; and "Presidential Candidates' Applications Will Be Considered after Feb. 7," *Vietnam Press* (Morning), January 19, 1961, H.4.

7. "President Inspects Central Provinces," *Vietnam Press* (Morning), January 18, 1961, H.1; and "President Inspects Phuoc Long Province," *Vietnam Press* (Evening), January 19, 1961, H.1.

8. "Civil Servants League to Conduct Course on Presidential Election," *Vietnam Press* (Morning), January 21, 1961, H.3.

9. "Attention Presidential Candidates," *Vietnam Press* (Morning), January 21, 1961, H.7.

10. "Seminar on Presidential Election Opens," *Vietnam Press* (Evening), January 23, 1961, H.3.

11. "People Learn Presidential Election Procedure," *Vietnam Press* (Morning), February 18, 1961, H.8.

12. "Study Session on Presidential Election Organized in Provinces," *Vietnam Press* (Evening), February 20, 1961, I 1.12.

13. "Film on Presidential Election Released," *Vietnam Press* (Evening), February 18, 1961, H.1.

14. "Preparation for Presidential Election in Tay Ninh," *Vietnam Press* (Evening), February 23, 1961, H.10; "Preparation for Presidential Election in Provinces," *Vietnam Press* (Evening), February 24, 1961, H.5; "Provinces Prepare for Presidential Election," *Vietnam Press* (Single), February 26, 1961, H.1; and "Provinces Prepare for Presidential Election," *Vietnam Press* (Morning), February 28, 1961, H.15.

15. "Film on Presidential Election Procedures Shown," *Vietnam Press* (Evening), March 17, 1961, H.17.

16. Ngô Đình Diệm received backing from the faculty and staff of the Schools of Liberal Arts, Law, Science, Pedagogy, and Advanced Architecture, while meetings in Bình Định, Khánh Hòa, and Pleiku provinces between January 29 and 30 produced twelve additional cables calling for a second term. Representatives from such organizations as the Ex-Servicemen's Association, National Revolutionary Movement, Women's Association, Association for the Study of Confucius, Buddhist Association, Republican Youth, Vietnamese Confederation of Christian Workers, Nung, Man, and Tho tribesmen, and the members of the Cao Đài signed cables, passed resolutions, and rallied in support of Ngô Đình Diệm for a second term. "University Teachers Request President Ngo to Run for Another Term of Office," *Vietnam Press* (Evening), February 3, 1961, H.1–H.2; "University Teachers Request President Ngo to Run for Another Term of Office," *Vietnam Press* (Evening), February 3, 1961, H.1–H.2; "People throughout Nation Request President to Stand for Re-Election,"

Vietnam Press (Morning), February 4, 1961, H.1–H.2; and "More Groups Call on President to Seek Re-Election," *Vietnam Press* (Evening), February 4, 1961, H.1–H.2.

17. "People in Province Ask President to Seek Re-election," *Vietnam Press* (Morning), February 1, 1961, H.2.

18. "People in Provinces Demand President Ngo Dinh Diem to Run for Re-election," *Vietnam Press* (Morning), January 31, 1961, H.1; and "People in Vinh Long and Binh Long Ask President Ngo Dinh Diem to Seek Re-election," *Vietnam Press* (Evening), January 31, 1961, H.1–H.2.

19. "People in Province Ask President to Seek Re-election," *Vietnam Press* (Morning), February 1, 1961, H.1–H.2; "More Civic Groups in Provinces Call on President to Seek Re-Election," *Vietnam Press* (Morning), February 2, 1961, H.2–H.3; and "More Resolutions Asking President to Seek Re-Election," *Vietnam Press* (Morning), February 3, 1961, H.2–H.3. Even if, as some historians of the period maintain, some of the crowd had been coerced into attending the events in support of Ngô Đình Diệm, one cannot justify the assertion that none supported the RVN president.

20. "Presidential Election Law Discussed at Study Sessions in Provinces," *Vietnam Press* (Evening), February 10, 1961, H.6.

21. "112 More Petitions Asking President to Seek Re-Election," *Vietnam Press* (Morning), February 6, 1961, H.1–H.3.

22. "Names of Presidential Candidates Kept Secret Till Tomorrow Midnight," *Vietnam Press* (Evening), February 6, 1961, H.1.

23. "Workers Unions—Many Other's Pledge Loyalty to Chief Executive—Ask Him to Stand for Re-Election," *Vietnam Press* (Morning), February 7, 1961, H.10–H.13.

24. "Workers Unions—Many Other's Pledge Loyalty to Chief Executive—Ask Him to Stand for Re-Election," *Vietnam Press* (Morning), February 7, 1961, H.13.

25. Durbrow to the Department of State, Telegram 1352, February 8, 1961, CDF 751K.00/2–861 HBS, RG 59, NARA. "President Ngo Seeks Re-Election," *Vietnam Press* (Evening), February 7, 1961, H.1. In January, Mendenhall had passed along rumors to Washington that Ngô Đình Nhu was working to damage the prestige of Nguyễn Ngọc Thơ in order to drop him from the ticket. These rumors, like many others that circulated in Saigon with an anti–Ngô Đình Diệm message, proved to be false. Mendenhall to the Department of State, Airgram G298, January 21, 1961, CDF 751K.00/1–2161 HBS, RG 59, NARA. On February 20, Durbrow met with Nguyễn Ngọc Thơ. The vice president told Durbrow that he did not look forward to remaining in his position but felt duty bound. He also told Durbrow in confidence that he had been asked to run against Ngô Đình Diệm but did not believe he could because, even if he disagreed with some of his action, Ngô Đình Diệm had done a great deal for the RVN. Durbrow to the Department of State, Airgram G-352, February 23, 1961, CDF 751K.00/2–2361, RG 59, NARA.

26. "President Ngo's Letter to the Nation," *Vietnam Press* (Morning), February 8, 1961, H.1–H.2.

27. A biographical sketch of Nguyễn Đình Quát and Nguyễn Thành Phương is available in enclosure 4 of Mendenhall to the Department of State, Dispatch 429, "1961 Presidential Election Campaign Gets Under Way," March 29, 1961, CDF 751K.00/3–2961, RG 59, NARA. Enclosure 5 of the same document contains a biographical sketch of Hồ Nhật Tân and Nguyễn Thế Truyền. See also "Six Candidates Slated for Elections," *Vietnam Press* (Morning), February 8, 1961, H.3. Nguyễn Đình Quát had approached the U.S. embassy in Saigon earlier in January seeking confirmation that his campaign would receive approval from the Americans. See Durbrow to the Department of State, Dispatch 315, "Possible Opposition Candidate in GVN Presidential Elections," January 24, 1961, CDF 751K.00/1–2461, RG 59, NARA. A January 11 Memorandum of Conversation between Mendenhall and Nguyễn Đình Quát is attached to the dispatch. See also Mendenhall to the Department of State, Airgram G-337, February 11, 1961, CDF 751K.00/2–1161 HBS, RG 59, NARA.

28. Added to the Socialist vote came messages of support from the Alumni Association of Vietnamese Architects and from Long An, the Việt Nam Phục quốc Hội and Cao Đài leadership. Buddhist and trade union pledges also came from the provinces of Vĩnh Long, Định Tường, Ba Xuyên, Quảng Trị, Khánh Hòa, and Ninh Thuận. See. "'We Vote for President Ngo Dinh Diem's Re-Election' Say Political Parties," *Vietnam Press* (Morning), February 8, 1961, H.4. For additional endorsements see, "Resolutions Continue to Pour into the Presidency," *Vietnam Press* (Morning), February 10, 1961, H.2–H.3; "66 More Resolutions Ask President to Stand for Re-Election," *Vietnam Press* (Morning), February 11, 1961, H.13; "Resolutions Pour in at Presidency," *Vietnam Press* (Evening), February 11, 1961, H.1; "People Want President Ngo to Seek Re-Election," *Vietnam Press* (Evening), March 2, 1961, H.11; "Nation Welcomes President's Decision to Seek Re-Election," *Vietnam Press* (Morning), February 23, 1961, H.1; "More Petitions Welcoming President's Decision to Seek Re-Election," *Vietnam Press* (Morning), February 24, 1961, H.1; "People Want President to Seek Re-Election," *Vietnam Press* (Evening), February 24, 1961, H.1–H.2; "People Want the President for Another Term of Office," *Vietnam Press* (Evening), February 25, 1961, H.3; and "People Want the President to Seek Re-Election," *Vietnam Press* (Morning), February 28, 1961.

29. "Tet Gifts Go to 1,250 Children at Independence Palace Party," *Vietnam Press* (Morning), February 9, 1961, H.1. Ngô Đình Diệm would also be seen at sporting events such as the February 12 soccer match between the Saigon Select Team and the Swiss Young Boys Champion Team, "President Visits Stadium, Fair, and Market," *Vietnam Press* (Morning), February 13, 1961, H.2.

30. "President Inspects Construction Projects in Tuyen Duc," *Vietnam Press* (Morning), February 10, 1961, H.1.

31. Durbrow to the Department of State, Airgram G-347, February 18, 1961, CDF 751K.11/2–1861 HBS, RG 59, NARA; and Durbrow to the Department of State, Dispatch 369, "February 24, 1961, WEEKA No. 8 for State, Army, Navy, and Air Departments," February 27, 1961, CDF 751K.00(W)/2–2761, RG 59, NARA; and Durbrow to the Department of State, Airgram G-361, February 28, 1961, CDF 751K.11/2–2861, RG 59, NARA.

32. "President's Decision to Seek Reelection Receives General Welcome," *Vietnam Press* (Morning), February 10, 1961, H.4–H5.
33. Mendenhall to the Department of State, Airgram G-337, February 11, 1961, CDF 751K.00/2–1161 HBS, RG 59, NARA. See also "Assembly Chairman Confirms Presidential Candidates' Names," *Vietnam Press* (Evening), February 10, 1961, H.1–H.2.
34. "President Makes Impromptu Market Visits," *Vietnam Press* (Single), February 14, 1961, H.1.
35. "Land Reform Benefits 126,027," *Vietnam Press* (Morning), February 25, 1961, H.7–H.9.
36. "21,733 Hectares of Waste Land Reclaimed since 1957," *Vietnam Press* (Morning), March 12, 1961, H.1.
37. "Presidential Candidates Choose Emblems," *Vietnam Press* (Evening), February 20, 1961, H.4.
38. "Election Campaign Committee to Meet on Tuesday," *Vietnam Press* (Morning), February 18, 1961, H.1; and "Central Presidential Election Campaign Committee Holds Second Work Session," *Vietnam Press* (Evening), February 21, 1961, H.2.
39. "Committee Discusses Election Campaign Procedure," *Vietnam Press* (Evening), February 22, 1961, H.6.
40. "President Visits New Airports," *Vietnam Press* (Morning), February 22, 1961, H.1–H.2; and "Vice President Opens Mekong Investigation Committee Meeting," *Vietnam Press* (Evening), February 22, 1961, H.1–H.3.
41. "Presidential Election Campaign Committee Meets," *Vietnam Press* (Morning), February 24, 1961, H.8; and "Election Campaign Committee Plans Contacts between Candidates and Voters," *Vietnam Press* (Evening), February 24, 1961, H.5.
42. Cunningham to the Department of State, Airgram G-363, March 2, 1961, CDF 751K.00/3–261 HBS, RG 59, NARA; and "Election Campaign to Start March 15," *Vietnam Press* (Single), February 26, 1961, H.1.
43. "Cost of Election Campaign to Exceed VN$3,000,000," *Vietnam Press* (Evening), February 27, 1961, H.4.
44. Mendenhall to the Department of State, Dispatch 381, "Conversation with Tran Van Dinh on Internal Situation in Viet-Nam," March 5, 1961, CDF 751/3–361 HBS, RG 59, NARA. A Memorandum of Conversation between Trần Văn Dĩnh and Mendenhall is attached to the dispatch.
45. "Election Campaign Procedures Explained," *Vietnam Press* (Morning), March 9, 1961, H.1–H.3. See also *Sài Gòn Mới* editorial, March 7, 1961, FBIS, G1.
46. "Voters' Cards to Be Distributed," *Vietnam Press* (Morning), March 7, 1961, H.1.
47. "April 9 Presidential Election 'A Success,' Predicts University Leader," *Vietnam Press* (Morning), March 13, 1961, H.4–H.8. See also *Dan Viet* editorial, March 10, 1961, FBIS, March 13, 1961, G2.
48. "April 9 Presidential Election 'A Success,' Predicts University Leader," *Vietnam Press* (Morning), March 13, 1961, H.6.
49. "First Posting Indicates 6,948,466 Voters," *Vietnam Press* (Evening), March 13, 1961, H.1.
50. Durbrow to the Department of State, Telegram 1475, March 17, 1961, CDF 751K.00/3–1761, RG 59, NARA. "Text of Address of the President of the Republic of Viet Nam, March 16, 1961," Dispatch 115, March 20, 1961, Folder 350 "Internal Political Affairs: Vietnam, 1959–1961," Box 5, Entry 3340B, RG 84, NARA.
51. "Text of Address of the President of the Republic of Viet Nam, March 16, 1961," Dispatch 115, March 20, 1961, Folder 350 "Internal Political Affairs: Vietnam, 1959–1961," Box 5, Entry 3340B, RG 84, NARA. See also *Dan Chi* editorial, March 20, 1961, FBIS, March 22, 1961, G1.
52. A summary of the campaign in its initial stages is available in Mendenhall to the Department of State, Dispatch 429, "1961 Presidential Election Campaign Gets Under Way," March 29, 1961, CDF 751K.00/3–2961, RG 59, NARA.
53. Memorandum of Conversation between Lê Trung Nghĩa and Cunningham, "Vietnamese Internal Situation with Particular Reference to Presidential Election April 9," March 23, 1961, Folder 14 "C GVN 1961—Elections," Box 2, Entry 5155, General Records of the Department of State, Bureau of East Asian Affairs, Vietnam Desk, Vietnam Subject Files, 1955–1962, RG 59, NARA.
54. A translation of Hồ Nhật Tân's address over Radio Saigon on March 20 is available as enclosure 3 in Mendenhall to the Department of State, Dispatch 429, "1961 Presidential Election Campaign Gets Under Way," March 29, 1961, CDF 751K.00/3–2961, RG 59, NARA. See also editorials in *Tieng Dan* and *Sài Gòn Mãi*, March 20, 1961, FBIS, March 22, 1961, G1; "Candidate Tan Holds Press Conference," *Times of Vietnam*, March 22, 1961, FBIS, March 23, 1961, G2–G3; "Ho Nhat Tan Platform," *Times of Vietnam*, March 22, 1961, FBIS, March 23, 1961, G3–G4; "Tan Talk on Radio Is Unsatisfactory," *Times of Vietnam*, March 22, 1961, FBIS, March 23, 1961, G4–G5; and "Quat Makes Broad Appeal for Votes," *Times of Vietnam*, March 23, 1961, FBIS, March 24, 1961, G1.
55. Memorandum of Conversation between Lê Trung Nghĩa and Cunningham, "Vietnamese Internal Situation with Particular Reference to Presidential Election April 9," March 23, 1961, Folder 14 "C GVN 1961—Elections," Box 2, Entry 5155, General Records of the Department of State, Bureau of East Asian Affairs, Vietnam Desk, Vietnam Subject Files, 1955–1962, RG 59, NARA.
56. "President to Address Nation Tonight," *Vietnam Press* (Morning), March 15, 1961, H.1.
57. "Address of the President of the Republic of Viet Nam," *Vietnam Press* (Morning), March 16, 1961, H.1–H.7.
58. "Address of the President of the Republic of Viet Nam," *Vietnam Press* (Morning), March 16, 1961, H.7.

Chapter 13

1. "Sub-Committee for Presidential Election Campaign Meets," *Vietnam Press* (Evening), March 15, 1961, H.2–H.3.
2. "Election Handbill Distribution to Start Next Monday," *Vietnam Press* (Evening), March 16, 1961, H.1.
3. See enclosure 2, "First Press Conference of Presidential Candidate Nguyen Dinh Quat and Vice Presi-

dential Candidate Nguyen Thanh Phuong," Mendenhall to the Department of State, Dispatch 429, "1961 Presidential Election Campaign Gets Under Way," March 29, 1961, CDF 751K.00/3-2961, RG 59, NARA. See also "Slate II Presidential Candidates Meet the Press," *Vietnam Press* (Evening), March 17, 1961, H.4-H.5.

4. "City Election Campaign Sub-Committee Issues Joint Statement," *Vietnam Press* (Evening), March 20, 1961, H.4.

5. "Provincial Sub-Committees of Presidential Election Campaign Meet," *Vietnam Press* (Evening), March 20, 1961, H.16.

6. "Slate II Presidential Candidates Meet the Press," *Vietnam Press* (Evening), March 17, 1961, H.5.

7. "Second Ticket's 14-Point Platform Broadcast over Radio Saigon," *Vietnam Press* (Evening), March 17, 1961, H.6-H.7.

8. "Slate II Appeals to Voters," *Vietnam Press* (Morning), March 24, 1961, H.1.

9. "City to Have 528 Polling Stations," *Vietnam Press* (Morning), March 21, 1961, H.1.

10. "Slate I on the Air—No Specific Programme Expounded," *Vietnam Press* (Evening), March 20, 1961, H.3.

11. "True Democracy for All; Slate I Candidates Offer Five Point Programme," *Vietnam Press* (Morning), March 23, 1961, H.1-H.2.

12. "Slate I Presents Eight Point Programme," *Vietnam Press* (Evening), March 25, 1961, H.6-H.7.

13. Durbrow via Mendenhall to the Department of State, Telegram G-41e, April 1, 1961, Folder 350 "Internal Political Affairs: Vietnam, 1959-1961," Box 5, Entry 3340B, RG 84, NARA. See also enclosure 1, "Press Conference by President Ngo Dinh Diem," March 23, 1961, Mendenhall to the Department of State, Dispatch 429, "1961 Presidential Election Campaign Gets Under Way," March 29, 1961, CDF 751K.00/3-2961, RG 59, NARA; and Durbrow to the Department of State, Airgram G-410, April 1, 1960, CDF 751K.00/4-161 HBS, RG 59, NARA.

14. Durbrow via Mendenhall to the Department of State, Telegram G-41e, April 1, 1961, Folder 350 "Internal Political Affairs: Vietnam, 1959-1961," Box 5, Entry 3340B, RG 84, NARA.

15. "Slate I Delegate Addresses Public," *Vietnam Press* (Evening), March 24, 1961, H.1.

16. "Civil Servants to Campaign for Massive Participation in Presidential Election," *Vietnam Press* (Evening), March 24, 1961, H.4.

17. "President Inaugurates Coal Washing Plant at Nong Son," *Vietnam Press* (Evening), March 25, 1961, H.1-H.2. On April 1, Ngô Đình Diệm had a similar trip to the Đa Nhim hydroelectric scheme at Đơn Dương district on the Dalat-Phan Rang road, "President Opens Da Nhim Construction Site," *Vietnam Press* (Single), April 2, 1961, H.1-H.10.

18. "Address by the President of the Republic at the Inauguration of the Coal Washing Plant of the Nong Son Coal Mine," *Vietnam Press* (Evening), March 25, 1961, H.3-H.5.

19. "Voters Fight for Loudspeakers at Campaign Talks," *Vietnam Press* (Evening), March 27, 1961, H.3-H.4.

20. "Candidates to Be Protected from Over Enthusiastic Voters," *Vietnam Press* (Morning), March 28, 1961, H.1.

21. Memorandum of Conversation, April 1, 1961, Folder 14 "C-GVN 1961 Elections," Box 2, Entry 5155, General Records of the Department of State, Bureau of East Asian Affairs, Vietnam Desk, Vietnam Subject Files, 1955-1962, RG 59, NARA.

22. "Slate I Meets Voters," *Vietnam Press* (Evening), March 29, 1961, H.3. See also "Tan Sobs at Unruly Press Conference," *Times of Vietnam*, March 27, 1961, FBIS, March 29, 1961, G2.

23. "Quat Would Not Seek Communist Coalition," *Tiếng Chuông*, March 29, 1961, FBIS, March 30, 1961, G1-G2. See also "Slate II Presidential Candidate Confuses Voters," *Vietnam Press* (Morning), March 29, 1961, H.3-H.4; and "Voters Press Slate II Candidate for Answers," *Vietnam Press* (Morning), April 6, 1961, H.1.

24. "Voters Make Suggestions at Slate I Campaign Speech," *Vietnam Press* (Evening), March 30, 1961, H.2-H.3. See also "Public Rally for Diem Ends in Fight," *Sài Gòn Mãi*, March 27, 1961, FBIS, March 29, 1961, G2-G4; "Paper Notes Disrupting Campaign Fights," *Sài Gòn Thời Báo*, March 27, 1961, FBIS, March 29, 1961, G4-G5; and "Diem Representative Question at Rally," *Times of Vietnam*, March 30, 1961, FBIS, March 31, 1961, G1.

25. "'Shortcomings Are Inevitable in any Policy and Government,' Vice President Says in Campaign Meeting," *Vietnam Press* (Single), April 2, 1961, H.11-H.12.

26. "President Ngo Dinh Diem Meets the Press," *Vietnam Press* (special edition), March 31, 1961, 1-21. See also "New Five-Year Plan Announced by Diem," *Times of Vietnam*, April 3, FBIS, April 5, 1961, K1-K2. It did not help Ngô Đình Diệm's opposition that scheduled meetings by the other candidates were canceled in order to campaign in other urban centers. See "Ticket No. 3 Cancels Press Conference," *Sài Gòn Mới*, March 31, 1961, FBIS, April 4, 1961, K4-K-6. Other newspapers, such as *Sài Gòn Thời Báo*, published negative articles about Slate II and Slate I which were never confirmed. See "Threats to Voters," *Sài Gòn Thời Báo*, April 3, 1961, FBIS, April 4, 1961, K6.

27. "Slate I Candidates Hold Third Campaign Meeting," *Vietnam Press* (Evening), April 1, 1961, H.2-H.3.

28. "City Election Campaign Committee Chairman Wants Apologies From Slate II," *Vietnam Press* (Evening), April 3, 1961, H.7; and "Voters Demonstrate Hostility to Slate II; Campaign Chairman Walks Out," *Vietnam Press* (Evening), April 3, 1961, H.8.

29. This incident reinforced an earlier *Sài Gòn Thời báo* editorial that expressed doubt about the revolutionary achievements of Hồ Nhật Tân and Nguyễn Thế Truyền; *Sài Gòn Thời báo*, March 31, 1961, FBIS, April 3, 1961, K1.

30. "Violence at Slate I Meeting," *Vietnam Press* (Evening), April 4, 1961, H.2.

31. *Thời luân*, founded by elements of the Cao Đài who at one time had supported Ngô Đình Diệm in his anti–Bảo Đại position, was occasionally in trouble with the Saigon government for being too anti–Ngô Đình Diệm. Nghiêm Xuân Thiện's role in the election does suggest that his criticism of Ngô Đình Diệm, while not welcomed, was tolerated. See Chapman, *Cauldron of Resistance*, 130.

32. "More Frustration at Slate I Press Conference," *Vietnam Press* (Morning), April 7, 1961, H.9–H.10.

33. "Election Campaign in Provinces: No Troubles Reported," *Vietnam Press* (Evening), April 4, 1961, H.3; and "Election Campaign in Provinces," *Vietnam Press* (Morning), April 6, 1961, H.2. Delegates for all three slates campaigned in Phong Dinh, Vĩnh Bình, Côn Sơn, Kiến Hòa, Long An, Bình Tuy, Phước Thành, Bình Định, Quảng Trị, Darlac, Quảng Đức, Long Khánh, Biên Hòa, Phước Tuy, Bình Long, Kiến Tường, and Kontom, with no reports of violence or misbehaving.

34. "Communist Victims Association Favours President Ngo Dinh Diem's Re-Election," *Vietnam Press* (Morning), April 4, 1961, H.3–H.4.

35. "Communist Victims Association Favours President Ngo Dinh Diem's Re-Election," *Vietnam Press* (Morning), April 4, 1961, H.4.

36. Mendenhall to the Department of State, Dispatch 437, "Madame Ngo Dinh Nhu Again in the Public Eye," April 3, 1961, CDF 751K.00/4-361, RG 59, NARA. A copy of Madame Nhu's March 22 address commemorating Hai Bà Trưng (Trung Sisters) in Saigon is attached as enclosure 1.

37. Durbrow to the Department of State, Telegram 1579, April 8, 1961, CDF 751K.00/4-861, RG 59, NARA; Durbrow to the Department of State, Telegram 1589, April 10, 1961, CDF 751K.00/4-1061, RG 59, NARA; and "President Ngo Meets Voters," *Vietnam Press* (Morning), April 7, 1961, H.1–H.8.

38. "Slate II Holds Last Press Conference," *Vietnam Press* (Evening), April 7, 1961, H.3.

39. "President Diem Appeals to Saigon Voters," *Times of Vietnam*, April 6, 1961, FBIS, April 7, 1961, K1–K2; and "President Ngo Meets the Press," *Vietnam Press* (Morning), April 8, 1961, H.1.

40. "U.S. to Stand by Free Viet Nam," *Vietnam Press* (Morning), April 8, 1961, H.7; and "Leading U.S. Senator Calls for More Aid to Viet Nam," *Vietnam Press* (Morning), April 8, 1961, H.9.

41. "National Assembly Protests against 'Tendentious and Malicious Allegations,'" *Vietnam Press* (Evening), April 8, 1961, H.1.

42. For more information on Operation Passage to Freedom, see Ronald B. Frankum, Jr., *Operation Passage to Freedom: The United States Navy in Vietnam, 1954–1955*.

43. "Saigon Begins to Vote in Calm," *Vietnam Press* (Morning), April 9, 1961, H.2–H.3. The two men were eventually released the same day.

44. "Like Any Citizen, President Goes to the Polls," *Vietnam Press* (Morning), April 9, 1961, H.1.

45. "Saigon Begins to Vote in Calm," *Vietnam Press* (Morning), April 9, 1961, H.2–H.3.

46. "70.7 Per Cent of Saigon Vote in at 3 P.M.," *Vietnam Press* (Evening), April 9, 1961, H.4.

47. "65–70 Per Cent of Registered Voters Go to the Polls in Provinces," *Vietnam Press* (Evening), April 9, 1961, H.2.

48. "The Election: Saigon Press Comments," *Vietnam Press* (Evening), April 9, 1961, C.1–C.2.

49. "Viet Cong Trouble-Making Scheme Foiled," *Vietnam Press* (Evening), April 9, 1961, H.4; and "Abortive Viet Cong Attempt to Sabotage Election," *Vietnam Press* (Evening), April 10, 1961, H.4–H.5.

50. "Viet Cong Fail to Prevent Vote Counting," *Vietnam Press* (Morning), April 11, 1961, H.5.

51. "The Security Situation during the Election for President and Vice President," *Vietnam Press* (Morning), April 12, 1961, H.3–H.6; and "Communist Sabotage Plan Uncovered," *Vietnam Press* (Morning), April 12, 1961, H.7. See also "Communist Plan to Sabotage Election Foiled, Foreign Press Notes," *Vietnam Press* (Evening), April 15, 1961, C.1–C.2 for press stories related to the Việt Cộng attempts to disrupt the elections.

52. See also Thomas Barnes, American vice consul in Hue, to the Department of State, Dispatch 20, "1061 Presidential Elections in the Hue Consular District," April 15, 1961, CDF 751K.00/4-1561, RG 59, NARA. Barnes described more severe attempts by the Việt Cộng to disrupt the elections as well as Cần Lao Party efforts to ensure proper results. Barnes' dispatch followed similar trends that had come out of Hue and Central Vietnam over the past year.

53. See also Durbrow to the Department of State, Telegram 1581, April 9, 1961, CDF 751K.00/4-961, RG 59, NARA.

54. Durbrow to the Department of State, Airgram G-427, April 13, 1961, CDF 751K.00/4-1361, RG 59, NARA.

55. "Voting in Saigon," *Vietnam Press* (Morning), April 12, 1961, H.10. See also "Preliminary Election Returns Announced," Saigon Radio, April 10, 1961, FBIS, April 10, 1961, K1.

56. "President Ngo Dinh Diem Re-Elected by 'Crushing Majority,'" *Vietnam Press* (Morning), April 10, 1961, H.1; "Returns From Provinces Show Clear Cut Victory for Slate I," *Vietnam Press* (Evening), April 10, 1961, H.1–H.2; "89.18 Per Cent of Voters for Slate I," *Vietnam Press* (Morning), April 11, 1961, H.1–H.2; Durbrow to the Department of State, Telegram 1593, April 11, 1961, CDF 751K.00/4-1161, RG 59, NARA; and Durbrow to the Department of State, Telegram 1594, April 11, 1961, CDF 751K.00/4-1161, RG 59, NARA.

57. "'No Pressure on Voters,' Candidates Representatives Say," *Vietnam Press* (Evening), April 11, 1961, H.1.

58. "Election Campaign in Quang Nam Reported Democratic," *Vietnam Press* (Morning), April 9, 1961, H.5.

59. "Singapore Daily Underlines President Ngo Dinh Diem's Victory in Election," *Vietnam Press* (Evening), April 10, 1961, C.1; and "President Ngo Dinh Diem's Reelection Hailed as Victory over Communists," *Vietnam Press* (Morning), April 11, 1961, H.3.

60. Singapore Reuters did report some Việt Cộng attempts to disrupt the election. See "Viet Cong Tries to Seize Ballot Boxes," *Singapore Reuters*, April 10, 1961, FBIS, April 10, 1961, K3; and Durbrow to the Department of State, Telegram 1582, April 10, 1961, Folder 350 "Internal Political Affairs: Vietnam, 1959–1961," Box 5, Entry 3340B, RG 84, NARA. See also "Diem Receives Nearly 6 Million Votes," *Times of Vietnam*, April 11, 1961, FBIS, April 11, 1961, K1.

61. Durbrow to Ngô Đình Diệm, Dispatch No. 465, April 12, 1961, Folder 350 "Internal Political Affairs: Vietnam, 1959–1961," Box 5, Entry 3340B, RG 84, NARA.

62. "Validation Committee to Examine Election Files," *Vietnam Press* (Evening), April 19, 1961, H.1.

63. "Validation Committee Announces Final Elec-

tion Returns and Victory of Slate I," *Vietnam Press* (Evening), April 24, 1961, H.1.

64. Executive Secretary to the Department of State Lucius D. Battle to Special Assistant to the Ralph A. Dungan, April 14, 1961, Folder "General, 4/1/61–4/24/61," Box 193, NSF: Vietnam, JFK.

65. "U.S. Ambassador Honored at Dinner," *Vietnam Press* (Morning), April 20, 1961, H.4.

66. "U.S. Ambassador Addresses Lions' Club," *Vietnam Press* (Morning), April 26, 1961, H.2–H.3.

67. "'U.S. Will Do Everything It Can to Support Viet Nam,' Mr. Dean Rusk Says," *Vietnam Press* (Evening), April 22, 1961, H.1.

68. Memorandum from Executive Secretary to the Department of State Lucius D. Battle to Special Assistant to the President Ralph A. Dungan, "Letter to President Ngo Dinh Diem of Viet-Nam," April 21, 1961, Folder "General, 4/25/61–4/30/61," Box 193, NSF: Vietnam, JFK.

69. "Saigon-Bien Hoa Highway Completed," *Vietnam Press* (Evening), April 26, 1961, H.4–H.5; "U.S. Ambassador Pays Farewell Visit to Assembly Chairman," *Vietnam Press* (Evening), April 27, 1961, H.6; and "President Open US$35 Million Saigon–Bien Hoa Highway," *Vietnam Press* (Evening), April 28, 1961, H.1–H.4.

70. "President Open US$35 Million Saigon–Bien Hoa Highway," *Vietnam Press* (Evening), April 28, 1961, H.2.

71. Hanoi, VNA, February 19, 1960, FBIS, February 24, 1960, E3.

72. "President Open US$35 Million Saigon–Bien Hoa Highway," *Vietnam Press* (Evening), April 28, 1961, H.4.

73. "Farewell Reception for U.S. Ambassador," *Vietnam Press* (Morning), April 29, 1961, H.11.

74. "Presidential Inauguration," *Vietnam Press* (Morning), April 29, 1961, H.1–H.6. See also the ninety-eight-page *Vietnam Press* inauguration special dated April 29.

Conclusion

1. Kahin, *Intervention*, 127.
2. Geoffrey Shaw, "Laotian 'Neutrality': A Fresh Look at a Key Vietnam War Blunder," *Small Wars & Insurgencies* 13, no. 1 (Spring 2002): 25–57. See also Ruby Abramson, *Spanning the Century: The Life of W. Averell Harriman, 1891–1986*, 606–626, for an analysis of Harriman's influence on American diplomacy in Southeast Asia during the Kennedy administration.

3. Stephen Pelz, "John F. Kennedy's 1961 Vietnam War Decisions," *Journal of Strategic Studies* 4, no. 4 (1981): 356–385; and Fred I. Greenstein and Richard H. Immerman, "What Did Eisenhower Tell Kennedy about Indochina? The Politics of Misperception," *Journal of American History* 79 (1992): 568–587. See also Cooper, *Lost Crusade*, 170–172.

Appendix

1. The official exchange rate of 35 Vietnamese piasters = 1 U.S. dollar was established in May 1953. All Vietnamese piaster amounts are followed by U.S. equivalents.

2. "Viet Nam Rubber Exports Soar," *Vietnam Press* (Morning), October 4, 1960, H.3; and "Rubber Keeps First Place in Viet Nam Exports," *Vietnam Press* (Evening), October 5, 1960, H.5.

3. "Vietnamese Rice Production Increased by One Third," *Vietnam Press* (Evening), October 3, 1960, H.23; and "Viet Nam Exportable Rice Surplus Amounts to 400,000 Tons This Year," *Vietnam Press* (Morning), October 6, 1960, H.6.

4. "Increased Vietnamese Rice Production and Exports Cited at International Rice Commission Meeting," *Vietnam Press* (Evening), November 16, 1960, H.9–H.12; and "Rice Cultivation Development in Vietnam Topic of Discussion at IRC Session," *Vietnam Press* (Morning), November 18, 1960, H.16–H.18.

5. "Viet Nam's Forestry and Farm Product Imports Top VN$1,278 Million," *Vietnam Press* (Morning), October 24, 1960, H.6.

6. "290,903 Tons of Fruit in 1959," *Vietnam Press* (Evening), October 6, 1960, H.3; "Phuoc Tuy Produces 1,200 Tons of Peanuts," *Vietnam Press* (Single), October 30, 1960, H.8.

7. "Ben Cat Dairy Farm to Supply Saigon with Fresh Milk," *Vietnam Press* (Morning), December 1, 1960, H.12.

8. "Food Situation in Viet Nam," *Vietnam Press* (Morning), December 5, 1960, H.10.

Bibliography

Primary Document Collections and Archives

Microfilm Collection, *Confidential U.S. State Department Central Files: Vietnam 1960–January 1963 Internal Affairs and Foreign Affairs* (A UPA Collection from LexisNexis)

Dwight D. Eisenhower Presidential Library, Abilene, Kansas
    Dwight D. Eisenhower Papers (Ann Whitman Files), 1953–1961. International Meeting Series. International Series. Name Series.
    Dwight D. Eisenhower: Records as President (White House Central Files, 1953–1961). Official Files. General Files.
    White House Office Files: National Security Council Staff Papers, 1948–1961. OCB Central File Series.
    John Foster Dulles Papers, 1951–1959. JFD Chronological Series.

Foreign Relations of the United States, Government Printing Office, Washington, DC.
    1958–1960, Volume I: Vietnam. 1961–1963, Volume I: Vietnam.

Hoover Institute at Stanford University, Palo Alto, California
    Samuel Tankersley Williams Papers, 1917–1980. Military Assistance Advisory Group (MAAG), Vietnam, 1955 October–1960 August.
    Papers of Edward Lansdale. Office Files from the United States Department of Defense, Office of the Secretary of Defense, 1957–1963.
    Papers of Elbridge Durbrow

John F. Kennedy Presidential Library, Boston, Massachusetts
    National Security Files: Country Files, Vietnam Files. National Security Files: Meetings and Memoranda. National Security Files: National Security Action Memoranda (NSAM). Presidential Office Files. Personal Papers of Theodore C. Sorensen. Personal Papers of James Thomson, Jr.

National Archives and Records Administration, College Park, Maryland.
    General Records of the Department of State, Record Group 59. Bureau of East Asian Affairs, Vietnam Desk, Vietnam Subject Files, 1960–1962. Bureau of East Asian Affairs, Vietnam Desk, Vietnam Subject Files, 1955–1962. Bureau of Far Eastern Affairs, Office of Southeast Asian Affairs, Vietnam Files, 1959–1960. Central Decimal Files, 1959–1960. Central Decimal Files, 1960–1963.
    Records of the Central Intelligence Agency, Record Group 263. Entry 24, Foreign Broadcast Information Service Daily Reports, 1941–1959. Entry 9, English Transcripts of Monitored Foreign Broadcasts Relating to the Vietnam War, 1957–1974. Entry 46D, Foreign Broadcast Information Service Daily Reports, 1959–1978.

Published Works

Abramson, Rudy. *Spanning the Century: The Life of W. Averell Harriman, 1891–1986.* New York: Morrow, 1992.

Adamson, Michael R. "Ambassadorial Roles and Foreign Policy: Elbridge Durbrow, Frederick Nolting, and the U.S. Commitment to Diem's Vietnam, 1957–61." *Presidential Studies Quarterly* 32, no. 2 (June 2002): 229–255.

Ahern, Thomas. *CIA and the House of Ngo: Covert Action in South Vietnam, 1954–1963.* Center for the Study of Intelligence, June 2000. Accessed on July 15, 2013, from the National Security Archives website: http://www.gwu.edu/~nsarchiv/NSAEBB/NSAEBB284/2-CIA_AND_THE_HOUSE_OF_NGO.pdf.

_____. *Vietnam Declassified: The CIA and Counterinsurgency.* Lexington: University Press of Kentucky, 2012.

Allen, Luther. "Crisis in Saigon: The Sunday Morning Visitor Returns." *Massachusetts Review* 3, no. 1 (Autumn 1961): 170–187.

Anderson, David L. *Trapped by Success: The Eisenhower Administration and Vietnam, 1953–1961.* New York: Columbia University Press, 1991.

Appy, Christian G. *Patriots: The Vietnam War Remembered from All Sides*. New York: Viking, 2003.
Bayless, Robert M. *Vietnam: Victory Was Never an Option*. Victoria, BC, Canada: Trafford, 2005.
Berman, Larry. *Planning a Tragedy: The Americanization of the War in Vietnam*. New York: Norton, 1982.
Blight, James G., Janet M. Lang, and David A. Welch. *Vietnam if Kennedy Had Lived: Virtual JFK*. Lanham, MD: Rowman and Littlefield, 2009.
Bouscaren, Anthony T. *Last of the Mandarins: Diem of Vietnam*. Pittsburgh, PA: Duquesne University Press, 1965.
Bradley, Mark Philip. *Vietnam at War*. New York: Oxford University Press, 2009.
Browne, Malcolm. *The New Face of War*. Indianapolis, IN: Bobbs-Merrill, 1965.
Bùi Diễm, with David Chanoff. *In the Jaws of History*. Boston: Houghton Mifflin, 1987.
Buttinger, Joseph. *Vietnam: A Dragon Embattled*. New York: Praeger, 1967.
_____. *Vietnam: A Political History*. New York: Praeger, 1968.
_____. *Vietnam: The Unforgettable Tragedy*. New York: Horizon Books, 1977.
Cao Ngọc Phuong. *Learning True Love: How I Learned and Practiced Social Change in Vietnam*. Berkeley, CA: Parallax Press, 1993.
Cao Văn Viên. *Leadership*. McLean, VA: General Research Corporation, 1978.
Catton, Philip E. *Diem's Final Failure: Prelude to America's War in Vietnam*. Lawrence: University Press of Kansas, 2002.
Chapman, Jessica M. *Cauldron of Resistance: Ngo Dinh Diem, the United States, and 1950s Southern Vietnam*. Ithaca, NY: Cornell University Press, 2013.
Chomsky, Noam. *Rethinking Camelot: JFK, the Vietnam War, and U.S. Political Culture*. Boston: South End Press, 1993.
Colby, William, and Peter Forbath, *Honorable Men: My Life in the CIA*. New York: Simon & Schuster, 1978.
Colby, William, with James McCargar. *Lost Victory*. Chicago: Contemporary Books, 1989.
Cooper, Chester. *The Lost Crusade: America in Vietnam*. New York: Dodd, Meed, 1970.
Dallek, Robert. *An Unfinished Life: John F. Kennedy, 1917–1963*. Boston: Little, Brown, 2003.
David Lan Pham. *Two Hamlets in Nam Bo: Memoirs of Life in Vietnam through Japanese Occupation, the French and American Wars, and Communist Rule, 1940–1986*. Jefferson, NC: McFarland, 2000.
Davidson, Phillip B. *Vietnam at War: The History, 1946–1975*. Novato, CA: Presidio Press, 1988.
DeGroot, Gerald J. *A Noble Cause? America and the Vietnam War*. London: Longman, 1999.
Dockery, Martin J. *Lost in Translation: Vietnam, a Combat Advisor's Story*. New York: Presidio Press, 2003.
Dommen, Arthur J. *The Indochinese Experience of the French and the Americans: Nationalism and Communism in Cambodia, Laos, and Vietnam*. Bloomington: Indiana University Press, 2001.
Donnell, John C. "National Renovation Campaigns in Vietnam." *Pacific Affairs* 32, no. 1 (March 1959): 73–88.
Dooley, Thomas A. *Deliver Us from Evil: The Story of Viet Nam's Flight to Freedom*. New York: Farrar, Straus and Cudahy, 1956.
_____. *The Edge of Tomorrow*. New York: Farrar, Straus and Cudahy, 1958.
_____. *The Night They Burned the Mountain*. New York: Farrar, Straus and Cudahy, 1958.
Duiker, William J. *Sacred War: Nationalism and Revolution in a Divided Vietnam*. New York: McGraw-Hill, 1995.
Elliott, Duong Van Mai. *The Sacred Willow: Four Generations in the Life of a Vietnamese Family*. New York: Oxford University Press, 1999.
Ernst, John P. *Forging a Fateful Alliance: Michigan State University and the Vietnam War*. East Lansing: Michigan State University Press, 1998.
Fall, Bernard. *The Two Viet-Nams*. New York: Praeger, 1964.
_____. *Viet-Nam Witness, 1953–1966*. New York: Praeger, 1966.
Fay, Paul B, Jr. *The Pleasure of His Company*. New York: Harper and Row, 1966.
Fisher, James T. *Dr. America: The Lives of Thomas A. Dooley, 1927–1961*. Amherst: University of Massachusetts Press, 1997.
_____. "The Second Catholic President: Ngo Dinh Diem, John F. Kennedy, and the Vietnam Lobby, 1954–1963." *U.S. Catholic Historian* 15, no. 3, Catholics in a Non-Catholic World, part 2 (Summer 1997): 119–137.
Fitzgerald, Frances. *Fire in the Lake: The Vietnamese and the Americans in Vietnam*. New York: Random House, 1972.
Fontaine, Ray. *The Dawn of Free Vietnam: A Biographical Sketch of Doctor Phan Quang Dan*. Brownsville, TX: Pan American Business Services, 1992.
Frankum, Ronald B., Jr. *Historical Dictionary of the War in Vietnam*. Lanham, MD: Scarecrow, 2011.
_____. *Operation Passage to Freedom: The United States in Vietnam, 1954–1955*. Lubbock: Texas Tech University Press, 2007.
Fulbright, J. William. *The Arrogance of Power*. New York: Random House, 1966.
Gardner, Lloyd C., and Ted Gittinger, eds. *Vietnam: The Early Decisions*. Austin: University of Texas Press, 1997.
Gelb, Leslie H., with Richard K. Betts. *The Irony of Vietnam: The System Worked*. Washington, DC: Brookings Institution, 1979.
Givhan, John B. *Rice and Cotton: South Vietnam and South Alabama*. Philadelphia: Xlibris, 2000.

Goodman, Allan E. *Politics in War: The Bases of Political Community in South Vietnam.* Cambridge, MA: Harvard University Press, 1973.

Halberstam, David. *The Making of a Quagmire.* New York: Random House, 1965.

Hall, Mitchell K. *The Vietnam War.* New York: Longman, 2007.

Hammer, Ellen J. *A Death in November: America in Vietnam, 1963.* New York: E.P. Dutton, 1987.

Haycraft, William Russell. *Unraveling Vietnam: How American Arms and Diplomacy Failed in Southeast Asia.* Jefferson, NC: McFarland, 2006.

Hearden, Patrick J. *The Tragedy of Vietnam.* New York: HarperCollins, 2008.

Henderson, William, and Wesley R. Fishel. "The Foreign Policy of Ngo Dinh Diem." *Vietnam Perspectives* 2, no. 1 (August 1966): 3–30.

Herring, George C. *America's Longest War: The United States and Vietnam, 1950–1975.* New York: McGraw-Hill, 2002.

Herrington, Stuart. *Silence Was a Weapon: The Vietnam War in the Villages.* Novato, CA: Presidio Press, 1982.

Hess, Gary R. *Vietnam and the United States: Origins and Legacy of War.* Boston: Twayne, 1990.

———. *Vietnam: Explaining America's Lost War.* Malden: Blackwell Publishing, 2009.

Hess, Martha. *Then the Americans Came: Voices from Vietnam.* New York: Four Walls Eight Windows, 1993.

Higgins, Marguerite. *Our Vietnam Nightmare.* New York: Harper and Row, 1965.

Hilsman, Roger. *To Move a Nation.* New York: Doubleday, 1967.

Hoàng Ngọc Thành and Thân Thị Nhân Đức. *President Ngo Dinh Diem and the US: His Overthrow and Assassination.* San Jose, CA: Tuan-Yen and Quan-Viet Mai-Nam Publishers, 2001.

Hoàng Văn Chí. *From Colonialism to Communism: A Case History of North Vietnam.* New York: Praeger, 1964.

Honey, P.J. "The Problem of Democracy in Vietnam." *The World Today* 16, no. 2 (February 1960): 71–79.

Hunt, Richard A. *Pacification: The American Struggle for Vietnam's Hearts and Minds.* Boulder, CO: Westview, 1995.

Jacobs, Seth. *America's Miracle Man in Vietnam: Ngo Dinh Diem, Religion, Race, and U.S. Intervention in Southeast Asia, 1950–1957.* Durham, NC: Duke University Press, 2004.

———. *Cold War Mandarin: Ngo Dinh Diem and the Origins of America's War in Vietnam, 1950–1963.* Lanham, MD: Rowman and Littlefield, 2006.

Jamieson, Neil L. *Understanding Vietnam.* Berkeley, CA: University of California Press, 1993.

Joiner, Charles A., and Roy Jumper. "Organizing Bureaucrats: South Viet Nam's National Revolutionary Civil Servants' League." *Asian Survey* 3, no. 4 (April 1963): 203–215.

Jones, Howard. *Death of a Generation: How the Assassinations of Diem and John F. Kennedy Prevented the Withdrawal of American Troops from Vietnam.* New York: Oxford University Press, 2003.

Kahin, George McT. *Intervention: How America Became Involved in Vietnam.* New York: Knopf, 1986.

Karnow, Stanley. *Vietnam: A History.* New York: Viking, 1983.

Kauffman, Christopher J. "Politics, Programs, and Protests: Catholic Relief Services in Vietnam, 1954–1975." *Catholic Historical Review* 91, no. 2 (April 2005): 223–250.

Kolko, Gabriel. *Anatomy of a War: Vietnam, the United States, and the Modern Historical Experience.* New York: Pantheon, 1985.

Krall, Yung. *A Thousand Tears Falling: The True Story of a Vietnamese Family Torn Apart by War, Communism, and the CIA.* Atlanta: Longstreet, 1995.

Labin, Suzanne. *Vietnam: An Eye-Witness Account.* Springfield, VA: Crestwood, 1965.

Lacouture, Jean. *Vietnam: Between Two Truces.* New York: Vintage, 1966.

Langguth, A.J. *Our Vietnam: The War, 1954–1975.* New York: Simon & Schuster, 2000.

Latham, Michael E. "Redirecting the Revolution? The USA and the Failure of Nation-Building in South Vietnam." *Third World Quarterly* 27, no. 1, From Nation-Building to State-Building (2006): 27–41.

Levine, Alan J. *The United States and the Struggle for Southeast Asia, 1945–1975.* Westport, CT: Praeger, 1995.

Lind, Michael. *Vietnam, the Necessary War: A Reinterpretation of America's Most Disastrous Military Conflict.* New York: Free Press, 1999.

Lindholm, Richard W., ed. *Vietnam, The First Five Years: An International Symposium.* East Lansing: Michigan State University Press, 1959.

Logevall, Fredrik. *Choosing War: The Lost Chance for Peace and the Escalation of War in Vietnam.* Berkeley: University of California Press, 1999.

———. *The Origins of the Vietnam War.* New York: Longman, 2001.

Lomperis, Timothy J. *The War Everyone Lost—and Won: America's Intervention in Viet Nam's Twin Struggles.* Baton Rouge: Louisiana State University Press, 1984.

Maclear, Michael. *The Ten Thousand Day War: Vietnam: 1945–1975.* New York: St. Martin's, 1981.

Maneli, Mieczyslaw. *War of the Vanquished.* New York: Harper and Row, 1971.

Mann, Robert. *A Grand Delusion: America's Descent into Vietnam.* New York: Basic Books, 2001.

Mecklin, John. *Mission in Torment*. New York: Doubleday, 1965.

Meyer, Harold J. *Hanging Sam: A Military Biography of General Samuel T. Williams from Pancho Villa to Vietnam*. Denton: University of North Texas Press, 1990.

Miller, Edward. *Misalliance: Ngo Dinh Diem, the United States, and the Fate of South Vietnam*. Cambridge, MA: Harvard University Press, 2013.

Morgan, Joseph G. *The Vietnam Lobby: The American Friends of Vietnam, 1955–1975*. Chapel Hill: University of North Carolina Press, 1997.

_____. "A Change of Course: American Catholics, Anticommunism, and the Vietnam War." *U.S. Catholic Historian* 22, no. 4, Catholic Anticommunism (Fall 2004): 117–130.

Morrison, Wilbur H. *The Elephant and the Tiger: The Full Story of the Vietnam War*. New York: Hippocrene, 1990.

Moyar, Mark. *Triumph Forsaken: The Vietnam War, 1954–1965*. New York: Cambridge University Press, 2006.

Murti, B.S.N. *Vietnam Divided: The Unfinished Struggle*. New York: Asia Publishing House, 1964.

Nashel, Jonathan. *Edward Lansdale's Cold War*. Boston: University of Massachusetts Press, 2005.

Neale, Jonathan. *The American War: Vietnam, 1960–1975*. London: Bookmarks, 2001.

Neu, Charles E. *America's Lost War: Vietnam, 1945–1975*. Wheeling, IL: Harlan Davidson, 2005.

Newman, John M. *JFK and Vietnam: Deception, Intrigue, and the Struggle for Power*. New York: Warner, 1992.

Nguyễn Đình Hoà. *From the City Inside the Red River: A Cultural Memoir of Mid-Century Vietnam*. Jefferson, NC: McFarland, 1999.

Nguyễn Ngọc Ngạn, with E.E. Richey. *The Will of Heaven*. New York: E.P. Dutton, 1982.

Nguyễn Quí Đức. *Where the Ashes Are: The Odyssey of a Vietnamese Family*. Reading, MA: Addison-Wesley, 1994.

Nguyễn Thái. "South Vietnam." In *The Asian Newspapers' Reluctant Revolution*, edited by John A. Lent, 234–257. Ames: Iowa State University Press, 1971.

Nguyễn Thị Định. *No Other Road to Take: Memoir of Mrs. Nguyen Thi Dinh*. Ithaca, NY: Cornell University Press, 1976.

Nguyễn Thị Tuyết Mai. *The Rubber Tree: Memoir of a Vietnamese Woman Who Was an Anti-French Guerrilla, an Aide to the First President of the Republic of Vietnam, a Publisher and a Peace Activist*. Edited by Monique Senderowicz. Jefferson, NC: McFarland, 1994.

Nguyễn Tuyết Mai. "Electioneering: Vietnamese Style." *Asian Survey* 2, no. 9 (November 1962): 11–18.

Nolting, Frederick, Jr. *From Trust to Tragedy*. New York: Praeger, 1989.

O'Leary, Bradley S., and Edward Lee. *The Deaths of the Cold War Kings: The Assassinations of Diem & JFK*. Baltimore, MD: Cemetery Dance, 2000.

Olson, James S., and Randy Roberts. *Where the Domino Fell: America and Vietnam, 1945–1990*. New York: St. Martin's, 1991.

Palmer, Bruce, Jr. *The 25-Year War: America's Military Role in Vietnam*. Lexington: University Press of Kentucky, 1984.

Palmer, Dave Richard. *The Summons of the Trumpet*. San Rafael, CA: Presidio Press, 1984.

Parmet, Herbert S. *JFK: The Presidency of John F. Kennedy*. New York: Dial, 1983.

Pauker, Guy J. "Political Doctrines and Practical Politics in Southeast Asia." *Pacific Affairs* 35, no. 1 (Spring 1962): 3–10.

Podhoretz, Norman. *Why We Were in Vietnam*. New York: Simon & Schuster, 1982.

Porter, D. Gareth. *The Perils of Dominance: Imbalance of Power and the Road to War in Vietnam*. Berkeley: University of California Press, 2005.

Prados, John. *Vietnam: The History of an Unwinnable War, 1945–1975*. Lawrence: University Press of Kansas, 2009.

Prouty, L. Fletcher. *JFK: The CIA, Vietnam and the Plot to Assassinate John F. Kennedy*. New York: Carol, 1992.

Race, Jeffrey. *War Comes to Long An*. Berkeley: University of California Press, 1972.

Record, Jeffrey. *The Wrong War: Why We Lost in Vietnam*. Annapolis, MD: Naval Institute Press, 1998.

Rosenau, William. *US Internal Security Assistance to South Vietnam: Insurgency, Subversion and Public Order*. London: Routledge, 2005.

Rust, William J. *Kennedy in Vietnam*. New York: Scribner, 1985.

Schandler, Herbert Y. *America in Vietnam: The War That Couldn't Be Won*. Lanham, MD: Rowman and Littlefield, 2009.

Schulzinger, Robert D. *A Time for War: The United States and Vietnam, 1941–1975*. New York: Oxford University Press, 1997.

Scigliano, Robert G. "The Electoral Process in South Vietnam: Politics in an Underdeveloped State." *Midwest Journal of Political Science* 4, no. 2 (May 1960): 138–161.

_____. "Political Parties in South Vietnam under the Republic." *Pacific Affairs* 33, no. 4 (December 1960): 327–346.

_____. *South Vietnam: Nation under Stress*. Boston: Houghton Mifflin, 1963.

Shaplen, Robert. *The Lost Revolution: The U.S. in Vietnam, 1946–1966*. New York: Harper and Row, 1965.

_____. *Time Out of Hand: Revolution and Reaction in Southeast Asia*. New York: Harper and Row, 1969.

Shaw, Geoffrey. "Laotian 'Neutrality': A Fresh Look at a Key Vietnam War Blunder." *Small Wars & Insurgencies* 13, no. 1 (Spring 2002): 25–57.

Sheehan, Neil. *A Bright Shining Lie: John Paul Vann and America in Vietnam*. New York: Random House, 1988.

Short, Anthony. *The Origins of the Vietnam War*. New York: Longman, 1989.

Smith, Ralph B. *Revolution versus Containment, 1955–61*. New York: St. Martin's, 1985.

Spector, Ronald H. *Advice and Support: The Early Years, 1941–1960*. Honolulu, HI: University Press of the Pacific, 2005.

Statler, Kathryn C. *Replacing France: The Origins of American Intervention in Vietnam*. Lexington: University Press of Kentucky, 2007.

Strober, Gerald S., and Deborah Hart Strober. *Let Us Begin Anew: An Oral History of the Kennedy Presidency*. New York: HarperCollins, 2003.

Sullivan, William H. *Obbligato: Notes on a Foreign Service Career*. New York: Norton, 1984.

Trần Văn Đôn. *Our Endless War*. San Rafael, CA: Presidio Press, 1978.

Tregaskis, Richard. *Vietnam Diary*. New York: Holt, Rinehart and Winston, 1963.

Trullinger, James. *Village at War*. New York: Longman, 1980.

Tucker, Spencer. *Vietnam*. Lexington: University Press of Kentucky, 1999.

Turley, William S. *The Second Indochina War: A Short Political and Military History, 1954–1975*. Boulder, CO: Westview, 1986.

Walinsky, Louis J., ed. *Agrarian Reform as Unfinished Business: The Selected Papers of Wolf Ladejinsky*. New York: Oxford University Press, 1977.

Warner, Denis. *The Last Confucian*. Baltimore, MD: Penguin, 1964.

Warner, Geoffrey. "The United States and Vietnam 1945–65: Part II: 1954–65." *International Affairs* 48, no. 4 (October 1972): 593–615.

Westheider, James E. *The Vietnam War*. Westport, CT: Greenwood, 2007.

Winters, Francis X. *The Year of the Hare: America in Vietnam, January 25, 1963–February 15, 1964*. Athens: University of Georgia Press, 1997.

Wintler, Justin. *The Viet Nam Wars*. New York: St. Martin's, 1991.

Woodruff, Mark R. *Unheralded Victory: The Defeat of the Viet Cong and the North Vietnamese Army, 1961–1973*. Arlington, VA: Vandamere Press, 1999.

Wurfel, David. "The Saigon Political Elite: Focus on Four Cabinets." *Asian Survey* 7, no. 8, Vietnam: A Symposium (August 1967): 527–539.

Young, Marilyn B. *The Vietnam Wars, 1945–1990*. New York: HarperCollins, 1991.

Zasloff, Joseph J. "Rural Resettlement in South Viet Nam: The Agroville Program." *Pacific Affairs* 35, no. 4 (Winter 1962–1963): 327–340.

Index

Agence France Presse 163
Agroville Plan 27, 29, 34, 38–39, 41–42, 44–45, 50–51, 62, 68, 70, 74–77, 81, 85, 87, 129, 166, 175, 210n23, 212n35, 212n43
Ah Chau Jih Pao 2, 76
Allen, Luther 116
American Trading Company of Vietnam 51, 81, 220n71
An Đôn 175
An Giang Province 163, 164, 172, 196
An Xuyên Province 188, 196
USS *Anacortes* 132
Anderson, Daniel 39, 60, 70, 135–136, 156, 159
Ansari, S.S. 80
Anspacher, John M. 232n43
Army of the Republic of Vietnam (ARVN) 17–18, 22, 25–27, 29–30, 33, 35, 39–40, 42–43, 45, 47–49, 66, 69, 71, 79, 83–84, 93, 95–96, 99, 101–103, 105–106, 109, 111–112, 114, 126, 128–130, 132, 137, 139–140, 159, 165
Askew, Laurin B. 57
Australia 97, 119, 206

Bà Rịa 93
Ba Xuyên Province 38, 165, 171, 172, 196
Bangkok 106, 124, 134, 161, 165, 167
Bảo Đại 7, 69
Barnes, Thomas 91, 241n52
Basic Counterinsurgency Plan for Viet Nam 148, 152, 154–155, 159–162, 164–167, 180, 197
Battle, Lucius D. 198
Bến Cát 206
Biên Hòa 75, 93, 95, 171, 198
Bình Dân Hospital 116
Bình Đông 195
Bình Dương 75, 143, 171
Bình Hưng 156–157
Bình Lớn Second Constituency 91
Bình Long 172, 188
Bình Thuận 171, 172

Bình Tuy 71
Bình Xuyên 7, 52, 72, 137, 140
Bloc for Liberty and Progress *see* Caravelle Group
Bonesteel, Charles H. 58
Boun Oum Na Champassak 196
Bowles, Chester 154–155
Brand, Vance 91
Brèthes, Jean 80
Briggs, Bud 228n22
Browne, Malcom 4
Brucker, Wilbur M. 22–24, 209n5
Bùi Quang Nga 12
Bùi Văn Lương 89, 171, 195
Bundy, McGeorge 236n1
Buổi sang (Morning Post) 2, 12, 37, 113
"Buy America" Plan 18, 167

Cà Mau 46, 156
Cabell, Charles P. 45
Cách mạng Quốc gia (National Revolution) 2, 27, 37, 56, 133
Calfo, George 80–81
Cambodia 3, 19, 21, 40, 45, 47, 52–53, 59, 61–63, 68, 91, 154–156, 162–166; border incidents and disputes with RVN 26, 47, 62, 163–166
Cần Lao Nhân Vị Cách Mạng Đảng *see* Cần Lao Party
Cần Lao Party 13–14, 35, 37, 45–47, 51, 54, 59–60, 62–64, 70, 72–73, 79, 117, 140, 156, 161–162, 186
Cần Thơ 38, 75, 98, 174
Cao Đài 7, 12, 52, 140, 143, 172, 174, 181
Cao Văn Trường 47, 142, 175, 177–178, 185
Cao xuân Vỹ 112
Capital Military Region 75, 97, 99, 107
Caravelle Group 4, 51–53, 55–56, 61, 69–72, 74, 77, 106
Caravelle Manifesto 4, 50–57, 59, 64–65, 67–69, 82, 95
USS *Card* 132
Câu Ngan District 151

Central Presidential Election Campaign Committee *see* Elections, Presidential (1961)
Cherne, Leo 209n1
Choi Duk Shin 121
Cholon 34, 96, 98, 102, 115, 166, 173, 175, 184–186, 188, 191
Chung Juo Jih Pao 2
Chuông Mai (Morning Bell) 2, 113
Civil Guard 17, 30, 32–33, 37, 39–40, 43, 46, 57–58, 68, 75, 78–79, 83–84, 87, 109–110, 122, 126, 129–132, 136–139, 148, 150, 152, 159, 195, 207n8, 208n29, 219n54
Cochin China *see* Mekong Delta
Colby, William E. 10, 93–95, 97–98, 113, 145, 150, 167, 208n11
Colegrove, Albert 52, 214–215n7, 215n18
Collins, John F. 144
Comstock, Richard 47–48, 51–52
Côn Sơn 174, 188
Constitutional Court (RVN) 142–143, 157–158, 171
Coster, Donald 68, 72
Country Team (U.S.) 8, 10–15, 23, 25, 31, 42, 48, 66, 83, 125, 144–145, 165–167
Coup d'état (Laos, August 1960) 76, 87–88
Coup d'état (November 1960) 4, 14, 35, 93–108
Coup d'état (November 1963) 4
Court of Appeals (RVN) 157–158, 172
Court of Cassation (RVN) 143, 157–158
Củ Chi 143
Cunningham, Francis 8, 81, 95, 115–116, 119, 131, 146–147, 150, 169–170, 180–181

Đa Nhim River 174
Đại Tâm Village 165
Đại Việt Party 78

249

Đại Việt Quốc dân Đảng see Đại Việt Party
Dalat 59, 71, 94, 98, 140, 174, 186, 196–197
Dân chúng (The People) 2, 59, 61, 71, 76, 86, 113
Danang 71, 154, 172, 186,
Đặng Độc Khởi 89, 134
Đảng Lao động Việt Nam (Lao động Party) 38
Đào Hưng Long 52
Darlac 171, 197
De Jaeger, Raymond J. 94
Democratic Republic of Vietnam (DRV) 14, 16–17, 22–23, 26–27, 29, 33, 38, 45, 81, 139, 141, 187, 211n7
Department of Civic Action (RVN) 153, 171
Department of Rural Affairs (RVN) 153
Diệm, Ngô Đình see Ngô Đình Diệm
Điện Biên Phủ 7, 216n30
Dillion, C. Douglas 32, 137
Dillon, James 64–65
Định Khắc Quyết 191
Định Tường 172
Đình Văn Huấn 158
Dixon, Ben 89, 134
Đỗ Văn Điển 100, 102
Dolan, John 62–63
Đồng Nai 133
Đồng Nai River 91
Động Tiên Canal 86
Douglas, James H. 109–110
Dulles, Allen 236n1
Dungan, Ralph A. 242n68
Dương Chí Sanh 133
Dương Văn Minh 66, 97, 101, 139–140
Durbrow, Elbridge 5, 8, 10–12, 14–15, 17–18, 20, 22–28, 31, 33, 35–40, 42, 44–46, 48, 50–53, 55–59, 61, 63, 65, 67–68, 70, 72–75, 77–79, 81, 83, 85, 87, 89–91, 93–95, 97, 99–101, 103, 105, 107, 109–112, 114–119, 121, 125, 127, 129, 131, 133, 135, 137–142, 144–149, 151–152, 154, 156–160, 162–169, 170–171, 176, 187–188, 201–204

Elections, National Assembly (1959) 8, 11–12, 14, 38–39, 77
Elections, Presidential (1961) 11, 14–15, 90, 139–142, 146, 151, 154, 165, 167–175, 177–198, 201, 203; Central Presidential Election Campaign Committee 175, 177–178, 182, 184–185, 188; election laws 142–143, 170–172, 175; public meeting schedules 182; radio broadcast schedules 181; results of 196–197; Slate I 174, 177, 181–182, 185–189, 192–194, 196–197; Slate II 174, 177, 180–182, 184–186, 189, 192–194, 196–197; Slate III 174, 177, 180–182, 185–186, 189, 192, 194, 196–197
Erhardt, Ludwig 184
Exodus, Operation 7, 55, 91, 194, 215n19

Felt, Harry D. 43, 104, 130–131, 137, 141, 144
Fink, Andrew 232n32
Fishel, Welsey 207$ch1n$3
Flesch, Joseph 61
Forsyth, William Douglas 89, 121
France 7, 54, 79, 112, 117, 119
Free Democratic Party of Vietnam 156
Free Khmer Radio 59
French, Jerome T. 111, 123–125, 137

Gandhi, Indira 192
Garcia, Carols P. 196
Garden City Plan see Agroville Plan
Gardiner, Arthur 55, 133, 146
Gates, Thomas 124, 132, 137
Geneva Conference and Agreements (1954) 5, 7, 18, 23–24, 33, 67, 91, 139, 156, 164, 192, 212n31, 215n19, 216n30
Geneva Conference and Agreements (1962) 203
Gia Định 166, 173
Gia Long 10
Gonder, Frank 51–53, 55–56, 72, 215n18
Gore, Al 11, 18–19
Great Britain see United Kingdom

Hạ Như Chi 142
Hà Tiên 194
Hà Tĩnh 174
Hai Bà Trưng 241n36
Hammarskjold, Dag 163
Hanoi 2, 17, 19, 57, 123, 137, 141, 191, 211n7
Hanoi VNA see Radio Hanoi
Harriman, W. Averell 203–204
Haznam, Basri 66
Heavner, Theodore J.C. 37, 73, 212n22
Helble, John J. 188
Herter, Christian 62
Hiệp Hòa Suger Refinery 63
Hồ Chí Minh 16, 70, 212n34
Hồ Nhật Tân 174, 177, 180, 184–189, 191–193
Hồ Tấn Quyển 95
Hồ Văn Nhựt 52–53
Hồ Việt Điều 52
Hòa Hảo 7, 52, 140, 208n9
Hỏa Lựu 38
Hoàng Cơ Thụy 95–97, 107, 140
Hoàng Đình Tú 94
Hoàng Huy 188
Hoàng Thủy Nam 19
Hohler, Henry A.F. 78–79, 86, 89, 132
Hood, Samuel 155
Houghton, Amory 79–80
Hue 71, 73, 91, 137, 158, 172, 182, 186, 197
Hưng Long Pagoda 176
Huỳnh Công Tịnh 102
Huỳnh Ngọc Diệp 189
Huỳnh Thành Vị 12, 133
Huỳnh Văn Cao 102

Interfamily Group program 33–34
International Conference on the Settlement of the Laotian Question see Geneva Conference and Agreements (1962)
International Control Commission (ICC) 23, 33, 211n7
International Supervisory and Control Commission 121

Johnson, Lyndon B. 165, 168
Joint Chiefs of Staff (U.S.) 82

Karnow, Stanley 114–115, 228n22
Kennedy, John F. 108, 145, 148–53, 159–160, 165, 167–168, 175, 178, 180, 187, 192, 198, 201, 203–204
Kent, Sherman 83
Khánh Hòa 172, 195, 237n16, 238n28
Khánh Hội 188
Kiên Giang 172, 194, 218n29
Kiến Hòa 137, 172, 195, 210n24, 241n33
Kiến Tường 164, 241n33
Kim Khánh 165
Knight, Robert 61, 64, 66, 123–124
Komer, Robert 152
Kông Khánh 171
Kong Le 76, 87
Kontum 197
Korea, Republic of see Republic of Korea

Ladejinski, Wolf 34–35, 46, 62, 72–73, 87, 149, 209n1, 231n29, 235n19
Lại Từ 157
Lalouette, Robert 62, 69–70, 78–79, 86, 89, 121, 222n34
Lâm Đồng 151

Lam Lê Trinh 72, 89, 163
Lâm Quang Thơ 98
Lâm Văn Phát 195
Lâm Văn Tết 52
Land Redistribution/Reform 7, 16, 71, 73, 85–86, 89, 154, 175–176, 205
Lane, Andre 231n25
Lansdale, Edward 10, 36, 38, 44–45, 48, 50, 55, 59, 61, 63, 65, 67–68, 72–73, 75–79, 83, 85, 87, 89–90, 93, 110–111, 119, 131, 133, 135, 144, 147, 149, 151–152, 154, 156–160, 163–164, 169, 201–202, 204, 208, 212, 214–215, 217–218, 220–221, 227, 233–237, 245–246
Laos 3, 21, 39, 45, 76, 81, 87–88, 91, 135, 139, 141, 145, 193, 203–204
Laspiur, Rufino 89
Lê Quang Tung 95
Lê Trọng Quát 90–91, 142, 157, 222n51
Lê Trung Nghĩa 147, 180–181
Lê Văn Đồng 34–35, 70, 79, 205
Lê Văn Đức 208n26
Lê Văn Kim 96, 140
Lê Văn Nghiêm 93, 102, 227n7
Lê Văn Tất 181
Lê Văn Ty 96–97, 100–101, 103, 139, 224n28
Leavitt, G. 228n22
LeMay, Curtis E. 132
Lemnitzer, Lyman Louis 123, 125, 153, 226n73
Lincoln, Franklin 78
Lộc Ninh 171
Lodge, Henry Cabot 204
Long An 37, 171–172, 197, 207n8, 210n24, 238n28
Long Khánh 37, 188
Long Xuyên 174
Loubassou, Louis 196
Lư Đình Sơn 100, 103
Luang Praband 76
Lưu Hưng 192

Madame Nhu 52, 75, 79, 87–88, 116, 119–122, 126, 145, 192–193, 223n5
Malaya 29, 42–45, 57–58, 61, 159, 165, 210n31
Manac'h, Etienne 70, 79
Mansfield, Mike 67, 193
Martin, Pepper 228n22
May, Jacques M. 55
May Jih Luan Zan 2
M'Ba, Leo 196
McGarr, Lionel C. 9–10, 67, 82–84, 88, 97–100, 103–107, 113–114, 118–119, 121–123, 125–126, 128–133, 135, 137–139, 141, 145, 150, 154–156, 160–162, 164, 166–168, 201, 204

McGee, Gale 19
McMillen, Harold 167
Mekong Delta 42, 46, 53, 58, 78–80
Mekong River 177
Mendenhall, Joseph 8, 10–11, 13–14, 52–54, 59, 69–70, 75, 78, 80, 91, 94, 97–98, 116, 119, 123, 125, 131, 134–135, 137, 140, 144–146, 150, 165–167, 181, 196, 203, 216n13, 215n18
Menon, Gopala 121
Merchant, Livingston 123, 136
Michigan State University Group 5, 7, 40, 207ch1n3
Military Advisor Assistance Group (MAAG) 15, 23–26, 26, 40, 47–48, 56, 67, 72, 83–84, 103, 105–106, 109, 118–119, 124, 127–133, 135, 138, 145–146, 148, 159–160, 166, 201, 209n9
Military Assistance Program (MAP) 42, 126, 152, 159, 161–162
Le Monde Diplomatique 120
Montagnards 53
Mounier, Emmanuel 208n23, 211n10
Mỹ Tho 98, 100, 211n34
Mỹ Thuận 79
Myers, Samuel L. 41

Nam Định 174
Nasution, Abdul Haris 165
National Assembly (RVN) 8, 11–12, 14, 28, 38–39, 47, 52, 76–80, 84–87, 89–93, 106, 109, 111, 116, 122, 133, 135, 138, 140–143, 156–158, 161, 164, 166, 168, 170–171, 173, 179, 191, 193, 195–197
National Assembly Elections (August 1959) *see* Elections, National Assembly (1959)
National Economic Council 122, 126, 138, 153, 158, 179, 190
National Liberation Front of South Vietnam *see* Việt Cộng
National Revolutionary Movement 11–12, 37, 70, 72, 109, 133, 187, 207ch1n4, 237n16
National Security Council (RVN) 74, 78
Nehru, Pandit 192
Nevard, Jacques 115, 228n22
Nghiêm Xuân Thiện 191, 240n31
Ngô Đình Cẩn 37, 70, 73, 116–117, 125
Ngô Đình Diệm 2–10, 12, 14–15, 17–18, 20, 22–28, 30–31, 33, 35–40, 42, 44–46, 48, 50–53, 55–59, 61, 63–65, 67–68, 70–75, 77–81, 83–85, 87–91, 93–95, 97, 99–101, 103, 105, 107, 109–112, 114–119, 121, 123, 125, 127, 129, 131, 133–135, 137–140, 142, 144, 146–152, 154, 156–160, 162–172, 174, 176–180, 182–183, 185–191, 193, 195, 197, 199–204
Ngô Đình Luyện 74, 193
Ngô Đình Nhu 2–3, 5, 17, 35, 37–38, 57, 63, 70, 75, 77, 79–80, 85, 87, 91, 93, 95, 97, 101, 103, 105, 107, 112, 114, 119, 121, 125, 127, 129, 131, 135, 137–139, 146–148, 150, 157, 168, 174, 193, 195, 207, 210, 213, 222, 230, 238
Ngô Đình Thục 116, 137, 193
Ngô Quận 133
Ngô Trọng Hiếu 227n7
Ngô Văn Tinh 208n26
Ngô Xuân Soạn 105–107
Ngôn Luận (Opinion) 2, 28, 34, 72
Nguyễn Chánh Thi 96–97, 101–102, 105–107, 115, 224n28
Nguyễn Đình Hoà 116
Nguyễn Đình Quát 174, 177, 180, 184–186, 189, 191–193, 238n27
Nguyễn Đình Thuận 18–19, 22–24, 39, 44–45, 47, 54, 60–61, 63, 65–66, 68, 72, 74, 78, 80, 87, 89, 94, 97–100, 102, 106, 113, 117–120, 122, 124–125, 130–133, 139–140, 147, 154–156, 159–167, 171–172, 212n40, 213n63, 213n66, 229n38
Nguyễn Duy Liên 175
Nguyễn Duy Quang 78
Nguyễn Khánh 40–41, 43, 75, 94, 97, 105, 139, 165
Nguyễn Lộc Hóa 156
Nguyễn Minh Mẫn 102, 104–105
Nguyễn Ngọc Bích 174–175
Nguyễn Ngọc Khôi 47–48
Nguyễn Ngọc Lễ 185
Nguyễn Ngọc Thơ 14, 18–19, 30, 36, 54, 73–74, 80, 87, 99, 109, 133, 137, 140, 147, 164, 166, 172–174, 176–177, 183–185, 187–189, 197–198, 238n25
Nguyễn Phước 172
Nguyễn Phương Thiệp 78, 135
Nguyễn Tấn 14
Nguyễn Thái 90
Nguyễn Thanh Lớp 185
Nguyễn Thành Phương 174, 177, 185
Nguyễn Thanh Sơn 185
Nguyễn Thành Tôn 207n8
Nguyễn Thế Truyền 174, 177, 186, 189, 191, 194
Nguyễn Tri Phương Market 188, 191
Nguyễn Triệu Hồng 97

Nguyễn Trúc Chi 158
Nguyễn Văn Bửu 73
Nguyễn Văn Cẩn 141
Nguyễn Văn Châu 227n7
Nguyễn Văn Chuân 102
Nguyễn Văn Đông 73
Nguyễn Văn Kiến 194
Nguyễn Văn Liên 12
Nguyễn Văn Lộc 97
Nguyễn Văn Lợi 97
Nguyễn Văn Lương 89
Nguyễn Văn Sỹ 89
Nguyễn Văn Thiện 95
Nguyễn Văn Thọ 140
Nguyễn Văn Thỏa 174–175
Nguyễn Văn Thời 78
Nguyễn Văn Y 12, 213n46, 227n7
Nguyễn Xuân Chữ 78
Nguyễn Xuân Khương 175
Nha Trang 48, 106, 172, 215n13
Nhu, Ngô Đình *see* Ngô Đình Nhu
Ninh Hòa 217n84
Nolting, Frederick E., Jr. 158, 168–169, 198–200, 203–204
Nông Sơn 187
Norodom Sihanouk 36, 59, 162–165, 212n25

O'Daniel John W. 118
O'Donnell, Edward 80
Osservatore Romano 232n41
Ouane Rattikone 76

Palmer, Williston 160
Parkes, Roderick 121
Parsons, J. Graham 9, 24, 44–48, 54, 60–61, 66–67, 70, 76–77, 83–84, 88, 99, 104–105, 120, 124–125, 129, 131, 135–139, 144, 148–150, 152, 156
Passage to Freedom, Operation 7, 18, 192, 194
Pathet Lao 76, 87, 203
Paul Nguyễn Văn Bình 137
Pauline Tho 140
People's Committee Against Communists and Rebels 112–113, 120–122, 125–126, 128, 134
People's Counter-Coup d'État Committee 111–112, 230n61
Personalism 13, 33, 77, 142, 169, 208n23, 211n10
Personalist Labor Revolutionary Party *see* Cần Lao Party
Phạm Đăng Lâm 223n12
Phạm Huy Cơ 156
Phạm Ngọc Vinh 37, 212n22
Phạm Văn Liễu 97
Phạm Văn Ngô 185
Phạm Văn Thùng 12
Phấn Ba Thực 187
Phan Huy Quát 106, 134, 214n2

Phan Khắc Sửu 11–12, 52–53, 56, 77, 91, 106, 134, 140, 208n20
Phan Phụng Tiên 106
Phan Quang Đán 11, 14, 77, 103, 134, 140, 231n27
Phnom Penh 54, 106, 163, 165, 216n43, 226n86
Phong Dinh 38, 62, 188, 197, 212n35, 241n33
Phoumi Nosavan 76
Phú Hòa Đông 210n24
Phú Lâm 96
Phú Lợi 93
Phú Thạnh 210n24
Phu Văn Lâu palace 172
Phú Yên 91, 195
Phước Long 100, 171, 195
Phước Thành 173, 188, 241n33
Phước Tuy 171, 205, 214n81, 241n33
Pinay, Antoine 164
Plaine de Joncs 211n34
Pleiku 91, 139, 171, 188, 237n16
Pope John XXIII 136–137
Pramote Chongehareon 234n3
Presidential Elections (April 1961) *see* Elections, Presidential (1961)

Quảng Nam 171, 196
Quảng Ngãi 195
Quảng Trị 73, 188, 238n28, 241n33
Qui Nhơn 91, 215n13

Rạch Giá market 194
Rach Lang 207n8
Radio Broadcasting Service 133
Radio Catinat 161
Radio Hanoi 138, 211n8
Radio Saigon 94, 96, 100, 239n54
Réalités Cambodgiennes 54, 213n61, 215n15
Republic of Korea 56, 61, 66, 69–70, 72, 119, 121, 218n19
Republican Youth 17, 27, 73, 75, 85, 88, 109, 144, 186, 187, 194, 208n29
Revolutionary Committee (November 1960 Coup d'état) 96–97, 99–103, 111
Robertson, Frank 228n22
Robinson, James 137, 228n22
Rostow, Walter 152, 168
Roux, Henri 79
Rusk, Dean 148–150, 152–153, 159–161, 165, 167, 198

Sài Gòn Mãi 2, 133, 162–164, 231n22
Sài Gòn Mới 2, 56, 71, 113, 194
Sài Gòn Thời Báo 2, 133, 194, 240n26

Saigon Military Mission 65, 208n9
Sam Sary 59, 63, 216n43
Sawin, John S. 115–116
Self-Defense Corps 30, 39, 136–137, 156, 208n29
Self-Defense Force 17, 37, 232n38
Senghor, Leopold Sedar 196
Sihanouk, Norodom *see* Norodom Sihanouk
Socialist Alliance 133
Socialist Union Group 90, 142, 157
Lẽ Sống (Reason to Live) 2
South Korea *see* Republic of Korea
Southeast Asia Treaty Organization (SEATO) 124, 165, 167, 193, 211n8
Souvanna Phouma 76
Sri Savang Vartthana 76
Steeves, John M. 62, 64–65, 137–138, 167–168
Stump, Felix B. 59
Sully, François 228n22
Superior (High) Council of the Judiciary (RVN) 153, 157–158, 179
Syngman Rhee 61, 72

Tân Lược 74
Tân Sơn Nhứt 93–95, 102, 106
Tao Đàn park 194
Tây Ninh 26–27, 30, 99–100, 141, 154
Temporary Equipment Recovery Mission (TERM) 23–24, 67, 209n9
Tết 174
Thái Quang Hoàng 97, 106, 139–140, 224n28
Thailand 234n3
Thanh niên Cộng hòa 17; *see also* Republic Youth
Thời luận (Commentary) 2, 191, 240n31
Thời Vĩnh 210n24
Thủ Đức 93
Thừa Thiên 172, 217n75
Thừa Thiên Citizen's Rally 37
Tiếng Chuông (Bell Toll) 2, 52, 61, 72, 138
Tiếng dân 194
Tin Mới (New Reports) 2, 61, 71, 76, 113
Tịnh Biên 163–164
Toland, Butler 95–96, 115
Tôn Thất Đính 75, 91, 101, 139–140, 219n33, 227n7
Trần Chánh Tranh 210n18
Trần Cửu Thiên 62
Trần Đình An 116
Trần Kim Tuyển 56, 79–80, 87–88, 112
Trần Quốc Bửu 79

Trần Quốc Dũng 47–48, 208n26
Trần Quốc Thái 208n26
Trần Tắc Lâm 158
Trần Thiện Khiêm 96, 98–99, 102–103, 105, 114
Trần Trung Dũng 89
Trần Văn Chương 36, 44, 52, 60, 63, 65, 90–91, 120, 136, 154–155, 167–168, 198, 219n54, 221n30
Trần Văn Dĩnh 89, 119
Trần Văn Đỗ 52–53, 106
Trần Văn Đôn 101, 139–140
Trần Văn Hương 52
Trần Văn Lắm 116
Trần Văn Sơn 188, 191
Trần Văn Thọ 113, 133, 228n17
Trần Văn Tuyên 56
Trần Văn Văn 52–53, 56, 69, 77, 106
Tràng Sụp 26
Trapnell, Thomas 168
Tri Tôn district 163
Trịnh Xuân Phong 132
Trúc Giang 210n24
Trung Lập 143
Trương Công Cửu 230n1
Trương Đình Dzu 170
Trương Vĩnh Lễ 36–37, 77, 106, 109, 111–112, 137, 140, 169, 174, 198
Tự do (Freedom) 2, 37, 86, 113, 212n31, 212n32
Tunku, Abdul Rahman 165
Tuyên Đức 171, 174, 196

U Minh forest 69, 71, 156; operation 70
United Kingdom 61, 112, 117, 119, 159, 228n12, 230n55
United States Information Service (USIS) 77, 145, 201
United States Operations Mission (USOM) 24, 40, 53, 55, 68, 77, 132, 145–146, 201, 209n14
Usher, Richard 44

VNS *Văn Đồn* 132, 231n14
Vị Thanh 38, 62
Vientiane 76, 106
Việt Cộng 16, 22–24, 26–30, 33, 35, 37–39, 41–43, 47, 50, 53, 56, 61–62, 69–71, 75, 78, 81–84, 86, 90–92, 95–96, 99–101, 104, 106–107, 111, 116, 124–126, 128–130, 132–133, 136–137, 139, 141, 145–146, 148, 151, 153–154, 156, 159, 163–165, 168–169, 181–182, 187, 191, 193–196, 198, 207n8, 210n24, 214n75, 214n81, 221n15, 223n18, 229n32, 233n63, 241n52, 241n60
Việt Minh 143, 156
Việt Nam Phục quốc Hội 238n28
Vietnam Press 2, 37, 90, 143, 170, 172–174, 185, 189
Vietnamese-American Association 116
Vietnamese Socialist Party 109, 174
Vietnamese Women's Solidarity Movement 75, 192
Vinh 45
Vĩnh Bình 151, 171
Vĩnh Lợi 172
Vĩnh Long 37, 74, 172
Vĩnh Tế1 64
Vịnh Thượng 174

Võ Văn Hải 35, 62, 100, 102, 124–125
Voice of the Republic of Vietnam 134, 228n16
Vũ Quốc Thúc 178–179
Vu Tien Tuấn 158
Vũ Văn Mẫu 160–162, 168, 198
Vũ Văn Thái 147
Vũng Tàu 93–94
Vương Quang Nhường 157–158
Vương Văn Đông 94–97, 100–103, 106–107, 113–115, 224n30

Walton, Frank 68
War Zone D 98
White, Isaac D. 33, 154, 209n1
Wilde, James 94, 228n22
Williams, Samuel T. 9–10, 15, 22–27, 29–30, 32, 35, 38–42, 44, 47–48, 55–56, 58–63, 65–68, 71–72, 74–75, 82–84, 88, 118, 128, 204
Women's Solidarity Movement 75, 192
Wood, Chalmers B. 43, 45, 60–62, 64, 70, 76–78, 120, 136, 146, 152–155, 159, 209n8
Woody Edwards 228n22

Xóm Côi school 194
Xuân Lộc district 37

Young, Kenneth 60–61
Yuen Tse Kien 135

Zasloff, Joseph 74, 212n29